W9-CDH-538

YOUR CHILD *CAN* READ AND *YOU* CAN HELP

other books by the author

THE JANE ERVIN READING COMPREHENSION SERIES

NEW PHONICS WORKBOOK D

A SHORT GUIDE TO THE NEW GRAMMAR

Your Child **Can** Read and **You** Can Help

A BOOK FOR PARENTS

by Dr. Jane Ervin

Doubleday & Company, Inc.
Garden City, New York
1979

Grateful acknowledgment is given for permission to include the following copyrighted material:

"In the Dark" from *Now We Are Six* by A. A. Milne. Copyright 1927 by E. P. Dutton & Company, Inc. Copyright renewal © 1955 by A. A. Milne. Reprinted by permission of E. P. Dutton and Methuen Children's Books Ltd.

Portion of "Ars Poetica" from *New and Collected Poems 1917–1976* by Archibald MacLeish. Copyright © 1976 by Archibald MacLeish. Reprinted by permission of Houghton Mifflin Company.

The drawing on page 117 is by Agatha Jaka

Library of Congress Cataloging in Publication Data

Ervin, Jane.
Your child can read and you can help.

Bibliography: p. 365.
Includes index.
1. Reading. 2. Reading readiness.
3. Children—Language. 4. Books and reading
for children. I. Title.
LB1050.E75 372.4′1
ISBN: 0-385-14141-6
Library of Congress Catalog Card Number 78-69656

Printed in the United States of America
First Edition

To My Parents

Who not only taught me to read and love books, but gave me the kind of home and childhood that I wish every child could have.

And to Johnny

And all the children with whom I have shared the adventure of learning to read.

ACKNOWLEDGMENTS

It is impossible to mention all the people—teachers, parents, psychologists, doctors, researchers, librarians, book sellers, friends, colleagues, and children—who have contributed in some way to this book as it has developed over the past several years. I thank them all.

I would, however, especially like to thank: Kathy Foster for her work on the book selections; Ann Buchwald for her enthusiasm, encouragement, and incredible ability to always make the right comment or suggestion—whether it be to clarify my thoughts, improve the text, or boost my morale; Karen Van Westering, my editor, for making the last part of the book's "journey" go so smoothly; and of course my husband, Charles, for being so enthusiastic, encouraging, understanding, good-humored, and unselfish during yet another one of my writing projects.

You will notice that I refer to he, his, and him throughout the book. This does not mean I favor boys over girls! I have done it purely to be consistent.

CONTENTS

NOTE TO PARENTS 1

INTRODUCTION: HOW DO WE READ? 4

PART ONE: A FEW THINGS YOU NEED TO KNOW BEFORE YOU START

Chapter 1: What's Involved in Teaching: Some Tricks of the Trade 11

Give Your Child Confidence and a Sense of Security 12

Give Praise and Encouragement 14

Motivation Is the Key 17

Let Your Child Learn by Doing 26

Success Is Essential: Hints for Teaching Specific Skills 29

PART TWO: PREPARING YOUR CHILD FOR READING: THOSE IMPORTANT FIRST FEW YEARS BEFORE SCHOOL

Chapter 2: When and How to Start 37

Begin the Day Your Child Is Born 37

Start by Doing What Comes Naturally 38

Get Your Child Interested in Learning 39

Your Child Is Innately Curious 52

Your Child Enjoys Learning 53

Chapter 3: The Importance of Emotional and Physical Well-being 56
Emotional Stability and Self-reliance 56
Physical Development and General Health 61

Chapter 4: Make Your Child Think: Developing Those Intellectual Skills 67
The Stages of Development 68
When Your Child Is a Baby 71
The Importance of Observation 74
The Need to Concentrate 80
Seeing Relationships and Associations Is Also Necessary 81
Logical Thinking Is the Key 82

Chapter 5: Talking Leads to Reading: Developing Those Language Skills 86
When Your Child Is a Baby 86
The Eighth Month Is Important 91
Your Child's First Sentences 94
At Three Your Child Is a Talker 98
At Four or Five Your Child Is the Wizard of Words 103

Chapter 6: When Your Child Is Ready to Read 107
Your Child Shows Signs of Wanting to Become a Reader 107
Making the Transition from Talking to Reading 108

PART THREE: TEACHING YOUR CHILD THE FUNDAMENTALS: THE READING LESSONS

Chapter 7: Stage I: The Very Basics 137

Chapter 8: Stage II: Some Variations 190

Chapter 9: Stage III: The Harder Ones 242

PART FOUR: NOW THAT YOUR CHILD CAN READ: SOME SUGGESTIONS FOR DEVELOPING INTEREST AND COMPREHENSION

Chapter 10: Getting Your Child to Read and Enjoy Books 277
When Your Child Goes to School 278
As Your Child Begins to Read 279
Choose Appropriate Books 280
Involve Your Child in the Choice 286
Make Trips to the Library and the Bookstore 286
Give Your Child a Library of His Own 287
Let Your Child Read Anything and Everything 290

Chapter 11: Ways to Help Your Child Get the Most out of a Book 291
Read the Book Yourself 292
Let Your Child Get a General Impression First 292
Ask Questions 292
Personalize It 294
Encourage Your Child's Own Interpretations 294
Help Your Child to Assume Certain Responsibilities 295
Your Child Must Have the Intention 296
Make Your Child Aware of the Author's Techniques 297
Make Your Child Aware of the Different Literary Forms 297

PART FIVE: WORKING WITH OTHERS TO HELP YOUR CHILD READ

Chapter 12: Working with the School 319
How to Evaluate a School's Reading Program 320
How to Evaluate Your Child's Progress and Reading Level 336

How to Work with the School to Improve Your Child's Reading 345

Chapter 13: Getting Help When There Is a Problem 347

Signs of Reading Disability 348

What to Do if You Suspect Your Child Has a Reading Disability 352

Diagnosis 353

Treatment 356

Where to Find Help 358

APPENDIX: BOOK SUGGESTIONS: SOME TIPS AND TITLES 363

INDEX 436

YOUR CHILD *CAN* READ AND *YOU* CAN HELP

NOTE TO PARENTS

You're concerned about your child's reading. You have a fourth-grader who is still struggling over the simplest one-syllable words. Or you have a sixth grader who is totally disinterested in reading. You can't persuade him to pick up a book, let alone read one! Or perhaps you have a preschooler and want to give him a head start.

You know reading is vital to his education. Johnny or Jane can't learn or succeed in the world today without it. But you're not sure how to help them. In fact, you're not even sure if you *should* help them. Should you get involved? Or should you leave it to the school? How do you know if they are making enough progress at school, or are reading at the appropriate level for their age? How do you know if they have a real reading problem, or if it's something minor that can be easily corrected?

These questions, and probably many more, are whirling through your mind. You have heard and read so much about reading lately that you don't know what to believe. You're unsure, confused, and frustrated. You want to do the best for your child but are uncertain just what "the best" means. If it's any consolation, you are not alone in your concern. Parents all over the country are lamenting, "Johnny is having terrible problems with his reading, and we don't know what to do." I not only hear this during my office consultations, but also at parent meetings, cocktail parties, chatting to total strangers on plane trips, and even, on one occasion, when walking my dog.

Children from all backgrounds can develop reading problems. They are not necessarily related to social and economic circumstances. A child from an affluent family can still be deprived of the necessary reading help, while a child from an extremely poor family can receive all the help he needs. A wonderful illustration of this is Abraham Lincoln, who became an avid reader despite his meager background. The children with whom I work come from every possible strata of society. They go to the most exclusive private schools, parochial schools, and the local public schools. Two of my recent students were David and Sally, both eleven years old. David is the son of a judge, and Sally is the daughter of a janitor, and yet both have similar reading-comprehension problems.

Reading problems need not necessarily result from lack of attention and care. David and Sally could not have more loving, conscientious parents. Nor are reading problems particularly related to intelligence. In fact, most of the children who come to me are of average, or above average, intelligence. A typical example is Adam, a nine-year-old who was doing well at school except in the subjects that involved reading. "He's always been quick to learn, and his teacher tells us he's bright," his parents told me. "He's getting good grades in math and science, but is having a terrible time with his reading. He's in the slowest reading group, but seems to be making no progress."

It is because of your concern about your child's reading, and the concern of these many other parents, that I have written this book. It is intended: (1) as a guide for parents of young children to help them *prevent* their child from developing reading problems, and, if they wish, give him a head start in learning to read; (2) as an aid to parents of older children to enable them to recognize their child's reading needs and problems, and help them decide when and how to help.

I have tried to answer the questions parents ask me about their child's reading, so I hope I have covered yours. However, a word of caution. I have given you as much information as possible about how you can help your child. But you, as the parent, must ultimately make the judgment *how* to use the information. You must rely, to some extent, on those wonderful gifts you have—common sense and parent intuition. You know your child better than anyone else—his strengths, weaknesses, temperament, and character—and you must decide just when and how to help him. Somehow you must achieve a balance, deciding when you should "push" your child and when to leave him alone. There can be various ways to solve a child's reading problem. You, as the parent, must decide what is best and appropriate for your child and family situation.

Before I get into the ways you can help your child, let me clear up some misconceptions that you, like many other parents, may have. First, contrary to what you may have heard, you don't need to be an "expert" to help your child to read. It's not difficult, and what's more, it needn't take any more effort or time than you normally devote to his upbringing. It is just a matter of organization and ranking priorities. This is particularly important to realize if you're both working, like so many parents are these days.

Another misconception that many parents have is that they can't teach their own child.

"I'm a parent, not a teacher," I am told over and over again. "My kid won't work with me. I can't teach him a thing!"

"Nonsense" is my reply. You have been teaching him since the day he was born. How do you think he leaned to speak, to feed himself, or tie his shoes?

You can help your child to read. It may call for a little patience and perseverance, but being a dedicated parent I know you have that. But really it's just a matter of KNOWING WHAT TO DO. I hope this book will give you that "know-how." Have faith:

Your child **can** read—and **you** can help.

INTRODUCTION

How Do We Read?

One of the reasons why you've hesitated to help your child with his reading is probably because you know nothing about reading. You have no idea what is involved in learning to read. Right? Well don't let that deter you. If the truth be known, even some elementary teachers start out that way. They teach themselves as they go along, and you can do the same.

What happens when you read? How do you manage to decipher meaning from those strange squiggles that confront you when you read a book, or the newspaper, or Penny's scribbled note from camp:

> Dear Mom and Dad,
>
> Mary and I got here alright. I saw a deer yesterday. Please send a pot or pan and some food for a cook-out. And I need some more money.
>
> Penny

Reading is an extension of talking. In fact, it's sometimes called "inner speech" because you translate the written words into "spoken" language in your mind to understand them. Reread Penny's letter slowly and you'll see what I mean. Notice how you first recognize the letters and hear the sounds they represent. Then you combine those sounds together into a word that has meaning. You not only blend the sounds together, but also recognize their sequence so you don't read "was" for "saw," "top" for "pot," and "nap" for "pan," which is a common error in beginning readers and a sign of a problem in older readers.

When you first learn to read you put the sounds together orally, but as you become more skilled and familiar with their combinations you do this silently to yourself. It is not until you can do this that reading becomes a truly mental process. One method I use to see if my students have reached this stage is to ask them to read a story to themselves. Then I watch to see if they're really doing this, or if they're whispering or "mouthing" the words. Watch your child sometime when he's reading and notice if he's moving his lips. If he is, it's likely he hasn't yet learned to make the changeover.

You Read in Gulps

Now think back to the first time you read Penny's letter—or any part of this book, for that matter. You didn't read word by word, but in big "gulps." You read the words in groups or phrases as they represented units of thought. "Gulp One" told you Penny and Mary arrived safely. "Gulp Two" told you Penny had seen a deer, and so on. This skill is crucial to comprehension and fluency, and is usually one of the first introduced in speed-reading courses. Try increasing your "gulps" by taking in more words at one time, and notice how much more rapidly you read.

Penny made it pretty clear in her letter what she wanted. But what if she had said:

> I can't join in the cook-out because I don't have a pan or any food of my own.

Or:

> I could go to the movies with the other kids if I had some money.

You'd still get the message, but you'd have to do a little "reading between the lines."

You often have to interpret a writer's subtle use of words to understand the special inferences and meanings he's trying to convey. Sometimes they're easy to understand. When he says, "He was no giant of a man," it's not too difficult to figure he's talking about someone small. But what about when he says, "He was a demon"? Is he talking about a devil, or describing a naughty boy? When he says, "There were *millions* of people there," does he really mean "millions"? What does he mean when he says, "The skies *wept* and the thunder *roared,*" and "Mother gave Sam a *piercing* look as he *wolfed* his food"?

Understanding the real meaning of what a writer is saying comes with experience. However, I am constantly amazed how even young children sometimes pick up subtle meanings. For example, many youngsters get the delightful humor of the poem *The Grasshopper and the Elephant*.

"That's silly," they say, but they laugh. Read it with your child and enjoy it together.

Way down South where bananas grow
A grasshopper stepped on an elephant's toe
The elephant said, with tears in his eyes,
"Pick on somebody your own size."

One way I test my older students to see if they can interpret more subtle meanings is to give them this poem by Christina Rosetti and ask them to give it a title. If they call it "Sheep" I know they're not there yet. If your child is ten or eleven, or older, try it out on him and see what he comes up with.

White sheep, white sheep
On a blue hill,
When the wind stops
You all stand still.
When the wind blows
You walk away slow
White sheep, white sheep
Where do you go?

If he's having a tough time, help him by asking such questions as:
"Have you ever seen a blue hill? No? Then what do you think the poet is really describing? Could the wind blow sheep? If he's not talking about sheep, what is he talking about?"

How's *your* reading comprehension? Did you pass the test and call the poem "Clouds"?

Reading Is like Talking to a Friend

How many times have you read something and then discovered you haven't taken in a single word? More times than you care to admit, I'm sure. It's really very easy to do, especially if you're tired. This is because reading requires *an alert mind.*

I tell my students that reading is like talking to a friend. You pay attention and respond just as though the words had been spoken. But you have to concentrate harder and put more effort into reading because you can't ask questions. You're left to figure out the meaning on your own. As you don't have such aids as tone of voice, facial expression, and body movements to help you, you must adapt and vary the way you read according to what you're reading. For example, imagine you've ordered Jimmy a bike for Christmas and it arrives in six nice, neat packages. How do you read the directions for putting it together? Slowly, carefully, and thoroughly—particularly if it's Christmas Eve! In fact, you even reread sections so you don't miss a single detail, for you know if you do, Jimmy will never ride that bike. But what if you're reading an ad in a magazine? You read that much more rapidly, even skimming parts, because you want only to find out the essential characteristics of the product and its price.

As you become more experienced, you also adapt your reading according to your purpose for reading. Think how you read the paper. Don't you read the articles that particularly interest you slowly, paying attention to all the facts and details? Then just scan the other parts in a rather cursory way to get the gist of what they're about?

I wonder how much you can remember of this explanation of reading, and how long it took you to read it. Did you absorb all the information in a few minutes flat? If so, you're a reading whizz. You can put together all the necessary skills so that you read quickly and effectively. But *how* did you learn to do this? And how can you get your child to read the same way?

Learning to read involves three basic aspects:

prereading skills
the "mechanics" or fundamentals
reading comprehension

In the rest of the book I will show you how each of these aspects can be broken down into specific skills that you can help your child learn.

PART ONE:

A Few Things You Need to Know Before You Start

CHAPTER 1

What's Involved in Teaching: Some Tricks of the Trade

Before you start to help your child with his reading, here are a few "tricks of the trade." They are teaching methods that have worked well for me in many situations, and I think they will work well for you also. They are the sort of things that stimulate children to learn; not just "book work" but any learning, and will help you teach your child all the important skills, abilities, and attitudes he needs to read well, even if you don't intend to teach him the actual fundamental skills of reading. They are not new or revolutionary. In fact, they are probably the very things you are doing instinctively as a parent as you teach your child to pick up his toys, eat without turning himself into a candidate for a detergent ad, and sit quietly in the back seat of the car as you speed down the freeway.

Why am I writing about these techniques if you are already doing them? First of all, like many other successful parents, you may be doing them so automatically you are not even aware of them. I want to call your attention to them so that you will *consciously* apply them to helping your child with his reading. Second, I want you to realize you are not starting in a vacuum—you already have the tools. There is no need to panic. You don't have to come up with all sorts of new ideas and gimmicks. Third, I want to give you a feeling of security and confidence so you will go ahead with your plan to help your child. In fact, I am "teaching" you exactly how you should teach him —by giving you assurance and building from there! Finally, I hope that you will find a helpful goodie or two that you had not thought of before.

Give Your Child Confidence and a Sense of Security

Yes, it's terribly important you give your child the feeling that he is capable, and that you have faith in his abilities. A child with confidence will be much more eager to learn and try new things. You must give him a sense of security so that even when he makes mistakes and everything goes wrong (which is bound to happen from time to time) he doesn't have the feeling he is failing and want to give up.

Imagine yourself in the following situation and you'll see what I mean. It's 6:30 P.M. and "one of those evenings." The children are fighting over a toy, the baby is throwing up, the telephone has started to ring, and your husband is tired and hungry, waiting for his supper. And what happens? You burn the hamburgers.

The man of your life looks up from the comfortable chair where he's reading the evening paper and says, "My God, woman, haven't you learned to cook a hamburger properly yet?"

What would be your reaction? You'd probably throw the hamburger at him, burst into tears, or tell him, "Fix your own wretched hamburger." You would not only be full of anger, hate, and resentment, but also thoroughly discouraged and demoralized. You would probably feel ready to quit feeding the family that night and every other night.

But it could have been worse. What if he had looked at the hamburgers and said scathingly, "Let me show you, dear, how to fix the hamburgers. You don't seem to be able to cope." Then you would have felt completely humiliated!

What if he had said, "My, you're getting it from all quarters tonight. The kids, the baby, the phone, and now the dinner. I don't know how you cope with all this each evening." Wouldn't that make you feel better? In fact, wouldn't it make you feel you really wanted to and could cope with the situation?

Something similar happens to a child facing the task of learning to read. Imagine that you are helping your daughter with her spelling and she gets every single word wrong. Don't make a big deal of it. Don't blow it out of proportion and don't let her either. Admit the disaster openly and laugh it off. Say, "Bad luck. Don't worry, things can't get worse, they can only get better!"

Then reassure her by saying, "Do you remember what a hard time you had learning your multiplication tables? You're a real whiz at them now." Or, "Do you remember how you thought you'd never learn to swim? Now you're a positive fish!"

It's no use scolding on occasions like these, for no one conscientiously sets out to fail. In their heart of hearts everyone wants to do well. Your child is probably far more disappointed with the results than you are. Don't, by the way, be fooled by his behavior. Not everyone shows frustration by crying. Your child could well become aggressive and belligerent, or morose, or even have a temper tantrum. But however he reacts, remember what he needs is the assurance that if he perseveres he will succeed in the end.

You should use the same tactics of reminding your child of previous accomplishments if he is hesitant about learning something new. You can also give him confidence by working along with him. I often do this when I am introducing a more difficult reader to one of my students. We glance through the book together looking at the pictures and then I read the first few paragraphs. We take it in turns until he realizes that he's not going to have such a tough time as he thought and is no longer hesitant.

One of the worst things you can do to undermine a child's confidence is to give him a task and then take over in the middle because he's having difficulty, or is not going as fast as you think he should. This sounds pretty obvious, but we are all guilty of doing it.

Come on, admit it: Haven't you done it? What about that time you were rushing for the bus?

"Hurry up and put your shoes on, dear," you call to Michael. "Mommy's got to go to the stores before they close."

Michael struggles with his laces, but it is getting late and the bus is due in a few minutes. "Oh let me do that," you say irritably. You push his fingers out of the way and quickly tie the bow. You catch the bus, but you have a demoralized child.

If your child is reading a story to you and is taking much longer than you thought he would because he's stumbling over nearly all the words, don't say, "Oh let me finish it or we'll never get through." Let him finish even if it means supper won't be on time that night or he will go to bed late.

If it looks as though he is going to take an impossibly long time, and you do have to interrupt him, say, "You're doing fine, but my, it's a hard story, isn't it? I bet you'd like a break. How about finishing it later?" This will prevent him from losing face and will still give him a chance to complete the story.

Give Praise and Encouragement

I have found by far the most effective way to teach is through praise and encouragement. They are the magic potions that bring out all the best qualities in a child, making him want to learn. They can turn a surly, unco-operative thirteen-year-old into an enthusiastic student, and help a shy, overly cautious four-year-old accept the challenge of new experiences.

You know the effect praise can have from your own experiences. When your wife compliments you on the marvelous job you did cleaning out the garage, doesn't it encourage you to keep it tidy? It might even spur you on to tackle the basement—or perhaps that is going a little too far! What about when someone says, "You sure look great with that new hairstyle." Doesn't it make you take a little extra trouble with your appearance?

Lets face it: We all flourish on compliments. However poorly a child performs, I always find something good to say before I comment on the aspects that need improvement. For example, when Susan brought me her dictation the other day I said to her:

"Well, Susan, let's see how you did. My goodness, your handwriting has really improved. I can read every word, and it's so neat." She beamed with pleasure as she had been working on her sloppy letter formation.

"Now let's have a look at the spelling," I continued. "Congratulations! You've got 'awkward' and 'awful' right. You've really had a struggle with those "aw" words, haven't you? But, now, Susan, what about these?" I pointed to several words she had misspelled. "You'll have to work on these now, won't you?"

I gave her a nudge in the ribs with my elbow and she grinned. She went off humming nonchalantly, but I could tell she was determined to get them *all* right next time. And she nearly did.

The one thing you must never—I repeat, never—do, is to tell your child he's stupid—however mad and frustrated you might feel. I know how infuriating it can be when you have gone over and over something with a child, such as teaching him to hold his spoon correctly, or to remember his telephone number in case of an emergency, and he *still* doesn't get it.

"How can you be so dumb?" You say to yourself, "And to think you're *my* daughter!" But keep it to yourself. Just a slip of the tongue can cause untold damage. What is the point in her making an effort, if you tell her she can't do it anyway?

You must still be encouraging and say, "You're sure having a hard time with this." This tells her, "Ah she understands." "Don't worry, you'll get it in the end. Lots of people have difficulty learning this." This lets her know she's not the only one who's had a hard time acquiring this skill. These comments won't make her learn the skill overnight, but they are more likely to encourage her to plod on until she does finally get it.

You should use the same approach if your child turns the tables on you and says "I'm so stupid. I can't read this book. I'm dumb."

Tell him, "You're not dumb. You're just having a tough time now. We all go through these periods."

Don't, however, do what one mother did. She was so intent on convincing her child he wasn't dumb that they got into quite an argument and she ended up by saying, "Don't tell me you're stupid, stupid!"

It is so easy to find fault and so easy to forget to praise. We tend to forget the effort put into the mastery of a skill and only scold when it is not achieved. Young Joe spills his milk at breakfast and you admonish him,

"Oh you clumsy boy! Can't you be more careful?"

But what about all the times he was careful and didn't spill his milk? Did you make any comment then?

You blasted him for his untidy room, but did you notice he remembered to put his bike away? Obviously you can't be constantly praising a child, or your praise would be meaningless. But do remember to acknowledge past accomplishments as you forge ahead with new ones. Also make sure you praise *efforts* as well as end products.

I watched a three-year-old in a restaurant one day. She struggled into her coat. Then she patiently and painstakingly tried to do the buttons up. She was having a terrible time, the buttons just would not go through those impossible holes, but she would not give up. Solemnly and slowly she persevered. At last she got one through, then the next, and then the next. Her face became one enormous smile. She tapped her mother on the arm to share her achievement. Her mother took one look and noticed the buttons were out of line.

"Oh for heaven's sake, Jenny," she cried, "you've done the buttons up all wrong. Here, let me do them up properly."

Jenny burst into tears, and I don't blame her. If only her mother had said, "Well done, Jenny, you've got three buttons done up. But do you notice you've still got one that isn't in a hole? Next time you put your coat on I'll show you how to do them all up."—and left it at that.

In order to be effective, praise must be specific. Don't say vaguely, "That's terrific," or "Well done." Instead say, "That's a terrific story you've just told"; and "You've done the exercise so well, you've got only one word wrong." You will notice I was extremely specific in my praise of Susan's dictation.

This applies to criticism as well. In order to be constructive you must not only tell a child what needs correcting but also *how* to correct it. For example, if he has helped you set the table for a dinner party and you see the forks are in the wrong place, the glasses missing, and the table mats upside down, you don't say:

"Oh you've done it all wrong!" No. You say: "I think there're a few things that need straightening out here. Put the forks here, change the mats so that you can see the pictures, and you'd better get some glasses from the cupboard." Now he can finish the job properly.

You should also be careful to avoid praising a child's personal characteristics and traits. Phrases like, "You're terrific," "You're an angel," and "You're such a great son" are not helpful. In fact, they are harmful, because they make a child feel that if he fails to acquire a skill he is failing totally as a person.

So stick to praising his efforts and accomplishments. What do you do when your child accomplishes nothing and has obviously made no effort? Do you do the opposite and bawl him out? Suppose you have asked him to take the supper dishes into the kitchen and he goes out to play. Or you have given him a short story to read and he watches television instead. What do you do then?

My usual approach if a child has not completed an assignment, or has done it so sloppily that he might as well not have done it, is to say:

"It's a pity you didn't do it, because I think you could have done it really well. I'll excuse you this time, but you'd better do it tonight or you'll fall awfully far behind."

I try to hit the happy medium. I don't praise, but I still try to be encouraging. I don't condemn, but I don't let him get away with anything—I expect the assignment to be completed by the next morning. If it is not, then I am cross.

You will have to decide when your child needs praise to help him learn, and when he needs that little kick in the pants.

Motivation Is the Key

If your child really wants to learn something, you can bet your last dollar he will. Do you remember when he got his first bike? Didn't he spend every spare moment enduring numerous gashes and bruises from the inevitable falls until he was finally whizzing around the neighborhood with the other kids? And what about that time he decided to swim the length of the pool? He came close to drowning as he struggled, gasped, and splashed, but he made it!

I have recently been watching one of my students, Matthew, who was determined to learn to skateboard. Each day he came early so he could practice on my driveway. If he fell once, he fell a hundred times, but this never deterred him. Each time he jumped up, rubbed the banged part of his anatomy, gritted his teeth, and mounted the board again.

"You really have given yourself a tough job learning to balance on that board," I said one day after he had had a particularly bad fall. He gave me one of his impish grins and replied, "Sure it's hard. But don't worry, Doc, I've nearly got it licked. I'll be the best on my block by the time I'm through."

I don't know if he was the best on his block, but by the time his classes with me were over, he could not only balance with one foot on the board, but he could also do many intricate maneuvers. And this was a boy whose teacher's report stated: "This boy is incapable of learning; his concentration is poor; he lacks initiative; he gives up too easily; and he never completes assignments."

How was it that Matthew demonstrated all these attributes learning to skateboard, and yet none of them in the classroom? He was motivated. He not only wanted to learn to skateboard, but he also wanted to do it well.

"But skateboarding is fun," I can hear you say. "It's very different from learning academic subjects." "Not necessarily" is my reply. Learning to read, or to write—or anything, for that matter—can be just as satisfying, challenging, and engrossing for a child if you go about it the right way.

Use Your Child's Particular Interests

How did I get Matthew to learn? I did what I do with all my students. I started with his particular interests. Often I have to prod and pry to find out what a student's interests are, but with Matthew, of course, it was a cinch. It was more than obvious what his passion in life was at that time! He had never written a composition or completed a whole book when he came to me. But before our sessions were through he completed a project on, you guessed it, "Skateboarding"! He researched the topic, read articles about it, and finally wrote a pretty good survey on how to choose the best kind of boards, how to perform the various maneuvers, and where the main competitions are held. He was stimulated to write, not only legibly, but also with good grammar and correct spelling, and his reading improved by leaps and bounds. I must say I was as thrilled with his progress as were his parents. And, although he probably wouldn't admit it, I think Matthew was as proud of his academic accomplishments as he was of his skateboard ones.

You will find, if you use your child's special interests as a vehicle for teaching him, or even for getting him to do something he doesn't want to, you will have much greater success. If you want to improve his reading comprehension and he is mad about football, go and get him an autobiography of a football star. If horses are his latest craze, find a story about horses like Marguerite Henry's *Misty of Chincoteague,* which is so popular with junior-high kids. If he has just started a shell collection, buy one or two inexpensive paperbacks on shells.

Relate the Reason to Your Child's Own Life

You probably find it fairly easy to motivate your child because you know what his interests are. However, it is also helpful if you can show him a *purpose* for what he is doing. For example, have you noticed how much more quickly and efficiently he cleans up the living room when you say, "Your favorite TV show is on in ten minutes. If you pick up your things by then, you can watch it"; than when you say vaguely, "I think you'd better clean up the living room now"?

A child can be stimulated to do even the most tedious academic chores if he sees a reason for doing it. Take Jimmy, another of my students. He had been having an uphill struggle with his multiplication tables for some time. Finally I said to him: "Tonight's the night. You've got to knuckle down and get these tables under your belt." To say that I met some resistance is putting it mildly. I had obviously failed miserably in motivating my young client!

"They're boring and dull," he cried, "they take too much time, and anyway, I've got more important things to do!" Casually, sensing that perhaps here at last was a clue how to reach him, I asked, "What sort of things?"

"Well, I'm designing this hovercraft," he began, "and I'm having a terrible time getting the dimensions right." Before I could utter a word, my nine-year-old student had whipped out his pencil and was hastily making sketches and describing all sorts of sophisticated—at least to nonmechanically minded me—engineering terms!

I couldn't believe my luck—or my stupidity. Why on earth had I not found out Jimmy's passion for boats and given him a definite purpose for learning those wretched multiplication tables? Fortunately it was not too late. Jimmy saw how they would save him time and effort designing his hovercraft and he learned them within the week.

The more you can relate the reason for learning a skill, or completing a task, to your child's own life, the more motivated he will be. If you can show him what it will do for *him,* as I eventually managed to do for Jimmy, he will respond much more readily. If you are having a hard time getting your son to eat his breakfast before school, do not say:

"Hurry up Mark. Eat your cereal for Daddy."

You will have much better results with:

"Gee, Mark, when you've finished all that cereal you'll have so much energy for that football game you're playing this morning, the other team won't have a chance."

Be Positive

I expect you noticed the last remark presumes Mark is going to eat his cereal. I find this positive approach more effective in motivating my students, as it conveys that I have confidence in them. It tells them there is no doubt in my mind that they can and will complete the task. This lessens any doubts they may have about their ability, as well as giving them a sense of pride, which encourages them.

Be Clear and Direct

I also find I get the best results when I am clear and direct in my instructions. There are no "ifs," "ands," and "buts" with me. I say what I mean, and mean what I say. When I give a math assignment I say, "Finish these sums by ten o'clock" and not "How about finishing this page of sums?" When I teach a phonics rule I say, "I'm going to give you this exercise to do tomorrow so make sure you know the rule," and not, "Isn't it about time you learned that rule?" I avoid open-ended questions because they suggest there is an option to learning the skill. They can produce indecisiveness and invite arguments, or even downright refusal.

Consider an everyday family situation that all parents have to contend with at some time or other—getting the kids to do their homework, or what I call the "Homework Hassle"—and you will see what I mean.

All is peace and tranquillity at the Finches' home. The kids are in the living room absorbed in, and enjoying, their activities. Jack is working on a strategy for his lastest passion, war-gaming, and has his model soldiers strewn around him. Josephine is knitting a sweater for her doll. And Susie is sprawled on the floor reading a Nancy Drew.

Mr. Finch puts his head around the door:

"How about getting your homework done, kids?" he asks.

"O.K., Dad," comes a triple response. But no movement.

He repeats this several times, but the children still continue with what they are doing. Finally he yells: "Didn't I tell you to go and do your homework? Now get going *this minute."*

This time he has an impact, and the children go to do their homework—but not before there is a nice "scene" with the children screaming they "hate homework," "it's a waste of time," and they "don't know what to do, anyway."

Mr. Finch has finally succeeded in making the kids do what he wanted—but at what a price! The peace and tranquillity of his home are disrupted, and the kids certainly are not motivated to do their homework well!

Now let's go across the street, and see how Mr. Suckley handles the situation. The kids have had supper and are outside in the garden. The twins, Paul and Lesley, are shooting baskets, while Billy is weeding his patch of garden. Mr. Suckley opens his bedroom window, and calls down, "It's 6:45 P.M. You've got fifteen minutes before homework time. You needn't start cleaning up just yet, but you are to be in your rooms *ready to work* [he emphasized these words] at seven o'clock. Does everyone hear me loud and clear?"

"O.K., Dad," comes the response from three upturned faces. "Good. Paul, you've got a watch. Keep the others informed of the time every so often so they can keep track of it."

"Right, Dad," Paul replied.

"I suggest you start putting your things away in five minutes," Mr. Suckley added as he disappeared from sight.

Every now and then Paul looked at his watch. He knew he was responsible for the time-keeping and he didn't want to let the others down by missing the appointed time. At six-fifty he called out. "Ten minutes to go. Time to pack up." He picked up the sweater he had thrown on a nearby bush and pulled it over his head. Lesley continued to shoot baskets because she knew she had only to wash her hands.

"Call me when I've got five minutes," she said to her twin. Billy, however, began to collect his tools together because he knew it would take longer to put them away. And then he had to change as he was in his "gardening" pants.

By 7:00 P.M. the three Suckley children were in their rooms. They had had a good time outside, but now they were ready to tackle their homework.

Have Faith In Your Child

If you respect your children, treat them as normal human beings with rights and feelings of their own, and do not "talk down" to them, you will have no problems motivating them. As long as they know what is expected of them, and your expectations are reasonable, they will not only do their darndest to meet them, but also will enjoy the challenge.

There will always be times when they are overtired, upset about something, or just in a plain, old-fashioned bad mood. Then you may have a hard time convincing them that anything is really worthwhile or important. However, if you are tactful, and careful about what you say, you should be able to reach them most of the time.

Then there are also those few occasions when *you* might not be in the best of moods! When this happens you must make a particular effort to keep your feelings under control, not to speak hastily, and avoid certain words and comments that could turn your kids off. Look at the following examples and you will see what I mean:

TURN-OFF AND TURN-ON REMARKS

TURN-OFF: *"You won't go to the movies with the others if you don't finish your lunch."*
Threatening your kid will get you nowhere.

TURN-ON: *"If you hurry and eat your lunch you'll just make the movie."*

TURN-OFF: *"Be quiet and listen to me for a change."*
Watch being too bossy.
TURN-ON: *"Settle down, honey. I want to tell you something."*

TURN-OFF: *"Don't tell me you know those words. You couldn't have learned them in that time."*
Don't accuse him—have faith in him.
TURN-ON: *"Wow! You've learned those already? Are you sure you want me to test you on them, or do you want to go over them again?"*

TURN-OFF: *"Stop crying, you stupid boy. You're a pain in the neck."*
You rebuke him for being impolite, but what about you?
TURN-ON: *"Come on, dear, there's no need to keep on crying like that."*

TURN-OFF: *"Haven't you heard what chairs are for yet?"*
Sarcasm is the lowest form of wit, goes the old saying; it is also the cruelest.
TURN-ON: *"Don't jump on the chair, dear."*

TURN-OFF: *"You're not nearly good enough to go into the next reader."*
He may not be, but you would encourage him if you were more tactful.
TURN-ON: *"You're not quite ready for the next book, but why don't we look at it together so you can see what you have to prepare for."*

TURN-OFF: *"I've told you again and again to wipe your feet when you come in the front door."*
Don't nag. If you've had to repeatedly tell him, you're obviously not getting through to him. Switch to another means of motivation.
TURN-ON: *"Go outside again and wipe your feet when you come in—you've forgotten again."*

Your Attitude Has an Effect

It is amazing how much your attitude and feelings can affect your child's attitude. I hate to admit it, but when one of my lessons doesn't go well, it's usually because I am not in the right frame of mind. So a word of warning: If you wake up in a grouchy mood, don't choose that day to tackle some new project with your child.

Your enthusiasm is also vital. If your kids know that you consider what they are doing important and worthwhile, they will feel it is too. For instance, if you don't feel it's mandatory for them to do their homework, they certainly won't. If they never see you with your nose in a book, its very unlikely they will be motivated to read.

Practice What You Preach

One of the common hassles in a family is getting the kids to wash their hands before mealtime. No wonder! Time and time again I have seen a parent stride in from the office or shopping and go straight to the table—often bawling out the kids en route for not going to the bathroom.

Children learn by imitating. They watch you smile and they gurgle. They see you walking and they struggle to stand up and put one foot in front of the other. You are the model. When they get older they dress up in your clothes. They imitate the way you talk and even your mannerisms. Later they experiment with your cigarettes and borrow the car, because this is "being grown up." So take a hint: PRACTICE WHAT YOU PREACH and you will get results.

Give Rewards—in Moderation

One of the best ways to get results is to give rewards. However, you must be careful how you go about this, as you don't want your child learning just to get a prize. The ultimate reward, of course, should come from the satisfaction of doing a job well. But let's be realistic about this. There are many tasks your children are going to have to do that they won't enjoy, or even want to do. So a surprise goodie, or a special treat now and then to help them on their way, or recognize their effort, is not going to cause any harm. In fact, on the contrary, it will probably be a terrific morale booster and provide an impetus to spur them on to bigger and better things.

The secret is not overdoing the prize-giving, and judging when it's appropriate. Take Mrs. Sternoff's predicament and you will see what I mean. She came to me last year perplexed, frustrated, and exasperated.

"I can't understand it, doctor," she said. "My husband and I have given Stanley everything he's asked for, and more. And still he's not working. His teacher says he's smart, but he'll have to repeat fifth grade if he doesn't improve. What can we do?"

Yes, Stanley was smart. He had recognized he was on to a good thing. He had figured out that if he didn't work, he got a prize.

What they did was send him to me. But I enjoyed Stanley, and we had a great deal of fun together. I called him my "prize collector" and made a joke out of the whole thing. However, I let him know right from the start that it was a joke, and from now on, prizes—at least in the tangible form he was used to—were out. I was quite frank and faced him with the problem.

"Look, Stanley," I said, "you've been on to a good thing, but now the party is over. You've really got to get down to work now, or you're going to have to repeat fifth grade. Right? You're going to find it tough at first, but you're smart. You can do it."

What I did do, though, was to give him plenty of praise and introduce him to my point system. I often use this with children who need an extra "crutch" to help them along. It provides an immediate reward and yet is intrinsic to the learning process. It can work in two ways. Sometimes I give the student the maximum number of points he can earn on an assignment or test, and he sees how near he can get to that number. At other times I give him points for all the work he accomplishes during a class period and he sees if he can beat his score the next day.

The points act as a bridge and I don't have to use them for long. For example, I used them only a week or two with Stanley, and only a few days with Ethel, another student who had been creating havoc at home by demanding presents for schoolwork.

I called sweet, quiet, but crafty young Ethel my basement bargainer. Her approach to gaining prizes was: "If you give me ______, then I'll ______."

I used the points a little longer with Shirley. She was the most aggressive of the prize collectors. I called her my prize fighter because she used the threatening approach: "If you don't give me ______, I'll ______."

The more immediate the reward or prize, the greater its motivating effect—the "You've done so well on the spelling tests, you can now read that book you've just got from the library" kind. Some of the best rewards are the surprise or unpredictable ones, such as the "I thought we'd go to the zoo today instead of doing our lesson as we're so far ahead" kind.

If you do decide to use a reward, make sure that you are offering it for a task you know your child can achieve. There is nothing more demoralizing than reaching for a star that cannot be plucked out of the sky. And don't make the mistake I made once of promising something you may not be able to deliver. I told one of my students I would take him on a picnic as he had worked so hard—and it rained!

If you use the lessons in this book to help your child to read, you will probably come up with your own plan of rewards and incentives to motivate him. For the more immediate, tangible rewards, you may decide points are most suited to his interests, needs, and temperament. Or you may use grades (A, B, C, D), numbers (eight out of ten right), smiling faces, stars, charts showing his progress, or just encouraging comments.

Hopefully there will be one or two lessons when he will be so motivated he won't need any incentives at all. You may be surprised. If you remember some of these "trade" tips, you could find you are in for an easier time than you think!

Let Your Child Learn by Doing

We learn best by doing. As the Chinese proverb says: "I hear and I forget. I see and I remember. I do and I understand." Imagine learning how to fix the car and you will see what I mean. Which do you think would be the easiest method to understand how the engine works:

Having someone tell you about the different parts;
Having someone point out the different parts;
Actually taking the parts out and putting them together again.

I remember learning to knit when I was quite young. It took me less than half an hour because a kindly old lady took the time to sit down with me, show me how to hold the needles and wool, and then coach me as I struggled to cast on and make the plain and purl stitches. Recently I have been trying to learn to crochet from an instruction book. And I still haven't fathomed it out.

I also remember how I learned to skate. A boyfriend took me to the middle of a huge, frozen pond—and left me. It was bitterly cold so I had no choice. If I didn't move I would freeze. I thought he was mean, and cruel at the time, but his method worked.

Teaching your child by doing is easy for you because you've been doing it ever since he was born. You didn't teach him to tie his shoes by saying: "Now, listen to me, Bobbie. You hold the laces in each hand, then you cross them over. . . ." No, you sat down on the sofa with him and actually tied the laces with him, saying: "Now hold the laces in your hand like this. Good, that's right. Now cross them over like this. No, hold them a bit tighter. . . ." You use exactly the same method when you teach him such things as counting, identifying colors, recognizing the letters, and, finally, to read.

Reciting Facts Doesn't Mean You Know Them

Don't be fooled, as I am afraid some teachers are, into believing that if your child can recite specific facts and details he knows them. This isn't necessarily so, as it was recently proved to me.

I had a call from the principal of one of our local schools. "I want you to test one of our kids," he said. "He's just arrived from another state. His report cards are terrific—mostly A's—and he has great recommendations from his former teachers. However, he's done extremely poorly on our tests—in fact, so poorly I can't possibly put him in the third grade, where he should be. I can't make it out. His parents say he's always been at the top of his class. Will you have a look at him?"

I duly tested Ted and came up with the same results as the new school. Ted knew very little. However, after talking to him for a while about his former school I discovered why. All his learning had been done by memorization. Each day he had been fed reams of information, which he was tested on the next day. Being a conscientious boy, he had studied hard and done well on the tests. However, the tragedy is that he never really understood what he was learning, or could relate it to his own life. The information was meaningless to him and so had soon been forgotten.

Information Cannot Be Learned in a Vacuum

Information cannot be learned in a vacuum. If Ted had used his multiplications to calculate how many pieces of gum he could buy with $1.50, instead of just reciting them parrot fashion, or if he had been able to re-enact one of the battles of the Revolution instead of memorizing its date, they would have had some meaning for him and he would not have forgotten them so easily.

Think about your child's experiences at school and you'll see what I mean.

One day he comes home from school, plonks down his school-books, and heads for the refrigerator.

"How was school?" you ask.

"O.K."

"What did you do?"

"Nothing much."

"Well, you must have done something. What did you do in social studies?"

"Oh we learned about the early settlers."

"My, that sounds interesting."

"Well, it wasn't. It was as dull as could be. I was so bored. I thought the class would never end. And look at the homework Mr. Richards has given us, five whole pages of this history book to learn for a test. It'll take me hours. I've got better things to do with my time."

Another day. The back door is flung open and your son runs into the house calling you:

"Mommy, Mommy. Guess what. We've been on a field trip to that museum you told me about. And we saw the houses the early settlers lived in, and the clothes they wore, and the things they used to cook with. It was such fun. I even got to hold some of the pots and pans, and they were so heavy. That's because they had to cook on open fires. They made the pots themselves. They were reddish because their soil had iron in it. Say, do you have a notebook I can have? We're all going to do projects on the early days, and I want to get started."

It's pretty obvious which lesson had more impact on your child. I expect he forgot the facts he learned from the history book pretty soon. But I bet he talked about the trip to the museum for weeks.

Of course, there is a place for memorization in learning, but it must be accompanied by plenty of practice. When your child learns to read or spell, for example, he has to memorize the basic rules before he can sound out the words correctly. But then he has to go over and over them before he has them down pat. Practice does make perfect! You know how important practice is if you have ever learned to type, ski, or cook. Have you ever tried to make popovers? It didn't take me long to memorize the recipe, but it has taken me literally years of trial and error to get them to pop!

Whatever it is you are teaching your child, make sure he becomes involved in what he is learning:

•Check to see that he really knows what he is doing and why he is doing it; ask him questions as you go along, and at the end ask him, "What did you learn today?"
•Encourage him to ask questions.
•Relate what he is learning to his life: "This will help you to do your math homework faster." "Did you notice the girl in the story is the same age as you? How do you think you would have acted if you were in the same predicament as she?"
•Finally, give him plenty of opportunities to *use* his knowledge.

Success Is Essential: Hints for Teaching Specific Skills

Children thrive on success, as we all do. Think about the time you tried to lose weight. Weren't you encouraged that first week, when you lost two whole pounds? But what about the next week, when you lost barely an ounce? Didn't you feel like quitting?

You like to do the things you are successful at. When you learn to serve without double faulting each time, you begin to enjoy playing tennis. But when you can't get a single backhand over the net, don't you feel like switching to golf? It's just the same with your child. You will find that he will enjoy learning if you help him to be successful.

So far I have talked in general terms about how you can help your child to learn. Now here are a few hints to teach him a specific skill, whether it's cleaning his teeth or riding a bike, developing those important prereading thinking and language skills, recognizing or writing the letters, or actually learning the fundamental reading skills.

•**Don't try to tackle too much at one time.** Don't try to teach your toddler ten words at once. One at a time is plenty. Teach the letters one by one. Don't try to cover all the short vowels in one session!

•**Break down each skill or task into smaller, manageable parts.** When you ask Cindy to clear up the yard, you don't push her outside and say, "Get on with it." You break the job into stages that she can do one at a time. "Pick up the bats and balls. Put your hot wheels in the garage. Then clear up the sandbox. And don't forget to bring your sweater in." When you play one of the games I give to develop logical thinking or one of the reading skills, don't give your child all the rules at once and immediately begin. Explain each rule, one by one, giving him time to absorb them and ask questions if necessary. Then play a "trial" game before the "real thing." When you teach him the short vowels, first make sure he can recognize the letters and their sounds. Then have him read them in simple, one-syllable words, and then in longer, more difficult words.

•**Work on only one thing at a time.** Don't progress to a new skill until he has fully grasped the previous one. Don't try to teach him the differences in shapes the same day you teach him the colors. Don't show him how to write the letters when you teach him their sounds. Don't introduce long vowels until he has the short vowels down pat.

•**Don't be the eager-beaver teacher and rush things.** Learning takes *time.* If you try to speed things up you create pressure and anxiety. This in turn leads to failure, so you defeat your own purpose. Some days your child's progress will be fantastic, and both of you will be elated. But on other days he will seem to be making no progress at all, and even appear to be forgetting some of what he has learned. This is nothing to be concerned about, unless, of course, it continues for a long period, for this is the way we all learn. I always tell my students when I am teaching them to read that it's like going up a slippery mountain slope. You make great headway, and then you have to stop to catch your breath. Sometimes, if you come to a particularly slippery part, you even fall back a little. But then you get your breath and energy back, and on you go again, until eventually climbing, resting, slipping, and climbing, you reach the top. You cannot rush the learning process. Your child needs the pauses to catch his breath (absorb new information), and the "slips" backward are merely a reorganization or "processing" of new information.

•**Don't always look for results.** Don't panic if he is not learning as quickly as you might like, and never, of course, show your child you are concerned with his slow progress. You can check to see if you are "result-oriented" by watching your reactions when your child does a task. Do you only give praise when he does it well, or do you pat him on the back for trying? Or, if your child is at school do you notice the A's and B's on his report card first, or the C's and D's? Do you first congratulate him on his good grades, or do you bawl him out for his low grades? Or do you ignore the grades and look for the comments on effort?

•**See that he achieves some degree of success at each session.** If he has had a particularly tough day and hasn't made much headway, make sure you end with something you know he can do well.

•**Let him know how he is doing—the sooner the better.** When he does something correctly, immediately say "Good, yes, that's right." If you are teaching him the letters or the reading lessons, or some other skill that entails "homework," correct it as soon as possible so he knows if he's on the right track. Prompt "feedback" not only reinforces learning but also prevents mistakes being repeated.

•**Choose carefully what you teach according to his ability and skill level.** You don't expect your child to climb the stairs to bed when he can't get up the front-door step. So don't have him draw circles and squares until he's had plenty of "scribbling" practice and can draw straight and curved lines. Don't teach him words until he has learned to deal with symbols, and don't play the games I give for seeing relationships until he has learned to observe accurately.

•**Teach toward his strengths rather than his weaknesses.** This should be easy because you know your child better than anyone else. You understand his temperament. You know his idiosyncrasies, fears, and special talents. You know what he can do best, so you can plan your teaching accordingly. If you know he finds it easier to learn visually by actually seeing a word written down, you know this will be the best way to first introduce him to the letters. Or if you realize he has a hard time speaking distinctly, you can teach him to pronounce words correctly by giving him catchy jingles and rhymes to sing.

•**Start with what he knows and build from there.** If you want to increase his vocabulary, begin with words he already knows.
Ask:

"What is this?"

"It's an apple."

"Yes, it's an apple. An apple is a fruit. Can you say fruit?"

"Fruit."

"Good! A pear is a fruit too. Can you think of anything else that is a fruit?"

And so on.

•**Use his particular likes and interests to introduce new skills.** If he loves to cook, use cookie baking to teach him the shapes. If he's a great milk drinker, use milk in two glasses to play the game I describe to develop his ability to think intuitively. If he's got a special hobby, relate it to the reading lessons. For example, when I taught Jimmy, who adored boats, the double vowels, I introduced them by using such words as "boat," "sail," "sea," "beach," and "breeze."

•**Don't make your sessions too long so he gets tired or loses interest.** The length of time will vary, of course, according to what you are teaching and your child's age at the time. If you are working on vocabulary development and he is still a toddler, a few minutes going over two or three words is plenty long enough. But if he is ten, you can spend twenty minutes or more. You can have him look up the words in the dictionary, read them in sentences, and then use them in his own sentences.

•**Be specific.** Make it absolutely clear what he is supposed to be learning. This is particularly important when you are teaching him the letters and the fundamental reading skills. Begin by explaining: "Today we're going to learn the letter 'b,' or how short vowels can be made into long vowels." Be precise when you give him a task. Ask him to repeat your directions so you know for sure he understands what he has to do. If you give him a written test, which you might do in the later stages of the reading lessons, remind him to read the instructions slowly and carefully before starting. This sounds obvious, but again and again I find a student forgetting to do this, to the frustration of both of us.

•**Don't try to outwit or catch him out.** Don't test him until you are pretty sure he can do the task or skill. You don't say, "Now see how quickly you can finish the jigsaw puzzle" when he's having a hard time putting the first pieces together, so don't give him a vocabulary test until he has had plenty of time to learn the words. If you give him a test, don't ask "trick" questions. Tests should be to air knowledge, not a trap, so make sure you cover all the topics with him beforehand and he is well prepared.

•**Give him your UNDIVIDED attention while teaching.** Don't try to teach your child the alphabet while you are cooking supper, and don't play the games I give to develop his vocabulary while trying to watch your favorite television program. If you are teaching him the reading lessons, even if he is working one of the exercises, resist the temptation to darn that sock he needs for sports tomorrow, or knit that sweater that has to be finished for Christmas. If you have important things that need to be done it is better to shorten the lesson. If you want him to concentrate and focus on the task at hand, you must too. There is no better way to teach than on a one-to-one basis. A child flourishes when he knows your only concern is to help him. You have a golden opportunity to perform miracles. Take advantage of it!

•**Enjoy your teaching sessions—and he will too.** Be relaxed. Don't feel you have to be serious all the time. In fact, if you can think up the odd joke to make a point clear, it will have much more impact. If you can have a good laugh at something, he is far more likely to remember it. Vary the activities for a change of pace. If he is having a hard time and making no progress, take a break. Start with the toughies while he is fresh, and always try to end on a fun note.

I really enjoy my sessions with my students. I hope these hints on teaching and learning will help you to enjoy your sessions with your child and successfully help him acquire the skills he needs to read, so that one day you will discover him on top of that slippery mountain, reading a book on his own with understanding and pleasure, for then you will know that you have indeed performed a miracle—he has become a fully fledged reader.

PART TWO:

Preparing Your Child for Reading: Those Important First Few Years Before School

CHAPTER 2

When and How to Start

Begin the Day Your Child Is Born

When do you start helping your child to read? As early as possible. In fact, the day he's born is not too soon! Often parents don't think I am serious when I tell them this. But this is usually because they are thinking of reading in terms of actually reading a book. They don't realize there are many skills, abilities, and attitudes a child needs to acquire *before* he's ready to read.

Nor do they realize what a crucial role they play in their child's reading development. Later on they are quick to blame the school for his reading problems, when actually it may be their own fault for not preparing him adequately.

"But that's what I thought kindergarten was for," they protest when I ask them what they are doing about getting their child ready for reading.

But kindergarten is too late. And so is nursery school. This is because the skills, abilities, and attitudes are so intimately related to a child's whole growth and development. They are not the sort of things that can be learned overnight, or even in a year or two. Nor can they be "taught" through regular means of instruction. However good the kindergarten, or nursery school programs may be, they cannot substitute for the important element, time. Nor can they provide many of the necessary activities and experiences that you can so easily and naturally expose your child to. All they can do is reinforce and build upon the solid foundation that *you* build, slowly and gradually, as he grows from a tiny infant.

Many parents also don't realize that their child learns more during the first five years of his life than at any other time, and that not only his ability to read but also his intelligence, behavior, and ability to learn generally are particularly influenced by the kinds of stimulation, and experiences, he is exposed to, especially during his first year.

You begin when he is born simply because he is ready. It may seem that the frail but gorgeous creature you have miraculously created is just a bundle of burps, gurgles, snuffles, and cries, needing only to be fed, diapered, and snuggled. But actually he is an intelligent little fellow, quite capable of learning. He can look, listen, make sounds (and how!), hear, and perform certain muscular co-ordinations such as sucking, grasping, and moving his body and limbs—all indications of highly organized systems of behavior. He also has all his faculties, they are only waiting like flowers in bud to unfold and reveal their colors. And, of course, you know he is quite capable of reacting to his environment from the way he bawled out your doctor for giving him that whack on the behind when he arrived on the scene.

Start by Doing What Comes Naturally

Your task is really quite simple. All you need to do is to see that the skills and abilities your child will need to read don't remain dormant. You cultivate them so they flourish as the flowers do when they are watered and fertilized. You start by doing what comes naturally as a proud parent. You cuddle your baby and smile at him. You quietly talk or sing to him. Make noises. Dangle a toy to attract his attention, and let him grasp your finger. For all these things awaken the senses that he will eventually need to read. When you talk and sing to him, you are getting him used to the sounds and rhythms of language. When you make noises, you stimulate his learning. When you dangle a toy in front of him, you help him focus his eyes, and when you let him grasp your fingers, you are establishing basic brain-muscular co-ordinations.

By doing these things you are also making him aware of his surroundings, so that in the future he will be able to react to them on his own accord. And you are making him aware of you, and building a rapport between the two of you, for, as you smile, cluck, and chat to him, and he smiles, gurgles, and reaches out to touch you in return, you are achieving your first bonds of communication.

Get Your Child Interested in Learning

The first thing you have to do to prepare your child for reading is to get him interested in learning. This is not as difficult as you might think, for you have a lot going for you.

To begin with, your home has many advantages. It provides an ideal teaching situation that no school can come close to duplicating. It is full of all the most marvelous stimuli and opportunities for learning imaginable. Glance around your home and you will see what I mean. Books, magazines, newspapers, television, radio, and perhaps a record player and a tape recorder. Clocks, telephones, thermometers, timers, measuring cups, and tape measures—all naturals for teaching. Then there are all those pots and pans, cups and saucers, kitchen utensils and equipment, cleaning materials, and any number of other household goods and foods that can also be used for all sorts of learning.

A child can learn much more easily and naturally in the home setting. Here he can truly learn by doing and experiencing. Take cooking. By making a simple batch of brownies, he learns, and practices all the mental skills he needs to eventually read a book. For he has to observe accurately, concentrate, remember information, see relationships, make associations, think logically, and reason. Not only is the learning effortless, it's also fun—and tasty!

At home you are not under the same pressure a teacher is at school. You don't have to stop an activity when the bell rings. If you want to spend longer doing something, you can change the time of dinner, or reorganize your day's plans. If you suddenly decide a trip to a special exhibit at the local museum would be especially beneficial, you can go. You have no red tape to cope with.

You have only one or two kids, or a handful at most to cope with, not twenty or more. Yes! I know you have a myriad and one other things to do apart from looking after the kids, especially if you have a job. But still, you do have a chance to be alone with your children. You are there to listen, watch, and reassure, all necessary when a child is learning, for he needs someone to show off a new skill to and someone just to talk to. Also, you can answer his questions as they arise. He doesn't have to raise his hand and wait his turn. And what is more, he is not afraid to ask at home.

Nor is your child afraid of making mistakes, or trying new things in the familiar setting of his home—that is, of course, as long as you encourage and support him in his efforts and don't make fun of him when things go wrong.

Learning also makes sense at home. There is a reason for acquiring the skills because they can be put *immediately to use*. Your child learns to concentrate so he can throw the ball through the hoop you have just attached to the garage wall. He acquires new words so he can tell you exactly what he wants for breakfast. And hopefully, he asks you to help him to read, so he can find out about the story in that exciting-looking book you gave him for his birthday.

Last, of course, you have a captive audience. You don't have to be a high-pressure salesman to get your child into your "classroom." He's right there. The poor kid can't escape you! Your task is to take advantage of this situation and provide the incentives for learning. And that is not difficult.

Providing a Home That Stimulates Learning

The first thing you need is a home set up for learning. This sounds as though it requires a lot of effort, but really it doesn't, for the average home usually provides the stimulation a child needs to learn. But for a little reassurance, here are the things I look for when I visit a student's house.

ARE THERE BOOKS AND READING MATERIALS?

I glance around to see if there are plenty of books. I don't mean just "learning" books such as history, science, or reference books, or even expensive books. I mean all kinds of books—some serious, but also fun ones, "escape" ones, the latest best seller, inexpensive paperbacks, and library books. I notice if they are neatly stacked on shelves, or behind glass doors, or lying around, obviously being used and read. Are there newspapers? Magazines? If so, which ones are they? What sort of information do they contain? Are there books for the children, and are they the kind that encourage a kid to read? (more about this later). This tells me the parents are curious and feel learning, particularly reading, is important—one of the most crucial factors in stimulating a child to learn and read.

ARE THERE PLACES FOR RELAXING, READING, AND TALKING?

I look to see if there is a suitable place, or one or two comfortable chairs or rugs, where the family can relax and enjoy the books. Is the sitting area set up so the family can chat easily together? Or are all the chairs directed toward the television set?

ARE THERE INDICATIONS OF HOBBIES AND SPECIAL INTERESTS?

I look for indications of family hobbies and interests. Is there a butterfly display, or shell collage on the wall? A stamp, or photo album on the coffee table? A hamster in a makeshift hutch in the kitchen? A bird feeder swinging from a hook outside the kitchen window? Or a plant box with sprouting seeds? A home with projects and situations such as these cannot help but stimulate a child to learn. They also provide plenty of opportunities for him to learn by doing, but only, of course, if he has a definite role to play, such as pasting the stamps, or photos, in the album; feeding the hamster or birds; or watering the plants.

ARE THE CHILDREN'S PROJECTS ON DISPLAY?

Does the refrigerator door have David's latest work of art stuck on it? Is Sally's mock-up of a colonial house on the mantelpiece? Are young Edgar's somewhat irregular woven placemats on the dining-room table? This shows the parents have pride in their children's work, which in turn encourages them to do other projects. I am pleased, by the way, to see efforts like Edgar's placemats on show, because this tells me that the parents are putting the emphasis where it should be—on effort rather than end result.

IS THERE A FAMILY BULLETIN BOARD?

I look to see if there is a bulletin board in the kitchen, or hallway, or some place where everyone regularly passes by. Are there newspaper clippings of events going on in the neighborhood or local area? Are the times the library is open posted? Is there a family schedule for the month, with key events, such as special family outings, school field trips, holidays, etc., written down? This says, again, that the parents are interested in expanding their children's experiences and horizons. But it also tells me that they—or at least one of them—is well organized, which is another very necessary factor if a child is to have the orderly, well-regulated kind of life that is conducive to learning.

IS THERE TELEVISION?

I check to see if there is a television set, and where it is located. Is it the focal point of the sitting area? How many TVs are there? Do the children have one of their own? I am not anti-TV at all. In fact, I think it can be a wonderful teacher, and stimulate much learning. There are some marvelous programs on these days, about animals, explorations and discoveries, travel or historic events, to name just a few. They are extremely informative and enjoyable. And they probably have more impact than a book because they present the material visually. Other benefits can come if the family watches television together, for it gives them a chance to share experiences and learn together, as well as providing a common topic for later family discussions.

What I try to determine is if the television predominates the family, and particularly the children's lives. Do the kids rush in from school, grab a cookie, head for the set, and remain glued to its screen until it's time for supper?

I also try to find out if there is discrimination in the choice of programs. Who chooses the programs? The parents or the children? The best method is for the parents and children to decide together. Each week they should discuss the programs and set up a viewing schedule. Both should express their views about specific programs, and if there is a conflict in opinions, compromises should be made. Time should be allotted for some fun programs, such as serials, game shows, and yes, even the odd cartoon, as well as specific learning and cultural ones. However, all programs involving violence, murder, and crime should be avoided. Deciding the programs ahead of time prevents daily "TV arguments," which seem to occur in so many families, and allows time to be scheduled for other important events such as homework, family chores, special projects, and outings.

DO THE CHILDREN HAVE A PLACE OF THEIR OWN?

Every child should have a place in the home that is especially his. So if he doesn't have the luxury of a separate bedroom, I look to see if he has been designated some other part of the house. It does not have to be a particularly large area; for example, it can be a corner of the den, or even the kitchen. But it should provide him with a place to keep his toys, books, and special possessions, and—if at all possible—some privacy so he can go off quietly on his own, knowing he won't be disturbed.

Many parents are surprised when I suggest they should provide their child with the opportunity to be alone. But kids are just like you and me, they need a chance to collect their thoughts. This is especially the case with older children, who not only need a chance to pursue their own interests, but also a quiet place, away from distractions, to do their homework.

Parents are also surprised when I tell them that children, even toddlers, can learn a good deal on their own! They don't need Mom and

Dad constantly hovering over them, feeding them information. They need time to ponder and absorb what they have learned and a chance to formulate questions to discover new things. Nor do they need to be exposed to stimulating situations every time the clock strikes, or have every part of their day structured and regulated. They need time and freedom to experiment on their own and to discover for themselves. They need to pursue avenues without interruption and the chance of chastisement—unless, of course, the "avenues" become hazardous or dangerous, in which case you do intervene!

If you haven't given your youngster opportunities to be on his own, try it. You will be surprised how long and hard he works and how much he manages to figure things out on his own without your guidance. Watch him playing with his bricks. It doesn't take him long to work out that he can build a taller pile if he puts the larger ones at the bottom and the smaller ones at the top. You will also find how working on his own develops his concentration, patience, and initiative.

IS THE HOME CHILD-ORIENTED?

My main concern when I visit a home is to see if it is set up for kids. Is it child-oriented? Or parent-oriented? By this I don't mean whether there are special facilities and equipment for the children, such as a doll's house or piano, or a sandbox or jungle gym in the garden. It's great to have these, and they can lead to all kinds of learning, but learning can take place without them. No, I am referring to the general organization of the house. Is it, for example, as neat as a new pin? Is it so immaculate and tidy that there is not a cushion out of place, a toy on the floor, a forgotten football in the corner, or dirty footprint on the linoleum? Is it like a movie set where the furniture is never disturbed? Or does it breathe life and activity? Does it tell me: Things are going on here—interesting things, fun things, creative things, *learning* things?

Whenever I go into what I call a movie-set home, I always think of Linda. She was a poor, pathetic child, with short, straight hair and large, woebegone eyes, who was a second-grade student in the school I was principal of. She was overly shy, barely communicating with her fellow students or her teachers. What was worse, she showed no interest in any subject, not even the fun ones like art and sports, and was obviously learning nothing. I had a conference with her parents. They were as concerned as I was, but could offer no reason for her disinterest.

One day her car pool failed to pick her up after school, so I took her home. We drove up to a lovely, new, expensive house. Her mother greeted me eagerly and invited me in. She was obviously very proud of her home, and offered to show me around. Linda, however, was greeted very differently. Within a minute she was told:

"Look at all that mud you've brought in. How many times have I told you to wipe your feet before you come in?"

"Don't put your books down there, I've just polished that chest."

There had been no "Hello, dear. How did school go today?" or even, "Well, I see you got home all right after all."

The more I saw, the more obvious it became. The house was the cleanest and tidiest I think I have ever seen, with many items that you and I would have to save years to buy. But it was also the most unwelcoming, barren, and unstimulating. Poor Linda, no wonder she had not developed an interest in anything.

Now I realize this is an extreme case, and later I discovered that Mrs. Cantley was completely neurotic about cleanliness. I am not suggesting that if you have a spic-and-span home you are neurotic, or your child's not going to learn. What I *am* saying, however, is that it's essential for your child to grow up in a stimulating household. Put the emphasis where it should be—on the kids, rather than the house. Accept the fact that if you have kids the house can't always be as clean and tidy as you would like. Help them to develop good habits such as putting their toys and games away at night, making their beds neatly, and cleaning the bath out. But do not be prissy about the odd forgotten marble or the dirty fingerprint on Grandma's photograph. Keep one room, or area of a room, that is "off bounds" so you have somewhere you can comfortably take an unexpected visitor, but, do not turn the den into a doctor's waiting room.

Finally, spend as much time as you can with your kids. Remember, they are young for only a short time, and these are their best learning years. Enjoy them, and let them enjoy you and their home, and see how they flourish.

Making Your Home Happy and Tension-free

Even more important than the physical setting of your home is the kind of atmosphere or "climate" you create. It must be positive and encouraging if your child is to develop positive and favorable attitudes to learning and reading. This means you must practice all the "tricks of the trade" I mentioned in the previous chapter: giving your child confidence and a sense of security; praising and encouraging him; motivating him; letting him learn by doing; and seeing he has success. But it goes beyond this to include every facet of your relationship with your child and affects your entire way of life. How can I tell if there is a good atmosphere in the home for learning? First, I try to determine if there are good family relations and if the home is happy, relaxed, and tension-free, for little learning can go on unless a child is at peace at home. Is the child accepted as an individual? Is he made to feel important? Are his opinions listened to and respected? Is he free from fear of ridicule? I can sometimes get an inkling of this listening to parents talk with their child.

Billy rushes in "Dad, Dad, I've just found a turtle in the garden. Quickly, come and see it."

NOT A GOOD SIGN: *"Can't you see I'm talking to Dr. Ervin? I'll come when I'm good and ready."*

GOOD SIGN: *"How exciting. I don't think you noticed Dr. Ervin is here. Go and give it some lettuce, and I'll come just as soon as we've finished talking."*

Tracy shows me the dress she has made for her doll:

NOT A GOOD SIGN: *"For heaven's sake, run along, Tracy. Grown-ups aren't interested in dolls."*

GOOD SIGN: *"Hasn't Tracy made it beautifully? She worked so hard at it. Can you see how neat the stitches are?"*

Seven-year-old Tom is sprawled on the sofa, totally absorbed in a book, sucking his thumb:

NOT A GOOD SIGN: *"Tom! If I've told you once, I've told you a hundred times. Stop sucking your thumb like a one-year-old."*

GOOD SIGN: *No comment—Tom is left to enjoy his book.*

I can also tell quite a lot from the tone of voice parents use with their children. When Mr. Brown says to his son: "Now, come on, let's try reading the next page" in a cheerful, firm voice, it's encouraging. But, when Mr. King says the same thing with a whine and a sigh, it's not. In fact, it's downright discouraging.

SITUATIONS THAT CAUSE TENSION AND DISCOURAGE LEARNING

All sorts of everyday circumstances can cause tension and hinder learning. Parents, often quite unconsciously, do things that stifle a child's desire to learn:

•**They're too demanding.** They push their child beyond his capabilities. For example, although Joan is still having a hard time with the second-grade reader, they persuade her teacher to put her in the third-grade one.

•**They make comparisons.** If a child is told, "John read this book when he was six. How come you can't?" it puts him under enormous pressure.

•**They're inconsistent.** They say one thing one day, and another the next, so the child never knows where he is. One night they are adamant he must be in bed by seven o'clock. And yet the next night they "give in" and say, "O.K., but be in bed by half-past seven."

Inconsistency can also come from the parents not working as a "team." If they don't back up each other's decisions the child not only becomes confused, but also learns the game of "playing one parent off against the other." For example, if you are both going to help your child to read, you must decide ahead of time which assignments are important. That way if you tell him one day: "You have to learn these words," your better half doesn't say the next day (after he has spent a good half hour struggling with them), "Oh these don't matter. You needn't bother with them."

•**They "nit-pick."** They focus on the little details that are wrong and ignore the true accomplishments their child has made. For example, if their child has made a great effort to dress himself neatly but forgot to brush his teeth, they will emphasize the fact that he forgot the teeth cleaning rather than that he got himself all spruced up.

•**They make unnecessary restrictions.** They are what I call the "don'ters." Everything becomes a no-no, so the child is constantly faced with the possibility of not doing anything right. They take him to a bookstore and say, "Choose a book for your birthday present." He spends considerable time, reviewing books and makes his decision. He hands it to his parents and then is told, "Oh that's a silly book to choose," or "You won't enjoy that" or "That's too expensive." If restrictions are necessary—for example, if there are certain books you don't want your child to choose—make the restrictions clear *beforehand*. But always try to limit such restrictions.

•**They punish.** Punishment should not be used in teaching, except perhaps, in very extreme cases. Like threats, it does not produce results, only fear and hostility. The emphasis should be on praise and encouragement. If you make it clear what you want from your child, and you are firm but reasonable, there should be little need for punishment. If an occasion does occur when your child deliberately and willfully disobeys, you must play it by ear and decide the best way to deal with the situation. However, never resort to physical punishment—it's demeaning for both of you. It may get rid of some of your frustration, but it will only increase your child's. If you do decide that some sort of punishment is in order, give it immediately, and then don't discuss or refer to the incident again.

If Jenny hasn't learned her words for the third night in a row, you might say:

"Jenny, this is the third night you haven't learned these words. I'm sorry, but instead of watching that Disney movie tonight you'll have to work on them."

However, the next time she has to learn some words, do not say:

"And this time I don't want to have to punish you like last time." Instead, just assume she'll learn them—and she most likely will.

•**They ridicule their child in front of others.** If parents want to reprimand or correct their children, they should do it in the privacy of the home, unless it is for something very minor such as a mispronounced word. Additionally, it goes without saying that they should never make fun of their child—in or out of the home. All parents will agree with this, but how many do it unconsciously.

Consider the situation where five-year-old Charles is telling a story, and he uses a word incorrectly, a real Mrs. Malapropism. His father roars with laughter and jokes to his friend, "What will he come up with next? Have you ever heard 'melody' used that way before?" He continues chatting, quite oblivious that he has not only embarrassed and humiliated his son, but also done untold damage to his vocabulary development. For Charles decides then and there: "I'm not going to try out any of those fancy words again, that's for sure."

•**They're disorganized.** A child cannot lead a happy, productive life without a certain order to his day. This doesn't mean that meals always have to be served at exactly the same minute each day, or your child must always take his nap at two o'clock whether he is ready for it or not. But it does mean there should be a regular routine, so that when he wakes up in the morning he pretty well knows what to expect. It's the same with teaching a specific skill. If you don't introduce it in an orderly manner a child will be confused. In teaching a child to write the letters, you first teach him to make straight lines, then curled lines and then show him how to put them together to make the letters.

•**They choose inappropriate times for teaching.** Parents should not try to teach their children all day and every day. "There's a time and a place for everything." There are, for example, certain occasions in each household that are already too full of tension to be appropriately used as a "learning situation." One such occasion is breakfasttime, when you are too busy getting the food on the table, the lunches packed, and the kids ready for the school bus, without trying to improve their vocabulary at the same time! Likewise, if you come home tired and tense from a day full of problems and catastrophes, this is not the time to give Sally her reading lesson—not at least until you have had time to unwind by having a shower, or a drink, or read the newspaper.

Dinner, by the way, should mainly be a time when the family relaxes together and enjoys each other. It can be used for learning general things through informal discussions of the day's events, but it should never be used for formal instruction, such as reviewing rules or practicing spelling.

•**They let their kids get the best of them.** There are times when our "loved ones" aren't always the angelic kids we would like them to be. In fact, let's face it, they are sometimes downright annoying, and even deliberately set out to disrupt things. The trick is not to let them! Imagine, for example, you are trying to teach your child something, and he starts drumming his fingernails on the table. What do you do? Say, "Don't do that, Michael"? If you do, you've had it! For this tells him, "Ah I've distracted her. If I do it again there probably won't be time to learn this today." And he will do it again. No, the best method is simply to ignore it. It will take a lot of patience and self-restraint on your part, but whatever annoying habit it may be—gritting teeth, cracking knuckles, tapping feet, chewing gum, or sniffing—*keep quiet!*

WHAT MAKES AN EFFECTIVE LEARNING "CLIMATE"?

Having discussed some of the negatives, let's look at some of the things that do create an effective learning "climate":

•**Being a good listener.** Instead of constantly feeding your child with facts and information, let him tell you things. Encourage him to chat about everyday occurrences, such as what he did at a friend's house, or at the zoo; the game he played with his rag doll; or what happened in a cartoon. Have him tell you his own stories. Ask him to give his opinions: "What did you think of that book?" "Why do you think the characters acted that way?" And above all else, let him feel free to ask you questions. For all these things encourage his interest and motivate him to learn, as well as force him to organize his thoughts and reason and develop his language skills.

•**Being willing to answer your child's questions.** How many parents have despaired at their children's endless questions, especially when they have already been asked—and answered—several times before. But this is the way youngsters learn. They ask because, fortunately, they are innately curious. They have a tremendous urge to learn. They repeat the question because they want to be assured that what they have learned is correct. By failing to answer your child's questions you turn down his curiosity valve. Be grateful that he wants to find out, and try to take time to answer his questions as fully as possible. Actually, I am constantly amazed by parents' patience. I followed a father and his son around the supermarket one day, and I am quite sure the young boy asked a dozen questions within a dozen minutes. But that fantastic father quietly answered each one, at times going into quite long explanations. Of course, you are not going to be able to do as this father did every time you go shopping. There are going to be days when you simply have to do it in fifteen minutes flat, or the family will not get supper that night. However, try not to cut your child short, and instead say: "That's an interesting question. Can you remember it, and ask me later, because Mommy has to do the shopping quickly today?" Then, if possible, try to remember the question, in case he forgets it.

•**Letting your child seek his own solutions.** It's easy to explain something by saying, "This happens because—." However, if you let your child observe for himself, and draw his own conclusions, he will be much more likely to remember. Instead of saying, "These flowers are growing taller than those flowers because they get more sun," ask, "Why do you think these flowers are growing taller than those flowers?" It takes longer to teach this way, but it's worth it, for it also develops his perception and his reasoning ability, and trains him to tackle problems in the future.

•**Being open-minded and receptive to your child's ideas.** Let him see that you respect his opinions. Don't be the "know-all" with all the answers, and be willing to learn from him. If you meet him halfway, he will go the other half. And you will then have a truly happy learning relationship.

Your Child Is Innately Curious

As well as having an ideal teaching situation, your home, you have another great advantage for getting your child interested in learning. As I said earlier but would like to emphasize, your child is born with an innate curiosity and a wonderful capacity for learning. He has a mind of his own, and he is eager to use it. It's literally like a sponge, ready and willing to absorb every little drop of information. His interests are unlimited. His potential, fantastic.

All you have to do is capitalize on this tremendous inquisitiveness and potential. Provide him with the opportunities, stimulation, and practice, and he will take it from there! Sometimes he will even provide his own opportunities and save you the trouble. They may not always be the most suitable, or quite the ones you would have chosen, but nevertheless they can develop many important skills. For example, he is doing a great job of developing his eye-muscle co-ordination when he scribbles all over his bedroom wall, or that best seller you have just purchased. And he is surely developing his ability to concentrate as he slowly and methodically unpicks your knitting!

As he grows older, tune up his muscle co-ordinations, tease his senses, tug at his mind, and tantalize that curiosity. Give him the widest variety of experiences you can. For every new activity, game, situation, and challenge stretches his world, stimulates his interests, and helps him to learn. The more he learns, the more he will want to learn. Ultimately every experience can stimulate his interest in reading and enrich his background for deeper understanding.

Whatever activity you choose, however, make sure your child sees it as being worthwhile and enjoyable. As soon as he is old enough, involve him in the planning, and let him make the choice sometimes.

Let your activities evolve from your normal daily activities. Don't feel you have to spend a lot of money to provide the experiences your child needs to learn. I have said it earlier, but I repeat: Your home is full of golden opportunities, and there are many things you can do in your community that don't cost a cent. You don't need expensive equipment or special materials to "turn him on" to learning. Of course, it's nice to have the odd game, educational toy, or piece of equipment to add variety, or save yourself the time and effort of making your own. But they are by no means "musts."

Even if money is no concern, don't overdo the buying, for it's been my experience, that the more excessive the amount of material goods lavished on a child, the less he seems to play and use his own initiative for learning. Blow it on a dishwasher instead, and spend more time with your child. Ultimately, it is the experiences that he shares with you and the fun he has learning with you that will make him want to learn more.

Your Child Enjoys Learning

Another advantage you have in stimulating your child to learn is that he *enjoys* learning. You won't find it hard to persuade him to learn, because learning is fun for him. It's a marvelous game.

"My, this is great," he says as he busily sploggles paint onto his colorful picture. "Aren't I clever? Isn't this the best picture ever? Wow, this learning biz is fun!" You can see the sheer joy in his face as he proudly shows you the finished product.

He rejoices in every new fact learned and revels in every new skill acquired. Learning is one fantastic adventure after another, even though it may not seem so to you especially if the adventure is pulling all the books off the shelf, or taking every ornament off the coffee table. If you are smart you will avoid as many of these situations as possible, and take away as many opportunities or stimuli that can cause problems, or disrupt the household, as you can. Recognize, as I said earlier, that you can't have a model home with a youngster around. For these early years, put away—or at least out of reach—that crystal ashtray Aunt Ethel and Uncle George gave you as a wedding present, and your beautiful book on America. You might even do what a friend of mine did and turn the book shelves to the wall. But hers was an extreme case. She was living in a small apartment in New York with three boys under four.

Of course, there will be times when your child finds that learning is more than just a joyride. He is bound to have upsets and failures that cause him frustration. But these times soon pass, and before you know it, the tears are gone, and he is chuckling happily again. Here again, however, you can help. You can minimize the chance of frustration by not asking him to do things that are too difficult, and giving him enough time to complete projects well. For example, don't have him write a "T" before he can draw a straight line, or draw a picture when supper is only ten minutes away.

All you have to do when you are helping your child learn is to take advantage of his enjoyment in learning, and approach your teaching with a sense of fun too. This won't be hard because you will find that his sheer joy of discovery will rub off on you. Of course, you too will have times of frustration, perhaps when you have gone over and over something and he still doesn't get it. And situations will arise that will irritate you to death, such as when he bangs away at his xylophone, hitting the same note again and again, on the day you have the most blinding headache. However, when this does happen, try to remember you gave him the xylophone so he would develop his muscle co-ordination and sense of rhythm, and he is doing just what you want. He is hitting that same note repeatedly to reinforce the correct movements and assure himself he has really learned the skill. When occasions like this arise, and you feel that if he bangs that note again you will scream—count to ten, or at least to three! Say to yourself, "He's learning. And he's having fun." It might help!

Take my word for it, usually you will find you really enjoy teaching your child. You will be just as thrilled with his accomplishments as he is. And you will rejoice with him every time he learns a new word, solves a difficult problem, or, finally, one day, manages to tell you what he wants in a complete, and coherent, sentence.

You will also find working with your child to be one of the most—if not the most—rewarding and satisfying experiences in your life. To me, nothing can compare with the opportunity of sharing the struggles and joys of achievement with a child. It will make your life fuller and more worthwhile. It will stimulate you and give you a new purpose and sense of direction.

Helping your child to learn will also bring you closer to your child.

You will come to know him as you would never have done: You will develop an intimate relationship and true understanding that will, hopefully, stand you in good stead for those rocky, perilous teen-age years ahead, and flourish into a lasting trust. Enough said!

CHAPTER 3

The Importance of Emotional and Physical Well-being

Emotional Stability and Self-reliance

"Hey Mom, look at me!" Sarah calls as she perilously perches on the top step of the ladder.

"Come and see the picture I've painted," calls Jenny proudly to her Dad.

"Look what I've done," says Jim, as he produces the chocolate-chip cookies he has made all on his own, for dinner.

Could this be your child saying these things? Do they have a familiar ring?

Could your child have been the one I met in the dentist's office the other day? A young mother had brought her two-year-old daughter, and to keep her quiet she (rather inappropriately for a dental visit!) had given her a piece of candy. The mother had picked up a magazine and was deeply engrossed in one of the articles. Meanwhile, the toddler had curled herself up in one of the big leather chairs, and when I entered the room was about to begin what was to become the great adventure of "getting the candy out of the wrapper." For ten solid minutes she tried every trick in the bag. You name it, and she gave it a go. First of all, she tried the conventional way of using her fingers, twisting and turning the candy, looking for its opening. But when this method didn't work, she resorted to trying to bite it open with her teeth, bang it open on the table beside her, and even grind it out with the heel of her shoe. When these brought no results, she threw it against the wall. And finally, as I was called for my appointment, she returned to the finger method.

I really should have helped her out, or at least drawn the mother's attention to her predicament. But, quite frankly, I was too intrigued by the child's tremendous patience and perseverance.

Would your child have gone to such great lengths as my young friend? Does he persevere until he finishes a task? Can he work fairly well on his own? Is he like Sarah, Jenny, and Jim, happy and confident, and proud to show off his accomplishments? Does he have faith in his capabilities? Is he self-reliant? And is he emotionally mature so he can tackle learning without introducing personal problems, control his feelings, and not blow problems out of proportion? If so, he is going to find learning to read pretty easy.

On the other hand, if he is nervous and tense and lacks self-confidence, he is probably going to have a tough time. As I described earlier, learning to read is like climbing a slippery mountain slope. Your child has to be prepared for the long trek up, and accept the inevitable slides back as a challenge rather than as a defeat. This means he must be patient, persevering, and capable of accepting frustration, and even failure, at times.

How to Tell if Your Child Is Emotionally Immature

You can tell if your child is emotionally immature and unsure of himself by noticing such signs as: rapid changes of mood; restlessness, depression; crying excessively, particularly over small problems; extreme unco-operativeness; temper tantrums; passiveness; nervous habits, such as eye blinking, stuttering, biting fingernails, thumb sucking, and teeth grinding; extreme shyness; and a feeling of insecurity, which shows itself by an inability or desire to help himself, or lack of initiative. Obviously, all children display these kinds of behaviors at some point—as they grow up—they are quite normal. It's when they are excessive and dominate that they indicate emotional immaturity.

The Importance of Love and Affection

It is in the emotional development of your child that you as parents play such a crucial role. Nothing can substitute for your love and affection. The knowledge that he is loved gives your child the wonderful sense of security that makes almost anything possible. It is the carrot that spurs him on to a new skill, the magic word that makes everything seem so much easier. It's what makes him stick in there when the going gets tough, and enables him to accept the defeats, but come up fighting again.

The longer I work with children, the more I realize that loving and learning are inseparable. Time and time again, it's illustrated to me when I compare the progress of a child who comes from a home where love and affection are Priority No. 1, with a child who comes from a home where it is not.

Most parents start off on the right foot and lavish attention and affection on their child for the first months, or year or two. But then, as he grows older, matures, and becomes more self-reliant, they tend to curtail it, fearful he'll become spoiled. Don't fall into this trap. You won't spoil your child. You are too sensible for that. It has been my experience that as a child grows older and needs less physical care, he needs *more* emotional attention. So keep the affection and attention flowing. Take my word for it, they are the two Big A's of the ABC of learning.

The Need for a Secure and Stable Childhood

Nothing can substitute for a happy, stable childhood. If your child feels wanted and accepted and can trust you, he will grow to trust himself. If he can depend on consistant behavior from you, he will learn to be consistent too.

If you practice the "tricks of the trade," and provide the kind of home "atmosphere" I suggest earlier, your child will grow up confident and secure. If you set certain standards of behavior so he knows what is acceptable and what is not acceptable, you will give a structure and stability to his life. And if you present them so they call for self-discipline and not conformity, they will help to develop his sense of responsibility.

Develop Your Child's Sense of Responsibility

Seeing himself as responsible will give your child a positive picture of himself, the kind of self-concept that will help him throughout life, but especially in learning—for learning demands acceptance of responsibility.

You can develop this sense of responsibility by gradually loosening your reins, and letting your child conquer his own worlds. Teach him *how* to do things, rather than doing them for him. At one, show him how to feed himself. At two, let him begin to dress himself. And at three, make him responsible for keeping his room tidy, and even making his bed. At first it will be much harder and time-consuming for you to have him do these things. But it will pay off 100 per cent in terms of his self-reliance and feelings of competence and worth. Be sure he can do what you ask him to, and that it doesn't take longer than his current attention span (see page 80). Give him enough time to complete the job satisfactorily. But don't expect perfection. If you have to redo it (and you will on occasion), do it when he won't see you, or you defeat your whole purpose.

You also give your child's sense of responsibility a boost if you give him the opportunity to make decisions as soon as possible. Start by having him make simple choices. For example, ask him: "Which book shall we read tonight? The one about Peter Rabbit, or Charlie, the monkey?" Or, "What shall we have for dessert? Apple sauce or bananas?"

Encourage him to give his opinion on things. "What did you think about that mischievous teddy bear in the story?" "What did you think of Mary's birthday party?"

As soon as he can toddle, give him responsibilities around the house. This makes him feel very needed and important. And it's a help to you! Give him jobs as they arise. Sweeping up the leaves.

Taking the newspapers out to the garbage. Laying the table, or stacking the plates away. When he's about three, give him a regular job that he is responsible for each day, such as emptying the dishwasher, or feeding the birds, or watering the plants. And, of course, tidying up his toys.

When your child is about four, if possible have a pet for him to look after. He will learn a lot by just watching another living being, but he will also learn what it's really like to be responsible for something. Naturally, you will have to do the bulk of the work at first, until he is old enough to cope on his own (probably not until he is eight). But he can be responsible for feeding and cleaning the dish out. Or if it's a cat or dog, help to train it. If a pet is not for your household, let him have his own plant, window box, or patch of garden, or some living thing that requires daily care.

Any job, activity, project, or game you give your child to do, if appropriate to his ability level and presented in the right way, can help to develop those personal qualities necessary for learning to read. The more informal the activity, the better. Any of the creative activities are great, for they give him an opportunity to express himself and provide an outlet for his frustrations. Let him paint, draw, model in clay and plasticine, and sculpture. But also let him dance, sing, and play "music." Let him play with mud, water, flour, and other gorgeously messy ingredients. But do this in a place that can be cleaned up easily, perferably outside, or in the kitchen or bathroom. Dress him in something that doesn't matter. And have the bath water ready!

Let him make and construct things, such as furniture for his dolls' house (matchboxes, thumbtack boxes, thread wheels, chestnuts, wool, string, odd pieces of wood, cardboard, and gift wrapping paper are all good for this). Or make a "present" from odd boxes, wrapping paper, and string. (When he is young let him give himself the present, as he will have just as much fun, or more, unwrapping it.) Or create a simplified cornhusk or clothespin doll, or, with your help, a puppet. Or construct his own musical instruments. A xylophone from several cans put upside down, tied together, and put on a tray. A drum from an old box, such as a cylinder oatmeal carton, or a large ice-cream container. A trumpet from a rolled-up piece of cardboard, or thick paper.

Finally, see that he has plenty of opportunity to express himself through dramatic activities, such as dressing up, role-playing, puppetry, acting out stories, and playing charades.

All the games your child plays with his manipulative toys call upon the same skill and characteristics, such as patience, perseverance, and concentration, that reading requires. So make sure he has plenty of time to fit his nesting buckets and boxes into one another. Sort out his beads and buttons into their colors and sizes. Thread his beads. Build his blocks into buildings. And complete his jigsaws.

The many family games such as puzzles, board games, and cards are also good, particularly as they help to develop your child's feeling of family and "togetherness."

All the activities and games I suggest in this book can be used to help your child gain confidence in himself and in his ability to learn. However, when it gets down to the nitty-gritty it is you and your attitude to your child that will have the most effect upon him.

If you trust and respect him, if you give him your best and expect the best from him, if you are consistent and set reasonable standards of behavior, if you help him to be independent and self-sufficient early on, and if you enfold him in love, you will have a happy, stable, and secure child ready for the challenge of learning to read.

Physical Development and General Health

It goes without saying that your child needs to be in good health to learn to read, as he does for all learning. If his body is in tip-top shape, he will be alert and ready to concentrate. Good health will help him be patient, persevering, and generally capable of coping with difficulties and problems as they arise. Your attention to his physical development will ensure that he can see and hear properly and perform intricate muscular co-ordinations.

See That Your Child Gets Plenty of Sleep

Make sure that your child gets plenty of sleep. The more I work with children the more I realize the importance of this. If they have been shortchanged of their "hours before midnight," they are grouchy, easily distracted, fidgety, and generally lack interest. In short, they not only yawn and put their fists in their eyes, they also are just not "turned on" to learning. Establish a regular bedtime hour, and make exceptions only for special occasions, so your child doesn't get into the disruptive habit of "negotiating" the time with you. Also if he is young see that he has an hour of quiet in the afternoon. This can be used as your special reading time together later on. But while he is a toddler, it should be a truly rest period. It's hard to say exactly how much sleep your child should have each night, as this is an individual thing and children vary in their needs. However, just to give you an idea, I would say a minimum of ten hours, at least until he is six.

Watch Your Child's Diet

A child (or anyone) with a rumbling stomach or even slight hunger pains isn't going to be in the mood for learning, however exciting you make it. Be sure he gets three good meals a day at *regular* times, and particularly ensure that he has a substantial breakfast, so he is well prepared to meet the challenges of the day.

But he also needs to eat the *right kinds* of food, for research has shown that diet can have a major influence, not only on a child's energy and endurance level and his general attitude to himself and the world around him, but also specifically on his intelligence and learning ability. For example, some studies show that a proper, well-balanced diet can change an I.Q. as much as twenty points, while an inadequate one can actually hinder mental development. Others show that "junk" food, and foods with additives and artificial coloring, can affect the learning behaviors of children, such as attention span, concentration and low tolerance for frustration and failure. Many others indicate that lack of sufficient protein results in poor physical development and learning ability. These studies show that other foods, such as carbohydrates (all those handy and tasty sugar and starch foods such as cookies, cakes, candy, and bread), even though high in calories, cannot provide the fundamental needs of the body.

So watch what you serve. Go slow on the potato chips, cookies, and soft drinks. And include proteins (meat, fish, poultry, eggs, cheese, and nuts) in every meal. This needn't affect your food budget, for there are many delicious, yet economical recipes available in newspapers and magazines, and many excellent paperbacks devoted to the subject. You can also get help from your county agricultural extension service, or you can call the local school nutritionist or nurse. You can also consult these sources to ensure that you provide properly balanced meals, which are also important. For example, you should include plenty of fresh fruit and vegetables, which supply lots of the vitamins and trace minerals; milk; fats; and some carbohydrates in the daily diet. If your child is in the habit of having a snack, and I am sure he is, have on hand plenty of carrot straws or other raw vegetables, fruit, cheese, and nuts. If he craves candy, have a special time each day when he can choose one or two from his candy canister. Preferably make it after a meal when he won't have much room left!

If you introduce him to a sensible diet from the beginning, you shouldn't, however, have this problem. A child's eating pattern, like his sleeping pattern, is a matter of habit. He enjoys what he is used to, and obviously he is used to what you provide.

See That Your Child Keeps Physically Fit

See to it that he keeps physically fit and has plenty of exercise. I don't have to tell you that your child is superactive. He is constantly on the move: pulling his truck, climbing the stairs, stretching up to reach his favorite book off the shelf, banging nails into a piece of wood, jumping up and down, and falling over. It's probably as much as *you* can do to keep up with *him!* But encourage the activity, for he needs to exercise all and every muscle in his body. Encourage him to play games or participate in activities, that provide opportunities for many kinds of movement and muscular co-ordination: running, jumping, hopping, skipping, dancing, stretching, bending, pushing, pulling, crawling, climbing, sliding, kicking, punching, pounding, balancing, hanging, throwing, carrying, lifting, steering, stacking, squeezing, taking apart, putting together, and any other moving "ing" you can think of. Make sure he not only develops all those big muscles, but increasingly, as he gets older, all those important smaller muscles. When he is around twelve to eighteen months, introduce him to nice fat pencils and crayons and of course even before this you can have him play with the letters of his plastic alphabet, and focus his eyes on the printed page as you read him a story.

It is also important for you to pay particular attention to your child's physical development, because it is closely related to his mental development. Many parents don't realize this. But the more efficiently your child uses his body, the more efficiently he uses his mind, for all his basic mental skills are built on his physical achievements. When he stretches his legs, sucks his thumb, reaches for a toy, rolls over in his cot, holds a spoon, crawls, stands, and walks, he is establishing the basic patterns in his mind that will eventually enable him to learn to read.

He learns to do all these physical skills by constant repetition, practice, and trial and error. As his motor development increases, so does his learning and ability to store knowledge, as well as many of the other skills necessary for reading, such as concentrating, observing, remembering information, and seeing relationships.

So remind yourself when your child bangs the spoon on his plate for the umpteenth time, pulls all the saucepans out of the cabinet, or drags the entire roll of toilet paper down the stairs and drapes it around the house, or whatever skill he happens to be practicing at the time, that he learns by his actions! And he can't acquire mental abilities until his body has developed sufficiently.

So if you want to help your child to read, here's a tip: Get in shape yourself, eat well and get plenty of sleep. If you are physically fit, you will be able to keep up with this dynamo you are living with.

Your child first learns through his senses. It is through seeing, hearing, touching, smelling, and tasting that he learns to move and control his body and make "SENSE" of the confusing world he has been brought into. I explain the importance of developing his senses more fully in the next chapter, "Make Your Child Think." However, in preparing your child physically for learning to read, you should pay special attention to his sight and hearing, for he must be able to focus his eyes on the page, and recognize the letters and words, and hear their sounds before he can read.

Check Your Child's Sight

Your child is born farsighted, but gradually he develops nearsight and standard-distance vision, until he achieves the normal 20/20 level at about five or six years.

Keep an eye on his vision as he grows up. Notice if his eyes turn inward, outward, or upward, involuntarily, or if he squints when he looks at a picture or a book; plays with his threading beads, or jigsaws; tries to catch a ball; or when you hand him something. Note if he tilts his head as you talk to him, or point something out to him. Notice if he frequently rubs his eyes; complains of headaches, or of not being able to see clearly; or seems particularly tired after doing activities or playing games requiring near vision and fine discrimination. Also watch for a reluctance to do these activities. Any of these signs may mean that he has trouble seeing.

If there is any doubt in your mind that your child may have a visual problem, play it safe and take him to a child's eye specialist. If it turns out that he has poor vision, astigmatism, or nearsightedness, this doesn't mean he is not going to learn to read, or even, for that matter, have more difficulty than Jack down the street, who has normal vision. In fact, it could well be that Jack may have terrible problems learning, despite his good eyesight. This is because some people with perfectly normal vision have difficulty noticing specific details. They find it hard to discriminate between similarities and differences. For example, they find it difficult to tell the difference between "b" and "d," or "d" and "g," or "p" and "q." They confuse "w" with "m." And read "no" for "on," "saw" for "was," and "tam" for "mat." It is quite normal for a child to confuse these at first, so don't be concerned if your child does. However, if they continue, it could be an indication of a problem. I talk more about this in the chapter, "Getting Help When There Is a Problem."

Check Your Child's Hearing

It is also important to detect if your child has a hearing problem, not only because he needs to hear well to identify the sounds of our language, but also because a child with a hearing loss usually develops other problems that hinder his ability to read. The sheer effort of watching and striving to hear can so physically exhaust a child that he becomes apathetic and defeatist, and may develop all sorts of emotional problems.

It's difficult to detect if a young child has a hearing problem. Even routine physical checkups don't always reveal it. And your child can't help because, not knowing what the sounds should be like, he doesn't realize he has a problem. However, there are some signs that might be a clue: frequent earaches; speaking in a loud voice; distorted or unclear speech; turning his head or cupping his ear to hear; not answering when his back is turned; not coming when you call; inability to follow directions; frequent inattentiveness; turning up the TV, radio, or record player; and preference for very loud and noisy toys. Again, if there is any question in your mind, take your child to an ear specialist, for it may be a serious problem. On the other hand, it may be something relatively simple, like the accumulation of wax, which he can deal with easily.

CHAPTER 4

Make Your Child Think: Developing Those Intellectual Skills

"I know I'm biased, but my child really is bright for his age." How many times have you been told that? And own up to it, how often have *you* bragged that?

But it's true. Your child can reason out all sorts of things on his own. Watch how quickly he figures out which peg fits into which hole when he plays with his hammer and peg toys. Or how soon he fathoms out that if a cookie canister has supplied one chocolate-chip cookie, it's likely to produce another.

Nurture your child's intellectual and reasoning abilities because they are crucial to reading. One of the most difficult and important aspects is being able to understand the meaning behind the words, and figure out exactly what the writer is saying. It is still not known exactly how we do this. But one thing is for sure: The better your child can think, the greater success he will have.

Give him plenty of food for thought and mind-stirring challenges. The more his mind is stretched, the farther it will reach, and the more inventive and resilient it will be. Ask questions so he learns to think for himself. Pose problems so he begins to wonder. Offer choices so he can weigh alternatives. Introduce him to ideas that make him question, and make him look at the world from the inside and the outside so his imagination is aroused.

But don't get carried away with your enthusiasm, for you don't want to be the "pushy parent." Don't expect too much of your child, or try to accelerate his rate of progress beyond what he is capable of achieving. He can absorb only so much at one time. This is because his mind develops in a series of stages, and he is not capable of performing the intellectual skills at one stage before he has acquired certain other skills at previous stages.

The Stages of Development

All children pass through these periods in the same order, but the length of time varies enormously. It depends on their innate abilities; their biological age (which takes a more or less standard time in all children); and the kind of environment they grow up in. You have already given your child his innate abilities, and he will pretty well take care of his biological age. However, by providing the right kind of experiences at the right times, you can see he progresses as quickly and smoothly from one stage to the next.

Knowing these stages will help you to choose the most appropriate experiences and will help you understand your child's responses better. It should save wasted time and a lot of frustration, and ensure that the time you spend working together is both beneficial and enjoyable.

The "Sensational" Stage

I call the first stage, which goes approximately from birth to two years, the "Sensational" Stage because your child's progress is so fantastic and because all his learning takes place through his senses. Through seeing, hearing, touching, smelling, and tasting, he sets his mind to work, and begins to make "Sense" of the confusing world he has been brought into.

At first literally nothing makes sense. Life is a succession of visual images, sounds, and feelings. In fact, he cannot even distinguish himself from his surroundings. Gradually, however, he begins to notice himself and realizes, "I'm me. I'm someone." Slowly but surely he learns to sort out all the various objects and people in his surroundings. But not until around the end of his first year does he develop the concept of the permanent character of objects. Things exist for him only when he can actually see them.

Try this game out on your baby and see if he has learned this concept yet. Dangle a toy, doll, or some object he is familiar with, in front of him. Then, while he is still watching, cover it with a cloth or handy diaper. Does he notice where it has gone? Does he look for it? Or does he lose interest?

It is a great intellectual leap forward when your child perseveres in looking for a hidden object. You can help him toward this by playing simple "hide and seek" and "peekaboo" games. Shake his rattle and then hide it behind your back. At first, make the intervals short between the disappearing and reappearing. But when he gets the idea, lengthen the time. Put your face near his, and say, "Hi!" and then bend down beneath his crib, out of sight. As he learns to wait for your reappearance, play the game farther away from him. Pop your head around the door, or from behind the curtains.

At first, a baby also has no concept of cause and effect. He will try to put out the light by screwing up his eyes, or make his musical box play by banging on his crib. Again, it takes time, trial and error, and experience for him to grasp the concept. You can help by increasing his powers of observation (more about this later), giving him plenty of opportunities to practice, and as he grows older, taking the time to point out the what, why, and how of things. Instead of saying, "Don't touch that hot stove," add, "because it will hurt your fingers." As you turn off the light at night, show him the magical switch, and let him be the magician who brings the darkness.

By helping your child develop the concepts of permanence, and cause and effect, you are making a tremendous contribution toward preparing him for reading, for they are crucial to comprehension.

The "Pre-operational" Stage

Somewhere toward the end of your child's second year, he enters what Dr. Jean Piaget (the Swiss psychologist who discovered these stages) calls the "pre-operational" stage. By "operational" he means the complex mental acts associated with more adult thinking—hence the "pre." This period usually lasts until your child is about 6½ to 7. I call the first part of this period, up to about 4 years, the "symbolic" stage, because he learns to deal with symbols. He now understands the relationship between an object and the symbol or word for that object. He will let you know loud and clear when he reaches this stage because this is when he begins talking.

In regard to helping your child prepare for reading, this is a crucial period. You should do everything you can to develop his ability to talk, since written language is simply recorded spoken language. You must help your child use the symbols of our language (words) orally, so he later can interpret them visually; and help him express himself coherently, so he can understand what a writer is saying when he "talks" to him.

At about four years comes the beginning of intuitive thought, and the development of the concept that objects have certain enduring characteristics. Your child learns that things are not always what they seem. Those senses he has relied on so heavily up to now sometimes let him down. For example, he learns that a piece of plastecine or clay is the same size whether it's in a round ball or a long, elongated sausage, and the amount of water is the same whether it's in a wide, shallow bowl, or a tall, deep one. Logic now asserts itself, and, although it has quite a battle to establish its supremacy, it eventually takes over. Then comes the day when your child turns to you and says, "Say Dad, I've just figured it out." When this happens you know you have a fellow thinker in the household, and a potential reader.

You can see if your child has reached this stage of development, and help him toward it, by playing some of these games. If he doesn't get the answer right, don't go into complicated explanations. Just say simply, "They're the same." Give him more chances to observe the similarities for himself, for this is the only way he will come to grasp the concept.

Have him look at the rods below. And ask him if they are all the same length.

Pour some milk, or orange juice, into two identical glasses. Ask him if each one holds the same amount. When he agrees, pour the liquid from one of them into a shorter, stouter glass. Ask again if each holds the same amount.

Make some bread dough. Cut out two biscuits exactly the same size. Ask if they are the same size. Then make one into either a ball or a sausage shape and ask, "Does this ball [or sausage] have the same amount of dough as the other one?" Do the same when you make the next batch of cookies.

Put equal amounts of the dough, or cookie batter, in identical bowls. Then put the contents of one bowl into a taller, deeper one and ask, "Do the bowls hold the same amount?" You can play this game using beads, buttons, candy, macaroni, rice, or any other such items.

You can probably think up many more imaginative games than these. But you get the idea.

When Your Child Is a Baby

Since your child first learns through his senses, and his ability to observe and listen are so important to thinking, talking, and reading, expose him to many sights, sounds, and experiences as soon as possible. Before he is born, go hunting for inexpensive toys and playthings. But also use your imagination and make a few. Or beg, borrow, or buy some from a friend whose child has outgrown them.

The First Classroom: Your Child's Bedroom

A child's bedroom is his first classroom. Set it up so it's cheerful, colorful, inviting, and stimulating. Hang a mobile, kite, hanging streamers, of ribbons or glass beads, or even a balloon or two, from the ceiling. A baby will react to these moving objects and follow them with his eyes, developing his ability to focus them, and stimulating him to observe. Put up interesting pictures or posters of bold shapes and patterns. Babies are particularly stimulated by patterns and graphic arts, so make plenty of checkerboard or bull's-eye types of designs. Change them frequently for variety. Stick up shiny tinfoil stars, bright yellow moons (yellow is the first color he will learn to recognize, by the way), or silhouettes of animals or birds. Place the odd stuffed animal, doll, or toy in strategic locations. And don't forget to hang a rattle, or bracelet of bells, from his crib. Be sure to have a clock near enough for him to hear its comforting tick-tock, and, if possible, a music box. A colorful, healthy plant or two also adds variety, as do a silvery or shiny ornament to glisten in the sun. Make sure he has a special shelf for his future "library," and stock it with Mother Goose, and storybooks so he grows up with books from the very start and they become a familiar and accepted part of his life. Then, of course, there must be a mirror, not only to reflect and reinforce the impact of all the objects in the room, but also to enable him to observe and get to know the most important person in the world—himself. Finally, place a lamp or night light in a corner to cast friendly shadows in the night.

None of these need be costly. In fact, most of them you can make yourself. For example, you can make the mobile from cardboard, or pieces of wood, or metal. All you need to make the posters are a few large cut-out pictures, or just some travel advertisements put out by the airlines. While an assortment of colored felt pens and some nice large swishes of your arm can take care of the patterns and graphic arts. The animals and moon can be made from shelf paper, and the lamp from an old wine bottle and cast-off shade. The clock need not keep regular time, and the ornaments can be those wedding presents you never did like. The only expensive item is the music box, which you could forgo, but which I urge you to splurge on. It will give your child endless hours of pleasure and is a wonderful vehicle for developing his hearing and sense of rhythm.

The Need for a Change of Scenery

Even though you make your baby's bedroom as imaginative and creative as possible, don't abandon him to it, and have him spend most of the time in his crib. He needs the stimulation of a change of scenery, just as you do. Often parents don't realize this, and think their baby is crying because he is hungry or wants his diaper changed. But probably he is just yelling, "Hey. I want to get out of here for a while. I want to see some new things. I've got a lot to learn. And I want to learn it—now!"

So give your child variety in environment and a chance to learn new things. Whenever possible, have him with you. You don't have to hold or nurse him all the time, and, in fact, you don't always have to play with him. Just pop him on a blanket on the floor (but be careful to avoid the drafts), or put him in his carry cot, or infant seat if he is four weeks, and he'll probably be quite content to listen to the noises you make, and watch you as you go around the room and about your business. Try, if possible, however, to chat or sing to him so he is developing his ear for language. (See Chapter 5, "Talking Leads to Reading: Developing Those Language Skills," for more on this.)

The kitchen is perhaps the best environment in your home for learning, as it is full of a wide variety of inviting stimuli to awaken the senses. There are those glittering pots and pans, flashing knives, sleek white refrigerators and stoves and oh so many different sizes, shapes, and colors to look at. And what about all those curious sounds to hear. Glasses clinking, water running, the dishwasher roaring, spoons tinkling, and mixers whirring. Then there is all the exciting activity: chopping, scraping, cutting, stirring, pouring, splashing, and just endless hustle and bustle.

If the weather is suitable, take your baby for a walk each day. He will have a great time watching the live mobiles: people walking, trees swaying in the breeze, and cars moving, to say nothing of the experience he will get listening to the sound of footsteps, the rustle of leaves, and the toot of car horns. You can push him in his carriage or pop him in a sling.

A young father in my neighborhood takes his new baby out in a sling every evening after he gets home from work. He strolls around the block, chatting away to his tiny replica happily nestled on his back. They obviously enjoy it, and I am sure Mommy appreciates the twenty minutes to quietly get on with supper.

Don't forget to keep up the chitchat as you walk. It shouldn't be incessant—a comment now and then is enough to keep his senses alive and the communication going between you. If possible try to get a carriage that enables your baby to face you, as they have in Europe. This makes it so much easier for your *tête-à-têtes*. I'm quite sure one of the reasons why European children seem to talk sooner and read earlier is because of this.

If you can't go for a walk for some reason, take your baby out into the garden. If you have no garden, hold him near an open window. He won't be able to see things too well, as his vision cannot discriminate among things in the distance, but he can hear the various sounds.

The Importance of Observation

As your child grows older, keep his ears tuned and his eyes popping, for only they can feed his mind with the necessary information to keep his wits about him. They are the windows that let in the rays of knowledge, illuminating the details of life so he comes to understand himself and the world around him. They are the means by which he learns to observe and note details, which is the first step in the thinking process. If he can't do this he can't make assumptions or come to conclusions. He can't figure out how to do his jacket up without noticing the buttons and the holes. He can't piece together his model rocket without observing the sizes and shapes of each part, just as later on, when he becomes an adult, he won't be able to work out how to replace the tire when he has a flat, or complete more intellectual tasks, such as figuring out his income taxes, deciding which candidate to vote for, or developing his point of view on pollution control without first noting the important details and facts.

The ability to observe is the core to all thinking and learning, but particularly to talking and reading.

I describe many ways in which you can increase your child's observation powers in conjunction with developing his language ability in the next chapter, on talking. This is the easiest and best way, for the acquisition of one reinforces the acquisition of the other. And, of course, he must combine the two when he learns to read.

However, here are some additional pointers that will help your child take a closer look at the things around him and, hopefully, stimulate his curiosity and arouse his imagination, so that as he grows older he raises questions about his findings; for when this happens, the time bomb in his mind is ignited and his thought processes are truly activated.

I can't give you a specific time when you should do these activities because, as I have just pointed out, children develop at different rates. You will have to rely on that great parent intuition you have to decide which stage of development your child is in, and try out the activities with him to see if he is ready.

You should, however, make a habit of pointing out interesting things to your child from the time he is a baby. At first you will obviously get no response, but eventually he will "sit up and take notice." As he grows older talk about the things you see, but don't bombard him with so much information that he doesn't have the opportunity to observe for himself. When he has started to talk, ask him what he noticed. Later, when he is capable of expressing an opinion, ask more perceptive questions. "Why do you think the streets look pretty in the snow?" "Why do you think the red vase is better to put these flowers in than the yellow one?" Encourage him to point things out to you, but always try to lead him to come to conclusions about what he has seen.

Sometimes show him new things. At other times point out special features of a familiar object. Show him the colorful design that makes the curtains so bright and cheerful. The scratch on the table that spoils its sheen. The way the dog's ears prick up to hear a sound. And, if you also want to get a message across about tidiness, how much more attractive he looks when his hair is brushed neatly!

Show him similarities. As soon as he shows signs of seeing relationships, have him match objects. Start off with easy ones to match such as cups, saucers, and plates in your china set, and the same-size forks, knives, and spoons of the cutlery. Point out the identical buttons on his coat, the same size blocks he needs to build similar constructions, the similar milk and cottage cheese cartons. Gradually extend his comparisons to more difficult and unfamiliar items, and eventually have him tell you why and how they are the same.

Show him differences. How the knife is sharp and the rock is blunt. How the shell of a nut is rough and the surface of a stone is smooth. And how the skin of an apple differs from the skin of an orange. Then show him how some of the things, which seem similar at first glance, often have differences. One cup might have a crack or a chip, one fork may be egg-stained, while each shell in his collection has its own special pattern and unique features.

Have him look at the trees. Ask him how they differ. What makes an oak different from an elm, or a pine tree? Have him compare their shapes and sizes. Then look at their leaves. How are they dissimilar? Is it just their shape? What about their color, texture, and intricate designs? Have him look at the same tree in different seasons. Ask him how he can tell what time of the year it is by looking at its leaves.

Extend his awareness by continually taking him one step farther in his observations. When he points out a tree, show him the squirrel scrambling up its trunk, or the bird perched on its branch. When he notices the squirrel, see if he spies the nut he is carrying to hide away for winter. Or if he finds the bird, see if he can discover its nest.

When he draws your attention to the dog going by, see if he can identify the characteristics that make it a beagle, rather than a Yorkshire terrier; or a Labrador, rather than a German shepherd.

The most effective and exciting way to broaden your child's perception and sharpen his powers of discrimination is to go on explorations together, such as walks, trips, and outings. However, here are some games and activities you can play with him that will stimulate his awareness. Some of these, incidently, are used on I.Q. tests.

Again, it is difficult to pinpoint a specific age for these activities. You can start with the simplist forms as soon as you think your child has entered the "symbolic" stage (two to four years) and gradually progress to the more complex. Make sure the activities are carried out in an atmosphere of play and don't become a "lesson." Lavish plenty of praise for correct answers, and never show disappointment when he answers incorrectly. But be sure to let him know what the correct answer is. Always end on a happy note when he has had success.

Play the old favorite, "I spy." Describe something in the room and have him guess what it is. Or have him describe something and you guess. Or have him identify all the items that are the same color.

For general perception of all the senses, play "blindfold." Put some articles of different shapes and textures into a paper bag, such as a smooth stone, fur, velvet, sandpaper, clay or plastecine, a roll or a cookie. Have him guess what they are. Give him various items that have very distinctive smells and see if he can identify them—for example, the soap he uses at bathtime, the cleanser you use to clean his tub, vanilla, lemon juice, chocolate, and so on. Make some familiar noises, knocking on the table with your knuckles, pouring water from a jug into a glass; tearing paper; scraping or chopping carrots, or turning on the mixer or vacuum cleaner. Or have him close his eyes and tell you the sounds he can hear. Play this in different places: in different rooms, sometimes with the window open; on the bus, or in the car; at the beach, or park, or other places you visit. This is also a useful game if he is getting excited or restless on a trip and you want to quiet him down.

"Follow the leader" is great for developing his powers of observation, and he will thoroughly enjoy it. Whatever movement you do, he has to copy. When he is small limit this to simply waving an arm, lifting a leg, bending down, or turning around. Later hop on one leg, turn your head, or scratch your face. Then progress to twiddling your thumbs, closing one eye, and changing the expression on your face. Another variation of this is "Simon says," when he must imitate your movements only when you say "Simon says."

As he gains dexterity have him imitate you making things. For example, take a paper towel, roll it up, connect it with cellotape, and put it to your eye as a "lookout" and see if he can do the same. At first have him do each movement at the same time as you do it. Later have him make the object after you have completed yours. Use paper napkins and fold them into different shapes. When he is a whiz with scissors (about four years), see if he can cut out fun shapes that are similar to yours.

When he is used to handling a paint brush, crayon, or pencil (about two years) have him copy very simple large shapes and designs. As his dexterity develops make a nice round circle, a straight line, vertical first, then horizontal, and eventually at right angles, and have him copy these. By the time he is around five or six he should be able to draw fairly neat squares and oblongs, and finally a star (six lines crossing). This is one of the games on I.Q. tests. The closer the child can duplicate the shapes, the higher his points. Draw pinmen and any other simple, familiar items like a house, an apple, an orange, a banana, an animal, or a tree, and have him copy them. And, of course, finally have him copy the letters. See page 116.

You can also play the imitating game by playing with his manipulative toys. Use his blocks and put them together in various ways for him to copy. First put them in a tower, six on top of one another. Then into a row of four. Then add a block on top of the second one. Put one block beside another, and then another on top of it to make a "seat." As he becomes adept at copying, proceed to more complex arrangements. This is another game included on I.Q. tests.

Play rhythms or "tunes" on his xylophone or drum. Or use a spoon on a glass, or a wooden mixing spoon on a saucepan, or his rattle, or his bracelet of bells from his baby days. And see if he can duplicate them.

"Hide and seek" is a perennial favorite and will keep him absorbed and happy for many play sessions. I am sure you will have many imaginative ideas, but here are a few suggestions. Hide a small article, like a marble, block, tiny toy, or better still, something edible like a cookie or candy and have him look for it. You can put it in the inner box or bucket of his nesting sets. Or get six matching cartons (cottage cheese, potato, or Jell-O containers are great) and put it in one of these. Or you can hide it somewhere around the house and give him "clues." Tell him he is "hotter" as he gets nearer to it, and "colder" when he moves away from it. You can also "hide" lengths of colored ribbons and wools, draping them on the furniture, windowsills, and wherever they are clearly visible, and see how many he can find in a certain time.

"Hide and seek" can also be played with pictures, particularly pictures in his storybook, because identification of items will help his understanding of the story. Ask him to: "Find the monkey who has escaped from his cage." "Which is the unhappy dog?" "Who stole the cooling cupcake?" "Where are the eggs that turned to gold?"

Another good game to play with pictures is "What is missing?" Find pictures of familiar objects. Cut off one part, such as the leg of a chair, the gate of a fence, the wheel of a car. Ask, "What is missing?" And then supply the missing part to pop into place when he tells you.

Do the same with simple jigsaws. At first complete it all except for one piece. Finally have him put all the pieces together. Be sure to tell him what the final picture will be before he starts.

Play the "matching" game. Start simply by holding up an item he has to match, such as a flower, fork, stone, coat, shoe (eventually see if he can pick out the correct matching one, but be happy with just a shoe at first), or can of soup. Or touch a chair, table, or another item in the room and have him touch another similar one. Touch parts of your body and have him touch the same part of his body. Put some food into a bowl—cereal, rice, macaroni, flour, or sugar. See if he can fill his bowl with the same ingredient. Later see if he can fill his bowl to exactly the same *level* as yours. You can practice this by filling a glass with juice and then have him fill his to the same height. There are lots of fun things you can do in the kitchen that help him observe comparable sizes, levels, and shapes. Cooking, of course, is a natural. He'll love measuring ingredients in the measuring cup, making similar-size pieces of dough, and cutting out similar shapes with the cookie cutter.

You can also play the matching game with his playthings, such as blocks, colored shapes, beads, and buttons. These are also great for playing "What's the difference?" Show him six blocks, all the same color except one. Ask him "Which one is different?" Or, "Which is the odd man out?" You can do this with numerous items. Food again is handy and familiar. Give him five cookies and one apple and tell him he can eat the odd man out. Or show him five pieces of macaroni and one piece of spaghetti. Or use clothes: five T-shirts and one pair of underpants.

As he grows older and his eyes become as sharp as a hawk's, show him items that are similar but with one special difference. You can do this by drawing simple pictures. Animals, all the same, but one with a part, such as an ear, missing. Or all facing the same way, except one. Items, such as buckets, all upside down, except one. Hats all with feathers, or the same brims, except one. Christmas trees with the same number of candles, or ornaments, except one. Fruit, with one that has had a bite taken out. Faces, with one with a differently shaped mouth, eye, or nose. Cups, with one without a handle. Or you can draw shapes, such as three triangles, and put a dot in one. Eventually draw simple patterns and designs and have him pick out the one that is different.

A variation of this game is to draw the items in different sizes and have him tell you which is the biggest or the smallest. But he won't be able to do this until he has learned the concept of size.

As he matures you can introduce him to observation games that also require memorization, another skill crucial to thinking and reading. Place a few familiar objects on a table. Let him have a good, long look at them. Then cover them and ask him to name them. Gradually increase the number of objects. Put some other items on the table. But this time, after he has seen the objects, take one away. Ask him which object is missing. As he gets the idea, rearrange the remaining items. Show him a picture containing several familiar objects. Remove the picture, and have him name as many of the items as he can. Do the same with a picture full of people doing things and have him name all their actions after you have hidden the picture. Show him a simple, large pattern and see if he can duplicate it from memory.

Describe an object and see if he can guess what it is. "I'm thinking of something that has a black, furry coat, two yellow eyes, a tail, four legs, that is about as big as your foot." (the new kitten you have just acquired). Gradually, as he grows older, progress to descriptions of more difficult and less familiar objects. As he learns to talk, have him describe things for you to identify. Sometimes make a mistake, and let him be one up on you. It will be great for the ego!

Don't overdo the games. Only play them when they fit naturally into your other activities. And don't let them usurp other creative activities like crafts or dramatics that so effortlessly and effectively heighten and develop your child's powers of observation.

The Need to Concentrate

All the games and activities I have described also develop your child's attention span and concentration, which are vital to the thinking process and essential to all learning.

It's generally accepted that the attention span of a one-year-old is approximately two minutes; a two-year-old, about ten minutes; and a six-year-old, around thirty minutes. However, I am constantly amazed how often I find youngsters concentrating for much longer periods than this. I have worked with two-year-olds whose interest has been sustained for a good ten to twelve minutes, and I have tested four-year-olds who have become so intrigued with the activities they haven't been distracted once during a full twenty minutes.

Watch your baby in his crib. Notice how long he focuses on that gently turning mobile. Or how closely he follows you as you move about the room. Or how long he plays with his rattle, or bracelet of bells.

Watch your toddler playing with his nesting buckets, or grappling with a jigsaw. Aren't you amazed sometimes how long he is willing to experiment until he has fitted each bucket, or piece, into its proper place?

And what about your older child? How long does he spend putting together that model plane he is determined to add to his collection? As long as it takes!

What makes children pay attention and concentrate for long periods? Doing things that *interest* them, and that is the only way your child will develop and increase his. If you give him plenty of enjoyable, exciting, and challenging activities, he will automatically and naturally *get into the habit* of focusing on what he is doing. If, on the other hand, you stand over him with a stopwatch and deliberately set out to make him do an activity for a certain length of time, you will get nowhere.

Seeing Relationships and Associations Is Also Necessary

Some of the games I have described also help your child to see relationships and make associations, another necessary ability for the trio of thinking, learning, and reading. Your child, however, won't be able to do this until he has learned the concept of cause and effect. As I explained in the description of the stages of development, and constantly stress (and cannot stress enough!), the best way to do this is through your normal, daily activities. Point out the why and how of things. Help your child see the relationships between one thing and another. And generally show him how the objects, actions, and events he comes into contact with fit into the general "scheme" of things.

However, if he enjoyed the other games, here are a few more that will particularly help him acquire these skills.

Cut shapes (such as triangles, squares, circles) out of heavy paper or cardboard, preferably in bright, solid colors. Have him sort them out into their colors. Then have him sort them into their shapes.

Collect together a variety of boxes. Four cartons like cereal or cake mix, raisin, rice, or macaroni boxes; shoe boxes; gift boxes; or paperclip or thumbtack boxes. Then add a tennis ball, an orange, a grapefruit, a round paperweight, and several other round shapes. Have him divide them into square and round shapes. Then do the same with cylindrical shapes, such as an empty cleanser can, soup or fruit cans, a bottle, and so on.

Collect together articles of two sizes. A big and small box; a big and small can; a big and small fork. And have him group these according to size.

Then have him differentiate among things in his collections. For example, mix up his shells and stones on the table and have him put them into two piles. Or use his colored beads, bricks, buttons, and other such playthings. You can also have fun playing this game blindfolded. Have him pick out all the same shapes from a hat and put them in a pile. Or divide all the large buttons from the small buttons. Or all the smooth items from the rough items.

As you can see, the possibilities of this game are endless. And you can easily make it more difficult as he "catches on." You can combine color with shape, and ask him to find the green triangles or the blue squares. Or add differentiating marks, like a dot or a line, on the shapes, so he has to find the green triangles with the dots on them, or the blue squares with a line on them.

Logical Thinking Is the Key

All the games and activities I have described in this section help your child to think logically, which is the key to understanding. All children, however, are logical. The more I work with them the more I realize this, for time and time again, they astound me with their clever and perceptive remarks. Their solutions to problems, or reasons for doing things, often make a good deal of sense, even though they may not always seem so to us all-knowing, sophisticated adults. For example, I couldn't imagine why the young fellow, who just paid me a visit, insisted on walking home in the rain without his shoes on. I found out later. They were brand new, and he was very proud of them. He didn't want to spoil them by getting them wet! It made sense.

Your child thinks logically because his mind is not cluttered with all the information you and I have gathered on the way to adulthood. You can encourage him to keep it orderly and precise by helping him to sort out and digest the knowledge he collects each day.

I firmly believe that the most effective and lasting way to do this is to see that he grows up in an orderly physical environment. It has been my experience that children who come from well-organized households tend to have more orderly minds, and a more sensible approach to learning.

Have a daily routine with regular mealtimes, bedtimes, and rest and play times. Establish clearly drawn boundaries, so your child knows what is expected of him, and what he can and cannot do. Provide him with plenty of pleasurable and meaningful activities, and encourage him to finish what he starts. See that he has places to keep his toys and that he puts them away neatly each night.

Involve your child in the family's affairs as he grows older, as this also helps him to develop the ability to think logically and sensibly. If you include him in family discussions and decisions (start with simple ones, such as where to go on a wet Sunday afternoon), and let him hear your reasons for doing things, and watch your actions based on those reasons, you give him an opportunity to see logical thought "in action."

Have him do some of the things I suggest for developing his self-confidence and sense of responsibility (in the chapter on the importance of emotional stability, beginning on page 56), for they also help him to think clearly. All the chores you give him to do around the house have to be done in a logical, orderly way, while each time you let him make a decision he has to "think through" the options and come to a conclusion. And be sure to give him plenty of time alone, so he can quietly "work things out" on his own.

In summary, create a balance at home. On the one hand, see that it is orderly and predictable. On the other hand, see that it is relaxed, and provides your child with the freedom to exercise his mind to the full, so he learns to *think for himself*.

Most of your child's toys and playthings help to develop his ability to think logically. All his manipulative toys are designed to do this. But even his playthings, such as his kiddy car, ride 'em truck, rocking horse, sandbox, and jungle gym encourage its development. As do his make-believe toys such as his wooden telephone, house-cleaning set, dress-up clothes, and doll's house. And, of course, all his construction toys and tools.

There are, however, many activities you can do with your child to develop his logic. Anything involving an orderly sequence, such as making things, or following directions, are great. Cooking, carpentry, sewing, sculpturing, and arts and crafts are all "naturals." So are such things as "scientific experiments," which you will find he loves when he is around five. Here is one for showing him how the energy of heat stirs water. Have him fill a glass with cold water, and another with hot. Then tell him to add two drops of food coloring to them both. Ask him what he notices. When he tells you the coloring has dropped to the bottom of the glass with cold water, and mixed with the water in the glass with hot water, ask him "What made the color mix in the glass with hot water?"

You can always play fun games like "hide and seek" when your child is still a toddler. Hide a "surprise" and then give him directions to find it. Or have him play "mail deliverer." Give him letters that have to be "delivered" to certain places in the house or garden. Later, when he is around three to four, you can cut out shapes, such as fish, and have him put them in the order of their sizes, or give him a set of mixing bowls, or saucepans; or his nesting boxes, or buckets, and have him put them in the order of their size. Or have him stack boxes, with the largest at the bottom. When he is about four to five give him six drinking straws; pieces of string, or colored wool; or pencils, and have him arrange them in the order of their length. Or cut out pictures from a magazine or cartoon, and have him put them in their correct sequence. This and other such activities I suggest in the next chapter, on talking, are great fun for developing his ability to follow the logical progression of events in a story.

Some of the best games for developing your child's ability to think logically when he is around five or six are the ones you play on family occasions, such as sitting around the fire on a cold winter's night or going on a long car trip.

"What if" is always a favorite. Ask "What would happen *if*":

we had no electricity or gas?
we had no cars?
you were an Eskimo?
you lived in the sea?
you were stranded on a desert island?

The "I wish" game is also popular. Give him three wishes and have him explain why he wished for each item.

Or play the "problem" game. Give him a problem, and have him tell you how he would solve it. The water pipe has broken. It's late at night, and you can't get a plumber. You have to get to Grandma's but there are no buses, and there is no gas for the car.

Or play the "mystery" story. Start off a story that involves some sort of mystery, such as a lost cat or treasure. And have him tell you where it was found, and how it was discovered. Sometimes have him give you the mystery to solve, so he can hear how logically you solve it!

Any game will help your child to think logically, for he has to figure out the "rules" and follow directions to play. So get out the cards, board games, and all those other games stored away in the attic, and, of course, think up as many riddles, puzzles, and mind-"teasers" as you can. If you run out of ideas have him think up some games. It will not only give him extra practice in logical thinking but also, if you have prepared him well along the way, you will probably find he will come up with some imaginative, inventive, and *sensible* ones.

CHAPTER 5

Talking Leads to Reading: Developing Those Language Skills

When Your Child Is a Baby

You probably first realized you had produced a great talker soon after you brought your baby home. He told you in no uncertain terms that he was hungry, had a stomach ache, or was wet. You didn't always understand exactly what he was talking about, but at least you knew he was quite capable of communicating his thoughts and feelings.

But I bet you didn't realize, as you were pacing the darkened house at 3 A.M., trying to settle down old loudmouth so you could get some sleep, that every scream—and, in fact, every coo and gurgle—he had made, was preparing him for reading. You probably didn't care much then either! But it's true, for reading, being an extension of talking, begins with the sounds of language.

Encourage Your Baby to "Talk" to You

Before your child is ready to read he must be at ease with language, and be able to speak and communicate his thoughts easily and naturally. So you should encourage him to develop his language skills and "talk" to you as soon as possible. This won't be difficult because he is pretty proud of those vocal cords of his, and is very happy to show them off when he gets a chance. Listen to him practicing in his crib, and you will be surprised how many sounds he can produce—screeches that raise the ceiling, groans that crash to the floor, and sighs, coos, and gurgles that echo off the walls.

You can encourage your baby to experiment with, and use, his voice by giving him different things to react to. Put your face close to his and smile at him. Tickle him. Joggle him up and down in your arms as you hum or play some music. Clap your hands or snap your fingers. Introduce him to the sounds around him. The jingle of his rattle or bells. The clink of a spoon against a glass. The tick-tock of the clock. And the notes of the music box. Hearing all these sounds will also develop his listening ability which, as I mentioned earlier, is so essential to all learning, but especially reading. However, be sure to introduce these sounds singly, for your child is not capable as yet of absorbing more than one sound at a time.

You can also stimulate and reinforce his own sound-making by responding quickly and positively so that he will repeat the sounds. Reward the gurgles and goos with smiles, cuddles, and words of approval. "Oh what a clever boy you are." "My, that sounded good." And so on. Of course, your baby won't understand the words, but he will get the message by your encouraging tone.

The more sounds your baby makes, the more he exercises his vocal cords, and the faster his voice box develops. This enables him in turn to control the sounds he makes which eventually makes it possible for him to talk.

Talk to Your Baby

It is, however, your words, your talking, that encourage the development of your child's language ability more than anything else. The "conversations" you have with him are the key factors in preparing him for reading. Nothing can substitute for them. This is because speech is not a skill your child is born with. He must acquire it through experience. He must learn to hear, recognize, differentiate, and finally attach meaning to sounds so he can imitate them. And he can only do this by hearing them in the context of meaningful words and phrases. By talking to your infant you accustom him to the sounds and rhythm of words, and the nuances of your particular language, so that he gradually and almost unconsciously learns to give them meaning and make them part of him.

Also, talking to your baby gets him involved in language. It teaches him how to communicate, and it stimulates him to react and respond to what is being said, which is an essential factor in learning to read.

The pleasure and fun you both derive from your little chats also help your child develop a good feeling about language and builds up his confidence in language, which in turn encourages him to use it. And they establish a rapport and understanding between the two of you that will make it easier for you to teach him the many other important prereading skills.

So if you're not a talker, start talking!

Talk to, with, at, and around your baby. Talk to him whenever you have the opportunity. As you bath him, bathe him in words. As you diaper him, powder him with words. And when you feed him, add a few to the menu. Chat to him as he lies in his crib, playpen, or swinging cradle in the kitchen. And don't forget the odd word or two when you take him for a walk. As I suggested on page 73, if possible try to get a carriage that allows your baby to face you, as they have in Europe. And, of course, talk to him as you indulge in those wondrous cuddling times. As he feels the warmth of your body and the depth of your love, and listens to your tender words, he will surely come to love language as he comes to love you. A baby, by the way, is greatly influenced by his emotional environment and experiences. If the environment is unpleasant, he may not be communicative. It's important, therefore, that you give him a feeling of security and constantly reassure him of your love. With a very young baby that means responding soon to his cries of hunger and unhappiness.

Tell Stories

If you run out of topics of "conversation," you can always recite poems, reminisce about those good old days, or "talk over" a problem you have on your mind. One friend of mine, a journalist, reads her latest articles to her baby, and says it helps *her* a lot. You can also start telling him short stories about his toys or dolls. This will give you practice for the not-too-distant future when your storytelling will be in great demand. If you include lots of interesting words and fun sounds he will really enjoy them. For example, a story about his wooden train could include the "chuff-chuff" of the engine, the "rickety-rackety" of the wheels, and the "choo-choo" of the whistle. You can encourage your baby to become involved in the story by repeating the sounds and trying to get him to say them, and by bouncing him up and down in time to their rhythm. All children are fascinated by sounds like these and, as they get older, they delight in repeating them over and over again. Before you know it, they are making up their own nonsense words, which are often better-sounding than yours! So include as many "clippity-clops," "ting-alinglings," "quack-quacks," "meow-meows," and "wuff-wuffs" to your stories as you can tolerate.

Sing

Then, of course, your baby will love you to sing to him. You can sing your old favorite songs, the latest pop one you have just heard on the radio, folk songs, lullabies, or even the odd commercial jingle if you get stuck. But the songs he will enjoy most are the nursery rhymes. (Better get those Mother Goose books out now and review them!)

Children from time immemorial have loved nursery rhymes, and I can assure you your child will be no exception. They are full of music; rhythm; delicious and delightful sounds and words; and lots of repetition. And your child will enjoy them long before he learns to appreciate their simple but appealing, stories. Later you'll find them one of your best aids in helping him first develop his language skills, and then his reading skills. They literally shriek out: "Listen to me. Come and play with me. Come and join in the fun." And before you know it, he is. He's hooked. When he's young he will just enjoy banging out the rhythms, which you can encourage by emphasizing them as you sing, or say, the words; or holding his hands and clapping them out with them. However, as he gets older and begins to talk, he will revel in repeating the sounds and words. And can you blame him? Who could resist getting their tongues around "hickory, dickory, dock," "diddlety, diddlety, dumpty," "knickknack paddy whack," and "bumpety, bumpety, bump, lumpety, lumpety lum"?

Then, before you know it, he will be repeating whole phrases. This is easier than you think, because the constant repetition almost forces the words into his mouth. For example, if you sing "The Mulberry Bush" enough times together, he will soon be chanting, "Here we go round the mulberry bush," or "This is the way we wash our hands."

Introduce Your Baby to Books

Begin to expose your baby to books when he is three or four months by cuddling him and reading a story aloud, or letting him look at the colorful pictures of a magazine. Don't worry if he is more interested in playing with your necklace, or chewing your sweater at first. Persevere, and it won't be long before his curiosity is aroused, and he will be eagerly pointing to the pictures or repeating your words. By the time he is about twelve months he will be able to identify the key characters in his picture Mother Goose book. By eighteen to twenty-four months he will be turning the pages as you tell the story. And by three years he will be so familiar with the words that he will probably know the stories better than you. And he will irritably be pointing out to you, "No, the book says Peter Rabbit then went into the *cabbage patch.*"

One of the best ways to help your child make the link between talking and reading is to refer to books as "talking books." When you speak about books, say; "Let's see what this book *tells* us." Or, "Wow that book sure had a lot to *say* for itself!" Or ask, "What did that book *say?*" Show your child that books are not props. They speak to us just like people. One book says one thing, another book says something else. But they all talk, talk, talk.

Name Things

As words grow out of the recognition of objects and actions, get into the habit of naming things as you use or do them. When you bathe your child name the main parts of his body. "Now we'll wash your *tummy*. What a big *tummy* you have." Touch each part as you say the word, and repeat it several times to reinforce it. When you dress him, point out you are putting on his "pants," "coat," "socks," and "hat." When you move him about, say, *"Up* we go." *"In* we come." When you hand him something, say what it is, "Here's your *rattle."* "Hold your *spoon."* "It's time for your *bottle* now." As you go about the house doing your chores, explain what you are doing. "Mommy's *cleaning* the windows." "I'm *drying* the plates." "I'm *setting* the table." Use *his* actions to introduce new words and make a game of it. For example, if you see him shaking his bells, hold his hand gently and shake the bells with him, and say, *"Shake, shake, shake."* Later do this with objects so he will associate the word with the actions, rather than the object.

Of course, you mustn't overdo the naming, just as you mustn't overdo the talking, which I perhaps overexaggerated earlier in my enthusiasm to get you to communicate with your child. Obviously, there must be quiet moments. Silence is golden at times. And there are occasions, such as when you are in a hurry, your child's diaper needs quick attention, or he is in a bad mood, that are not the most appropriate times for vocabulary-building! However, when the time is right, seize your opportunity. And whenever possible, make it into a game. It must be fun if you are going to have any impact.

Naturally, at first the words won't have any meaning for him. But continue to play the game anyway, for gradually, over the months, as he matures and you continue to repeat the words, they will. Don't think just because he can't pronounce the words, he doesn't understand them. He is a smarter cookie than he lets on. Language comprehension precedes language production by several months. So although he can say only a few words by the time he is one, he understands *many* more several months before this.

The Eighth Month Is Important

An especially crucial time to emphasize words, and talk to your baby, is around the eighth month. Studies have shown that this is the time when the mode and rate of his speech development are most influenced by his "language environment." During this period, continue working on the now familiar words you have been practicing. But also introduce a few new ones. Remember, though, he is still in the "sensational" stage, and can think only in terms of concrete objects, so stick to nouns and verbs that name the things he can see, touch, and do.

Change your tactics now and concentrate on teaching him one word at a time. Say it again and again, doing the action, or touching, or pointing to the object, as you did before. For example, give him some nice resounding kisses and say, *"kiss kiss*. Mummy, *kiss, kiss* Tony." You may feel like a stuck record, but if you want results, that is the way to do it. So keep going. And remember that every word he learns to say will be an easier word for him to read when he sees it in print. Just look ahead a little.

Actually, these sessions don't take up much time. Three to ten minutes are plenty. But if they get too much for you, or you don't have time, try enlisting one of your older kids, or that teen-ager up the street who baby-sits for you. You will find they have a great deal of patience and will probably enjoy themselves as much as Junior. A friend of mine tells me her older daughter, aged eight, spends up to fifteen minutes playing "names," as she calls it, with her eleven-month-old brother. In fact, it was Mary who taught him his first word, by saying "bye-bye" and waving to him for a solid ten minutes.

Don't always expect results like Mary's, though. And don't get discouraged when he doesn't immediately become a walking thesaurus. Even though you may seem to be making no headway, rest assured that you are! Remember, learning takes *time*. Just hang in there. Relax. Enjoy the word games. But again, don't overdo them. Your child can absorb only so much. If you overwhelm him with too many words, he will learn none of them. So focus on a few. You will probably find that his vocabulary develops in spurts, with perhaps the most dramatic increase when he is about 18 to 24 months. All children develop differently, but to give you an idea what to expect, the average 1-year-old knows (which means he understands and speaks) approximately 3 words. At 15 months he knows 19 words. At 18 months, 22 words. At 21 months, 118. At 24 months, 272. And at 3 years he has a speaking vocabulary of more than 1,000 words, and an understanding of more than twice that many.

Praise Each Word

Of course, when he does learn to say a word, make a big "to-do" about it. Smile. Praise him. Hug him. Repeat the word. And encourage him to use it again, particularly during the next few days. For these all help to reinforce the word in his mind and make it truly a part of his vocabulary. You should especially wave the flag, blow the horn, and generally make whoopee when he says his first word. For this is indeed a landmark in his life. It is a truly fantastic achievement and a giant step toward reading. It is not quite the time to get out your set of encyclopedias, but you might consider dusting them off.

Speak Distinctly and Avoid Baby Talk

When you are teaching your youngster words, whenever possible speak directly to him, so he can see your face. And be sure to enunciate distinctly and slowly, but naturally, so he hears the words correctly. I don't know if you realize it, but you have produced a great mimic, as good as any you will see on television. And he will repeat the words as you say them. In other words, he learns the speech he hears, so it is important to avoid using baby talk. Always give the real name for something, so he learns the correct words from the start. And however delightful and "cute" his first babyish words may be, don't be tempted to repeat them because this will encourage him to use them. Don't tell him he is pronouncing them incorrectly, for this will only discourage him. Instead, repeat the words correctly and clearly. If he says "cu-cu" for cup say, "Yes. This is a *cup,*" and emphasize the "p." This will give him a good feeling. And he will be so pleased with himself that before you know it, the word will pop out the right way.

At first your child's words will be enmeshed in what seems meaningless gibberish, and he will be almost impossible to understand. However, encourage him to keep up the "talk." Let his tongue wag and the "conversation" flow, for these seemingly nonsense sentences actually have the characteristics of adult language. They have rhythm and fluency, and use all the various sounds of our speech. Respond to what he is saying, and compliment him. "My, what a great talker you are." Sometimes invite him to come and talk to you. "Come and sit on Daddy's knee and tell me what you did today." By doing this, you not only increase his language facility, but also build up his confidence in himself, and in his power to communicate —all of which, of course, stimulate him to make further strides in his language development.

Your Child's First Sentences

By eighteen months your child, with your help, will have built up a pretty good vocabulary of what I call the "concrete" words of our language—nouns (the "naming" words) and verbs (the "doing" words). For example, he can say "dog," "mama," "ball," "play," "eat," "do," "go," and so on. Now, however, comes the truly exciting time when he begins to put these words together to make sentences. Mentally this is an incredible achievement. It means he can think logically, figure out sequences of behavior, and express them. And it shows he has entered the symbolic stage (see page 70). Although the sentences are made up of just two words, "Toy give," "Ball gone," "Daddy come," "Eat cookies," they are actually very much like abbreviated or "telegraphic" versions of adult sentences.

At first he talks in a sort of monologue. Sometimes he chats happily away to himself, just for the sheer delight of using his newly discovered words. At other times he carries on "conversations" with you, which often have no relationship whatsoever to what you are talking about. For example, you may be telling him what he's going to have for supper, while he will be speaking about his teddy bear. Your job, as before, is to encourage his flow of language. But, at the same time, guide him into "proper" conversations, so he learns to react and respond to what others say, as he must do later on when he reads. Ask him questions. "What did you see when you went out in the car with Daddy?" Or "what did you buy when you went to the store?"

Stretch Those Sentences

In regard to helping your child develop his language ability and subsequently his ability to read, the years from eighteen months to three or four years are *crucial.* You should make his talking your No. 1 priority. Your motto now should be: "Children should be seen and *very much heard!*" Encourage his sentence development as you did his vocabulary development. When he says, "Give cookie," respond by repeating his thought in an adult way. "Yes, I will give you a cookie. Here is your cookie." Also help him to expand his sentences and enhance the meaning of what he is saying by getting him to use the more descriptive and specific words of our language. Teach him to use adjectives. When he says, "Want ball," ask him, "What color is the ball?" Or, "How big is the ball?" When he tells you it's "blue" or "big," say, "Here is your blue ball." Then have him repeat what you've just said. Do the same with prepositions, and help him to say, "*Under* the table." "*Inside* my toy box." "Come *in* from the yard." Whenever possible, have him act out the words, as this will greatly help him understand their meanings. This is especially the case with prepositions, as they convey abstract concepts that are difficult to grasp. Have him crouch *under* the table. Step *inside* the closet. Go *outside* and come *in* from the yard. He will really enjoy this because he is very action-oriented at this stage.

You can also play "hide and seek" with him, using a doll or a hand puppet. Make it jump *over* the vase. Go *under* the table. Slide *down* the table leg. And climb back *up* again. Then hop *inside* the vase and sneak *out* slowly. As you do the actions give a running commentary so he associates the correct words with them. Then have him make the toy, or puppet, do the actions as you call them out. Finally have him describe the actions as he makes them do them. Don't introduce too many prepositions at one time. Two are plenty at first, such as up and down, or in and out.

You can use many of his toys to help him understand these concepts, particularly the ones that involve placement problems, such as nesting buckets, shape sorting boxes, shape stacker, blocks, and hammer-and-peg toys. They all call for your child to put things, in, out, over, under, through, and so on. Other playthings can also help, such as a jump rope. He can skip *over* it. Duck *under* it. Tie it *around* his middle. Stretch it *across* the lawn. Put it *inside* a paper bag. And take it *out* again. Hang it *up on* a hook. And pull it *down off* the hook.

Pictures are great for drawing your child's attention to these words. Cut them out of old magazines, or draw a few (if you've got the talent). And, of course, use the ones in his nursery rhyme and storybooks. Point to the cow jumping *over* the moon. And the dish running *away* with the spoon. Then ask him, "Who jumped *over* the moon?" Or "What did the cow do?" Then follow this up with more "conversation" about the words. "You can jump over things, can't you? Let me see you jump over the stool." And so on.

You can have a lot of fun teaching adjectives. Have him "go and sit in the *red* chair." "Find me a *round* plate." "Look in the garden for a *small* leaf." Or have him name all the *big* things in the room, and then all the *small* things. Or all the *blue* things. At supper ask him which food he's eating is *hot,* and which *cold*. Have him sort his beads, buttons, or blocks into *big* or *small* piles. Or into their colors. Have him describe things to you. His clothes: "I have on a *nice, clean* sweater." His food: "This orange is *tasty* and *sweet*." The flowers: "This flower has a *lovely* smell." Sometimes ask him how many words he can think of to describe one word. And gradually help him to use more specific words, such as scarlet for red, tiny for small, enormous for big, and so on.

You can use many of the same activities, toys, and games you used to teach him prepositions. The fit-together toys give you a great chance to talk about things that are "bigger than" and "largest." The new hammer-and-peg toys that feature pegs in varying geometrical shapes give you a chance to say to your child, "Now hit the square peg," "now the round one," and "now the star-shaped one."

You both can have a wonderful time acting out the adjectives. You can take it in turns being happy, sad, cross, old, funny, and hungry. Sometimes you can use "props" to help you get into the mood. They don't have to be fancy. Things you have around the house will do nicely: the clown hat left over from trick or treat; a stick (for the old man); an empty plate, a broken doll, or a candy bar. You can also introduce him to some adverbs this way. The old man can walk *slowly*. The clown laugh *loudly*. And the girl sob *noisily* over her broken doll.

Drama is a particularly useful way to help your youngster develop his vocabulary and stretch out those condensed sentences. Encourage him to play with his train set, tea set, doll house, playhouse, toy soldiers, wood telephone, and minikitchen, and have imaginery conversations as he does so. Suggest he is the train driver checking out his route, the general telling his soldiers the next campaign, and mother and father discussing how to arrange the furniture on moving day. Suggest he "talk things over" with his dolls and stuffed animals. Or make the toys talk to each other. And, of course, keep your conversations with him going.

Also, this is a particularly important time for story-telling, as it exposes him to words and sentences being used correctly. Lengthen your reading-aloud time, for his attention span is longer now. You have probably already introduced him to the fun cloth and touch books, so now introduce more "meaty" books (see my recommended list in the Appendix). Have him repeat phrases or even whole sentences, particularly if they have fun-sounding words or catchy rhythms. Have him retell parts of the story in his own words. Ask him about things that happened, when they happened, and how they happened. Ask his opinion, but be sure to make it an open-ended question, such as, "Why did you like the story?" rather than, "Did you like the story?" to which he could reply with a simple "Yes" or "No." Stop sometimes and ask him, "What do you think is going to happen next?" Or leave off before the end and have him predict the outcome of the story.

By familiarizing your child with books early on, you get him used to handling them correctly. He learns to hold them up the right way, turn the pages, look at the left page before the right one, and follow the sequence of events in their proper order. As you read, however, be sure to have him "read along" with you, and have him turn the pages so he synchronizes your words with the pictures.

Reading aloud to your child is also a marvelous way to improve his listening skills, for he knows if he doesn't listen intently, he might miss the most exciting part of the story. It also develops his attention span and concentration, which are so vital in reading.

Be sure to read slowly and distinctly, and as *naturally* as possible, so it seems the book is talking to him. Adopt a confidential, quiet tone, but try to convey a feeling of suspense, wonderment, or humor at the appropriate times.

You should also continue telling your own stories. He will still love listening to them, particularly if you now make them up about him or the family or things he has done. He will also especially enjoy mystery or suspense stories. So if you can combine the two, "How David got lost in the magic wood," you have it made.

Now is also the time to get your child to tell stories. You have already started him off by having him predict outcomes in his storybook. Help him along by starting a story and having him finish it. Let him tell you how he eventually got out of the wood. Or have him start off and you finish. Or if the family is together, tell a "round-robin story." Have one person start off the story and then stop midway through a sentence and point to someone else, who has to carry on with it. This is a great game, by the way, for tedious waits at the bus stop or long trips. You can also encourage him to tell stories by playing the "let's pretend" game. For example, say "Let's pretend you've just landed on the moon. Tell me about your adventures there." Or "Let's pretend you're Mrs. Squirrel and it's wintertime. What would you be doing?" If he has a hard time thinking up things to say, discreetly give him suggestions. "I wonder if you would find robots on the moon." Or "I bet you'd be busy storing up things to eat."

Your Child Imitates You

As I said earlier, Junior is a great imitator. One of the ways he learns to develop his language ability now is listening to your conversations with each other and the rest of the family. He unconsciously absorbs your grammar, use of speech, vocabulary, *and* your speech habits! No, don't get out that grammar book left over from your high-school days, nor rush out and buy one of those "vocabulary builder" paperbacks. Continue to speak as you normally do, or your talk will be forced and unnatural. But once in a while, cock an ear, listen to yourself, and ask, "Did I say that clearly?" Or "Could I have used a better word to describe that?"

At Three Your Child Is a Talker

During your child's third year, you realize he is obviously going to be a politician, a salesman, or a disc jockey. Because it's talk, talk, talk!

If you were worried he wasn't talking earlier on, you now wonder why on earth you did. Anything for a little peace and quiet! He talks to the mailman, the checkout lady at the supermarket, the dog, the birds, his toys, his imaginary friends, and himself. He even talks to the pictures, flowers, and furniture. And, of course, he talks to you, you, you.

He has a comment on everything. His food. His clothes. What he wants for his birthday. When he will go to bed. And even a few on the neighbors and your friends—not always the most complimentary or made at the best of times. I will never forget a youngster turning to me at a party, pointing her finger at an attractive blonde, and saying in a *very* loud voice, "I've seen Mrs. Keen with her teeth out. She does look funny."

And, of course, with every other breath, out pops a question. How? Who? When? Which one? Where? And why, why, why? "Why must I eat my peas?" "Why are you going out?" "Why are tomatoes red?"

Do Things Together

This is the time he can become a real companion, and you can have a great time together. Involve him in your life. Do as many things together as you can. When you have common interests, his questions won't seem so irritating, and your conversations, discussions, story-telling, and games—all the things you need to do now to develop his language skills—will be far more meaningful. His talking will develop quickly, easily, and naturally, and before you know it he will be more than just a companion. He will be a full-fledged member of the family, ready to contribute his thoughts and feelings. What is more, he will be ready to pick up that book and READ!

Go for walks together. They create a wonderful feeling of "togetherness" and are marvelous for *tête-à-têtes.* I wonder how many confidences have been told, and secrets shared, during a stroll in the woods, or along a riverbed, or even down a city street, despite its hustle and bustle. You can talk about all sorts of things. Who he will invite to his birthday party. What clothes he will need to take on vacation. What the nursery school he is soon going to will be like. But the best things to talk about are the things that are around you. Point them out as you go along, especially if your child has not come into contact with them before. When you comment on something, be sure to name it *precisely* now. Don't say, "That's a nice coat in the shop window," but "That's a *warm leather jacket* in the *dress-shop* window." Or "That man looks cold," but "That *pretzel vendor* looks cold." If the words are a bit tricky or difficult, like pretzel and vendor, add a few words to explain them. "Who is *selling* those *cookie-like* things?"

After you have pointed something out, ask questions about it. Be sure they are ones, though, that encourage a comment, rather than a short "Yes" or "No." Ask, "Why do you think the vendor (repeat the new word for reinforcement) is cold?" A child can give a variety of answers to this question, but however he does answer it, show interest, and respond with an encouraging remark. "Yes, you're right, he doesn't have a very thick coat on." Or even, "That's interesting. I hadn't thought of that."

Encourage your child to point things out to you. Have him explain things to you. Ask, "What is that funny thing over there?" (a fire hydrant). He may not know what it is. But even so, get him to have a guess. You will be amazed how inventive—and articulate—he becomes when you do this. Children love to use their imagination, and I bet your child will come up with some pretty good, and amusing, uses for a fire hydrant. Also, sometimes when he asks you a question, turn it back to him. Say, "My, that's an interesting question. I don't know. *What do you think?*"

When you get home, keep the conversation going by reflecting on what you have seen. "Wasn't that old lady having a hard time carrying all those packages? Do you think she made it to the bus stop?" "Which store window did you think was the most interesting?" And so on.

There are all sorts of short expeditions you take routinely that provide good opportunities for talking: going to mail a letter, taking the dog for a walk, or visiting a neighbor, for instance. When you drive in the car turn off the radio and get into the habit of pointing things out as you go along, or better still have your child do this. Then he will get plenty of practice, and you can keep your eyes on the road.

The expeditions he will love most are those that take him away from the familiar setting of his neighborhood. Visits to the zoo, or circus, a camping trip, or a day at the beach will all excite him beyond words. But they will also help him learn many new ones. At the same time, they will broaden his experiences, so that when he comes to read, "The lion roared in his cage" or "The sea lapped against the shore," he will know what they mean.

It doesn't have to be a special event for you to talk together. The best opportunities are right at home—at mealtimes, bedtimes, and as you go about your chores. If, however, you are busy and don't have time, invite another child to come and play with him. He is just at the right age for guests. And they will have a whale of a time chatting nineteen to the dozen as they play.

Encourage "Self-talk"

A child doesn't always have to have a companion to practice his speech. In fact, it is a good idea to give him the opportunity now and then to practice on his own. He can then try out words and experiment with ways of saying them, without any embarrassment or fear of being laughed at.

There are many activities that stimulate one-sided "conversations." Give him dress-up clothes—hats, masks, clothes you no longer wear, and even your shoes—and let him impersonate people, talking as they would. Encourage your child to play doctors, house, trains, storekeeper, pilot, and act out the conversations the people involved would have. Provide a mirror so he can actually talk to his characters, or just talk to himself. Suggest he be a character he has read about in a story, or one he has seen on television. Or that disc jockey he might eventually be.

Get out the puppets you bought him in earlier days or teach him how his fingers can have conversations with each other. Show him how to make the finger of one hand talk to the fingers of the other hand. Or at night in his partly darkened bedroom, show him how he can put his fingers together in different ways to form animal or creature silhouettes on the wall, who can talk.

Suggest he make telephone calls, using his own toy phone—yours if it plugs out, or an imaginary one. Give him some definite people to "call," and topics of conversation such as, "Call Grandma and tell her all about your trip to the vet's with Fido. Tell her about the different animals you saw in the waiting room." Or "Call up the doll hospital, and explain what has to be done to Teddy Bear."

One of the activities he will love most is using a tape recorder. At first he will be shy and embarrassed. But aren't we all when we are first told, "Say something into the speaker"? Help him to get started, as you should do with all the activities, by giving him something specific to talk about. Give him a picture of a scene with lots of people doing things (such as a street scene, people at the beach, etc.) and have him describe what the people are doing. Or have him retell a story you have read to him recently. Or have him make up his own story about some characters or animals he has read about. Of course, he will be absolutely fascinated hearing his own voice. But don't worry if you don't have a tape recorder. He will get nearly as much fun out of a "pretend" one, especially if you can come up with a good replica of a speaker.

Stress Speaking Distinctly

If your child has a speech problem, help him to correct it by saying the sounds with him in front of a mirror. Enunciate the sound first, showing him how to synchronize his mouth, lips, and tongue. Have him do it with you. Then have him do it alone. After this, practice words with the sound, still in front of the mirror. If he is telescoping words, say each syllable of the word slowly and have him repeat the word in exactly the same way. Do this as many as ten to twelve times at a stretch and he will soon be saying the word correctly.

A tape recorder can also be very useful in helping your child correct sloppy or incorrect speech habits. It is so much easier for him to recognize what he is doing incorrectly if he can hear it "outside" himself. Children of this age may still have difficulty in pronouncing some sounds. They may say "w" for "r," as in "wead" (for read); "v" for "th" as in "muvver" (for mother); "f" for "th" as in "fin" (for thin); and "kw" for "c" as in "k*w*oss" (for cross). Or they may miss out letters and say "bend" for "blend"; and "sen" for "send." Or they may telescope words, condensing the syllables, as in "favwite."

You certainly should not expect perfect speech from your youngster yet. But you should encourage him to speak as distinctly as possible, because good speech habits are so vital in learning to read. If you speak a dialect, or use regional pronunciations in your conversations at home, help your child become familiar with the more generally accepted "formal" forms of pronunciation. This will help greatly with his reading, because our written language is based on this way of speaking.

Singing with your child is a good way to develop his facility with words and general language fluency now, and you will find he will enjoy it as much as he did when you first introduced him to the nursery rhymes. He may not be able to sing in key yet, but now that he knows most of the words he is singing, he will be more conscious of the rhythm and music of the words, and particularly of the similarities of some of them.

Singing is also good language practice because it provides a nicely disguised drill in words. As well as requiring clear pronunciation, it requires careful listening and teaches the discipline of using words in rhythm.

Sometimes alternate the singing so that you sing one line or verse, and he sings the next. Sometimes have him do the actions of the song. And then, of course, let him be the prima donna—or the masculine equivalent of that!—and sing solo. He will love this and it will encourage him to learn the words.

At Four or Five Your Child Is the Wizard of Words

It is when your child reaches his fourth or fifth year that his vocabulary explodes. If you have been helping him in the ways I have described, he truly becomes the wizard of words. He obviously has the gift of gab, and now you are quite convinced he is going to be a poet or a writer. He amazes and enchants you with his strange, but unusually vivid suggestive descriptions. There is music in his words (you see, the songs do help!). His speech is as vibrant and alive as he is. The words pop out with the crack and speed of a shotgun hitting the bull's-eye of expression. Sometimes they even emerge with the rat-tat-tat of a rifle, ripping through the code of conventional speech, but nevertheless conveying their meaning.

Sample some of the beauties I have collected over the years and you will see what I mean. I particularly love these descriptions of colors. "Yellow is sizzling sunshine." "Green is always in a hurry." (This could have come from constantly seeing the green "Go" of traffic signals.) "White is open and black is closed." "Red is hot." "Purple shouts," and "Pink is quiet." And these: "Someone's buttered the flowers" (daffodils). "The outside is taking a shower" (rain). "The lawn is covered with ice cream" (snow). "The rosebud smiled open." "He munched on mushy marshmallows." "His frown fell down to his knees." I also like the way one small boy described sandwiches as "sandboxes." "Because you put lots of things into them."

Words obviously give your child great pleasure at this stage. He loves them for themselves, as well as for the power they give him to communicate his thoughts. Listen to him when he is in the tub or riding his bike up and down, and you will probably hear him repeating a word over and over again. I know one 4½-year-old who learned to say "superfragalisticexpialidosis" and came out with it at every opportunity.

A 4- or 5-year-old collects words just as enthusiastically as he collects shells, stones, bottletops, and insects. Your job now is to encourage the collecting, and, at the same time, help your child to use words appropriately, without destroying the beauty and creativity of his language.

Do not fall into the trap some parents do at this stage and try to do this by "vocabulary building" exercises, word lists, or drills. Just continue as you have been doing, gradually and naturally showing your child what words are for and what they can do, by broadening his experiences, talking, and reading aloud to him.

Broaden Your Child's Knowledge of Words

Continue to take your child about with you, for the more people he meets, the more words he will be exposed to. For example, when he overhears the friend you meet while shopping, say, "I really was quite perturbed." And he asks, "What does 'perturbed' mean?" He adds a new word to his word bank.

Broaden his knowledge of the world by giving him new experiences and expeditions to new places, but also by giving him more detailed information and explanations of things he is already familiar with. Explain how the car engine works. How insects, like ants, live in communities like human beings. Why the bird bath freezes over. And why insulating the house makes it warmer. Talk about topical issues, such as the fuel shortage, and air pollution. And introduce him to more abstract ideas and concepts, such as beauty, truth, and values. He will find them difficult to grasp, but you lay the foundation now for later understanding.

Use more sophisticated words when you talk to him. Make him aware of synonyms (words that have the same meaning, such as big, huge, gigantic, enormous); antonyms (words that have the opposite meaning, such as big and small, or hot and cold); and homonyms (words that have the same sound but different meanings and spellings, such as bear and bare, or break and brake, or see and sea). If you are a bit rusty on these, turn to page 271, where you will find a list of the most common ones. Or buy yourself a paperback thesaurus. It won't cost much and is a great standby. Show him the flexibility of words and how they can change their meaning according to their context, for this is the key to reading comprehension. Give him sentences to compare: "He played the record on his record player." "He ran the race in record time." And "He recorded his score in his notebook."

When he asks you the meaning of a word, don't just give him the definition. *Put the word into a sentence,* and then make *him* use it in a sentence. If he misuses a word, point it out kindly by saying, "I didn't quite understand you. The word you used [give the word] doesn't mean what you want to say." Don't say, "That's not the right word to use," for this will discourage him from trying out new words. And don't tell him the correct word before giving him the chance to produce it.

Children today often have a larger vocabulary than their predecessors because of their exposure to television. Many people think television is a deterrent to reading, and it can be if you let your child sit passively watching it hour after hour. However, if you use it wisely, and in moderation, selecting the programs carefully, it can be a great way to broaden a child's vocabulary. Programs such as the Jacques Cousteau's underwater documentaries, which intrigue many youngsters of this age, expose your child to all sorts of words he might not otherwise come into contact with—words such as "exploration," "treasures" of the sea, "equipment," "technology," "oceanography," and the names of many different fish. There is no need—and, in fact, you should *not* try—to explain the meaning of all the new words, for this would take all the enjoyment from watching. Just hearing the words helps him get an idea of their meaning. If you include them in your conversations afterward, the meanings will gradually become clearer to him. It will take some time, but have faith, one day he will surprise you and actually use the word correctly.

Always try to find time after watching a program to discuss it, as this will give you a chance to immediately use some of the words. Also, it enables you to clear up any misunderstandings he might have. If he watches a program alone, have him tell you what it was about. This is marvelous in helping him become more articulate generally, but also gives him a chance to air any new words he may want to "show off."

"Sesame Street" and "Electric Company" are, of course, naturals for your child to watch, as they are specially designed to develop youngsters' language skills. Some cartoons are also good because their stories are simple and the words can be easily related to what they are describing. Some of the commercials, let's face it, can and do add the odd word or two to your child's vocabulary. Actually, it is to be expected, because they employ all the best teaching techniques: the constant repetition of the words; catchy rhymes and jingles; showing the object (product) many times as the name is said; and generally conveying "good things" about the word.

I see the impact of commercials on youngsters' vocabulary development more and more these days. A four-year-old recently advised me of the best canned food for my dog, telling me, "It's the most nutritious [and she got the pronunciation perfectly correct], because it's full of protein." And a youngster who came to stay gave me very precise instructions, explaining what he would like for breakfast. He named the exact cereal, the type of bread and orange juice, and even the kind of margarine, telling me authoritatively, "Margarine is better than butter because it causes less cholesterol!"

Keep Up the Reading

Continue to read aloud to your child, but as he is so active now, choose a time when his energies are spent and he is ready to settle down and listen. Keep a good supply of books from the library, because he will get through them much more rapidly now. If possible, try to buy him some books of his own to add to his library, for once you have read them together, he will want to return to them again and again.

Keep up the good work of broadening his knowledge of the world and expanding his vocabulary by introducing him to more informative and factual books, such as ones about the sea (a good follow-up to the Cousteau programs), insects, the forest, airplanes, and, of course, as many as possible on his "collection" of the moment.

If he hankers after his old familiar friends, don't worry. Be grateful he enjoys them so much. Strike a happy compromise. Get him into the habit of beginning your reading time together with a new book and ending with a favorite. Or vice versa. Whatever you do, though, keep him involved, thinking, and constantly searching for the meaning behind the words.

CHAPTER 6

When Your Child Is Ready to Read

Your Child Shows Signs of Wanting to Become a Reader

It is not hard to tell when your child is interested in learning to read. He will beg you to read to him. Watch the clock until your special reading time together. Strut around importantly carrying books, or printed matter. Pretend to read, and even boast he can read.

By this time (usually when he is about four or five, but it may be as early as three, or, if he is a late developer, around six, or even seven) he has had so much exposure to words and language that he chats away effortlessly and coherently, and pretty well understands everything you say. The spoken word has become part of his life, but now he becomes intrigued with the printed word. He notices the signs on the street. The words that flash on the screen in a commercial. The name on a cookie package. His eyes wander from the pictures in the book you are reading to him, to the words below. He scrutinizes the squiggles and strange shapes, and wonders how you can be so clever to decipher their meaning. Ever the imitator, he wants to be like you. Still full of that innate curiosity, he decides to find out for himself. So finally there comes that wondrous, exciting day when all your hard work is rewarded and he asks, "What does that word say?"

Ring the bells, hit the gong, clap your hands, and smile—just as you did when he said his first word, for your child has indeed passed another milestone. And give yourself a big pat on the back, because you have obviously done a great job preparing him for reading. You have not only given him the tools, but you have also aroused his *desire to read*. You haven't forced it on him. It has developed naturally, out of the stimulating environment you have created.

Once your child decides he wants to read, he is already halfway there. You can rest assured it won't take him long to learn. Just a few more steps and he'll be ready.

But before going on to those steps, a quick word about what you do if your child shows no interest in learning to read. The answer is short and sweet. You don't panic, push, or turn the situation into a problem. You stop worrying, continue working on the skills mentioned in the preceding chapters in the section—and wait. He will get around to it when he is good and ready.

Making the Transition from Talking to Reading

Awareness of Written Words

There are several ways you can easily, and naturally, as part of your normal day's activities, make your child conscious that written language is spoken language, and at the same time help him to recognize printed words. The most obvious is making him aware of the words in print around him. Point to the billboards, the names of the streets and stores, the words on the mailbox, the ice-cream vendor's van, and trucks, and casually say the words. As you drive, point out the road signs and say, "I'd better go slowly now. That sign says 'slow.'" After a while, have him pretend he is the driver and see if he can identify the signs. At first he will recognize them by their shape, but gradually he will learn to recognize the words too.

Continue to use the supermarket. Did you ever imagine how useful it would be in preparing your child to read? Point to the names of the products and say, "That is the *peanut butter* you like." Or call his attention to the "specials" signs. "I notice they have your favorite *cookies* on sale," and put your finger on the word. As he becomes accustomed to this, ask him what a word says, such as, "What is the name of this cereal?" But be sure it is a word he is familiar with and you know he will recognize easily. Sometimes ask him to find an item. "See if you can find your favorite *chocolate* ice cream." The supermarket and other stores are particularly good for helping your child make the association between the printed words and what they stand for, because the actual articles are there for them to see, and—whoops!—touch.

There are also endless opportunities at home to familiarize a child with written language. Not only books, newspapers and magazines, but also mail-order catalogues, sales brochures, calendars, grandparents' letters, and even your shopping list stuck on the refrigerator door. Packages boldly naming their contents, "milk," "butter," "eggs," are just waiting for your child to identify them. Ask him to get you the products as you cook, or prepare a meal. Tell him, "I need the eggs, milk, and a package of butter." At first he will pick them out by their cartons. But, in time, he will notice their names, especially if you give him a felt magic marker, or heavy crayon, and have him circle "eggs," "milk," and "butter." Another game you can play in the kitchen is to have him pick out a package of frozen or canned vegetables and ask him to guess what kind they are. He will find it easy, because all he has to do is look at the picture. However, follow this up by pointing to the word and have him circle it.

Obviously, one of the best methods for helping your child learn to recognize written words is to use his own books, since he is familiar with the stories. And, if the truth be known, he probably knows some of the words already. Start pointing out a few key words as you read. Explain, "That says 'dog.' That is the word for 'dog.'" Pronounce "dog" slowly and distinctly. Then have him point to the word and say "dog." Then have him point to the dog. However, be careful not to overdo it, nor interrupt the progression of the story. And do it casually, so it doesn't become a "lesson." Remember, at this stage, you are just helping him to associate spoken language with written language. You are not teaching him to actually read.

Whatever activity or game you use, limit the words you introduce to the very basic ones he comes into contact with each day or is likely to use himself. On the other hand, if he asks what a strange or difficult word says, always tell him. Don't be like the mother I overheard who, when her daughter asked what "homogeneous" meant, snapped, "That's a much too difficult word for you. You wouldn't understand it even if I told you." No, she probably would not have understood it. But, even so, her interest and curiosity deserved to be recognized positively, so that in the future she will be encouraged to ask what other words mean.

There are endless games and activities you can play with your child to help him recognize words. A friend of mine made signs out of large pieces of cardboard, labeling various articles in the house, such as "bed," "desk," "table," "chair," and "stove." She placed them on the appropriate articles and then had her daughter "read" the words. My friend pointed to the word and said, "This is the word for 'bed.'" Then she had her repeat the word. After a few sessions of doing this she took away the labels and had her put them back. Her daughter thoroughly enjoyed trotting around the house importantly holding her signs. And after a week of this, my friend was amazed to find she had to start making new labels. Her child not only knew all the words, but also was beside herself with eagerness to learn some more.

This same friend also made a large outline of Nancy, and labeled the main parts of her body. She then hung it up in her room and each day went over the names with her: "head," "neck," "arm," "leg," and "foot." Next, she put these names on cardboard and had Nancy cover up the appropriate word on the poster with them. After a while, she held up the cardboard signs and had her touch the appropriate parts of her body.

You can use labels for helping your child learn all kinds of words. You can make a "menu" for supper. Label the shells in his collection. Post the days of the week on the refrigerator door. However, the label that will interest him most is the one with *his name* on it. This should be one of the first labels, if not the first label you introduce him to. Write it in big, bold letters and hang it up in a prominent place in his room. Or better still, stick it on his door.

You can also use labels, or word or "flash" cards, as they are usually called in school, to start off a *real* word collection for him. He will thoroughly enjoy shuffling through the cards, and will be especially proud of them if you give him a special box or folder, labeled "David's words," to keep them in. Let him color the cards, and if his dexterity is good enough, even crayon over the letters. Have him make a drawing or stick on a picture of the word on the back of the card—where he will have more room. An alternative is to have him paste the cards in a scrapbook. He will have more room for his drawings and pictures, but he won't be able to play with the cards, which most kids like to do. One four-year-old child I know spends literally hours trotting importantly around the house with his cards in an old purse of his mother's (his briefcase, he told me), looking for articles to match his cards with. Sometimes he takes them to his grandmother's and tries to match the cards with things in her house. This boy also likes to play "offices" with his cards. He sits at the dining-room table and stacks them into "in" and "out" baskets (shoe box cartons), which I presume he has seen on his father's office desk. He carefully scrutinizes each card, passing them back and forth between the cartons. And now and then uses them as notes to "dictate" to his secretary.

Don't worry if your child is more absorbed in playing with the cards than learning their contents. As long as you see that he understands the meaning of the words *before* you add them to his collection, the activities will help to reinforce them in his mind.

Add more "sight" words (the term given to words that are read in a "gulp" and not first broken down into their letter sounds) very gradually. Again, let me stress. Include only simple, everyday words. Remember, the name of the game is not how big you can make his collection, but how useful.

Another way you can introduce your child to sight words that will thrill him literally "beyond words" is to create his *own* book. Draw, color, or paste the pictures of familiar objects, printing the words beneath. But arrange them in a sequence that tells a story. Include him in it and he will love it even more. Give the book a swish, colorful cover and bind it with pretty ribbon. And you will find it will occupy him for hours. And before long, he will be pleading for more. So be prepared!

You can help your child see the relationship between spoken and written language by having him "help" you make the shopping list, write instructions to the baby-sitter, or answer the grandparents' letters. Better still, have him dictate his own letter to them, while you act as his "secretary" and write it down. He can then actually watch his words going down on paper. And if you read them back to him, he will realize they say exactly what he has just said.

You can follow this up by having him tell you a story to write down. It can be his own, or, if he is stuck for ideas, one he has read recently. Or you can start keeping a diary, and record an event he tells you each day. You can also have fun making up poems and rhymes together, such as the one a youngster made up for me: "The naughty boy/broke his toy." Or you can even make up a commercial jingle advertising your own imaginary products.

Learning the letters

When your child has learned to identify a pretty good number of sight words (about twenty to thirty) and is eager to learn even more, it is time to introduce him to the letters. Some parents do this much earlier, before their child has learned to "read" words. In fact, I know some parents who have introduced them to their eighteen-month-old. However, it's been my experience that children have much more fun, and learn them much more easily, if you wait until they are genuinely interested in words and their meanings (which I said earlier is when they are about three or four, but could be earlier or later than this). It then also becomes the natural culmination of all the other activities you have done with him, for the rhymes, songs, story times, games, and fireside chats have accustomed his ear to the sounds of the letters, and the activities building his sight vocabulary have introduced him to their form and shape.

Your child will revel in the role of being the letter detective, which a friend of mind encouraged by giving her daughter a magnifying glass. She found the culmination of being Sherlock Holmes and the excitement of learning the letters helped her to learn the whole alphabet in a few weeks.

You can introduce the letters in any order. But teach them one by one. Don't progress to a new letter until your child has the one you are working on down pat and can recognize *both* its sound and shape. As usual, make the lessons seem like games. As soon as you detect his interest waning, stop. Then pick up where you left off when he is eager to learn again. At first make your sessions fairly short (about four to five minutes), but gradually lengthen them as his attention span and interest increase. For more hints on teaching, refer to the "Tricks of the Trade" chapter, especially pages 29–34.

One good way to begin introducing the letters to your child is to choose letters that seem to particularly interest him. If you hear him singing "Sing a Song of Sixpence," or he seems fascinated with a word such as "Snodgrass" (a name that fascinated a child I know), start with "S."

However, you can also begin by playing a game, such as the "name it" game. Put five or six items on a tray, or find pictures of several items, beginning with the letter you want to introduce. Then ask him to "give their name."

LEARNING THE SOUNDS OF THE LETTERS

Whichever method you choose, begin by drawing his attention to the sound of the letter. Say, "Did you notice that the words began with the same sound?" Then make the "S" sound. Repeat the words, emphasizing the "S" sound. Then ask him to repeat the words, emphasizing their beginning sound.

Next, ask him if he can think of any more words beginning with the "S" sound. He will probably come up with plenty. But if he is having a hard time, point to some objects in the room and have him name them. Or give him an "S" word, like "snail," and say, "Does 'snail' begin with the sound?"

You can play all sorts of games to give him practice in identifying words beginning with the sound. "I Spy," finding as many items in the room as possible, is always popular. So is "I'm Going to Market to Buy," naming as many foods, clothes, or other products as possible. Then there is the "naming" game, thinking of as many boys' or girls' names as possible. Also the "Rhyming" game. In this game, you give him a word like "mat" or "bit" and he has to give you a rhyming word, like "sat" or "sit." You can show him a picture and have him point out everything beginning with the letter, or you can have him draw or paint objects that begin with it. For more activities for all aspects of introducing the letters, see the end of this section.

It is important to introduce the letter sound initially as part of a word, as this immediately establishes in your child's mind that letters are parts of words and don't function as isolated entities. Introduce only the simplest and most common sounds of the letter. For example, the *c*ake sound of "c" and not the "ni*c*e" sound. And the *s*un sound of "s" and not the "ro*s*e." But you can introduce both sounds of the vowels (a, e, i, o, u). For example, c*a*ke and c*a*t.

The Simplest and Most Common Sounds of the Letters

a	apple	apron	b	bat
c	cat		d	dog
e	egg	each	f	finger
g	girl		h	hand
i	igloo	iris	j	juice
k	kite		l	leaf
m	man		n	nuts
o	October	open	p	pan
q	queen		r	rain
s	sock		t	toe
u	umbrella	uniform	v	voice
w	window		x	box
y	yellow		z	zoo

As soon as your child can quickly and easily identify words beginning with the sound, give him a few words with an "odd man out" and see if he can pick it out. "Sam, sneakers, toe, smile." This is to teach him to differentiate the sound from other ones. Then have him try to trick you with some odd-man-out words.

After this, help him to identify the sound at the end of words. You can have lots of fun doing this using rhyming words, poems, songs, and jingles. Have him recite the nursery rhymes he knows by heart. And then ask him to, "Pick out the words that have the same sound at the end." Recite a poem or sing a song he knows, leaving out one of the rhyming words, and have him give it to you. Ask him, "Which word does it rhyme with? What sound do they both end with?" Give him a word like "bat" and see how many rhyming words he can come up with. This is also good practice for differentiating among beginning sounds. Play the "naming" game, but this time have him think of names that begin with the last letter of the previous one. "Ethel—Linda—Ann—Nan."

After a while, you can start giving him "homework." Little projects he can do on his own. He will love this and feel very grown up, particularly if he has an older brother or sister at school. Have him find pictures, or collect items, that begin or end with the sound. Or have him draw, crayon, or paint pictures of the items. Have him make a tape recording of the words.

When you are pretty sure he can identify the sound in words, focus on the sound itself. Help him to pronounce it correctly by standing in front of the mirror with him. Show him how you use your tongue, lips, and mouth to make the sound. Then have him copy you. And, if you can associate it with an animal noise, or some other familiar sound, so much the bettter. The "hi*ss*" of a snake. The "bu*zz*" of a bumblebee. The "*p*urr" of a cat.

LEARNING WHAT THE LETTERS LOOK LIKE

When you know he has the sound of the letter down pat, show him what it looks like. Or, if he is tiring of the hearing games, do it sooner. The best way to introduce the shape of the letters is to show them individually (not as part of a word). Print them, nice and large, on the same kind of flash cards you used to introduce the sight words. Or make big, stiff letters from corrugated cardboard so he can actually handle the letters. Or buy some plastic ones, or magnetic ones, which are great for sticking on the refrigerator door for your kitchen learning sessions. Did you ever imagine it would become your teacher's chalkboard? Of course, you can use a chalkboard and draw the letters, or a flannelboard with felt letters, or a large poster and use a colorful magic marker. Or you can use them all!

Each time you introduce a letter, say it by its name and remind him of its sound. "This is the letter 'c,' which stands for the 'c' sound in *c*ake, *c*ream, *c*offee, and *c*rumpet." Then ask him, "Give me some more words beginning with the 'c' sound." When you introduce the vowels, remind him they have two sounds. "This is the letter 'A.' It's the letter that makes the 'c*a*ke-b*a*ke-t*a*ke' sound. And the 'c*a*t-b*a*t-s*a*t' sound." Again, ask him to give you words with the sounds.

Whenever possible, give him an object he knows that he can associate the shape of the letter with. "O" looks like a ball, or orange. "I" like a stick. "S" like a snake. "M" like two mountaintops. "J" like a candy stick upside down. And so on. If you can make the example edible, so much the better.

Let him touch, feel, and even be the letters. He will love trying to bend his body into an "O." Or stretch his arms and legs to make an "X." Or curl up to be a "S." You can get him to draw the shapes of the letters in the air with his fingers. Or draw them in the sand. Or trace over your letters. The best way, however, to establish the shapes well and truly in his mind is to have him write the letters himself.

LEARNING TO WRITE THE LETTERS

The most usual method of writing first taught to youngsters is called "manuscript writing." It has two forms, capital letters and small letters, but you don't have to teach him both at the same time. Some kids can't cope with two letters for one sound for a while, though for others, it's a cinch. It doesn't matter which type you introduce first. Some kids find it easier to write the capital letters, while others find it easier to make the small letters. You will just have to play it by ear with your child. He may not even be interested in writing at all, in which case, leave it for a while. Don't force it upon him, as it means he is not ready. Don't attempt to teach him unless he has the dexterity and fine motor co-ordination to hold and manipulate a pencil or crayon. But if he has done plenty of finger painting, drawing, painting, crayoning, and coloring, he should be ready.

Start him out by having him draw straight and curved lines, and circles, for all the letters are formed from these. Make it interesting for him by giving him special things to draw. "Draw me ten nice, big, fat, juicy oranges." Or "Draw a house with the straightest walls you can, with the curliest smoke wafting into the sky, and a big hot sun beaming its rays out." Or "Draw the sky at night, with lots of sparkling stars, a half moon, and a witch riding on her broom."

Give him a large, fat pencil, or crayon, and show him how to hold it correctly—between his second finger (on the side) and thumb so it slants and rests in the groove between the thumb and first finger and is supported by the first finger (see drawing). The grip should be easy (not grasped for dear life, which he'll probably do at first), and note that the pencil should not be held upright, or in the fist.

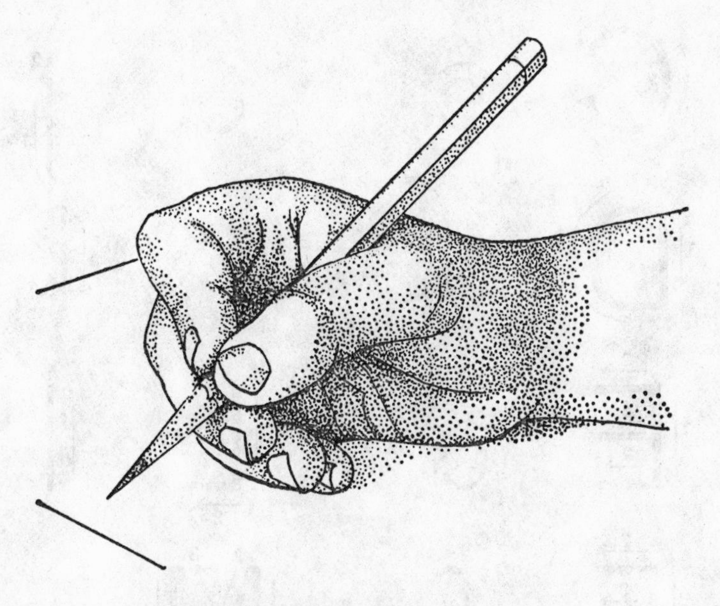

Hand turned slightly on the side to show the pencil grip.

At first teach him to write the letters on his drawing paper so they can be made nice and large. Then use the ordinary eight-by-eleven-inch paper, with one centimeter between the lines. Draw the letters so they take up two lines, as shown on pages 118–19. And be sure to follow the direction of the arrows, and order of the numbers, so you teach him to form them the correct way.

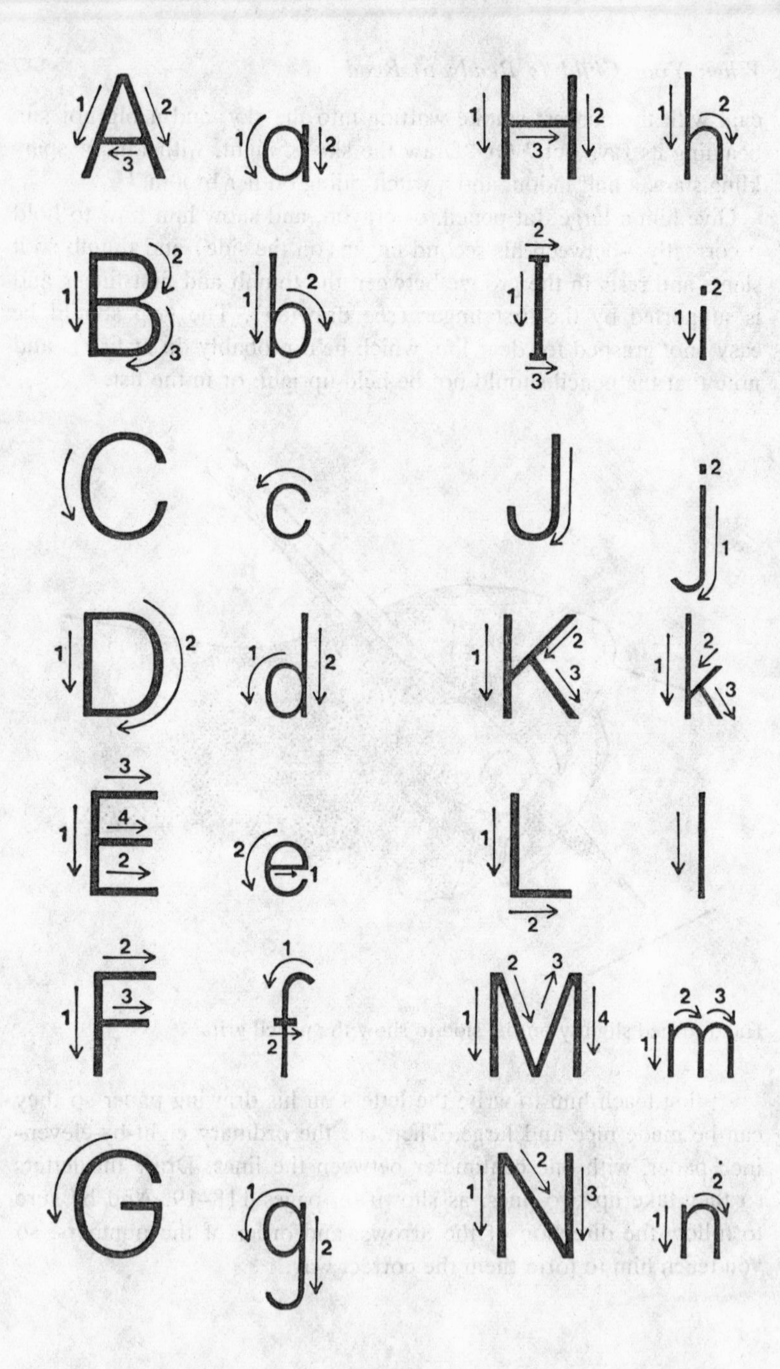
A a H h
B b I i
C c J j
D d K k
E e L l
F f M m
G g N n

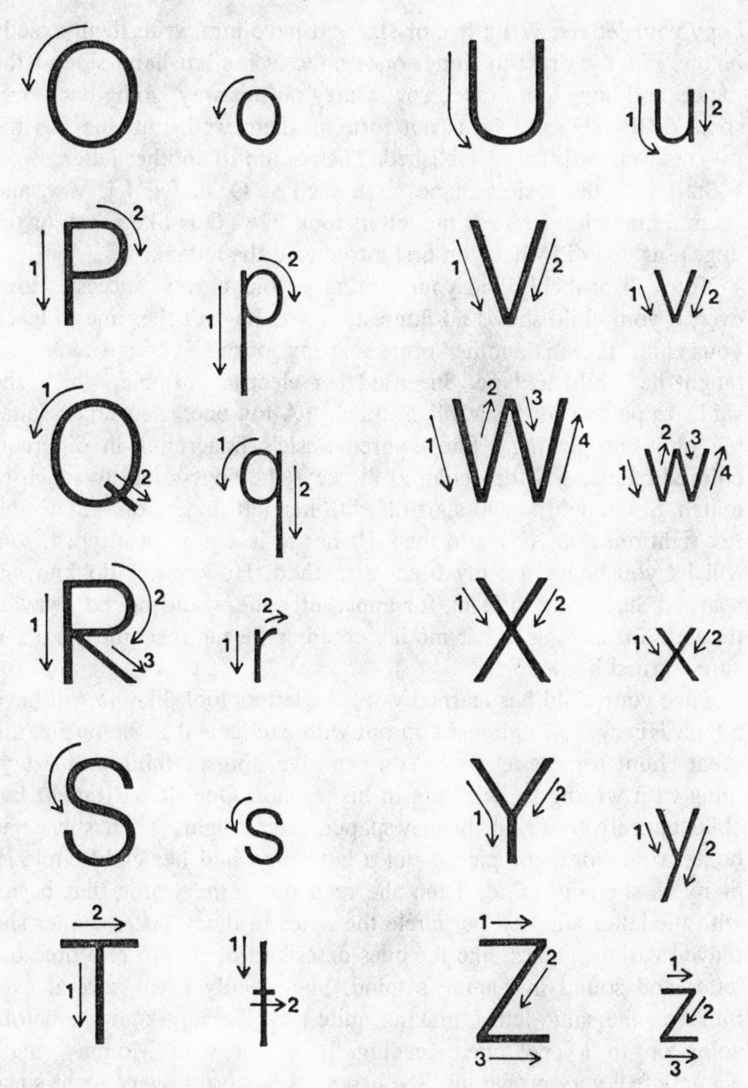

How to write the capital and small letters of manuscript writing.

First, draw the letter several times. Second, have him trace over your letters. Third, make the letter several times with dotted lines. Fourth, have him go over these, joining the dots. Fifth, have him copy your letters. Write five or six, and have him write them exactly below. Finally, draw the letter once only, at the left-hand side of the paper, and have him draw a row. Carry on this way, going back over some of the stages if he is not forming them well, until he has the process well and truly established. Then go on to another letter.

Start with the easiest shapes first, such as O, o, I i, J j, V v, and remind him what some of the letters look like (O is like a ball or orange), as you did when you first introduced the letters.

You will probably find your writing lessons a great success. However, if your child shows no interest, or you haven't the time to teach your child, there is another route that my journalist friend took. She taught her child to type. She used her electric portable, which she said was perfect for Susie's light touch. (A toy one, she said, is suitable only for playing.) She colored Susie's fingernails in different-colored paints, and then colored the keys the fingers had to touch to match. She taught her to start off with her left fingers on ASDF and her right ones on JKL, and then left her to it. I am not a typist, so I will let you figure out my friend's method. However, I do know it sparked Susie's enthusiasm, for apparently she would pound away at the keys for as long as her mother could spare the machine. And she sure learned her letters.

Once your child has learned what the letters look like he will have a ball. His eyes will almost pop out with excitement as he begins the great "hunt for the letters." You can give him anything and everything with writing to help him in his pursuit. One parent taught her child entirely by using the newspaper. Each night, when she came home from work, she picked out a letter and had her child circle as many as she could find. Then she read out some words that began with the letter and had her circle the letter in them. After dinner she played various games, like the ones described below, to reinforce the letter and sound in Tammy's mind. She usually spent several evenings on the same letter, making quite sure Tammy knew it, before going on to a new one. Reading the paper with Mommy made Tammy feel very grown up. She had seen her do it every night since she was a baby, and now she was doing it too. Each evening she would greet her at the door with the words, "Come on, hurry, Mommy, we've got to read the paper before supper." Believe it or not, it was not too long before Tammy *was* actually reading the paper. She was so stimulated by these sessions that, as soon as she knew her letters, she was urging her mother to teach her what the words were saying.

You will probably find the ABC books are the easiest and best way to teach your child the letters. There are many colorful, original, and captivating ones on the market today (see specific recommendations on page 365) and, of course, they are designed for this very purpose. If you choose one like *Gyo Fujikawa's A to Z Picture Book* you will probably find it becomes not only your child's favorite book, but also his most prized possession. It will be thumbed through and examined again and again. It could also inspire him to create his own ABC book, which will help to expand his "letter vocabulary." If it does, have him write the letters and copy simple words with the letter, such as, "tub," "train," "top," and "tacks" and either draw, or paste in, the pictures, as he did in his earlier books.

You can also draw your child's attention to letters around the house. You can start with his initials on the silver mug Cousin Mildred gave him when he was born. These will be easy to identify because he has already learned his name. Then there is the "h" and "c" on the water taps, the "s" on the sugar, and the "f" on the flour containers. And what about those macaroni alphabets you put in the soup? They could not be better, because he can actually cook and eat the letters after he has picked them out. There are many interesting ways he can create the letters himself. He can cut them out after writing them first. He can make them in plastecine, or modeling clay. Or he can make cookies in their shapes, and again have the delight of eating them.

The possibilities for making your child aware of the letters are endless. But if you think you will run out of ideas, don't worry. Before too long, he will be pointing out the letters to you and thinking up ways to practice them.

ACTIVITIES AND GAMES FOR LEARNING LETTERS

1. **Have "red-letter days."** Choose a letter, or have your child choose one, at breakfast each morning. This becomes the "letter of the day," and you display it in several prominent places: on the table

where you have your meals; on the mantelpiece in the sitting room; on the chest in the hall; on the mirror in the bathroom; and, of course, you guessed it, on the refrigerator door. Concentrate on this letter all day, and gear all your word games and activities to practicing it. On special days, such as Halloween, use the letter the name of the holiday begins with.

2. **Posting game.** Make a letter box (an old shoe carton is ideal) and have your child mail small objects beginning with the letter. Or he can mail his plastic letters as you call out their names. One parent made a large felt kangaroo, which she hung on her child's bedroom wall. Each day she pinned a letter to its chest. Then she had her child put articles beginning with the letter, or the letter itself, into its pouch.

3. **Filing game.** Make a file cabinet (from old match or thumbtack boxes). Label each one with a letter. Then have him "file" the letters into the correct boxes.

4. **Fish.** Put all the letters into a box, or a bowl, or just a heap on the floor, and have him "fish out" the letters as you call them out. Then have him give you letters to fish out, and tell you if you have found the correct one.

5. **Hunt and seek.** Hide the letters around the house. When he has found them all, have him hold up each one, and give its name, sound, and three words beginning with the letter. At first give him a plastic letter to take around with him, to remind him which one he is looking for.

6. **Matching.** Jumble up two sets of the alphabet and have him pair off the letters. Or point to a letter in his storybook or newspaper and have him hold up the appropriate one. Give him a tray of objects, or set of pictures, and have him put the letter that each one begins with, beside it. Or have him go around the house putting the letters on appropriate articles, as he did with his sight words.

7. **The action game.** Say, "I want you to: Skip, hop, jump. Do what the word beginning with 'h' tells you to do." Or play "Simple Simon," and have him do only the things that start with the letter. Say, "Simon is thinking of 'S.' Simon says, 'Kneel down,' 'wave your hand,' *'sneeze,'* 'cough.' "

8. **Find the odd man out.** Give him several letters and have him pick out the one that is different from all the others. Then have him

do this with the names of articles, or pictures. Or, ask him which words don't begin with the same letter in jingles such as "Peter Piper picked *a* peck *of* pickled peppercorns." He will love this, and, if you have him repeat it after you, he will be able to practice his "p" sound.

9. **Lotto.** Make letter lotto cards, and call out letters instead of numbers.

10. **Listing.** Let him "order" from a catalogue or sales brochure. Have him go through it picking out items beginning, or ending, with the letter. Or have him dictate a shopping list, or menu, made up of words with the letter.

Comprehension: Putting It All Together

Once your child has learned to recognize the letters and their sounds, he is ready to put them together to read words. But before he can truly read, he must be able to give meaning to words and understand them in their context. Your child should have no problem, for all the things you have been doing with him since he was a baby have prepared him for this. All he has to do is *put them all together*. It's just as though he were making a cake. You have given him the flour, sugar, and eggs, and even the bowl and mixing spoon. Now he has to stir them together and produce the cake.

He is familiar with words. He understands all the common ones and can use them appropriately. They roll off his tongue in an effortless flow. He has had so many different kinds of experiences he recognizes what a writer is talking about when he refers to such things as the monkey who escaped from his cage at the zoo, or the family that went on a picnic in the country. But, if he is not familiar with the subject he is reading about, there is no need for concern. He has learned how to think and use his mind, so he can have a good try at making sense of it. If it's particularly tough, he will struggle with it, because he has also learned to concentrate, and be patient and persevering. Also, don't forget he has been listening to stories, and "reading" books with you for several years now. So he is used to looking out for special clues to the meaning, and following the sequence of events to their logical conclusion.

WORDS AND THEIR RELATIONSHIPS

You can help your child "put it all together" by drawing his attention to words and their relationships, particularly at the same time he is learning sight words, and the letters and their sounds. Do this as you read to him, but, as usual, don't overdo it and spoil the story.

For example, when you read sentences such as the following, ask questions that pinpoint the *key words and their significance.*

"The lion *escaped* from his cage." Ask: "What did the lion do?" When he tells you, ask: "If he hadn't escaped, how would the story be different?"

"The little boy was *hungry.*" Ask: "What was the little boy?" When he tells you, ask: "What did his hunger make him do? Would he have done that if he hadn't been hungry?"

"The children landed on a *desert island.*" Ask: "Where did the children land?" When he tells you, check if he knows what "desert island" means. If he doesn't, don't tell him. Have him read on and try to guess from the rest of the story. It will be more fun this way, and it is what he will have to do when he is reading a story on his own.

Help him to recognize *word order,* so that when he meets a sentence like "The cat pounced on the mouse," he knows who is likely to be eaten. Point out the words that go together, so that when he reads, "Jane's dress is blue," he understands the dress is blue, and Jane's not suffering from the cold. Finally, help him to see combinations of words as they relate to *phrases of meaning*—those "gulps" I talked about earlier—so that when he reads, "John skateboarded down the path while Joan biked," he knows who went on the skateboard and who went on the bike.

You do this by raising questions that call on those wonderful powers of observation he now has, make him think through the answers on his own, and come to his own conclusions. For this again is what he will have to do when he reads.

THE MEANING OF THE STORY AS A WHOLE

You can also improve your child's comprehension by helping him interpret the meaning of the story as a whole. This is much more difficult, but as you talk over what you have read, you can draw his attention to: (1) the main idea, so he understands generally what the story is about, and realizes the significance of everything that happens; (2) the key events, or aspects, so he doesn't miss an essential part; (3) the order and sequence in which the events occur, so he follows the writer's train of thought and reasoning; (4) the important facts and details, so he sees them exactly as they are presented, and understands their relationship and how they contribute to the story as a whole.

You can also help him to "read between the lines" and draw conclusions by having him summarize in his own words what you have read, predict outcomes, and offer solutions. You can encourage him to be critical and make judgments by asking such quesions as: "Why did you like the story?" "Do you think it was sad?" This is an extremely sophisticated level of reading, which only comes after much experience, so don't worry if his replies aren't always what you would expect. Never tell him he is wrong, though. Show interest in his viewpoint, and tell him yours. Continue to ask for his opinions, and he will gradually become more perceptive.

When your child has learned to think about what you have read to him, and he is familiar with the letters and their sounds, he is ripe and ready for reading. He will slip effortlessly into the world of print, and before you know it, he will be reading the bedtime story to you, looking up the recipe for making his favorite cookies, and finding out how his favorite football team fared by searching the sports page of the paper.

Learning to read will not be a big deal, or an ordeal. It will just be a natural step in his progress toward coming to grips with the world and fulfilling his potential.

PART THREE:

Teaching Your Child the Fundamentals: The Reading Lessons

Teaching Your Child the Fundamentals: The Reading Lessons

You can use these lessons to teach your child to read whether he is a complete beginner, or needs help because he is having difficulty in school. They are easy to teach, don't require any expensive equipment or materials, and need only take up a short amount of time each day. All you have to do is follow the simple directions, and before you know it, your child will not only be learning to read, but you will both be enjoying the sessions too.

But a word of caution. If your child is a preschooler, consider these questions before you start teaching him:

•**Is my child READY to learn?** Has he acquired all those vital prerequisite skills, abilities, and attitudes described in Part II, "Preparing

Your child for Reading"? If you have not read this part of the book, do so NOW!

•**Is my child EAGER to learn?** I explain the importance of this in the last chapter of Part II, "When Your Child Is Ready to Read," but can't emphasize it enough. Does he really want to learn, or is it *you* who wants him to learn? In other words, whose goals are you working on—yours or his? If there is any likelihood of putting your child under pressure, don't attempt the lessons.

•**Should I give my child a head start?** This is a tough one to answer. The school is in business to educate your child, and the teachers should be specially trained to teach reading, so it's probably best to leave it to them. On the other hand, if your child is ready and so enthusiastic to learn that you feel he will be frustrated if he doesn't, go ahead. Introduce him to the first few lessons. See how he enjoys them and how easy you find them to teach. If all goes swimmingly, carry on. If not, wait.

If your child is older, an eight- or nine-year-old still struggling with the first readers, check with his teacher to see if he feels it is a good idea for you to help him. As I point out in Chapter 12, "Working with the School," your role should be to work with him to reinforce his program, not set up in competition. However, if you are convinced the school is not doing a good job teaching your child to read (see Chapter 12 again as to how to go about evaluating this), go ahead with the lessons.

Be sure, also, that your child understands why he is doing the lessons and is willing to put effort into them. This may take a little ingenuity on your part, but you should not have a hard time convincing him if: (1) you are positive and frank and explain, "It really is time you got this reading business licked because it will make your schoolwork so much easier. And think of the fun you'll have reading books like the one Grandfather gave you for your birthday"; (2) *you* are enthusiastic, and reassure him the lessons will be "a cinch" and, even, "enjoyable."

A Few Suggestions for Presenting the Lessons

The best way to teach the lessons is to set aside a specific time each day that you call "lesson time." This establishes a learning pattern, makes the lessons part of the daily routine, just like mealtimes, and prevents arguments and excuses about "having other things to do."

You will have to decide on the length of the lessons according to your child's age and attention span. However, at first, make them short (no more than ten minutes for a preschooler); and then gradually increase the time as his concentration and interest increase. At all times, though, be sure not to tackle too much at one time.

Give him homework each day to reinforce the skills you have taught and to see that they have really "sunk in." It needn't be much, just a few words to learn, or an activity to practice the skill is fine. You will have to play it by ear, though, depending on the lesson. If your child is a preschooler, treat the homework as a "special" and "grown-up" activity. If he's older, make it clear why you are giving it to him so that he sees it as important and not a "chore." Hopefully, he will then do it cheerfully and happily.

Use all those teaching methods and "tricks of the trade" I mention in the part, "A Few Things You Need to Know Before You Start," particularly those on pages 29–34. If you haven't read them—do so! And remember to always finish on a happy note, so your child is enthusiastic for the next lesson.

What You Need to Teach the Lessons

First of all, set up a special area where you can work peacefully. See that it has a table with plenty of "elbow room" for writing, and space for the materials you will need for the lesson if you don't have a handy shelf or windowsill to put them on. Have chairs for both of you that are comfortable and a suitable height for the table. I sit beside my students and write all my examples on paper; however, you may wish to use a chalkboard. If you do, see that it is placed so that your child can read it easily.

The materials you need will vary from day to day according to the activities you decide to use. But here are some daily essentials:

1. Plenty of paper. I find the best is the eight by eleven inches, with approximately one centimeter between the lines (This is the same paper that I suggested you use to teach your child to write), with holes so they can be kept in his notebook.
2. Lots of sharpened pencils, and a sharpener so you can keep them that way.
3. An eraser to get rid of those little items you want to forget and to keep *both* of your writing neat and tidy.
4. Crayons for underlining or writing a particularly important point, or even for writing the rules so they stand out in his notes. (Avoid using felt-tip pens, as they can't be erased and make the notes messy.)
5. A three-hole notebook for your child to store his notes and the exercises and activities you want him to keep.

Sometimes you will be able to use the activities and stories as they are presented in the book (but if you do, remember to cover up the answers!). Mostly, though, you will have to do a little prior preparation and write them out. When you do this, or any writing, such as making flash cards or notes for his notebook, use the method of writing your child is used to. Most schools teach the method I describe on page 116, but if your child is at school, check with his teacher to see which method he is using. An alternative is to type, but if you go this route first, teach your child the few differences in the letter shapes, such as a and t and sometimes g and q.

Outline of the Lessons

The lessons teach the basic sounds of our language and at the same time build reading comprehension. This is important because, as I have stressed so often, reading is not merely recognizing words but also *understanding their meaning*. From the very beginning, your child learns to combine the "mechanical" skills with identifying words in their context and to read "stories" to find answers to questions.

The lessons are taught in three stages. Stage I is the most important, as it introduces the very basic and essential sounds of our language. Stage II teaches some of the variations in the sounds of our language, while Stage III gets down to the real "toughies."

Each step is broken down into several steps (eighteen in all, which I call my "Dozen and a Half Steps to Success"), which, in turn, are sometimes broken down into a number of lessons. The time it will take your child to learn the skills of each step will depend on the length of your sessions, and, of course, how quickly he grasps them. None of the skills, though, is difficult to teach, even in Stage III. If you just go slowly and carefully, and follow the lesson outlines, you should have no problems.

All the lessons follow the same procedure. You begin by reading aloud to your child the rule necessary to learn the particular skill. Then you explain it by using the examples that immediately follow. Finally you give him some of the suggested activities and exercises so he can practice identifying and using the skill, and develop his reading comprehension.

I have included activities and exercises that appeal to youngsters of all ages. You will have to decide which ones are most appropriate for your child. I have given you plenty to choose from, particularly in the first lessons, so you should not be at a loss for things to do. Also, I am sure, as you progress, you will come up with some creative and fun ones of your own.

If you do run out of activities, I suggest you use the *New Phonics Workbooks,* which have excellent exercises children enjoy. Book D should be particularly helpful in reinforcing the skills of Stage III.

When your child has learned most of the rules, and you need more reading materials for him to practice his reading comprehension, I suggest you start into my *Jane Ervin Reading Comprehension Series.* The first workbook is at the third-grade reading level, and the series progresses to the twelfth grade, so they should keep up your child's reading skills for some years to come! (Both sets of workbooks are available from the publishers.*)

If you are using the lessons to help your older child, start off by using the notebook. Have him write in the rules and examples, or if it takes him a long time, do it for him. (I often do this, even with my

* *New Phonics Workbooks*
Modern Curriculum Press
13900 Prospect Road
Cleveland, O. 44136
The Jane Ervin Reading Comprehension Series
Educator's Publishing Service, Inc.
75 Moulton Street
Cambridge, Mass. 02138

fourth- and fifth-grade students, so we can quickly get on to learning the skill.) If you are working with your preschooler you will naturally have to introduce the skills orally. But as soon as possible, start writing the rules in his notebook—even if he can't read all the words—so he has them as a reference later on, when he can.

Also use the notebook as soon as possible to keep some of his activities and exercises, but be discriminating or the book will soon be bursting. Choose his best efforts so he has good examples to refer to when he reviews the skills, and, of course, include his own stories, as he will want to read these again and again.

The most effective way to teach the lessons is to follow the order of the steps as I present them, as they are carefully designed to build upon and reinforce previously learned skills. However, if your child only needs to work on specific skills (for example, if his teacher gave you a list when you met to discuss your child's reading progress), by all means zero in on just these. Look up the skills in the outline on pages 135–36 and get to work.

If, on the other hand, you are not sure which skills he needs to learn and practice, I suggest you start at the beginning and work your way through, skipping a skill he obviously knows. But a word of caution once again. Don't be fooled if he says, "Oh I've done that one." Yes, he may have "done it," but does he *know* it? Say, "Great, then this lesson won't take long at all." Or perhaps even better, to save him losing face, if he clearly doesn't know it, "Gee, are you sure it's the same one you're talking about? Let's check it out just to make sure."

You can have a good deal of fun and success teaching your child to read, as long as you don't expect him to become a reading expert overnight. Whether he is a complete beginner or an older child having difficulty, he will need a lot of practice, repetition, reinforcement, and *time* to absorb each lesson. Don't give yourself a deadline or make any rash promises, such as, "You'll learn to read in six weeks." Relax. Let your child progress at his own rate and don't go on to a new skill until he is a whiz at the one you are working on.

At the same time, keep his mind ticking and his tongue wagging, for remember, the ability to think and the development of language are the two most important elements in the reading process. Also, have a plentiful supply of leisure-type reading so he continues to read for fun.

Outline of the Lessons

Stage I: The Very Basics

Steps: 1. *Introducing the Letters* 138
2. *Vowels and Consonants* 140
3. *Short Vowels:* 142
LESSON 1: The Short A 142
LESSON 2: The Short I 146
LESSON 3: The Short O 150
LESSON 4: The Short U 154
LESSON 5: The Short E 159
4. *Some Sight Words:* is, his, as, has; the, to, of; he, she, they 163
5. *Consonant Blends* 165
6. *Long Vowels:* 169
LESSON 1: Noticing the Difference Between Long and Short Vowels 169
LESSON 2: The Magic E 170
LESSON 3: Vowel Teams 178
7. *Syllables* 186

Stage II: Some Variations

Steps: 1. *Consonant Teams:* SH, CH, TH, WH 191
2. *Vowels with R:* 196
LESSON 1: OR, AR 196
LESSON 2: ER, IR, UR 199
LESSON 3: AIR, ARE, EAR 201
3. *Y as a Vowel* 203
4. *C and G* 208
5. *Some Tricky Vowel Teams:* 213
LESSON 1: OO 213
LESSON 2: OI, OY 217
LESSON 3: OW, OU 219
LESSON 4: AW, AU 223
LESSON 5: EW 226
LESSON 6: EA 228
LESSON 7: Syllables and Review 232
6. *When Endings Are Added to Words* 235

Stage III: The Harder Ones

Steps: 1. *Silent Letters* 244
2. *Some Consonant Variations:* 247
LESSON 1: The F Sound 247
LESSON 2: The K Sound 249
LESSON 3: The Sounds of S 251
3. *Some Vowel Variations:* 252
LESSON 1: Unusual Long Vowels 252
LESSON 2: More Word Families 254
4. *Some Tough Sounds:* 256
LESSON 1: Those IE and EI Words 256
LESSON 2: More Words with the OO Sound 258
LESSON 3: Different Sounds for OU 259
LESSON 4: More Vowels with R 259
LESSON 5: Some More Unusual Vowel Sounds 263
LESSON 6: Some Special-ending Sounds 265
LESSON 7: More SH Sounds 266
5. *Increasing His Vocabulary:* 270
Sight Words 270
Homonyms 270
Prefixes and Roots 272

CHAPTER 7

Stage I: The Very Basics

These first steps in Stage I are the most important because they lay the foundation upon which you build all the other skills. So it's particularly vital that you don't hurry through them. They are mainly concerned with teaching:

(1) the simple, regular sounds of our language, which have no alternative pronunciation, and (2) the concept that letters and their sounds combine in various ways to give us *words that have meaning*. And it is *the way we combine letters* that is important. If you can get this idea across from the very beginning you will establish that reading involves comprehension, and is not just a mechanical process of sounding out the letters.

Step 1: Introducing the Letters

This lesson will pose no problem because you have already introduced your child to the sound and shape of the letters. You have shown him how to identify them in both spoken and written language. But it is just as well to check to be sure he has them firmly in mind. So go systematically through the alphabet (still focusing only on the most common, simple pronunciations of the letters). Be sure he can identify each letter at the end and middle of a word, as well as at the beginning. If he has difficulty with a letter, review it *before* going on to Lesson 2. You can use the activities he is familiar with, or try some of the suggestions listed here.

Also, be sure he can write all the letters, because he must write the words as he learns them.

If you have not yet introduced your child to the letters, turn to page 112 for ideas.

RULE:

Every letter has its own sound. The sounds of the letters combine (blend together) to make words that have special meanings.

EXAMPLES:

You cook in a PAN | You can sit on a LAP
When you're tired you NAP | You have a friend who's a PAL

ACTIVITIES:

1. Play the riddle game. Choose a letter, such as "p," and ask him a riddle that has to be answered with a word beginning with that letter.

Something you sleep on (pillow)
Something you like to eat (popcorn)
A color (purple)
An animal that turns into bacon (pig)

2. Give him words without the beginning letter and see how many letters he can use to complete them:

__at (mat, sat, pat, bat, cat, fat)
__it (mitt, sit, pit, bit, fit, hit)
__ig (big, fig, dig, pig, wig, rig)

3. Give him simple three-letter words and have him change the last letter to make a new word. Give him a clue if necessary.

Sam (sat—the opposite to stand; sad—the opposite of happy)
dot (doll—you push her in your baby carriage; dog—he barks a lot)
cub (cup—you drink out of it; cut—a knife does this)

4. Have him pick out a letter card from a box and give you six words beginning with the letter as quickly as possible.

5. Write the letters on a "clock" with a hand. Have him spin the hand. When it points to a certain letter, have him give you a word beginning with it, and then a word ending with it. Don't use more than ten to twelve letters each time. You can make the clock from cardboard and attach the letters around the edge with paperclips. Or draw the clock on paper and erase and change the letters. Or use a chalkboard or a flannelboard.

6. Play "home run." Draw a baseball diamond and put a letter at each base and two letters between the bases. To get a home run he has to give you a word beginning with each letter.

Step 2: Vowels and Consonants

Make sure he learns to say the names correctly. Sound them out slowly, emphasizing their syllables, "con-son-ants," and "vow-els." Have him repeat them until he has them. They may seem difficult, but he has learned harder words than these. I bet he can say "elevator" and "astronaut."

It is most important he learns these terms (don't worry, he needs to learn only a *very* few), because you are going to be referring to them constantly from now on. Vowels and consonants are going to be his "hooks" to hang his phonics hat on, and his "crutch" when he learns a new rule.

RULE:

There are two kinds of letters in our language:
VOWELS AND CONSONANTS.

EXAMPLES:

The vowels are: A E I O U.
The consonants are: all the other letters.

ACTIVITIES:

1. After you have pointed out the vowels (you can write them, use his plastic alphabet, or letter cards), have him say their two sounds. Before you start the following activities, ask: "What are the letters A E I O U called? What are the other letters called?" Then reverse the questions and ask: "What are the vowels? What are the consonants?"

2. Have him pick out the vowels from his plastic alphabet or his letter cards. Then have him write them.

3. Write these letters, and tell him to cross out the letter that does not belong:

A I T U O E
S P C K U M
H E Y B D R
O U A X I E

4. Scatter the letter cards upside down. Have him turn up a card and tell you if it's a vowel or a consonant.

5. Mix the five vowels with five consonants, and have him divide them correctly. He can put them in piles, or "mail" them into their correct boxes. Or you can write them, scattered on a page, or chalkboard, and have him draw a line from one vowel to another, connecting them up.

6. Show him six letters, one being a vowel. Have him tell you which one is the vowel.

7. Hold up a letter card, and ask him if it's a vowel or a consonant. Then show him a picture of an object and ask which it begins with. Read, or point to, words from the paper, or his storybook, and ask which these begin with.

8. Write sets of four words, and ask him to circle the word beginning with a vowel:

make	hat	wig	eat
frog	ant	hill	cot
pay	sock	nut	uniform

After he's completed each line, read the words to him.

9. Play the clock game. But this time when the hand lands on the letter, have him say if the letter is a vowel or a consonant before he gives a word.

10. Play the "stepping" game. Mark off seven or eight "steps," or actually use the stairs. Have him start at the starting line, or bottom stair. Hold up a letter, or word card, or call out a word. He can only take a step when the letter is, or the word begins with, a vowel. Or you can play "Simon Says" and he can only do the action when a word begins with a consonant.

Step 3: Short Vowels

Lesson 1: The Short Aa

This step is exciting because your child learns to read his first words. But watch it, because you are now getting down to the nitty-gritty. He will need *a lot* of practice and reinforcement.

As he already knows the short A sound, he should have no difficulty identifying it. But don't take any chances. Ask him to give you the two sounds for "A." Then explain that the "A" sound in "Apple" is called the "short A" sound. Use the activities given below but also think up your own so that he has as much practice as possible in: listening to words with the sound, and repeating them; thinking up his own words; identifying objects, pictures, and words with the sound; and finally—at last! *reading* words with the sound.

RULE:

Short A has the sound as in Apple.

EXAMPLES:

at bat am and can gap dad pal sad
sat mad tan cat pan tap nap man ran

ACTIVITIES:

1. Have him say the short A sound several times and repeat "apple," stressing the short A. Write the example words nice and large. Then point your finger at each one, and read it to him. Pronounce each letter very distinctly. Then have him repeat it after you. Say "Isn't this exciting? You've now read your first word. Wasn't it easy? Now see if you can read the rest of the words after me." Then say each one for him to repeat. Do this several times, repeating them one by one. Then, the moment of truth! Point to a word, without saying it, and see if he can read it. Don't worry if he can't. Continue with other short A activities, and come back to the words later. For example: Practice identifying the sound again. Give him six words beginning with A, and have him pick the odd man out:

ant, attic, apron (long A sound), Ann, and

then six words with A in the middle of the words:

cat, candy, lamp, cake (long A sound), pal

2. Have him "go fishing." Write short A words and other words on word cards. If you want to be more realistic, cut them out in the shape of fish. Have him fish for a card. Read the word to him, and ask him if it has a short A sound. If it does he has to tell you its meaning, and put it in a sentence.

3. Play "word families." Ask him, "How many words can you think of that rhyme with ______":

BAD (cad, Dad, fad, had, lad, mad, pad, sad)
CAN (an, Dan, fan, man, Nan, pan, ran, tan, van)
JACK (back, hack, lack, pack, quack, rack, sack)
HAM (am, dam, jam, ram, Sam, Tam, yam)

4. Have him make words by adding a short A. Tell him you're going to make "sandwiches." You're going to give him two consonants for the bread and he has to give you a short A for the filling. Write the letters and have him write in the missing A.

p__n p__l b__g m__p l__nd f__n m__n n__p
l__mp t__p b__d r__t p__ss c__mp b__nd f__st.

Then play the "naming" game. Say, "We're going on a camping trip and these are the people we'll take. Can you name them? If you add a short A, you'll be able to.

P__t S__m M__x M__c D__n D__d N__n V__l
J__ck P__m __nn T__m M__t

Have him pronounce each word as he completes it. Tell him to sound out each letter, and then *blend the letters together* to make the word. After he has finished all the words have him go back and read them all again.

5. Play the "magic" game, making new words from old words. This game is very important because it shows him how it's the *way letters are put together* that gives a word its meaning. Explain this to him, and have him give the different meaning for each of the words. Then have him put each word in a sentence to show he really understands it. You can use a plastic alphabet or letter cards for this. But you can also write the letters and have him rewrite them in the new order.

pan (nap) Pat (tap) pal (lap) tan (nat)
bad (dab) Tam (mat) dam (mad) Pam (map)

Always have him read the words back to you.

6. Now tell him he's really got to be a magician, because he's going to have to make entirely new words. So have him put his magician's cape on. Give him the A from his plastic alphabet, or the A letter card, and then give him two consonants from which he has to make a word. When he can do this easily, mix all the consonants into a magical hat, or bowl, and have him pick out two consonants. He then has to see if they will work with his A to make a word. Another fun game for making new words is this "riddle" game. Have him change the first, or last, letter of a word to answer a riddle. Read the riddle to him and have him give you the correct word.

You find it at the beach	band	(sand)
You can put things into these	tag	(bag)
	rack	(sack)
Water comes out of this	rap	(tap)
You can cook in this	pat	(pan)
You can take a ride in this	cat	(cab)
Sam plays with him	pam	(pal)

7. Now progress to activities that require more reading. Play "couples." Give him four rhyming words he has to match. Write them down, saying them as you do so. Then point to each word, and say them again. Have him repeat the words, and draw a line between the ones that rhyme. Or you can play this with word cards, and have him match the pairs.

band cab Max wax cap pad man rack Sam yam
nab sand wag tag sad tap Dan sack hand land

8. Write three words. Read the words to him. Have him read the words. Then ask him to circle the one you call out. Or use word cards, and have him pick out the correct one.

can, cat, cap; mat, man, map; tag, tan, tab; fan, fad, fat; hat, hand, ham; map, lad, mad; wag, wax, Max; pat, pan, pal.

9. Read these sentences to him. Then have him read them. Ask him questions to see if he understood what he had read. (REMEMBER: YOU MUST DEVELOP COMPREHENSION ALONG WITH THE PHONICS.)

Dad had a nap.	What did Dad do?
Nan ran a last lap.	What did Nan do?
Pam had a tan hat.	What did Pam have? What color was it?
Sam had a pal, Max, at camp.	Who was Sam's pal? Where were they?
Pat had a bad hand.	What did Pat have?

10. Now see if he can read words by himself, without hearing you say them first. Remind him again to sound out each letter distinctly, but to *blend* them together. Have him read each word. Underline the short A. Say the word again, and give its meaning. And then put it in a sentence.

map rat tap fat wag gap sack
ran sag wax fan yam lag ax

Then have him find a rhyming word for each one. He can write these down with its "partner," or make them into word cards to play the rhyming game.

11. See if he can read these sentences by himself. Have him reread each sentence several times and then draw the sentence. He'll have a lot of fun doing this, especially if you tell him to make his drawings funny. Afterward have him write the sentence beneath his drawing and read it to you again.

Fat Pam had a hat. Jack had a cap. A bad rat had a ham. A mad cat had a bat. Dan pats a tan cat. An ant had a bag and a sack. Max and Ann ran fast. Pat had a pan.

12. Have him read these sentences, and then choose the correct word to complete them.

Max and Dan had yams and ______	hat, ham, had
A cat had a ______	rap, mat, rat
Mac can pass ______	fast, last, lap
Can Dad land a ______	pass, bass, band
Ann had a ______ at camp	pat, past, pal
Jack had an ______	bat, jam, ax

13. Have him read these riddles and tell you the answers. There are several answers he can give. These are only suggestions. The point is to get him to read the questions and figure out what they're asking (helping to develop that comprehension of his).

A cat can wag a _______?	(tail)
A van and cab can _______?	(take you places)
A lamp can _______?	(give light)
A hand can _______?	(hold things, wave)
An ax can _______?	(chop)
A map can _______?	(tell you where to find places)
A bat, a rat, a cat, and an ant can _______?	(breathe, move, live, eat, sleep)

14. Try giving him simple, jumbled sentences and have him put the words in their correct order. If he finds it difficult, leave it. But this game is great for developing comprehension and seeing words as units of meaning.

nap Pam had a	(Pam had a nap)
Dad pan a pass	(Pass Dad a pan)
Fat, bat, had a Max	(Fat Max had a bat)
Cat a had rat a	(A cat had a rat)

15. Dictate these words to him, pronouncing each letter distinctly, and see if he can write them. Then have him read them back to you.

pat, cat, bat, rat, mat	an, can, fan, man, ran
tap, cap, gap, map, nap	bad, dad, had, pad, sad
am, ham, jam, Sam, yam	ax, lax, Max, tax, wax

16. See if he can write his own story to read. Make it as easy as possible at first by suggesting topics and words. Have him first draw the story, and then write the key words at the bottom. If he can make these into simple sentences, so much the better. As this is his first attempt at writing, he can even "plagiarize" a little and "borrow" one of the sentences he has read with you. Make it a fun project, and at this stage of the game, don't worry too much about the "story"!

Lesson 2: The Short Ii

Every lesson will be a little bit easier now. Watch how your child bursts with pride as he gets hold of these short vowels—for they open the door to so many new words for him to read.

You can use the same activities, with the odd variation now and then to add variety, as you used to teach him the short A. This saves him from learning new procedures and allows him to concentrate on learning the sound and reading the new words.

RULE:

Short I has the sound as in igloo.

EXAMPLES:

it bit pin win big dig sip zip rib
lid did him rim kick sick pill hill kit

ACTIVITIES:

1. Have him say the short I sound several times, and repeat "igloo," stressing the short I. Then write the example words nice and large, as you did with the example short A words. Point to each one as you say it. Then have him point to the word and read it. Repeat this several times. If he has problems, practice some more short I activities and return to the words again later.

Practice identifying the sound. Call out two words, one with the short I sound, and the other with the other I sound. Have him give you the word with the short sound.

rid—ride pin—pine hid—hide bit—bite kit—kite
din—dine did—died mitt—might fit—fight dim—dime

2. Call out two words, one with the short I and the other with the short A, and have him tell you which one has the short I. (This gives him a little extra practice with his short A words too.)

pan—pin sick—sack bit—bat hat—hit wig—wag
bad—bid tip—tap zip—zap lad—lid big—bag

3. Go "fishing." Put short I, and short A, words in a bowl. Have him take out a word, and if it has a short I, have him ask you to read it to him. Then have him repeat the word looking carefully at it, give the meaning, and then put it in a sentence.

4. Play "word families." Ask him, "How many words can you think of that rhyme with ______?"

HIT (it, bit, fit, lit, mitt, pit, sit, wit)
WIN (in, bin, din, fin, kin, pin, sin, tin)
LIP (dip, hip, nip, rip, sip, tip, zip)
DID (bid, hid, kid, lid, rid)

5. Play the "sandwich" game. Give him the "bread" (the consonants), and have him put in the "filling" (the short I). Then have him read the word he's made. Compliment and praise him for creating each new word. Make sure he blends the letters together and have him repeat each word several times.

d__d h__m p__ck s__p f__x d__n h__t m__x
f__ll l__p p__n t__ck b__b f__g s__x k__ck

6. Play the "naming" game. Ask, "Who is on the baseball team?"

B__ll D__ck T__m S__d J__ll J__m W__ll R__ck
K__m V__c L__z

Play the "magic" game, making new words from old words. Remind him each time you play this game (as you teach him the other short vowels and rules) that it's the order of the letters that gives a word its meaning.

pit (tip) nip (pin) dim (mid) mit (Tim)

Then give him the I from his plastic alphabet or letter cards, and give him two consonants from which he can make a word.

big did mix win dip kit lid lit wig pin

If he enjoys this, put all the consonants in a bowl, hat, or heap on the floor, have him pick two consonants, and see if he can make a word out of them.

7. Play the "riddle" game. Have him change the first, or last, letter of a word to answer the riddle. Read the riddle, and have him give you the correct word.

He lives on a farm	wig	(pig)
When you don't feel well you are	lick	(sick)
A saucepan has this	kid	(lid)
It can keep things together	pit	(pin)
When you garden you do this	din	(dig)
When you are first in a race	wit	(win)

8. Now progress to the activities that involve more reading. Play "couples." Give him four rhyming words to match. Read the words to him first, then have him read them, and tell you the pairs.

miss hip did sick kill fit zip hip him pin
dip kiss hid tick lit will mix six rim tin

9. Write three words. Read them to him. Have him read them. Then ask him to circle the one you call out.

big, dig, did; rip, sit, six; fit, fig, fin;
miss, kiss, pill; bid, lid, lip; sick, sin, sip;
hit, him, rim; lick, rid, pick

10. Read these sentences to him. Then have him read them. Ask him questions to see if he *understands* what he is reading.

Tim will hit Sid.	Who will Tim hit?
Bill will fix it.	Who will fix it?
Dick will kick six lids.	What will Dick kick?
Jill will miss Vic.	Who will Jill miss?
Bill sits in a big pit.	Where does Bill sit?

11. Now see if he can read short I words on his own, without you saying them first. Give him your usual reminders about sounding out the words. After he's read each word, have him give its meaning, and then use it in a sentence. Try to use some unfamiliar words so he's always increasing his vocabulary. Explain the word if it's new to him.

wit tin fin fig rig nip rip bid rid dim rim
wick rib kit hiss miss jazz sill mill gill

12. Pick out some of these words, and have him give you a rhyming word. Have him copy the original word, and then see if he can write his new word underneath.

13. See if he can read these sentences, and then draw them. Have him write the sentence beneath his drawing. Then have him read the sentence to you. Draw his attention to the fact that these sentences also have short A words.

Jack can lick six figs.	Jim will fix ham and yams.
Nan hid Tim's big cat.	A cab hit a tan pig.
Jill had a wig.	Dick will dig a big pit.

14. Have him read these sentences, also with short A words, and then choose the correct word to complete them.

Sid had six ______	fat, fits, figs
A cat licks Sam's ______	band, hand, land
Tim will pack the ______	ham, nap, sack
Ann had a mad ______	sip, sat, cat
Can a rat hit a ______?	man, mitt, pill
Can Bill ______ a ham?	Six, fix, mix

15. Have him read these "stories" and then answer your questions.

A pig had a fit and bit a man.

What happened to the man? Why did the pig bite him?

Jack and pal Dick will picnic. Jack will pack a ham in a bag, and jam it in a big sack.

What will Jack and Dick do? What will they have for lunch?

Dad had a big ax. Dad hid it.

What did Dad have? What did he do?

Bill ran fast. Bill will win.

Why will Bill win?

A mad bat bit a fat ant.

What did the bat do? What did the ant look like?

The bad rat licks its lips. It had a big ham, yams, figs, and jam.

Why is the rat licking his lips? Do you think "bad" is a good word to describe him? Why?

16. See if he can "unscramble" these sentences. Remind him that it's the order of the words in a sentence that makes it have "SENSE."

pigs ran pink six	(Six pink pigs ran)
Dick cat sick a had	(Dick had a sick cat)
fast can pass Bill	(Bill can pass fast)
a can Jack bag pack	(Jack can pack a bag)

17. Dictate these words to him and see if he can write them. Be sure to pronounce them slowly and distinctly. Then have him read them back to you.

lit	six	in	hid	sip	pig	hit	him	lid
did	win	wit	bin	rid	mix	sit	dip	wig

Lesson 3: The Short Oo

Things should be going with a swing now. But if your child is getting bored, or not progressing too well, slow down. Make your sessions shorter. Or if you think he needs a complete break, leave it for a day or two. Don't make it too long, though, for at this stage he may forget what he has learned. When you return to work, review what you have covered before going on. It's a good idea to do this now and then, even if you don't take a break.

RULE:

Short O has the sound as in October.

EXAMPLES:

got hot not nod rod mop pop top
sob rob Bob Tom box fox rock sock

ACTIVITIES:

1. Have him say the short O sound several times and repeat "October" stressing the short O. Then write the example words. Read them to him, pointing to each word, as you've done before. Then have him read each word to you. Repeat several times. If he needs more help identifying the short O, play more games practicing this.

Call out two words, one with a short O sound and one with the other O sound. Have him tell you which is the short O word.

cot—coat got—goat not—note hop—hope mop—mope
rod—road rob—robe cop—cope pop—Pope rot—rote

Explain the meaning of any words he doesn't know so you keep filling his word bank—for example, mope, cope, rote, and Pope. Call out a short O word, and either a short A, or short I word, and have him tell you which is the short I word.

lot—lit pad—pod rid—rod hop—hip cat—cot

Then give him three words to choose from.

sick—sock—sack hat—hit—hot pot—pit—pat
kick—tack—tock

2. Go "fishing." Put short O, I, and A words in a hat or box. Have him take out a word. This time have him try to read the word first before asking you to read it. If it has a short I sound have him give you the meaning of the word, and then put it in a sentence.

3. Play "word families." Ask him, "How many words can you think of that rhyme with ______?"

HOT (cot, dot, got, jot, lot, not, pot, rot, tot)
HOP (cop, mop, pop, top)
SOB (Bob, dob, job, lob, mob, rob)
SOCK (cock, dock, lock, mock, rock)

4. Play the "sandwich" game. Give him the bread (the consonants) and have him write in the filling (short O). Then have him read his words to you.

l__t b__x r__d B__b d__g s__ck n__t p__p
r__ck d__ll l__st j__b f__x m__b c__st T__M

5. Play the "magic" game, making new words. Have him pick out the I from his plastic alphabet or his letter cards. Then put the consonants in a box, and have him take two out, and see if he can make a word. Have him write the word and then read it to you.

Play the "riddle" game. Have him change the first, or last, letter of a word to answer the riddle. Read the riddle to him, and write down the word to be changed. This time see if he can spell, or write, the new word for you.

It's the opposite of cold	pot	(hot)
You can put things into it	fox	(box)
Peas live in this	rod	(pod)
A baby sleeps in this	cop	(cot)
Thieves do this	rot	(rob)
You do this to the floor to clean it	mob	(mop)

6. Now progress to the activities involving more reading. Play "couples." Give him four rhyming words to match. See if he can read the words now, without you reading them first. Use word cards, or write them, or have him write them.

not sock job top ox pod lock rock
pot dock hop cob box nod jot lot

Now play the game with short A and I words.

pan pin sock lick hot pot
top Nan tick sack hit cat
tin cop tack lock hat bit

7. Again see if he can read these words without you first doing so. Write three words, and have him circle the one you call out.

pop, job, jot; pod, lock, sock; sob, got, nod;
dot, Tom, on; dog, cot, lot; doll, fox, job.

Give him these words to read and have him underline the vowel, and then tell you what kind of words they are: Short A, I, or O words.

dot dab dig lick sack pill doll hop rat Tim
pig pass nod Bob hill fast rot sock back Tom

8. Have him read these sentences, but help him out if he begins to stumble. Then question him to test his comprehension.

Can a rat sit on a hill?	He can give various fun answers to this.
Jan got a doll in a box.	What did Jan get? What did it come in?
Jim hid a ham in a pot.	What did Jim have? Where did he hide it?
Tom and Tim sat on a mat.	Where did Tom and Tim sit?
Dad got a fox in a sack.	Where did Dad put the fox?

9. Have him "play detective," and complete these sentences by adding the correct letters to the words. Have him read the whole sentence before deciding on the letter, and then read the sentence again at the end.

Don __ost a sock in a pond.	m c l
Ann hid a rock in a __ox.	f b c
A bad __og bit Sam's hip.	b l d
Nan will fix Tom's __ocks.	t r s
Bob will jog, and Tod will __op.	m h n
A ham will fit into a __ot.	p l r

10. Have him read these phrases, and then make up a story from each one.

______ in a box ______ in a pond A big log hit and ______
Tom lost a ______ A bad fox hid in a pit and ______
Bob got a ______ Jack will fix ______

In case he runs short of ideas, help him out by saying, "What would you find in a box that might be exciting? Or, could there be something magic in the box? What would happen if it got out? Perhaps the box has a jumping Jack inside." And so on.

11. Have him read these sentences, and choose the correct word to complete them.

An ant can ______ on a box.	hot hob hop
A big rat sat in a ______.	pond, fond, bond
Bob ______ a hot rod.	pot lot got
Tod's ______ bit six pigs.	log dog fog

Bill can ______ fast. cot jot <u>jog</u>

A ______ hit Sam. sock <u>rock</u> rob

12. Have him read these "stories" and then answer your questions:

Don got hot. Don sat in a pond, and lost his socks. Don will hop back.

Why did Don sit in the pond? What happened? How did he get home?

Sam will hit and toss Ann's doll in a box. Tom will fix Ann's doll.

What is Sam going to do to Ann's doll? Who will fix her doll?

Todd had six sick pigs. A dog bit Todd's six pigs.

How many pigs did Todd have? Why were they sick?

Bob had a rock. Bob's rock hit Dot. It hit Dot's hip. Dot bit a lip. Doc will fix Dot's hip and lip.

What hit Dot? Where did it hit her? What did she do?
Who will make her better?
See if he can unscramble these sentences:

job had a Dad	(Dad had a job)
Nan fix a ham will	(Nan will fix a ham)
bit fox a a pig	(A fox bit a pig)
socks packs a in bag Tom	(Tom packs socks in a bag)

13. Dictate these words to him, and see if he can write them. Then have him read them back to you.

got hot not pot mop pop Tom
nod pod ox box job sob rob

14. Let him write his own "story" and then illustrate it.

Lesson 4: The Short Uu

You are making good progress. Three down, and only two more to go. Then he will have the short vowels taped! Be sure to keep your activities as games, and your sessions fun.

RULE:

Short U has the sound as in Umbrella.

EXAMPLES:

bug rug rut but us bus sum gum
fun gun cup duck luck bud cuff fuss

ACTIVITIES:

1. Have him say the short U sound several times, and repeat "Umbrella," stressing the short U. Instead of first reading the words to him, see if he can read them "cold." Have him point to the word, and pronounce it distinctly, blending the letters. After he's worked his way through the list, have him go over it several times more. The second time around have him underline the short U in each word. If he needs more help identifying short U words, play more games practicing this.

Call out six words, five with the short U, and one with the other sound of U. Ask, "Which one is the odd man out?"

tug mud tuck huge tub cut

Call out four words, three with other short vowels and one with a short U. Ask, "Which is the short U word?"

hit, lot, hut, hat; sock, suck, sick, sack; tick, tock, tact, tuck

2. Have him change the short vowels in A, I, and O words to short U. Point out how the short U now gives these words a *new meaning*. Write the word down and have him read it. Then have him underline the vowel. Have him rewrite the new short U word beneath it. Then ask him to pronounce both words so he can hear the difference in their sounds. Ask him the meaning of each word.

bat (but) ham (hum) tag (tug) mad (mud) hit (hut)
dock (duck) bin (bun) ran (run) rig (rug) cop (cup)

3. Go "fishing." Put short U, O, I, and A words in a box. Have him take out a word and read it to you. Then ask him, "Which short vowel does it have?" If it has a short U he must give the meaning and put it in a sentence.

4. Play "word families." Ask, "How many words can you think of that rhyme with ______?"

TUB (cub, dub, hub, pub, rub)
CUT (but, gut, hut, jut, nut, rut, tut)
RUG (bug, dug, hug, jug, lug, mug, tug)
SUN (bun, fun, gun, nun, pun, run)

5. Play the "sandwich" game. Give him the bread (the consonants) and have him write in the short U filling. Then have him read the words to you.

b__s n__t t__g b__d c__ff g__m __s __p
s__m b__t d__ck b__g c__p p__p

6. Play the "magic" game, making new words. Have him pick out the U from his plastic letters. Then pick two consonants and see if he can make a word.

7. Play the "riddle" game. Have him change the first, or last, letter of a word to answer the riddle. Read the riddle to him, and write down the word to be changed. Then have him write the new word and read it to you.

They have hard shells, and you can eat them	cuts	(nuts)
Another word for mat	tug	(rug)
Some kids like to play in it	bud	(mud)
Another word for we	up	(us)
Another word for pull	tum	(tug)
You drink from one	cub	(cup)

8. Play "couples." Give him four rhyming words to match. Have him read the words out loud, and listen to their sounds, before deciding which ones go together:

hug	puff	sun	run	bus	us
huff	jug	bun	sum	pup	cup
cuff	duck	dull	fun		
muff	luck	bun	gull		

Now see if he can do this with all the short vowels he learned so far.

mud	ran	pin	win	fan	fun	sob	lug
pot	lot	bus	lost	fill	can	hug	bad
pan	bud	cost	us	gun	hill	sad	rob

9. Have him read these words out loud. And then circle the one you call out.

Suck, up, rug; mud, gum, buzz; hum, bun, fun;
bus, dug, but; puff, duck, sun; nut, rum, run.

10. Have him play "detective" and complete these sentences by adding the correct letters to the words. Have him read the *whole* sentence before deciding on the letters. And then read the sentence again when he's found the missing word.

Gus had a mug, a __ug, and a cup.	l	j	k
Tom got a __ug in a box.	g	b	d
The __up got up on Ann's lap.	g	p	q
Jack's dog got __ud on him.	n	m	h
A big rat sat on a __ug.	s	t	r
Max and Tim can __un fast.	r	m	t

11. Have him read these sentences. Then underline all the short U words, and write them down, as this reinforces them in his mind.

It's fun to dig in mud.
A big bug's in a cup.
Can a duck jump?
Can an ant run?
Pat had a pup and a doll.
Tom will sup on a bun.

12. Have him read these sentences, and choose the correct word to complete them. Be sure he reads the whole sentence before deciding on the word.

Tim will ______ up a hill.	rug,	run,	rum
Nan had gum and ______.	cups,	cuts,	nuts
Jill's dog had a ______.	hug,	bug,	but
Jan will ______ and kiss Dot's doll.	sum,	mug,	hug
Bill can ______ a song.	hum,	hut,	hug
Jim's cat can jump in a ______.	tub,	tum,	gum

13. Have him read these "stories" and then answer your questions.

If Dan runs fast up a hill Dan will puff.

What makes Dan get out of breath? Which word means "out of breath"?

Cut up a ham, and Judd will sup on it. Dot will sup on nuts and yams. Nan will sup just on jam.

What will Judd have for supper? Dot? Nan? Who do you think will have the best supper?

Gus and Pat sat on a rug. Pat had a doll in a cot. Gus had a pup. Gus's pup bit Pat's doll. But Gus got a rod and hit it. Gus will hug and kiss Pat's doll.

What did Pat have? What did Gus have? What did the pup do? What did Gus do to the pup? What will he do to Pat's doll to make up for what the pup did?

A duck cannot run fast. But a bug can hop. And an ant can jump. A dog can dig. A fox can rob. And a cat can nap.

Tell me what each of the animals or insects can do. There is one you don't know what he can do. Which one is this? Which animal or insect would you like to be? Why?

14. See if he can unscramble these sentences:

rug Ann on sat a	(Ann sat on a rug)
jump can a pup	(A pup can jump)
Pam tub rub can a	(Pam can rub a tub)
bug fun a had	(A bug had fun)
Gus a jug had	(Gus had a jug)

15. Dictate these words to him and see if he can write them. Then have him read them back to you.

cup rub run gum us nut sun up
nun tug tuck sum fun but us bus

16. Let him write his own story and illustrate it.

Lesson 5: The Short Ee

I leave the Short E to last because it's the most difficult sound. Give him lots of practice saying it after you. And particularly make sure he can differentiate it from the short I sound.

RULE:

Short E has the sound as in Egg.

EXAMPLES:

red bed ten men pet met get bell well fell
web fed yes less mess peck neck egg pep hem

ACTIVITIES:

1. Have him repeat the short E sound lots of times, and repeat "Egg," stressing the short E. Have him read the example words slowly, sounding out each letter. Then have him say them faster and faster. This will help him to blend the letters. Make a game of it, and have a race with him. Take the first four words and see which of you can say them faster but *also* more *clearly*. Then do the same with the next four, and so on.

If he needs more help identifying short E words, play more games practicing this.

Call out two E words and have him tell you which one has the short E sound.

fell—feel bead—bed Ben—been set—seat weed—wed
teen—ten net—neat sell—seal need—Ned met—meet

Call out three words, two with other short vowels and one with short E. Ask, "Which is the short E word?"

big bug beg pin pen pan rid rod red
tin ten tan deck Dick duck din Dan den
lid led lad lit lot let sit sat set

2. Have him change the short vowels in A, I, O, and U words to short E. Again, point out how changing the vowel changes not only the sound of the word but also its meaning. Write the word down. Have him underline the vowel. Then write his new word

beneath the original word. Be sure to have him read both words aloud.

nut (net) fill (fell) bad (bed) man (men) got (get)
pin (pen) pat (pet) tin (ten) duck (deck) lad (led)

3. Go "fishing." Put all the short-vowel words in a box. Have him take out a word and read it to you. Then have him tell you which short vowel it has. If it's a short E word, have him tell you its meaning and put it in a sentence.

4. Play "word families." Ask, "How many words can you think of that rhyme with ______?"

WET (bet, get, jet, let, met, net, pet, set, vet, yet)
TEN (Ben, den, hen, Ken, Len, men, pen)
BED (fed, led, Ned, red, Ted, wed)
SELL (bell, fell, jell, Nell, tell, well, yell)

5. Play the "sandwich" game. Give him the bread (the consonants), and have him give you the short E filling. Then have him read the words to you.

b__d l__g s__t y__t w__ll w__t t__n
b__g m__n r__d g__t y__s t__ll p__g

6. Play the "magic" game. Have him pick out the E from his plastic letters. Then pick two consonants and see if he can be a magician and produce a word. If he can make a word, ask him if he can change the consonants around to make yet another word.

7. Play the "riddle" game. Have him change the first, or last, letter of a word to answer the riddle. Read the riddle to him, and write down the word to be changed. Then have him write his new word and read it to you.

The opposite word for dry	bet	(wet)
It means more than one man	hen	(men)
Another word for crimson	led	(red)
It has the opposite meaning of "no"	yet	(yes)
You sleep in this	ben	(bed)
You use this to walk	let	(leg)

Give him plenty of these kinds of riddles, as they're great for increasing his vocabulary.

8. Play "couples." Give him four rhyming words to match. Have him read the words aloud, and listen to their sounds, before deciding which ones go together.

bet bell   peg beg   peck tell   red ten
wet well   ten hen   sell deck   Ben Ted
met pet
pen men

Now see if he can do this with all the short vowels.

tin rat   peg lag   sick luck   well fit
den bug   sum leg   dock back   tan cup
hug win   rag lot   duck tick   up fell
bat Ken   cot rum   sack tock   lit fan

9. Have him read these words aloud, and then circle the one you call out.

get ten hen;   peck bell tell;   yes web fed;
den led red;   neck net bed;   Ned Ted Nell

10. Have him play "detective" and complete these sentences by adding the correct letters to the words. Remember to have him read the whole sentence before deciding on the letter. Then have him read the completed sentence.

Ted's pet fell into a __ell.   w m n
Bev met Ben at __en.   p t j
Ten men __ed six pigs in a pen.   h q f
Nell will __end Pat's hem.   s t m
Ben's pet hen can __eck.   b p q

11. Have him read these sentences. Then underline all the short E words and write them down. If the sentence is true have him write "yes" beside it.

A duck gets wet.
Jeff's hen had ten eggs.
Ben can lend Ted a pen.
Kent met a red dog.
Meg fell in a pond and got wet.
A fox can yell.

12. Have him read these sentences and choose the correct word to complete them. Be sure he reads the whole sentence before deciding on the word.

Bev had a nap in ______.   let, bed, bet
Ted went fast in a ______.   let, wet, jet

Jeff will ______ ten red hens.	bell, sell, tell
Bess had ______ ham, but six eggs.	mess, last, less
Dan had a red ______.	peck, ness, neck
Tom bet Ben he'd get ______.	will, well, bell

13. Have him read these "stories" and then answer your questions.

Tom fell in a pond and got wet. Ed will get a net and help Tom. Tim will run and tell Tom's Dad.

Who got wet? How did he get wet? What will Ed do? What was Tim going to do?

Nell, a red hen, had ten eggs in a nest. Ted, a big, bad fox got Nell's eggs. Ted fed on Nell's ten eggs. Ted went to bed and slept well. Nell wept.

How many eggs had Nell laid? What happened to them? What did the fox do after he had eaten the eggs? What did Nell do?

Ted's pet dog can beg. If it's fed ham, it will ring a bell. If it's fed nuts, it will jog up a hill. If it's fed eggs, it will jump on Ted's lap. But if it's fed hens, it will lick its lips.

What was Ted's pet. Do you think he was a usual kind of dog? Why not? What did he do if he was fed ham? Nuts? Eggs? Hens?

14. See if he can unscramble these sentences:

pet get Nan a will	(Nan will get a pet)
Ed hens red ten fed	(Ed fed ten red hens)
cat a had Peg pet	(Peg had a pet cat)
mop wet get a	(Get a wet mop)
fell well a in Ben	(Ben fell in a well)

15. Dictate these words to him, and see if he can write them. Then have him read them back to you.

set	met	led	den	sell	web	yes	leg
hem	men	wed	beg	red	tell	neck	jet

Let him write his own story and illustrate it.

Step 4: Some Sight Words

Teaching these sight words won't take up a full session. In fact, it's a good idea to introduce them as you teach the next lesson on blends. There are many blends to practice, so it would change the pace nicely.

Once you have introduced the words you can practice them as you go for walks, drives, or rides on the bus.

You will be amazed how these few sight words enable him to read so many more sentences. And how much easier it will be for you to make them up!

RULE:

Sight words cannot be sounded out. You have to learn them in one big gulp.

EXAMPLES:

is his as has; the to of; he she they

ACTIVITIES:

1. Read the first four words to him first. Point to each one as you say it. Then read each word one-by-one and have him repeat it after you. Then have him read each word on his own. Don't go on to the other words until he's got these under his belt.

Then take the next three words and do the same, and then the last three. Then put the words into sentences and have him say "beep" each time you use one.

Next take a newspaper, magazine, or some printed material, and have him find the words and circle them. Don't use his storybooks too often for this, or they won't remain storybooks for long.

If he needs more practice you can play some games with him.

2. Playing the "matching" game. Make out two sets of cards with the words. Jumble them up, and have him pair them off. Be sure to have him read aloud each word as he picks it up. Or write down three of the words in one column and have him match them with the same three in a different order in another column.

the	as	of	has	he	they
as	is	to	to	she	he
is	the	has	of	they	she

3. Jumble up the sight words with short-vowel words and put them face down on a table or on the floor. Have him read each word as he picks it up. When he picks up a sight word he gets a point. If he reads it correctly he gets another point.

4. Give him sentences with the sight words left out. Have him put in the correct word.

5. Have him write a story using his new sight words and illustrate it.

Step 5: Consonant Blends

This lesson will be a breeze. But it's going to take *time*. Don't tackle all the words at once, or it will become tedious! Do a few. Then go on to the next lesson. Then come back and do a few more. And so on. Vary the activities to teach each group of words so each lesson is different and interesting.

He shouldn't find these words difficult. It's just a matter of practicing blending the consonants together. Actually, he has already had a taste of some of them, as they were introduced in the last lesson or two.

Learning these words will not only help his pronunciation, it will also improve his fluency, and—if you take time to explain the meaning of new words—greatly increase his vocabulary.

RULE:

A blend is two or three consonants sounded—blended—together.

ACTIVITIES:

1. Beginning blends:

bl:	black, blend, block	gl:	glad, glass, glum
cl:	clap, clip, clock	pl:	plan, plant, plum
fl:	flag, fled, flock	sl:	slap, sled, slip
br:	brand, bring, brick	gr:	grass, grin, grip
cr:	crack, crib, cross	pr:	press, prick, print
dr:	dress, drink, drum	tr:	trick, trip, truck
fr:	Frank, Fred, frog		
sm:	smack, smart, smell	st:	stand, step, stop
sp:	spank, spend, spill	sw:	swam, swim, swing

Ending blends:

ang:	bang, rang, sang	ong:	long, song, strong
ing:	ring, sing, wing	ung:	rung, sung, stung
nd:	hand, send, pond	ft:	gift, lift, soft
nk:	bank, pink, sunk	mp:	lamp, camp, jump
nt:	plant, sent, hunt	st:	fast, nest, dust

As he says each word, be sure he sounds out each consonant, *blending,* but *not* slurring, them together.

The first time you introduce a word, say it for him, always remembering to point to the word at the same time, so he sees it in his mind as he hears its sound. Then have him repeat it several times.

Here are some suggestions for activities.

2. Give him several words with different blends and have him pick the word with the blend you ask for. Write the words and have him underline the blend in each word. Then have him read each word, and circle the correct one.

3. Play the "couples" game. Give him several blend pairs jumbled up, and have him match the words with the same blends. Be sure to make him read the words aloud so he gets used to the sounds of the blends and so you can check that he has got them right.

4. Play the "odd man out." Write four or five words with the same blend, and one with a different blend. Have him spot the different one. Don't let him make his choice until he has read all the words to you.

5. Put the blends on cards, and have him pick a card and give you three words beginning with the blend. Or call out a blend, or write the blend down, and have him give you a word using it.

6. Write down blend words without their blends, and have him put them in. Make him read his word aloud.

__em (stem) __ill (still) __ist (twist)

7. Give him a blend word—verbally or written down. Have him tell you what the blend is, and then give you a word with the same blend.

8. Play "lotto." Make out a lotto card with the blends, and call out blend words. This could be a good family game.

9. Play "round we go." This is another family game. Choose a blend, and go around in a circle with each person saying a word with that blend. When someone can't think of a word he has to drop out.

10. Play the "rhyming" game. Give him rhyming words with, and without, a blend. Have him read both words, then underline the blend and tell you what it is.

fat—flat	dip—drip	tuck—truck	plan—pan
crop—cop	black—back	gas—grass	Tim—trim

11. Give him riddles that have to be answered with a blend word.

People leave their money with one (ba<u>nk</u>)

This is a bird's home (ne<u>st</u>)

12. Have him write down the answer so he can underline the blend. You can do many of the activities you used to teach him the short vowels.

Word "families." For example:

SUNG (hung, lung, rung, sprung, stung)

HAND (band, land, sand, stand)

13. Have him play "detective" and complete sentences by adding the correct blends to words. Limit your sentences to short-vowel words so he can read them. Include as many of the blend words as you can so he gets plenty of practice.

Frank will se___ Jim a gift.	nt	<u>nd</u>	mp
Fred will run, but Ned must li___.	nd	<u>mp</u>	st
Bess sang a song in a black ___ess.	br	cr	<u>dr</u>

14. Have him read sentences, circle the words with blends, and then write them down and underline the blends. You can also make these funny, or into riddles, to liven things up.

Can a pink frog sing a soft song?
Can a cross crab spring across a pond?
Can a strong ant spank a slim rat?
Is a wet dress damp?
Can a clock run?

15. Here are some sentences you can use for various games. Or you can just give them to him to read.

Jack drank his milk from a glass. But Fred drank his from a mug.

A flock of ducks fled from a red fox.

Dad will clip the stems of his plants.

Jump up! Get in the truck.

Ted's fist hit Ron. Ron got a bump on his skull. But the doc will fix it.

Pam has a red dress. It has a pink frill and black trim.

The sun sinks in the west.

Mom can crack a crab fast.

Dad had a nap in bed. Dot slept in a cot. And Nan had a rest in a crib.

"Honk," went Dan's truck. It hit a bump. The truck had a flat.

A gust of wind will snap Dad's plants.

Judd will spill the milk if he drops his glass.

"Run to the pond and get me twelve frogs."

Jan had the best gift. It was a pet dog.

Dan is in a sulk. Dad has his gum.

Jack is slim, but he is strong.

16. Dictate some blend words, and have him write them down and then read them back to you. You can use the words from the examples, or, if he's pining for some new ones, here are a few.

plod	plus	blank	slim	drop	grab	track	trod
frost	skim	snip	stick	still	bring	swing	felt
must	went	limp	lump	ask	last	best	west

17. Don't forget to have him write a story or two along the way.

Step 6: Long Vowels

Lesson 1: Noticing the Difference Between Long and Short Vowels

Now you come to the other sound of the vowels. Long vowels are easy to identify because they have the same sound as their name.

There are three rules for long vowels (two given in this step and one in the next step). Explain them slowly and carefully, give lots of examples, and practice activities. Don't go on until he has each rule licked. If you do this, it will be a cinch. But if you try to hurry things up, it could lead to trouble.

RULE:

Long vowels say their name.

EXAMPLES:

cake	rain	boat	road	pie	five	meat	beets
cube	suit	street	tail	soap	kite	coat	tune

ACTIVITIES:

1. Read the example words and ask him which vowel they contain. Have him repeat the words after you.

Then play games differentiating between the long and the short sounds of each vowel in turn. Begin by giving him two words. Then give him four words with the long vowel, and one with the short vowel, and ask, "Which word has the short vowel?"

A: bake, cane, <u>can</u>, made, hate

I: bike, tie, pie, <u>big</u>, ice

O: bone, <u>cot</u>, rope, toad, cone

U: rule, mule, cute, tube, <u>sun</u>

E: Pete, leaf, key, <u>egg</u>, bee

Another variation of this game is to give him four words with different long-vowel sounds and one with a short vowel. Or vice versa —four words with short vowels and one with a long vowel.

tree	seat	dime	<u>bug</u>	joke
cut	lock	<u>kite</u>	hit	hand

2. The "rhyming" game is great for helping him to note the differences in the sound of the two kinds of vowels. Give him a word and have him give you another that rhymes with it. Or give him four words (two long and two short) and have him pair them off. Be sure to have him tell you which pairs have the long vowel and which have the short.

ride	coat	key	bat	feet	den	suit	pot
boat	side	hat	he	pen	beat	cot	fruit

3. You can play "I'm thinking of." Describe something you're thinking of, and have him guess what it is. Make the answer a simple, one-syllable word. You can tell him whether the answer will have a long or a short vowel. Or have him tell you when he's guessed the word.

I'm thinking of something you can eat, and it rhymes with bake (cake). I'm thinking of something you can hit a ball with (bat).

4. Then you can play games pointing to things in the room, or in a magazine, or as you do chores around the house, or go for a walk, or drive. Have him name the object, and tell you which kind of vowel it has: a long A, a short I, and so on. But be careful not to overdo it, or he won't look forward to his lessons.

Lesson 2: The Magic E

Kids really love this rule, because the E *is* magic. It has no sound, but can work wonders, for it changes both the sound and the meaning of a word.

I often use an imaginary magician called Marvin to introduce this rule. You may like to do the same. He adds variety. He can wave his wand and pop on that E, and *wow!*—a new word. Then, of course, your child can put on his magical hat or cloak, become the magician, and do the same.

RULE:

When a SILENT, "MAGIC" E is added to a word, it can make the vowel LONG. It also changes the meaning of the word.

EXAMPLES:

pin—pine	cub—cube	tap—tape	dim—dime	kit—kite
mad—made	hat—hate	at—ate	cap—cape	pet—Pete

ACTIVITIES:

1. Have him read the examples to get a feeling for the rule. Ask, "What does the magic E do to the words?"

Answer: It changes the *sound* and the *meaning* of the words.

After you're quite sure he understands the rule, take each vowel separately (except E, as few E words have the magic E) as you did with the short vowels. You can play all sorts of games. For example:

2. Write three short-vowel words, one magic E word, and have him circle the magic E word.

3. Write magic E words without their first consonant, and have him complete them. Be sure to have him read his word to you.

4. Give him jumbled magic E words. You can use his plastic alphabet, letter cards, or write the letters in the wrong order.

5. Play the "matching" game. Give him a magic E word, and ask him for a rhyming word. Write the magic E words on cards, in duplicate. Give one set to him, and keep one set. Show him one of your cards. Have him read the word and tell you which long vowel it has. Then find its partner in his set.

6. Then play "snap." Both turn up a card at the same time. If they have the same word, shout "snap." The one who says "snap" first takes both the cards. The winner is the one who has more cards at the end.

7. Play the "upside down" game. Now put both sets of cards face down on a table, or the floor. Take it in turns to turn up two cards. If the words on the cards match (or they could just rhyme), you take the cards. If they don't, you put them face down again. When no cards remain, you add up the cards you have. The winner is the one with the most. Again, remember to have him read the words as they're turned up. This game is also great for increasing his concentration and memory, for the trick is to remember where each card is after it's been turned face down again.

8. Play "word families." See how many rhyming words he can come up with.

9. Then, of course, include riddles, sentences to complete with missing words, or missing letters to words—and jumbled sentences to be put in their proper order.

10. Now also include games and activities to widen his vocabulary: Synonyms—see how many words he can come up with that have the

same meaning; and antonyms—how many words with the opposite meaning.

11. Dictate magic E words to him from the lists I give and have him read them back to you.

12. Have him continue writing his own stories. Now he may prefer not to illustrate them. Let him decide. Also have him start a special "word book," in which he writes examples of each new rule as he learns it. Make sure he understands the meaning of each word. He can also write his stories in this book, and illustrate both stories and words.

13. Have him do the following activities I give for each vowel, making sure he always reads the words aloud first.

LONG A WITH THE MAGIC E

Have him:

(a) Read these words aloud:

bake, take, cake	same, game, lame	sale, pale, tale
gate, hate, late	save, gave, wave	came, tame, flame
cape, tape, grape	Jane, pane, plane	made, wade, fade

(b) Compare these words:

mad—made	hat—hate	can—cane	rat—rate
tap—tape	pan—pane	cap—cape	fat—fate

(c) Circle the long-vowel words:

cat	cave	wag	can	mad	late
tale	pal	rake	tame	haze	tag
ham	cape	skate	had	make	pave

(d) Find the rhyming words:

state	wade	rake	lake	drape	kale	Jane	wave
made	plate	same	lame	sale	tape	pave	pane

(e) Read these sentences and complete them with one of the words:

Dave will take the lame man a ______.	take, sake, <u>cake</u>
Jane ______ a wave to Jake at the gate.	pave, <u>gave</u>, pane
Kate will ______ in the lake.	wave, <u>wade</u>, made
Dale came ______ to the sale.	rate, lame, <u>late</u>

Ted will save the ______.	lame, game, gate
Jane's red cape will ______ in the sun.	fade, fate, wade
Sam ate a ______ and a date.	sale, tape, grape
Abe will ______ on the lake.	make, skate, state

(f) Read the story. Then have him underline all the long A, magic E words, and write them in his word book. See if he can spot the one long O word:

Jane came late. She met Dale at the gate. She had made a cake to take to the lake. It had dates in it. Jane gave the cake to Dale.

Dale had a rake, and a net at the end of a cane, to get frogs from the lake. He had to wade into the lake. He got six frogs, but he had a spill. He fell in and got wet. Jane had to save him. And she got wet.

Jane and Dale ran back and ate the cake at home.

(g) Give the opposite meaning of these words.
unlike (same) love (hate) early (late) in danger (safe)

LONG I WITH THE MAGIC E

Have him:

(a) Read these words aloud:

fine line pine mine bite kite site nine
ride side stride tide mile smile pile five
like hike pike strike prize size life fire

(b) Compare these:

bit—bite win—wine Sid—side Tim—time
fin—fine dim—dime twin—twine spin—spine

(c) Circle the long-vowel words:

mile lid file win trip side Mick dime
hide him wide size Mike Dick slim hike
trim string

(d) Find the rhyming words:

side ride prize time fire wife kite bite
mine fine size dime life hire hide wide

(e) Read these sentences and complete them with one of the words:

Ike had a fine ______ at the game. — dime, time, dine
Mick had a flat ______ on his bike. — fire, hire, tire
A grape is the ______ of a dime. — site, size, side
Mom and Dad drink ______ from a glass. — wine, wide, nine
Nick got ______ on his tie. — side, pie, pile
If Jack saves ______ dimes he can ride the bus. — live, fire, five
Dick will ______ if he gets a prize. — stride, pride, smile
The King will ______ at nine, not five. — time, dime, dine

(f) Read the story. Then have him underline all the long I, magic E words and write them in his word book.

Mike lost his fine, pink kite. A gust of wind swept the line from his hand. He had a time to get it back. It made a dive into Dad's prize plants. It hid in his vine of ripe grapes. And at last it went up, up, up into a big pine on a hill.

Mike had to ride his bike five long miles. He had to stride up the hill and strike the pine. But the kite still hung in the pine.

Mike had to get help. He got on his bike, and went back to get his Dad. Dad got an ax. They went to the hill in Dad's truck.

Dad made five strikes at the pine. And snap! A big branch of the pine fell, and Mike's kite fell as well. Mike gave a smile the size of his kite, and ran to pick up his prize.

(g) Give a long I, magic E word that has the *same* meaning as:

good, nice (fine) a long walk (a hike)
a grin (a smile) to enjoy (like)
ten pennies (a dime) heap (pile)

LONG O WITH THE MAGIC E

Have him:

(a) Read these words aloud:

Coke, joke, smoke	bone, stone, cone	hope, rope, slope
stove, drove, cove	hole, pole, stole	robe, rode, froze
strode, broke, vote	woke, role, code	globe, mole, spoke

(b) Compare these:

rod—rode hop—hope cod—code pop—Pope not—note

(c) Underline the words below. Ask him, "What makes the first nonsense word into a real word with meaning?" Answer: the magic E:

stor—store bon—bone stol—stole glob—globe vot—vote

(d) Circle the long-vowel words:

drove	box	code	lot	stone	top	slop
slop	role	cone	Coke	hole	froze	role
slope	dog	sob	pod	mop	slope	stole

(e) Read these sentences and complete them with one of the words:

The dog ______ a bone, and hid it in a hole.	spoke, stole, smoke
Don ______ into the pond, and hit a stone.	dove, drove, cove
Dot can swim nine ______.	slopes, strokes, stoves
Dad made a ______ to be home at five.	hope, vote, note
Mom will fix the ham on the ______.	stove, froze, stole
Jack stole Mike's bike as a ______.	broke, Coke, joke
Ted ______ a bone in his hand.	Coke, broke, slope
Jan drank a ______ and ate the pie.	robe, rode, Coke

(f) Read the story. Then have him underline all the long O, magic E words and write them in his word book.

Tom awoke to the smell of smoke. It was no joke. The smoke got in his lungs. He got into his robe, and strode from his home to his pal Don.

He woke up Don: "Help! Help! Get help. And bring buckets and a rope."

Don got nine men, and they drove to Tom's home. The fire had made a big hole in the side. The men ran inside fast. "I hope the stove will not explode," spoke up a man.

But it did not. The men got buckets and jugs and wet Don's things. And, in time, they got the fire to stop. They did a swell job.

Don gave the men Coke and cakes. He gave a smile. He had lost his home. But he still had his pals.

(g) Give a long O, magic E word that answers these riddles.

People laugh when you make one of these.	(a joke)
It can be any size but it's made of nothing.	(a hole)
A fire makes this.	(smoke)
If you slip, you might break one.	(a bone)
Every hill has one.	(a slope)

LONG U WITH THE MAGIC E

Have him:

(a) Read these words aloud:

tube	cute	rule	use	cube	tune
mule	rude	prune	pure	Luke	yule
cure	fumes	fuse	duke	flute	dude

(b) Compare these:

us—use cut—cute cub—cube tub—tube

(c) Underline the words below. Ask him, "What makes the first nonsense word into a real word with meaning?" Answer: the magic E.

rul—rule rud—rude cur—cure flut—flute

(d) Circle the long-vowel words:

tune	duck	pure	Luke	lump
run	fuse	mule	swum	cube
duke	hut	gum	tube	rule

(e) Find the rhyming words:

use	fuse	tube	rule	cute	cure
duke	luke	cube	yule	flute	pure

(f) Read these sentences and complete them with one of the words:

Ted sang a ______ to June.	cube, tube, tune
Doc will ______ the lump on Luke's hand.	pure, cure, cute
The fumes from a fire are not ______.	prune, cube, pure
Dan made a ______ joke.	rule, rude, tube
Dad will ______ his plants in June.	fuse, yule, prune
The game had nine ______.	rules, tunes, cubes
Duke rode a black ______.	flute, mule, yule
Pat can use his ______ and June can sing.	tune, prune, flute

(g) Read the story. Then have him underline all the long U, magic E words and write them in his word book:

Dad gave June a cute pup. It had a fine name—Duke. The pup sat on June's lap, and she sang a tune to him.

June fed Duke cubes of ham, and gave him a big bone. The pup ate the ham, and hid the bone in a hole.

Duke had a lot of life in him. He gave June a bad time. He ate June's tube of paste. He got Mom's robe and made a hole in it. And he sat on a pie Mom had just made.

Mom was cross. She spoke to Dad. "June must cure Duke. He is a bad dog."

June gave Duke a smack and made a list of rules. And bit by bit, Duke broke his bad habits.

(h) Give a long U, magic E word that describes:
impolite (rude) clean, unsoiled (pure) Christmastime (yuletime) an animal like a donkey (mule) a musical instrument (a flute)

Lesson 3: Vowel Teams

Make sure you do your homework on this one! It's not a hard rule, but it needs to be explained clearly. The rule applies to syllables but you needn't mention this at this stage, as all the words he's dealing with have only one syllable.

You can use my definition of the rule, or you may prefer this catchier one:

When two vowels go a-walking,
The first one does the talking—
And says its name.

Once he has learned these vowel teams, he will make great strides. (As there are very few I and U vowel team words, and most of them are too difficult, I've not included them.) You will notice that Y and W can be vowels, but don't draw his attention to this yet.

RULE:
When two vowels come together, the FIRST ONE SAYS ITS NAME (is LONG), and the second one is silent.

EXAMPLES:
say, paid boat, snow, toe pie beets, meat

ACTIVITIES:

1. Have him read the examples to you as you teach him each long vowel team. Then have him underline the two vowels. Ask him to give you the rule. Then ask, "Give me the vowel that is sounded. Which is the vowel that is silent? Put a slash mark through it if it has no sound." Then have him read the word again.

2. You can use all the activities and games described in the magic E lesson. Now, however, put more and more emphasis on identify-

ing the words in printed matter. Have him read the newspaper with you at night. Look through magazines together. Give him a set of colored felt pens, and have him circle the vowel teams in different colors—red for the A vowel teams, green for the O, and so on.

3. Keep his word book going, and see that he continues to write his own stories. Don't forget to use some of the words for dictation, as this reinforces them in his mind.

Now go over the long vowel teams one by one.

A. LONG A VOWEL TEAMS

There are two vowel teams for long A

AI AY

RULE:

Y IS SOMETIMES A VOWEL. When it follows another vowel or comes at the end of a word it is a vowel.

Have him:

(a) Read aloud these words:

day say mail wait may fail pail
paid nail ray laid rain may sail
tail gay main tray way pain hay

(b) Answer these riddles by putting in the correct letter:

The opposite to night.	__ay	(day)
A boat can have one of these.	__ai__	(sail)
You can carry things on this.	____ay	(tray)
Most animals have one.	__ai__	(tail)
You get out your umbrella when it does this.	__ai__	(rain)
A month that comes in spring.	__ay	(May)
You sometimes have to do this for the bus.	__ai__	(wait)
It can take you places.	____ai__	(train)

(c) Find the rhyming words:

sail pail paid gain mail way train wail
hay pay laid pain tray nail rain tail

(d) Read these sentences and complete them with one of the words:

Jane got wet in the hail and ______.	sail, rain, ray
The frail man had a ______ in his side.	main, pail, pain
A big ______ ate Dad's best plants.	wail, snail, sail
Dad will ______ Jay's home gray.	paint, faint, fail
Bob laid the ______ on the tray.	sail, main, mail
The ______ went way up the hill.	tray, train, trail
The ______ of sun lit up the gray day.	trays, rays, ways
______ the rain stops.	way, say, pray

(e) Read the story. Ask him the questions, and some of your own, to test his *comprehension*. (Remember that is the *key* to reading.) Then have him underline all the words with long A vowel teams and write them in his word book. Introduce a new sight word: WAS

Jay went away to spend nine days at his pal's home in Maine. His name was Craig. It was time he went to Craig's as he had paid Jay a visit in May.

Jay went on the train. But he had to wait, as it was late. He had fun on the way, but was glad to get to Craig's.

The next day Jay and Craig went to play in the hay. They had a swell time. But Jay fell and got a sprain in his leg. It gave him a lot of pain. But he was brave, and did not faint. Craig came to Jay's aid and gave him a hand home. And his Mom laid a wet rag on it. It made the pain less. Jay had to limp for the rest of his stay. But he still had fun playing with his best pal, Craig.

Questions:

Give the story a title (for example, "Jay's Vacation." "Jay Has an Accident").

How many days did Jay spend with Craig?

Where do you think Craig lived: in the country, or in a city?

What makes you think that?
Who had the accident? Which day did it happen on?
What did Craig's mom do to help take the pain away?
Did Jay enjoy his visit?

(f) Introduce him to homonyms, those tricky words that have the same sound but different meanings and spellings. Say to him, "Both these words have the long A sound. Which is the vowel team word, and which is the magic E word? They both have the same sound, don't they? But they have different meanings. See if you can give me the two meanings. And then we'll write the words, and their meanings, in your word book."

mail—male	sale—sail	pail—pale	pain—pane
plane—plain	tail—tale	maid—made	vane—vain

B. LONG E VOWEL TEAMS

There are two vowel teams for Long E
EE EA

Have him:

(a) Read aloud these words:

ee: bee see feet feel seem beef seen seed sleeve
peel deep week need keep peep feed tree

ea: beat sea weak leaf meat read real pea team
lead bean bead meal lean mean cream speak

(b) Answer these riddles by putting in the correct letter:

You find it on trees.	_ea_	(leaf)
You walk on them.	_ee_	(feet)
It comes from a cow.	_ _ea_	(cream)
It's fun to swim in it.	_ea	(sea)
You do this at mealtimes.	_ee_	(feed)
They make a nice necklace.	_ea_ _	(beads)
The opposite to fake.	_ea_	(real)

(c) Find the rhyming words:

sea	feed	meal	speak	beef	peek	deep	leap
lead	bee	steal	week	leaf	weak	cream	seem

(d) Read these sentences and complete them with one of the words:

Will Tom's team ______ Jack's team?	meat, beat, seat
Dave got his ______ wet in the sea.	feel, feet, meal
Mom gave Dad a real feast of ______ and peas.	bead, beef, peel
The ______ fell from a tree.	feed, lead, leaf
______ came from the pot of ham and beans.	steam, stream, team
Joe dreams as he ______.	weeps, sleeps, beets
Dad went back ______ last week.	sea, eat, East
It's a treat if Mom ______ to Jane.	weeds, reads, feeds

(e) Read the story. Then ask him the questions and some of your own. Then have him underline all the words with long E vowel teams and write them in his word book.

Mom and Dad had a plan to take Steve to see the sea. It was a real treat as Steve had not seen the sea.

They got up at five on the day as the sun came up from the East. Dad woke Steve up from a deep sleep. He was dreaming of his day at the sea.

Steve got up fast. He gave Mom a hand and made up the picnic to eat at the sea. He made a feast of a meal: lean beef; sweet ham; cream buns; and tea in a flask.

At six, they got in Dad's van. Steve sat in the back seat. They went past trees, a stream, and a beehive. And, at last, they came to the sea. Steve gave a beaming smile. He ran along the sand, and got his feet wet in the sea. He gave a scream, "It's grand."

It was indeed a day of treats. He swam. He lay in the heat of the sun, and got a tan. He made heaps of sand, and had a fine time jumping on the heaps. And he got a sting on his heel from a bee. But it did not take long to heal.

At last it was time to leave. Steve was beat. And he went to sleep in the van on the way home.

Questions:

Where did Steve's parents take him?
Why was it a special treat?
What did they take to eat?
What did Steve do first when he got there?
What other things did he do during the day?
What did Steve do on the way home?

(f) Homonyms: Have him read both words. Then tell him their meanings. Have him write the words, and their meanings, in his word book, or he can illustrate the words.

see—sea	heel—heal	dear—deer	week—weak
beet—beat	meet—meat	peek—peak	seam—seem

C. LONG O VOWEL TEAMS

There are three vowel teams for long O
OA OE OW

RULE:
Sometimes W can be a vowel. It is always a vowel when it follows directly after another vowel.

---

oa: coat road loaf soap load moan toast
roast goal soak toad boast coast goat
oe: toe hoe Joe roe woe foe
ow: snow slow grow own bowl low blow
row glow crow tow grown bow flown

Have him:

(a) Answer these riddles by putting in the correct letter:

You often eat it at breakfast. __oa__ (soap)
You use it at bathtime. __oa__ __ (toast)

It comes in winter, and is white.	__ __ow	(snow)
The wind does this.	__ __ow	(blow)
Part of your foot.	__oe	(toe)
You can mix things in it.	__ow__	(bowl)
You put it on when you go out.	__oa__	(coat)
The opposite of fast.	__ __ow	(slow)

(b) Find the rhyming words:

row	hoe	roast	own	grown	groan	bowl	crow
toe	blow	boast	loan	flow	grow	glow	coal

(c) Read these sentences and complete them with one of the words:

Mom will ______ the meat.	toast, roast, boast
Joe will cut the ______ and make the toast.	goat, loan, loaf
Dad will let Jean ______ the boat.	sow, row, glow
Dan will ______ the grass, and sow the seeds in a row.	row, mow, grow
Jean will ______ the seeds if they grow.	hoe, toe, woe
The team will boast as they have five ______.	goats, boats, goals
The ______ ate the oats in the snow.	blow, crow, bow
Dick will ______ the boat he owns.	flow, loan, load

(d) Read the story. Then ask him the questions and some of your own.

It was snowing and the wind was blowing. Joe got on his coat and went into the snow. He had a tow truck. And a truck had hit a van. He got his truck and drove fast. The man in the truck was O.K. But his load of bags of oats was in the snow, on the road. Lots of crows had flown low to eat the oats.

The man from the van was moaning and groaning on the pavement. His coat was soaking from the snow. And he had been hit. He had cut his leg. But it was not bad. Joe got him in his truck and drove him to the doc.

Joe drove back to help the truck man. He gave him a hand loading his bags of oats.

It was dusk as he got home. He got a cup of hot tea to heat up, and had a big meal of ham and eggs on toast. He had spent half a day helping the truck and van men. But he did not boast. It was his job.

Questions:

What was Joe's job?
What time of the year was it? How do you know?
Who was hurt?
What happened to the truck driver's load?
How did Joe get warm after being out in the cold so long?
How long was he out in the cold?

(e) Homonyms: Have him read both words. Then tell him their meanings. Have him write them in his word book.

tow—toe	row—roe	road—rode
loan—lone	groan—grown	moan—mown

Step 7: Syllables

This is a *very important lesson.* So if you are in a hurry, or it's not nice and quiet because they are working on the street outside or all the other kids are home, don't tackle it.

There are five main rules for learning syllables. Take them one by one, not progressing to the next one until you are sure he has a good grasp of the one you are working on.

Being able to hear the syllables in a word is the key to sounding it out (and the key to spelling, by the way).

Your child has already learned to pronounce the syllables in words in his everyday speech. However, you have to *make him aware* of what he is doing, so he can transfer what he does naturally when he speaks, to reading the words.

Teaching him the syllables will not only improve his speed and fluency, it will also help him to decide if a vowel should be pronounced short or long.

RULE I:

Words are made up of syllables.

EXAMPLES:

dog cat boat tail went say pie snow (all one syllable)
pancake kitten visit into singing sixteen (all two syllables)

ACTIVITIES:

Explain to him that every word is made up of syllables. You can hear the syllables if you listen carefully.

Say "syllables," emphasizing its three syllables. Clap your hands or knock on a table as you pronounce each one. Say, "'Syllables' has three syllables. Did you hear them?" Repeat this. Then have him say, "syllables," emphasizing the three syllables, and clapping or knocking. Do this until he's got it.

Then have him read the top line of the examples, clapping as he says each word aloud. Ask, "How many syllables do they have?"

If he gets the answer correct, and he seems to have the idea, have him read the bottom line of the examples. Again, ask him how many syllables they have. If he has difficulty with the one-syllable words, give him more. Continue to give him words with one to three syllables until he can identify them without hesitation. Then ask him to give you words. Say, "I would like a two-syllable word beginning with P." Or, "Find something in this room that has a three-syllable name." Or, "Make up a menu for supper with only one-syllable words." And so on.

RULE II:

Every syllable has a VOWEL SOUND.

A syllable must always have a vowel. It can have more than one vowel as long as they make ONLY ONE SOUND.

EXAMPLES:

rab-bit mit-tens bot-tom bas-ket (two syllables)

coat sail time meat tie bake (one syllable)

ACTIVITIES:

Explain the rule. Have him look at the top line of examples and underline the vowels. Then ask him to read the words and tell you how many syllables they have. Point out to him: "ONE VOWEL SOUND MAKES ONE SYLLABLE."

Then have him *first* read aloud the bottom row of examples. Ask him how many syllables they have. Then have him underline the vowels. Ask, "Why don't the words have two syllables if they have two vowels?"

Answer: The two vowels make only one sound. The second vowel is silent in all the words. (You may wish to review the two long-vowel rules here.)

After lots of practice identifying the syllables in long-vowel words, give him games like these. Have him:

(a) Write the number of vowels he sees, and the number of syllables (the number of vowels he hears) in these words. Have him *underline all the vowels first:*

	VOWELS seen heard		VOWELS seen heard		VOWELS seen heard
kitten		bonnet		kite	
coat		lemon		second	
singing		rake		snow	
pie		beets		dime	
cake		seven		window	
ribbon		sailboat		mealtime	

(b) Find the rhyming words, and say how many syllables they have:

roast	kitten	basement	sweep	singing	bee
mitten	boast	pavement	deep	pea	ringing
planted	bone	fastest	weep	sadness	made
loan	hunted	sleep	slowest	paid	madness

(c) Draw a line between the syllables that make a word:

cab	side	rain	cake	sad	ing	but	el
cam	in	pan	man	yel	ness	bow	ton
in	el	mail	bow	sail	low	mel	on
sud	on	snow	day	wag	on	rain	gain
dis	den	rob	flake	pic	cross	a	on
drag	like	sun	in	a	nic	lem	coat

RULE III:

When a syllable ENDS IN A VOWEL it is LONG.
(This is the third rule for long vowels.)

EXAMPLES:

a-pron	mu-sic	ba-con	tu-lip	i-ris
li-on	pi-lot	e-ven	o-pen	di-et
he	she	we	be	the

ACTIVITIES:

Explain that this is the last rule to learn for long vowels. Read the top line of examples, stressing the first long-vowel syllables. Have him underline the long vowels, and then read the words to you. Then have him read aloud the bottom row of syllables and, again, underline the long vowels.

RULE IV:

When a syllable has ONLY ONE VOWEL and it ENDS IN A CONSONANT, the VOWEL IS SHORT.

EXAMPLES:

bat cot hit sock cup land-ed sing-ing
bump drop bas-ket mit-ten doll rab-bit

ACTIVITIES:

After you have explained the rule, have him underline the vowels in the examples and look to see if they are followed by a consonant. Then have him tell you, *before* he reads the words, if the syllable has a long or a short vowel. After he has read them all, ask, "What kind of vowel do all the words have? Why?"

Then have him read words with both long and short vowels. Have him put a slash mark between the syllables (Da/vid, tu/lip), and tell you if the vowels are sounded long or short.

lion	bacon	David	acorn	across
visit	singing	she	tulip	hunted
began	broken	melon	petal	he
insect	lemon	apron	open	cabin

RULE V:

When a word has the SAME TWO CONSONANTS COMING TOGETHER, you usually divide between them.

EXAMPLES:

rab-bit kit-ten but-ton hap-pen bot-tom
yel-low sud-den sad-dest swim-ming can-not

ACTIVITIES:

This is the last rule he needs to know about syllables. It's useful because it helps him to immediately identify that the first syllable has a short vowel.

After you've given him the rule, have him read the examples to you. Then ask: "What kind of vowel will the first syllable always have in words with 'twin' consonants?" Then have him give you the rule that tells him: If a syllable ends in a consonant, the vowel is short.

CHAPTER 8

Stage II: Some Variations

Now that you have given your child a good foundation in the basic reading skills, you are ready to proceed to some of the variations in the rules. Don't panic. They are no more difficult to teach. As long as you go step by step and take your time, your lessons will continue to go smoothly.

Explain to your child you are now going on to the next stage because "you've done so well." And to make it seem more special, have him start a new word book. I am sure the old one must be bursting and somewhat dilapidated by now anyway. This time have him write in only the words he does not know the meaning of. Encourage him to write stories in it using the new words, and continue to give dictation if you find it's helpful.

You can use the same kind of activities you used to teach the Stage I skills. But emphasize more and more, *actual reading,* for remember: Phonics is only useful when it helps COMPREHENSION.

Step 1: Consonant Teams

SH, CH, TH, WH

This lesson is a case of "practice makes perfect." But it can also be lots of fun, especially if you include plenty of tongue twisters, and games playing with the sounds of the words.

The important point to get across is that when these two consonants come together, they make *one* sound. This is in contrast to the consonant blends, in which each consonant is sounded.

RULE:

When SH, CH, TH, and WH come together, they make ONE SOUND.

EXAMPLES:

SH: ship shut shade fish dish shell sheep shall shine wish shake mash show plash finish sheet

CH: chop chain chin rich such cheek chase Chuck teach check lunch peach chicken much beach cheat

TH: that with teeth this tenth throw bath them thick bathe thank sixth cloth clothe thing beneath

WH: When whale which white whip whipe while wheel

ACTIVITIES:

1. (a) Take each consonant team one by one. Say the first word of the examples. For example, when you teach SH say "ship," so he first hears the sound in a word. Then say the sound "sh" alone several times. Have him repeat the sound several times, and then the word several times. Ask him, "Where does the sound come in the word?"

Next have him underline the sound in the example words before he reads it. Each time ask him where the sound comes. If he is having a hard time with the sound, stop and repeat it alone again. When he has read the examples twice, have him circle all the words ending with the sound. Then have him read four words several times, trying to get faster and faster; then make it six; then eight. Make it into a fun game. You take a turn and try to beat him.

(b) Check to make sure he really has the sound by playing some games. Give him five words beginning with S, C, T, and W according to the sound you are working on, and one with the consonant team. See if he can spot it.

(c) Call out words and ask him where the consonant team comes in the word. Then have him circle words in a newspaper or a magazine and tell you where the team comes.

(d) Write down a word with a blend and one with a consonant team, and have him tell you which one has the team.

spell—shell	slop—shop	spine—shine
clip—chip	crain—chain	creek—cheek
trash—thrash	trick—thick	twill—thrill
swim—whim	steel—wheel	scale—whale

(e) Next play some games, such as "I spy" or "I went shopping." You can vary the latter one by including things to eat, wear, use, and do, and places to go.

(f) Play the "describing" game. Have him think of as many words as possible beginning with the sound to describe something. I have had more fun playing this with my students, and you can too, especially if you involve the rest of the family and make the things to be described as amusing as possible. Have one person choose what is to be described. Then he either chooses another person to describe it, or everyone has a turn. Start with something easy like a train going through a tunnel, a jet taking off, or someone walking through the snow. Then try the funnier ones like turning a jelly mold onto a plate. Eating an apple, or a carrot. Or a mouse gnawing a cracker.

(g) Have him make up tongue twisters, and then try to say them as fast as possible. Make some up for him, and see how fast he can say these. If you have a tape recorder, tape him, and let him hear himself.

Here are a few to start you off:
Shall Sherry shut the shoe shop?
Chattering Chuck chopped chips of chilling chicken.
That thing thinks this is a thrilling Thanksgiving.
Whim, wham, whum, the white whale whipped the wheel.

(h) When you are sure he knows each sound, play games using

them all. The "clock" game is good. When the hand lands on one of the consonant teams, he has to give six words beginning with that team. The "Upside down" game, the "snap" game, and the "mailing" game—putting the words into their correct boxes—are also great.

Then give him activities like these to do:

2. Answer these riddles by completing the words with a consonant team:

You give this when someone gives you something.	____anks	(thanks)
A large boat.	____ip	(ship)
The opposite of poor.	ri____	(rich)
The opposite of black.	____ite	(white)
A lot of something.	mu____	(much)
It swims in the sea.	fi____	(fish)
It's round, and you have two of them on your bike.	____eel	(wheel)
The opposite of open.	____ut	(shut)

3. Find the rhyming words:

ship	such	bath	path	teach	slow	fish	rich
much	whip	chop	shop	throw	reach	dish	which

4. Read these sentences, and complete them with one of the words:

Chip had a ______ to be rich.	dish, wish, which
The chipmunk ______ the nuts with his teeth.	bench, lunch, munches
Mom had a ______, but Dad had chicken.	shop, crop, chop
Josh thinks he can catch ten ______.	fins, fits, fish
"Get a thick ______ to mop up the milk."	cloth, froth, moth
Dad likes shellfish when he can get ______.	this, that, them
Trish will ______ them when she gets back.	thick, think, thank
Nick had to ______ his bike home.	feel, wheel, steal

5. Read the story, then have him answer the questions, and some of your own. Then have him underline all the words with consonant teams, and write them in separate columns under SH, CH, TH, and WH.

Introduce four more sight words: **have, do, you,** and **said.**

It was Thanksgiving. But Mom was sick. So Chip and Dad had to get the meal.

They had to dash to the shops and get lots of things, as Mom had not had time to get them. They got a chicken, as it was cheap, and they did not have much cash. Then they got a white loaf, nuts, three yams, and a peach pie.

When they got home, Chip said, "Which jobs shall I do?"

Dad said, "I shall roast the chicken and heat the peach pie, while you can fix the stuffing and the yams."

So Chip began to shell the nuts and chop them up. Then he cut up the white loaf. He gave the yams a wash and began to bake them.

When the chicken was roasted, Dad shifted it onto a big dish. It had a chip, but it did not show. Chip gave the yams a mash.

It was a rush to finish the meal on time. But they did it. Mom got on a bathrobe and had it with them.

"This is the best Thanksgiving lunch I have had in a long while," she said. "Thank you, Dad and Chip. I shall let you do this again!"

Questions:

Why did Chip and Dad get the Thanksgiving meal?
Why did they get a chicken and not a turkey?
What did Chip make the stuffing from?
Who heated up the peach pie?
What did Mom say?

6. Increase his word bank. Have him give another similar word for these words (synonyms):

close (shut) seat (bench) wealthy (rich)
hurry (dash, rush) store (shop) cut up (chop)

Step 2: Vowels with R

In this lesson you teach your child that vowels are not always long or short. It won't take him long to catch on to the rule, and it sure will help him (and you?) spell tricky words with R. However, have him concentrate on *reading* the words, rather than spelling them at this stage.

RULE:

When vowels are FOLLOWED BY R, they have a DIFFERENT SOUND.

EXAMPLES:

OR, AR	car corn
ER, IR, UR	letter bird purse
AIR, ARE, EAR	pair stare bear

ACTIVITIES:

Start with the OR and AR words (Lesson 1), and then go on to the ER, IR, and UR words (Lesson 2). And finally tackle the tricky "air" words (Lesson 3). Have him practice the example words over and over until he has the sound. Next, have him compare OR and AR words, and then OR and AR words with ER, IR, and UR words. And finally have him compare all these words with the "air words." You can use the same activities you used to teach him the consonant teams. Don't forget to have him use the words as much as possible in his conversation, and writing his own stories. Also, be sure to encourage him to be the "word detective" and hunt for the words in the newspaper, magazines, and books around the house. And of course, give him plenty of practice reading stories that contain a nice lot of these words.

Lesson 1: OR, AR

EXAMPLES:

OR: or for corn north pork more born
storm sore store porch horse worn morning

AR: car arm are yard hard sharp farm
part card barn start bark dark art

ACTIVITIES:

Have him:

1. Answer the riddles by changing the underlined letters. Be sure he reads aloud the original word before changing it, and then his own word.

In a farm he's a pig, on your plate he's this.	cork	(pork)
You see it twinkling at night.	jar	(star)
You can play here.	lark	(park)
It's good to eat.	torn	(corn)
Dogs do this.	dark	(bark)
You can blow it.	born	(horn)
You shop here.	more	(store)
A piece of something.	cart	(part)

2. Find the rhyming words:

mark	bark	corn	yard	port	car	hard	pork
more	sore	born	card	bar	fort	lard	fork

3. Read these sentences, and complete them with one of the words:

We had a ______ chop and corn for lunch.	fork, cork, pork
Carlos came back for ______ corn.	sore, more, store
Dad had a ______ time starting the car.	hard, lard, lord
Art wore his best pants and ______ them.	tar, star, tore
Lorna made a cornhusk doll ______ Martha.	nor, for, sore
Mom started to fill the ______ with jam.	jars, cars, starts
It's not far to go to the ______.	port, part, park
Marc was starving. "I can eat a ______," he said.	horn, horse, harp

4. Read the story. Then have him answer the questions, and some of your own. Next, have him underline all the OR words, and circle all the AR words, and write them in separate columns.

Carl's home was on a farm. He had fun on the farm. But it was a hard life and he had lots of jobs to do. In the morning and e-ven-ing, he had to feed the pigs and his horse. He gave the pigs cornhusks. He got them from the barn. He gave his horse hay, which he got in a cart from a haystack. Then he had to sweep up the yard and weed the garden.

Carl was playing his horn when Dad gave a yell,

"The haystack is on fire!"

Carl ran onto the porch. Yes, the haystack was on fire.

It was dark, just three stars shone. So he darted back inside for his torch.

"A spark from the tractor, or car, must have started it," said Dad, as he marched across the yard. "We must stop the fire be-fore it gets to the barn."

The corn was stored in the barn, and Carl's horse was inside.

It was morning when Carl and Dad got the fire to stop. Carl was stiff and sore, and his coat was torn. And he was starving. But he was pleased. He and Dad had saved the barn, the corn, and his horse.

Questions:

Did Carl enjoy living on the farm?
What jobs did he have to do?
Who first spotted the fire?
What caught fire?
What was in the barn?
How long did it take Carl and his Dad to put out the fire?
Give a title to the story.

5. Increase his word bank. Have him give you words that have the opposite meaning of these words (antonyms):

light (dark	whole (part)	south (north)
dull (sharp)	stop (start)	soft (hard)
less (more)	evening (morning)	

Lesson 2: ER, IR, UR

EXAMPLES:

her sir fur girl purse Bert first letter
nurse stir fern church shirt sister curve dirt
fir after better third burn skirt dinner curl
winter whirl turkey summer chirp ruler Kirk clerk

ACTIVITIES:

Have him:

1. Answer the riddles by changing the underlined letters. Don't forget to have him read aloud both the original and the new words.

It's a tree that keeps its leaves in winter.	s̲ir	(fir)
You keep money in it.	n̲urse	(purse)
You write these.	b̲etter	(letter)
No. 3.	b̲ird	(third)
Fire does this.	t̲urn	(burn)
You can have these on your head.	h̲url	(curl)
Girls wear these.	fl̲irt	(skirt)
A top does this.	g̲irl	(whirl)

2. Find the rhyming words:

shirt	clerk	burn	turn	girl	fur	third	curve
skirt	jerk	dinner	winner	stir	curl	herd	swerve

3. Read these sentences and complete them with one of the words:

Martha wore a dark shirt and ______.	stir, skirt, sir
Dan will ______ the cake with the whirling mixer.	fur, fir, stir
A ______ perched in the fir tree was chirping.	herd, bird, girl
The nurse will fix Bert's ______ hand.	burn, hurt, dirt
Jack came first, and Tom came ______.	third, thirst, burst

Carter had turkey and corn for ______. winter, winner, dinner

Carlos got ______ on his shirt. hurt, dirt, turn

Kirk was a ______ in a store. clerk, stern, stir

4. Read the story. Then see if he can answer the questions, and some of your own. Next underline all the ER, IR, and UR words, and write them in separate columns. Then ask him to reread the story, and circle all the words with more than one syllable. (Some have been hyphenated to help him sound them out.)

It was Jane's birth-day. She had lots of cards, let-ters, and pres-ents. Her first present was a nurse's u-ni-form from her mom. Her last present was from her dad. It was the best. For it was a dar-ling kit-ten. It had black and white fur in stripes. So Jane named him "Ti-ger."

Tiger had lots of fun. He got Mom's yarn. He gave Jane's hand a scratch, and hurt it. He hid in the cur-tains, and e-ven start-ed to eat Jane's birthday cake.

"Tiger," said Jane, "you will have to be-have better than this. You have been a real tiger today."

Tiger gave a purr. Then he curled up on the carpet and went to sleep.

Jane, and her sister, and her mom and dad, then had sup-per. Mom served tur-key for a treat. And they ate the birthday cake for des-sert. When Tiger woke up, Jane gave him a bit of birthday cake, and he gave a purr again.

Questions:

Give three presents Jane got for her birthday.
Who gave her the nurse's uniform?
Who gave her the kitten?
What color was the kitten?
What did the kitten do?
What did Mom serve for supper?
What did Jane give Tiger when he woke up?

5. Increase his word bank. Have him give you words that have the opposite meanings of these words (antonyms):

summer (winter) brother (sister) before (after)
clean (dirty) last (first) straight (curly)

Lesson 3: AIR, ARE, EAR

EXAMPLES:

air	hair	care	pear	bare	dare
chair	pare	fair	stair	ware	tear
wear	pair	stare	bear	share	swear

ACTIVITIES:

The way I get my students to remember the three vowel combinations for the "air" sound is to give them this jingle. It seems to help them a lot, so I hope it works for you.

I'm going to PARE (peel) a PAIR (two) of PEARS (the fruit).
Have him make up his own jingles with the homonyms listed at the end of this lesson.

Have him:

1. Answer the riddle by changing the underlined letters. Be sure to have him read both the original and the new words.

You sit on this.	hair	(chair)
You pay this on the bus.	pare	(fare)
You do this to clothes.	pear	(wear)
You go up these to bed.	fairs	(stairs)
Another word for look.	dare	(stare)
You brush and comb it.	chair	(hair)
A nice juicy fruit.	bear	(pear)

2. Put these words in their correct order so they make sense:

pear ate Ted a	(Ted ate a pear.)
up stairs the went Jack	(Jack went up the stairs.)
sat Clare the in chair	(Clare sat in the chair.)
Jan coat wears a	(Jan wears a coat.)
had pair mittens he a of	(He had a pair of mittens.)
rabbit hare a a is	(A hare is a rabbit.)

3. Read these sentences and complete them with one of the words:

This _____ needs to be repaired.	stair, fare, chair
The _____ dared to stare at Clare.	bear, care, ware
Martha takes care of her fair _____.	pair, hair, bare
Dad has a _____ wheel for his car.	stare, pare, spare
Beware of the bear, it can _____ you.	scare, tear, wear
Dot will _____ her pear with Mom.	care, pair, share
Ted likes his meat red and _____.	bare, rare, fair
"Don't you dare _____ these pants," said Mom.	wear, tear, swear

4. Increase his word bank. Give him the correct meanings for these homonyms so he can complete the sentences. Have him read aloud each sentence.

stare Pat's home has no _____.
stair "Joan, you must not _____ like that," said Mom.

fair The _____ on the bus is a dime.
fare "It's not _____," he said.

bare The shelf was _____.
bear The _____ had white fur.

pear Dad had to _____ the fruit for des-sert.
pare Mom had a _____ of stockings on.
pair Jane had a _____ for sup-per.

hare The _____ ran across the grass.
hair The wind was blowing Norma's _____.

ware I shall _____ a pink shirt and a yellow skirt.
wear Dad went to the hard_____ store to get a hammer.

Introduce THERE and THEIR and explain these two words also have the air sound and give their meanings.

There "Go _____," said Mom.
Their They got _____ coats.

Step 3: Y as a Vowel

You have already introduced your child to this rule when you taught him the AI and AY vowel teams. However, this lesson goes into it in more detail.

DON'T go on to this lesson until your child's a real whiz at syllables, for he must be able to tell how many syllables a word has to apply the rule.

RULE:

When Y comes at the END of a word, it is a VOWEL.
When Y is the only vowel at the end of a ONE-SYLLABLE word, it has the sound of LONG I.
When Y is the only vowel at the end of a word with MORE THAN ONE SYLLABLE, it has a sound like LONG E.

EXAMPLES:

Long I: my cry try why by sky fly dry
Long E: penny happy baby funny puppy sleepy windy

ACTIVITIES:

1. (a) Have him read the long I words and clap his hands. Ask, "How many syllables do these words have?" Next, ask him, "Which vowel sound do they have?" Then say, "Now, what is the rule when Y is the only vowel at the end of a one-syllable word?" If he can't give you the rule, give him more practice. Don't try the long E words until he has the long I ones down pat. When he has the long E words, play games differentiating between the two sounds.

(b) Give him two words, one of each sound, and ask him, "Which has the long I sound?" Then give him several words, all of the same vowel sound but one, and ask which is the odd man out. Give him words to match. Ask him for rhyming words.

bunny—funny sleepy—weepy windy—Cindy

(c) Ask him for as many words as he can think of that rhyme with "my." (Most of them are in the examples.)

(d) Have him make "describing" words (adjectives) from "naming" words (nouns).

luck—lucky hand—handy mud—muddy rock—rocky

(e) Give him nouns and have him give you a word ending with Y to describe it.

baby—sleepy clown—funny throat—dry girl—shy

Any activity that makes him THINK about the words and their meanings is great, for he needs to do this to understand the words in their context as he reads. Never let your lessons become merely the identification of the sounds of the words. Remember: COMPREHENSION AND PHONICS MUST GO HAND IN HAND.

(f) Have him read aloud these words. Then tell him to go back and circle all the words in which Y is a consonant. Next, tell him to put I over the long I words, and E over the long E words. After this have him write out the words in separate columns. Then have him check over the words to make sure he has them in their correct columns.

cry	yellow	silly	yes	fly	windy	puppy
yard	why	candy	thirty	yard	my	party
baby	sky	lady	sadly	by	yet	teddy
yarn	Mommy	twenty	yank	shy	pony	try

Then choose a few of the words and have him make up sentences with them.

Follow that with activities like these:

2. Answer these riddles by adding Y to the words. Have him say the word and then tell you if Y is a consonant or a vowel. If it's a vowel have him say which sound it has.

If you look up you can always see it.	sk__
A lovely, bright color.	__ellow
Another name for a rabbit.	bunn__
You use this word to ask a question.	wh__
You can grow things here.	__ard
You sometimes have this on your birthday.	part__
Ten of these make a dime.	penn__
One way to cook eggs.	fr__

3. Find the rhyming words:

fly	Kenny	yellow	fly	Willy	Billy	sky	thirty
cry	penny	dry	fellow	sadly	badly	shy	dirty

4. Put these words in their correct order so they make sense:

skirt Betty yellow had a	(Betty had a yellow skirt.)
hit the Patty fly	(Patty hit the fly.)
was it birthday Freddy's	(It was Freddy's birthday.)
crying was Baby	(Baby was crying.)
plates dry will the Mommy	(Mommy will dry the plates.)
is puppy Bobby a	(Bobby is a puppy.)

5. Read these sentences, and complete them with one of the words. Make sure he reads the *whole* sentence before choosing the word and that he reads *all* three word choices before making his selection:

Jack will try to make a fire from the _______ branch.	cry, dry, my
Willy gave a _______ as the fly buzzed by.	sly, sky, cry
The fat lady went _______ up the hill.	slowly, lonely, homely
Mom will _______ the fish for supper.	try, shy, fry
Dad gave Kelly a _______ for his birthday.	lumpy, jumpy, puppy
Joan wore a _______ scarf with her dark coat.	pillow, yellow, fellow
If you _______ you can do it.	my, by, try
Billy went into the _______ to play.	yank, yarn, yard

6. Read the story and answer the questions, and some of yours. Then underline all the words with Y, and write them in separate columns: Y as a consonant (only two words); Y as long I; and Y as long E.

This is a sad tale, so try not to cry! If you get weepy you had better get a hanky.

There was a sly and crafty fox. His name was Freddy Fox. He was fond of his tummy, and liked to eat.

It was a fine, sunny day. The sky was blue. But it was windy. So Freddy was flying his yellow kite on the top of a hill. Sud-den-ly he spot-ted Mrs. Gray Bunny going by with a load-ed basket.

"My. This is lucky," said Freddy to himself. "Mrs. Gray Bunny will make me a fine dinner. I will try to get her to my home. I will dress in a bonnet and long skirt so she thinks I am a lady."

Mrs. Gray Bunny was shy. She did not like to chat. But Freddy seemed so helpful.

"Hel-lo, Mrs. Gray Bunny," he said. "Can I help you with that big basket? You must be wea-ry. Why do you not rest at my home for a while?"

Freddy sat Mrs. Gray Bunny in a chair and gave her a cup of tea and a candy. Mrs. Gray Bunny liked the candy. She ate three more. And then more and more!

Freddy smiled. Mrs. Gray Bunny was getting plump.

Then Mrs. Gray Bunny felt sleepy from eating so much candy. When she was asleep, Freddy popped her in a box and shut the lid.

Then he got his frying pan and began to heat it. Next he went into the yard and got plenty of peas and corn to add to his meal.

Sud-den-ly Mrs. Gray Bunny woke up. It was dark inside the box. She banged and banged and gave a cry,

"Let me go! Let me go!"

Freddy o-pened the box. But just then a fly buzzed by. Freddy gave it a swat. And slick-ity-slick Mrs. Gray Bunny got away. She ran and she ran. At last she got home.

"I was silly," she said. "Next time I go to the market, I will not stop on the way home."

Questions:

What kind of day was it?
What was Freddy doing when he saw Mrs. Gray Bunny?

Why did Freddy want Mrs. Gray Bunny to come to his home?
What did he give her to eat?
What did she do after she had eaten the candy?
What did Freddie do after she went to sleep?
How did Mrs. Gray Bunny escape the frying pan?

7. Increase his word bank. Have him give a word with the opposite meaning for these words (antonyms) ending with Y:

big (tiny) serious (funny) wet (dry)
laugh (cry) sad (happy) man (lady)

Step 4: C and G

Don't rush this one. It's an important lesson, as it unlocks many words. If you explain the rule slowly and carefully, with lots of examples, he will probably learn it in one lesson. But don't worry if he doesn't. If he gets muddled, leave it. Do something else, and come back to it fresh tomorrow.

I call C and G the "terrible twins," because they get up to all sorts of annoying tricks. But they are also like twins in that they are identical. Once you know one, you know the other. So tell your child that if he gets the hang of one, the other will be a breeze.

RULE:

When C or G are followed by E, I, or Y, they usually have a soft sound.
C sounds like S. G sounds like J.

EXAMPLES:

C: ice force city nice race slice price cent since
lace rice place mice center space fence Grace
dance pencil fancy twice

G: gem page stage large huge George cage
ginger urge wage charge hedge bridge magic
fudge Gene ledge pledge budge bulge

ACTIVITIES:

1. (a) Begin with the soft C words. Have him read aloud the examples, underline the C, and tell you which vowel makes it have the S sound. Then ask him for the rule. If he knows it, have him compare hard and soft C words, and tell you which have the S sound. Do this orally at first, but as you include more words, write them down. (But make sure he can read them all!)

Begin with just two words. Then give him six, with an "odd man out." Then about twenty. Jumble them up, have him underline the C in each word, and write them under two headings: hard C and soft C. Be sure to have him read each word aloud before he decides which heading to put it under. Then, when he has finished, have him read each column. This will help to reinforce the sound in his mind.

(b) Next, ask him to give you as many hard C, and then soft C, words as he can. You can play "I spy," variations of "I went to market," and all those other listing games, to make it fun.

(c) Have him "read" a newspaper or magazine and circle all the C words, and have him tell you if they have a hard or a soft sound. Then read the word to him and ask him if he guessed correctly.

(d) Have him make up tongue twisters, and say them faster and faster.

(e) Give him a word and see how many C words he can come up with to describe it. Then have him tell you if they have a hard or a soft C.

(f) Then you can play all those "matching games," "couples," "Upside down" game, rhyming pairs, and so on.

When he's got ahold of C and has *absolutely no difficulty* identifying the two sounds, go on to G. He'll find G much easier because he just has to apply what he's learned for C. But still, take G slowly, and play lots of the games you used for C.

(g) You can also include this activity, which you can't use for C. And it's great for reviewing the magic E:

Circle the soft G words and say: what makes the G soft, changes the sound of the vowel (ask: Is it long or short?), and gives the word a new meaning. Answer: the magic E.

rag—rage hug—huge wag—wage sag—sage

(h) When he's got both C and G down pat, play games differentiating among the four sounds. Use the "baseball diamond" game. First base is hard C; second is hard G; third is soft C; and home base is soft G. As he goes from base to base he must give you one, two, or even six words with the sound.

(i) Then give him lots of chances to use the words. Remind him to use them in his conversations. If he asks for a "bit" of bread, remind him of that more descriptive word, "slice." Or if he talks about something being "big," nudge him into using "large," or "giant," and so on. Have him write lots of stories. And, of course, practice *reading* the words as much as possible.

And do these activities with him. Have him:

2. Underline all the words with C, and circle all the words with G. Then write them under the headings hard C; soft C; hard G; and soft G. Some words can go under two headings.

rice	coat	face	giant	cuff	cell	page
gate	huge	cone	gem	go	city	Coke
ice	cage	leg	magic	lace	dog	large
candy	egg	fence	fudge	game	slice	huge

3. Fill in the missing C or G in these words, and then use the words to answer the riddles. Be sure to have him read out each word he makes. If the word can have either C or G, have him give both words:

i__e	(ice)	ed__e	(edge)	__ame	(came, game)
fen__e	(fence)	__em	(gem)	__oat	(coat, goat)
ri__e	(rice)	e__ __	(egg)	__ent	(cent)
pa__e	(page)	__ave	(cave)	hu__e	(huge)
sli__e	(slice)				
ca__e	(cage)				
__iant	(giant)				
__ity	(city)				

You can eat it. It's white. And it rhymes with nice.	(rice)
Someone who is very, very large.	(giant)
Another word for town.	(city)
People often have these for breakfast.	(eggs)
They are fun to play.	(games)
A loaf can be made into these.	(slices)
A book has these.	(pages)
Yards sometimes have these around them.	(fences)

4. Find the rhyming words:

mice	page	face	lace	came	place	rice	cage
ice	stage	coat	goat	race	game	wage	slice

5. Read these sentences and complete them with one of the words:

Cindy paid six ______s for the ice-cream cone.	cake, cent, center

Mom gave Gene a large helping of ______.	mice, slice, rice
George had fried eggs on a ______ of toast.	price, slice, dice
Dad cut the ______ and did the edges of the grass.	ledge, wedge, hedge
______ Gary came first in the races.	Rice, Twice, Mice
Grace will sing and ______ at the concert.	dance, fancy, fence
The large ______ was a huge price.	urge, magic, gem
The mice ate a giant slice of ______ cake.	fudge, budge, bulge

6. Read the story and answer the questions, and some of yours. Then have him underline all the C words and circle all the G words. Then write them in separate columns.

As he reads the story, try to get him to now read in phrases—those gulps I talked about earlier. This will help both his fluency and his comprehension a lot.

It was going to be an ex-cit-ing day. Cindy and Gene were going to the cir-cus.

They drove in the car with Mom and Dad across the city to get there.

My, there was so much to see. A band was playing mu-sic on a stage in the center. Gym-nasts were tumbling, and bal-an-cing on the edge of a bar. A man was doing magic tricks. Dogs were having races. Horses were jumping over fences. Girls in fancy, lace dresses were dancing. A camel had a girl, with gems on her dress, on his huge hump. Lions were in a cage. A pair of midgets had a wedding, and got rice thrown at them. A giant man on stilts went by. And there were lots of com-ic-al actors with painted faces, wearing funny clothes.

And there was so much to eat. But at a price! There were:

popcorn; candy; gum; ice-cream cones; cupcakes; slices of fudge cake; cups of hot coffee; and Coke with ice cubes.

Dad gave Cindy and Gene fifty cents. Cindy had a Coke and a cupcake. Gene had popcorn and an ice-cream cone. Mom had a cup of coffee. And Dad had a slice of fudge cake.

"I have not had such a good time since I went to that concert you danced in, Cindy," said Mom.

The rest of them agreed with Mom. It *had* been an exciting day.

Questions:

Why was it such an exciting day for Cindy and Gene?
How did they get to the circus?
What did the gymnasts do?
What did the horses do?
Where were the lions?
Was the man on stilts really a giant?
Who were the comical actors with paint on their faces?
Describe some of the food that was for sale.
What did Gene have?
What would you have chosen?
Which act would you like to see most?

7. Increase his word bank. Have him match the meanings with the correct words. Write the words down in a column. Read the meanings to him. Have him circle the word and read it aloud to you. Then have him tell you what kind of C, or G, it has.

gem center bulge urge ice fancy stage huge

Water that is frozen	(ice)
A very precious stone	(gem)
Another word to describe something that is large	(huge)
The middle of something	(center)
Actors perform on this	(stage)
A word that is the opposite of plain	(fancy)
A lump does this	(bulge)
To try to get someone to do something	(urge)

Step 5: Some Tricky Vowel Teams

Sorry, but this one is a real toughie! Forewarned is forearmed, though. Read through the lessons carefully before you teach them. Make sure you have the rules and sounds straight before you tackle them with your child!

He may dash through these tricky vowel teams. But I doubt it. Most kids take quite some time to learn them. Don't be surprised, by the way, if he picks them up quickly, and does beautifully for a while, and then suddenly forgets them. That's all in the game! Just be patient, and, as usual, go step by step. Don't go on to a new sound until he REALLY KNOWS the one you are working on.

RULE:

Sometimes when two vowels come together they do not always follow the rule, "When two vowels come together, the first says its name, and the second one is silent."

EXAMPLES:

oo:	foot, boot	oi, oy:	oil	boy
ea:	head	ow, ou:	clown	cloud
ew:	threw	aw, au:	saw	auto

ACTIVITIES:

You can use most of the activities and games you have introduced so far to teach these vowel teams. In fact, it's best to play the "old-timers" and favorites, as he's familiar with their procedures and so can concentrate on the sounds he has to learn.

Lesson 1: OO

RULE:

OO has two sounds. You can remember them by this: "You put your FOOT in your BOOT."

EXAMPLES:

FOOT words:	foot	wood	wool	book	stood	hook
	cook	shook	good	hood	look	took
	brook	nook	rook	crooked	cookie	soot

BOOT words:	boot	food	soon	cool	room	roof
	broom	root	tool	fool	moon	noon
	too	pool	zoo	spoon	goose	tooth

ACTIVITIES:

1. There is only one way to learn which sound the OO should have—practice! Have him go over, and over, the example words and other OO words, using different activities to keep up his interest. Tell him when he sees a word with OO, to first try one sound, and if that doesn't seem to make a word, to try the other sound. But the best way is to have him READ THE WORD IN ITS SENTENCE and see which sound MAKES SENSE.

When he can quickly and easily recognize which is a "foot" word and which is a "boot" word (call them by this—I always do, and it really helps my kids), try him out on these activities. Have him:

2. Read aloud each word and tell you if it's a "foot" or a "boot" word. Then underline the "foot" words and circle the "boot" words. Then write them under the headings of "foot" and "boot" for reinforcement.

book	zoo	stood	wood	cool	soot
spoon	foot	pool	good	boot	crooked
cool	cook	shook	room	hood	tool
brook	wool	food	cookie	soon	roof

3. Find the rhyming words:

spoon	look	wood	fool	zoo	took	foot	soot
took	croon	good	stool	book	too	root	toot

4. Read these sentences and complete them with one of the words. Then have him go back, reread the sentences and words, underline the foot words, and circle the boot words.

Joan took a ______ for her lunch.	crooked, cookie, cook
Amy's ______ coat had a hood.	hood, wood, wool
Mom sat on a stool, while Dad ______ up.	soon, stood, spoon
The pool was still cool by	noon, moon, croon

Jack took a ______ at the baby raccoon.	soot, cook, look
Tom felt foolish when he fell in the ______.	book, brook, crook
______ cooks do not need cookbooks.	Wood, Good, Goose
Tim ate his ______ with a spoon.	tool, fool, food

Read the story and answer the questions, and some of yours. If he is not sure how to pronounce the OO words, tell him to reread the sentence to see which sound MAKES THE MOST SENSE.

Nan likes to visit Pat. There are such a lot of things to choose to do. There are books to read. Wool and yarn to make place-mats and dolls' dresses. And e-ven tools and wood to con-struct things.

Pat has a large, sunny bedroom. It has nooks for storing her books. Hooks to hang up her coats. And painted, wooden chests to keep her clothes in.

Pat's mom and dad are nice. They take Nan on trips with Pat. They took her to the zoo. And, on a hot day, they took her to a cool pool to swim.

Nan had the best time when they took Pat and her to the woods. They went along a path with giant trees on each side. They had huge roots, which made bumps in the path. It was dark and gloomy at first. But then Pat's mom said,

"Listen. The birds are singing." And Nan spotted a rook and a woodchuck perched in the nook of a tree. And then she spotted a woodpecker, pecking away at the trunk of a tree.

Then Nan's mom said, "Look over there." And Nan spotted a raccoon fam-il-y: Mom and Dad and a baby raccoon.

Soon they came to a grassy patch. Chipmunks were playing

and chattering by a brook. Pat and Nan were hot. So they waded barefoot in the brook. My, it was good! It was so cool!

Then Pat's dad took a look at his watch.

"My goodness!" he said. "It's noon. We must get lunch."

So Nan and Pat gave him a hand getting dry wood to make a fire. Mom got the food to cook from the picnic basket.

After they had fin-ished their meal, they had a snooze. When they woke up they had a cookie and packed up their things.

They got home just as the moon was showing over the roof-tops. Nan was pooped. But she had had a good time.

Questions:

Why did Nan like to visit Pat?
Where did Pat keep her books? What is a "nook"?
Where did Pat's mom and dad take Nan before the trip to the woods?
What did Nan hear in the woods?
What did she see?
What did Nan and Pat do to cool off?
How did they cook their lunch?
When did they get home?

5. Increase his word bank. Write down these words, and have him read them to you. Next, call out one of the meanings, and have him circle the correct word. Then have him read the word aloud again and tell you if it's a "foot" or a "boot" word.

book boot wood moon cook cookie crooked spoon

Someone who gets the food ready to eat. (cook)
It tastes good, but is fattening. (cookie)
You read this. (book)
You wear this on your foot. (boot)
You use this to eat with. (spoon)
Something that is not straight. (crooked)
A tree is made of this. (wood)
It changes its shape at night. (moon)

Lesson 2: OI, OY

RULE:

OI and OY have the sound as in

OIL BOY

EXAMPLES:

oil boy toy boil soil joy join coy broil
coin foil spoil point enjoy Roy coil moist voice

ACTIVITIES:

1. Read several of the example words to him. Then say the rule, and repeat the OI, OY sound several times. Have him do the same. Next have him read all the example words and then go back and underline the vowel team. Finally, have him reread the words several times, getting faster and faster. Play several games helping him to identify the sound, and then differentiate it from other sounds, such as OO words and OW words.

Then do these activities with him.

2. Find the rhyming words.

spoil toy point join oil coy coin Joyce
Roy toil joint loin boy boil voice join

3. Fill in the missing letters in the words to answer the riddles.

The end of a pencil has one.	_oint	(point)
You plant seeds in this and they grow.	_oil	(soil)
Kids like to play with them.	_oy	(toy)
If you're not a girl, you must be this.	_oy	(boy)
You do this when you put things together.	joi_	(join)
You can do this to a rope.	coi_	(coil)
You can cook chops this way.	broi_	(broil)
A word for a penny, a nickel, or a dime.	coi_	(coin)

4. Read these sentences and complete them with one of the words.

Have him read the whole sentence and all the words before making his choice. And then read his completed sentence.

Mom laid the chicken on tinfoil and ______ it.	coiled, soiled, broiled
"Will you ______ us for lunch at noon?"	coin, join, joint
If you boil corn, it will ______.	soil, spoil, foil
Roy ______ digging in the soil.	enjoys, toys, boys
Mom gave Boyd six ______, five dimes and a penny.	coil, coins, join
Joyce pointed to the ______ in the store window.	boil, boys, toys
Dad will ______ Ann's toy train.	broil, soil, oil
The hamburgers were nice and ______.	voice, moist, point

5. Read the story and answer the questions, and some of yours. Then go back and underline all the OI and OY words. Next, write them down and practice reading them. And finally, put them in his own sentences. Then have him read these sentences to you.

Joyce and Roy had an a-part-ment in the city. They enjoyed life in the city. When it was sunny, they joined their pals in the park. They took Royal, their dog. Royal enjoyed running on the grass. And he liked to dig in the soil and make large holes for his bones.

"You must not do that," said Roy in a cross voice. "It will spoil the grass. If you do that you will have to stay at home."

When it was wet, Joyce and Roy went to the stores. They often went to the toy de-part-ment. That was fun. Joyce pointed to the toys she liked best. And Roy took a look at the prices. They were not cheap!

"When I get a lot of coins in my piggy bank," said Joyce to Roy, "I will get a toy for you and a toy for me."

Joyce and Roy's mom and dad had jobs. So they often got

the meals. They were good cooks. Joyce's hamburgers were so moist. She brushed them with oil and broiled them on tinfoil. And Roy was a whiz at boiling eggs and cooking a roast.

In the e-ven-ings Joyce, Roy, Mom, and Dad liked to play games or read their books. Joyce coiled up on the so-fa beside Mom, and Roy and Dad sat in the chairs. They were a happy family. And they enjoyed living in the city.

Questions:

Where did Joyce and Roy live?
Where did they go when it was sunny?
What was the name of their dog?
What did Royal like to do in the park?
What did Joyce and Roy do when it was wet?
What did Joyce tell Roy she would do?
How did Roy and Joyce help out at home?
What was Joyce particularly good at cooking?
What was Roy good at cooking?
What did the family do in the evenings?

6. Increase his word bank. Ask him to give you a word with the opposite meaning of these words (antonyms):

dry (moist) happiness (joy) to like (to enjoy)
link (join) wind up (coil) ruin (spoil)

Lesson 3: OW, OU

RULE:

OW and OU have the sound as in
CLOUD CLOWN

EXAMPLES:

cloud	clown	now	found	house	out	how
brown	our	down	loud	owl	count	bow
town	ground	cow	foul	flower	sound	south
mouth	mouse	round	gown	pound	about	powder

ACTIVITIES:

1. Give him the OW, OU sound, and say "cloud" and "clown" very distinctly, emphasizing the sound. Do this several times, and then have him do the same.

Next, write "cloud" and "clown," and underline the team vowels. Ask him what sound they have. Then ask him:

"What other sound have you already learned for OW?" Let's hope he says "long O"!

Remind him that when OW says long O it is following the *usual* rule for double vowels: "When two vowels come together the first one says its name, and the second one is silent." Then explain that there are some OW words that do not follow the rule. Then have him read the example words aloud, and afterward go back and circle all the OW words. Tell him that these are some of the exceptions. Then explain, as you did with the OO words, how he must figure out which way to pronounce OW words when he reads them.

Play games that help him to recognize the difference in the two sounds.

Then have him reread the example words, and remind him that "OU" also has the same sound as irregular OW.

Then have him do these activities. Have him:

2. Read aloud these words, and circle the long OW words, and underline the irregular OW words. Then write them in separate columns.

low	how	grow	ground	show	shower	lower
snout	snow	sour	yellow	clown	glow	found
follow	own	brown	slow	sound	now	flown
about	bowl	slow	count	window	shout	thousand
flow	cow	row	house	flour	pillow	flower

Have him write a story using some of the words and read it to you.

3. Find the rhyming words:

sound	slow	brown	town
pound	know	tow	bow
flour	shout	house	bow
out	flower	crow	mouse

4. Fill in the missing letters in the words to answer the riddles.

It's a drab color.	__ __own	(brown)
When you add up you do this.	__ount	(count)

Birds fly here in the winter.	_outh	(south)
You put them in a vase.	__owers	(flowers)
Actors do this at the end of a show.	bo_	(bow)
Lemons are this.	sou_	(sour)
You make bread and cakes from it.	flou_	(flour)
A funny person at the circus.	clow_	(clown)

5. Read these sentences, and complete them with one of the words:

Mom needs a ______ of flour to bake the cake.	sound, hound, pound
"I can ______ up to a thousand," said Ted.	clown, count, cloud
The brown owl had a ______ in his mouth.	howl, house, mouse
Jack left his towel in the ______.	sow, shower, shout
The ______ are A, E, I, O, U; and Y and W can be too.	vowels, towels, tower
The player made a ______ and the crowd shouted.	flower, foul, found
There was a cloudburst and ______ came the rain.	town, down, gown
The flowers were growing in the ______.	sound, round, ground

6. Read the story. Then have him answer the questions, and some of yours. Next have him circle all the OW and OU words that have the sound of "clown" and "cloud," and underline all the OW words with the long O sound. Finally, have him write the words in their appropriate columns and read them to you.

Ann and Sam liked to dress up. They had a grand time.

Sam liked to be a clown. He painted his face with snow-white powder and made his mouth red with his mom's lipstick. He got a brown pencil and gave himself big eyebrows and lines to look like a frown. Sam liked to be a King as well. He made a cape from a large towel, and a crown from a plastic bowl.

Ann liked to dress up in her mom's clothes. She had given Ann a long yellow gown with brown flowers, a blouse with a bow at the neck, and a row of beads. Ann felt grown-up and proud when she wore them.

Ann and Sam often gave their mom and dad a show. They dressed up, and they acted out lots of things. Mom and Dad had to guess the things they were. They pre-tend-ed to be: A farmer milking his cows and plowing the ground. A cowboy rounding up thousands of bulls. Mom pounding flour to make a loaf. And Dad mowing the grass, and sowing seeds, and wetting them to make them grow.

At times they made it funny. They pre-tend-ed to be: A lady tieing a bow on a cow. A mouse going up a mountain. A crow slipping on the snowy ground. Or a sow eating a bowl of pop-corn.

Mom and Dad found it hard to guess these!

Questions:

What did Ann and Sam like to do?
What did Sam especially like to be?
How did he make his face look like a clown's?
What had Mom given Ann?
What did Ann and Sam do for their parents?
Who did they pretend they were?
What were the funny things they pretended to be?

7. Increase his word bank. Have him give you an OW, OU word meaning the opposite of these words (antonyms):

lost (found) sweet (sour) country (town)
north (south) in (out) quiet (loud)

8. Give him the meaning of these homonyms. Then have him read aloud and write down these sentences, and complete them with the correct word.

flour flower

The ______ had come out of the ground.
A cake cannot be made without ______.

Lesson 4: AW, AU

RULE:

AW and AU have the sound as in

SAW AUTO

EXAMPLES:

saw	auto	draw	claw	yawn	dawn	paw	hawk
crawl	raw	lawn	haul	law	August	because	straw

ACTIVITIES:

1. Teach him the sound as you taught him the other vowel teams. Play plenty of games to reinforce the sound, and words, in his mind. Then have him do these activities.

2. Find the rhyming words:

dawn	law	haul	crawl	straw	cause	raw	Paul
jaw	lawn	fault	vault	pause	saw	paw	haul

3. Give as many words as possible to rhyme with SAW (law, draw, raw, paw, claw, flaw, thaw, straw, craw)

4. Fill in the missing letters in the words to answer the riddles:

Grass that has been dried.	___aw	(straw)
A baby deer.	_awn	(fawn)
You use these to eat with.	_aws	(jaws)
They are made to be obeyed.	_aws	(laws)
It brings the first light of day.	daw_	(dawn)
A baby does this before learning to walk.	craw_	(crawl)
It needs a lot of mowing.	law_	(lawn)
You can go places in it.	au__	(auto)

5. Read these sentences and complete them with one of the words:

Dan must cut the ______ and haul away the weeds.	pawn, <u>lawn</u>, law
The hawk had sharp ______.	paws, <u>claws</u>, laws
Jan saw the ______ crash into the van.	August, awning, <u>auto</u>

Paul yawned ______ he was sleepy.	pause, because, draws
The dog hit Maud on the ______ with his paw.	jaw, craw, claw
The tiger ate the ______ meat.	craw, draw, raw
Dad will ______ the wood on the grass.	straw, saw, thaw
There is not a strawberry to be found in ______.	cause, pause, August

6. Read the story and answer the questions, and some of yours. Next, have him underline all the AW, AU words, and write them down. Then have him read them to you, and see if he can write his own story using them.

Paul and his dad set out in their auto on a hot August day. They had been waiting for this day for a long time, because they were going on a camping trip.

They had gotten up at the crack of dawn and packed up the auto. Then they had driven into the mountains to look for a good place to pitch their tent.

At last they came to a stream with willow trees. It looked cool and in-vi-ting.

"This looks like a good spot," said Dad, "This will do us fine."

Paul helped his Dad haul the tent and food out of the back of the car. Then they pitched the tent. It made them hot.

"Let's pause for a while," said Dad, "and have a swim in the stream."

After this they had lunch, and sprawled under the willow tree to rest. Dad looked up and saw a nest with a baby bird in it. It was chirping, "Craw, craw."

"Let's crawl under this bush and see if its mom will re-turn," said Dad.

They did not have to wait long. Soon they saw a large black hawk flying in the sky. She had a rabbit in her sharp claws. It was to be her baby's lunch.

Then sud-den-ly they saw a deer and its fawn. They were wading in the stream and drinking. The fawn was sweet. It had soft brown fur.

"I wish there was a law to stop deers being killed," said Paul. "It's awful to kill them."

"I agree," said Dad.

Next they saw a chipmunk sitting on its haunches eating a nut, and all sorts of birds, and e-ven a snake crawling on the ground. They then collected wood for a fire, and ate their meal just as the sun was sinking in the sky.

Soon Paul began to yawn. The fresh air and ex-cite-ment had made him sleepy. He crawled into his sleeping bag, leaving the flap of the tent open to see the moon and stars. But he was fast asleep before they came out.

Questions:

Which month did Paul and his Dad go on the camping trip?
Where did they pitch their tent?
What did they do to cool off?
What did Dad spot in the willow tree?
What kind of bird was it?
What did it have for its lunch?
Who came to get a drink from the stream?
Who else did Paul and his dad see?
Why didn't Paul see the moon and the stars when they came out?

7. Increase his word bank. Have him give you an AW, AU word for these meanings.

uncooked (raw) a sharp nail (claw) to pull (haul)
animal's feet (paws) terrible (awful) to stop (pause)

Lesson 5: EW

RULE:

EW has the sound as in NEW.

EXAMPLES:

new few chew stew flew drew news
blew crew screw dew grew threw jewel

ACTIVITIES:

1. Teach him the sound just as you taught him the other vowel teams. Play plenty of games, as usual, to reinforce it in his mind. Then have him do these activities.

2. Give as many words as possible to rhyme with NEW (see the examples).

Fill in the missing letters in the words to answer these riddles:

It's good to eat in cold weather.	__ __ew	(stew)
They usually sparkle and women wear them.	jew__ __ __	(jewels)
You do this to food.	__ __ew	(chew)
It tells you something.	__ews	(news)
You can see it on the lawn early in the morning.	__ew	(dew)
A small number.	__ew	(few)
When you just buy something, it's this.	__ew	(new)
They work on a boat.	__ __ew	(crew)

3. Read these sentences and complete them with one of the words:

The wind ______ the leaves from the trees.	grew, flew, <u>blew</u>
"I will get you a ______ coat," said Mom.	stew, few, <u>new</u>
Jan made the ______ from ham, beans, and celery.	crew, <u>stew</u>, screw
I will eat just a ______ nuts.	dew, <u>few</u>, new
Dad turned on the TV to watch the ______.	new, <u>news</u>, chew

This meat needs a lot of ______ing. screw, crew, chew

Ted needed a ______ to fix the broken chair. screw, stew, mew

The game ______ a large crowd. few, drew, blew

4. Put these words into their correct order so they make sense:

dress a Joan had new	(Joan had a new dress.)
hair the wind blew her	(The wind blew her hair.)
bird the into flew sky the	(The bird flew into the sky.)
chewed gum Dan	(Dan chewed gum.)
the the crew boat sailed	(The crew sailed the boat.)
in plants garden the grew the	(The plants grew in the garden.)
Mom stew a made	(Mom made a stew.)

5. Read the story and answer the questions, and some of yours. Next, have him underline all the EW words, and write them down.

While Dad and Paul were camping, Mom and Linda went to stay with Granddad. His home was on the West Coast, so they flew there in a jet. It was a big ad-ven-ture for Linda, as she had not been on a plane be-fore.

The day they were to leave, she wore her new pink dress and a brown coat. Mom wore a new coat, and a hat.

They took a cab to the airport, and checked in their bags. Then Mom got herself a newspaper, and a book for Linda, to read on the plane. Linda had saved a few coins for the trip, and she spent three on a packet of chewing gum.

At last it was time to get on the plane. The crew looked smart in their blue u-ni-forms. A stew-ard-ess gave Linda a seat by the window.

Soon they were on their way. Up, up, up into the sky the jet flew. Linda looked down. The homes now looked like dolls' houses. The streets like strings. And the hills like bumps. They went over a lake. It was spark-ling like a jewel in the sun.

Then they were in the clouds. Mom began to read her news-paper. Linda got out a notebook, and drew. Then the stew-ard-ess gave them lunch on a tray. It was stew, salad, and a slice of cake for des-sert.

Just as Linda grew restless, it was time to land. The jet got lower and lower. And then, wham, they were down.

Granddad was there to meet them. He was happy to see them safe and sound. And Mom and Linda were happy to be with Granddad.

Questions:

Who were Linda and her mom going to see?
How did they get there?
What did Mom and Linda buy at the airport?
Describe what Linda saw from the plane window.
What did she do while Mom read the newspaper?
What did she have for lunch?
Who met them when they arrived?

6. Increase his word power. Have him give an EW word that has the same meaning as these words (synonyms):

sketched (drew) chop up (hew) not many (few)
never used (new) killed (slew) bench (pew)

Lesson 6: EA

RULE:

EA can have the sound of short E as well as of long E as in
HEAD BREAD

EXAMPLES:

head	bread	dead	deaf	read	heavy	ready
breast	lead	dread	meant	instead	health	wealthy
tread	spread	steady	sweater	weather	leather	meant

ACTIVITIES:

1. Ask him to give you the sound he has already learned for EA. When he tells you "long E," ask him to give you some words with EA as long E:

seat beads meat sea leaf heap team

Then tell him that EA can have the short E sound sometimes. Ask him to give you the sound of short E. Then read the example words to him and say, "All these words have EA as a short E." Next, have him read the words to you. If he's having a tough time, have him underline the vowel team, and say the short E sound alone, and then read the word as a whole.

Then play games to help him recognize both long E and short E EA words.

Remind him that the only way to tell if an EA word has the long E or the short E sound is to try both sounds out and see if they make a word he knows. Then read the word *in its sentence* to see if it makes sense. Point out that "read" and "lead" can be pronounced both ways. But it's easy to tell which words they are "if you see how they fit in with all the other words."

I like to read books. He read a book.

John will lead the band. The heavy box was made of lead.

Then have him do these activities:

2. Read the words aloud, circle the long E words, and underline the short E words. Then write the words in two columns:

beads	bread	teach	heavy	sea	head	hear
real	death	east	meant	mean	weak	wealth
leather	leaf	breast	eat	ready	year	dread
dear	sweater	seat	reach	healthy	thread	clean
deaf	meat	heaven	ear	weapon	peach	spread

3. Find the rhyming words:

bread	peach	seat	meat	meant	seen	breast	team
beach	dread	health	wealth	mean	bent	test	cream

4. Fill in the missing EA vowel team in the words to answer the riddles. Then have him say the word and tell you if EA has the long or the short E sound.

When you can't hear you are this.	d__ __f
It's made up of twelve months.	y__ __r
When you are fit and well you are this.	h__ __lthy
You can sit on it.	s__ __t
Trees have a lot of them.	l__ __ves
When something is hard to lift, it's this.	h__ __vy
The opposite to west.	__ __st
It keeps you warm.	sw__ __ter

5. Read these sentences and complete them with one of the words:

Can you help me with this ______ bag?	wealthy, healthy, heavy
I ______ to eat my peach first.	dead, meant, bread
The team wore thick, red ______s.	spread, sweater, threat
Ted's jacket is made of ______.	leather, feather, weather
Being ______ meant he had a hard time hearing.	heavy, wealthy, deaf
Mom got the meat and peas ______ to eat.	steady, ready, read
He was so heavy, he got out of ______ when he ran.	breath, health, wealth
Dick likes to ______ peanut butter on his bread.	steady, stead, spread

Ask him which sound all the "choice" words have. Next, have him circle all the short E EA words in the sentences, and then underline all the long E EA words.

6. Read the story and answer the questions, and some of yours. Next, have him circle the short E EA words, and underline the long E EA words, and write them in two columns. Then have him read the words to you.

Mrs. Robin Red Breast had a lot to do. It was spring cleaning day. Each year she took a whole day to ti-dy up the house after the winter.

She got up at the crack of dawn so she had plenty of time. She looked out of the window to check the weather.

"Yes. It's a perfect day for spring cleaning," she said to herself. "There's a nice breeze to air the carpets and blankets, and the sun will dry the curtains."

But first she had to get breakfast for Mr. Robin Red Breast. She sliced the bread for toast, and made him a bowl of cream of wheat.

Mr. Robin Red Breast was still asleep, so she shouted out in a loud voice, "Get up! Get up, sleepyhead! Breakfast is ready!" She had to yell because he was a bit deaf.

Then she flew out to get the newspaper, as her husband liked to read the headlines as he ate his breakfast.

As soon as he had left for his job, Mrs. Robin Red Breast began to clean. She washed, and brushed, and dusted, and cleaned, and *cleaned*. She swept out the dead leaves that had blown in. She beat the carpets. She shook the blankets. She scrubbed the bathtub with cleanser, and even mended the leaking faucet. She washed the curtains, and spread them out to dry on the branch of a tree. She turned out the closets. And she washed the windows.

She was just lifting a heavy chest when there was a scream and a squeal. Then a voice said,

"Please do not hurt me. I meant you no harm."

Mrs. Robin Red Breast bent down and saw a spi-der looking up at her.

"You can't stay in my house," she said firmly. "In fact you'd be better dead." But instead of treading on him, she swept him into her dustpan, and threw him out of the window.

By lunchtime she was weary, and beads of sweat ran down her forehead.

"Time for a meal and a rest," she said. And she sat down to a slice of meat and a peach.

Next she ironed the curtains.

"Oh deary me," she said, "they have lots of holes. I must get my thread and mend them." She got out her leather bag, and found the thread, and mended the holes.

Then she ironed the bedspread and made up the bed.

At last the house was neat and tidy. Mrs. Robin Red Breast looked around with pride.

She had a bath, and dressed in a clean skirt and sweater. Then she began to get supper ready. Soon she saw her husband flying over the nearby meadow.

"How pleased he will be to see the house so clean," she said. And she hummed a happy tune and fluffed up her feathers as she went out to greet him.

Questions:

What time of year was it?
Why did Mrs. Robin Red Breast get up so early?
Why did she have to shout when speaking to her husband?
What did she give him for breakfast?
Give four things she did to get the house clean and tidy.
What did she find under the chest?
What did she do to him?
What was the first thing she did after lunch?
What was the matter with the curtains?
Give the story a title.

7. Increase his word bank. Have him match the words with their meanings:

wealthy	stretch out
spread	to walk or step
heavy	rich
tread	a lot of weight

Lesson 7: Syllables and Review

RULE:

Vowel teams are NEVER SEPARATED when you divide a word into syllables.

EXAMPLES:

All these words have ONLY ONE SYLLABLE because they have ONLY ONE VOWEL SOUND:

moon, cook, moist, joy, crowd, shout, paw, Paul, blew, head

ACTIVITIES:

Have him read aloud the following words, and underline the vowel teams. Then have him write the number of vowels he sees, the number of vowel sounds he hears, and then the number of syllables.

This should be a good review of the vowel teams. If he seems to have difficulty with one or two of them, review them before going on to the next lesson. And if he has problems breaking the words into syllables, give him as many words as he needs to learn how to do it!

	vowels you see	vowels you hear	number of syllables
feather			
broom			
yawn			
look			
clouds			
pool			
boiling			
threadbare			
chew			
because			
bookstore			
screw			
around			
enjoying			
zoo			
withdrew			
breakfast			
frown			
headline			
spoon			
sweater			
flower			
goodness			
ointment			
laws			
threw			

	vowels you see	vowels you hear	number of syllables
toothpaste			
boiling			
strawberry			
woodshed			
shower			
woodpecker			
towel			
August			
noon			
auto			
downtown			
toys			

Step 6: When Endings Are Added to Words

Watch this lesson! Tread carefully. It's tricky!

These are important spelling rules. But they will help your child's reading because they show him how to break words into their syllables and pronounce them correctly.

Even though I call this lesson one of my "heavies," it does bring a bonus. You will find that once your child has learned it, he is not only a much more fluent reader, but a terrific speller as well!

RULE:

Some words change their spelling when an ending is added. There are three kinds of words that do this:

1. ONE-ONE-ONE words. Words of one SYLLABLE, with one VOWEL, followed by one CONSONANT, double the last consonant when an ending beginning with a vowel is added.

EXAMPLES:

hop—hopping skip—skipped

ACTIVITIES:

This rule should pose no problem. In fact, you can even skip it, unless you want to give his spelling a boost. I include it mainly for you, so you can analyze, and understand, the words you are teaching better.

The reason why he doesn't need to know this rule to improve his reading is that he can already divide and pronounce most of the one-one-one words by applying one of his syllable rules:

"When a word has the same two consonants coming together, you usually divide between them."

In case he has forgotten the rule, have him read these words aloud, and divide them into syllables.

Before you do, point out to him that ED can be pronounced in three different ways: after T and D it has the sound ED; at other times it has the sound of T or D.

For example: planted (ed) plodded (ed) jumped (t) smiled (d)

Have him put a slash mark to show where these words divide, and then write the number of syllables they have. If a word ends with ED, have him write the sound it has.

swimming	saddest
hottest	rushed
sender	swimmer
planning	begging
planted	searched
maddest	wagged
asked	hopping
slimmer	landed
passes	biggest
finished	opened
nodded	shopping
running	stopper

2. MAGIC (silent) E Words: Words ending in the magic E DROP THE E when an ending beginning with a vowel is added.

EXAMPLES:

hope+ing=hoping   time+ed=timed

ACTIVITIES:

1. This rule *is* important for his reading. He needs to know it to pronounce the magic E words with a long vowel sound when they have endings added to them. For example, he must recognize that "hoping" has a long O, because it comes from "hope." (If it had come from "hop," it would be "hopping.")

You will have to explain this rule to him slowly and carefully, with lots of examples. Begin by giving him a lot of *oral* practice so he doesn't have to worry about the spelling of the words. Give him magic E words with endings, and ask him to give you the original (called "root") word. Next, have him add endings to magic E words and pronounce them. Then do the same mixing the magic E words with one-one-one words. When he can do this easily orally, give him some reading activities like these:

2. Read the words aloud. Put a slash mark to show where these

magic E words are divided. Then write the number of syllables they have. If a word ends with ED, have him write the sound it has.

liking	ruler	whitest
rides	smiling	hiker
baked	finer	raked
hoping	timeless	homeless
used	hiding	ripest
safest	skated	shapely
driving	catcher	joked
closed	chased	dining
waving	wiping	traded
biked	piled	saving

3. Take off the endings on these magic E words and give the original (root) words:

using	dined	hoped
finest	saving	skating
bakes	smiled	cutest
liked	driver	shining
ruling	biking	riper

4. Underline the magic E words in these pairs:

rip—ripe lick—like can—cane pin—pine dim—dime
hoping—hopping dinner—diner taped—topped
ratting—rating

5. Match the rhyming words:

running	pruning	sinning	shining
tuning	sunning	winning	dining
rocking	raking	later	matter
blocking	baking	batter	hater

6. Divide these words into syllables by putting a slash mark, and say if they have a short vowel sound (are one-one-one words) or a long vowel sound (are magic E words):

baked	begged	dining	clapping	finest	sender
maddest	biting	chopped	saved	hottest	useful
skating	dipping	waded	jumped	raked	stopping
canning	taking	dimmest	wiper	badly	making
hopeless	tagged	liked	stepping	hiker	biking
shaped	trimmed	grabbed	rudely	cooler	traded

7. Give the original (root) word of these words, and say if it is a one-one-one word or a magic E word:

hottest	pinned	swimmer
skating	tasting	making
stopped	fattest	waved
hated	riding	dripping
hoping	madly	shaving
hopping	timing	begged

8. Fill in the missing letters in the words to answer the riddles, and tell you if they have a long or a short vowel sound. Then have him underline all the words with endings in the sentences, and tell you which sound they have:

A way to cook.	___aking	(baking)
You can only do this in water.	___ ___imming	(swimming)
When something is larger, it is this.	___igger	(bigger)
The opposite to standing.	___itting	(sitting)
The way to get the leaves up.	___aking	(raking)
He tries to strike the ball.	___atter	(batter)
It helps you draw straight lines.	___uler	(ruler)
Another word for dinner.	___upper	(supper)

9. Read these sentences and complete them with one of the words. Be sure to have him read aloud the whole sentence and all the words first.

Jack was ______ his bike so fast, he crashed.
hiding riding sliding

"This is the ______ banana," he said, eating it.
sickest fastest biggest

Mom is ______ cupcakes, and making pies for the party.
raking backing baking

"We'll go ______ when we've washed the dishes."
mopping sloping shopping

The dog ______ up, begging for the bone.
bumped jumped camped

Tom ______ jogging to keep fit.
biked licked <u>liked</u>

Marc is ______ than Jim. But Joe is bigger.
batter <u>fatter</u> fattest

Joan slipped when she was ______.
<u>skating</u> shaping taking

Have him reread the sentences and underline all the words with endings. Then have him say which vowel sounds these and the choice words have—long or short.

3. Words ENDING IN Y: Words ending in Y CHANGE THE Y TO I when ANY ending is added EXCEPT one beginning with I, IF there is a CONSONANT BEFORE THE Y.

EXAMPLES:
cry—cried funny—funniest happy—happiness

ACTIVITIES:

1. This rule will particularly help him pronounce two syllable words like "funny" with the long E sound when they have an ending added, and will help him break down words ending in Y into their correct syllables.

Begin by giving him plenty of oral practice, as you did when you introduced the magic E rule. Give him Y words with endings, and ask him to give you the original word. Next, have him add endings to Y words, and pronounce them. Then give him Y words with, and without, endings, and ask him how many syllables they have. When he finds this a cinch, give him reading activities like these:

2. Read these words aloud. Say how many syllables they have. Then give the original word:

cries	hurried	luckiest
silliest	tried	copying
flying	babies	emptied
flier	drying	candies
cookies	carried	chilliest
happier	stories	fried

3. Find the rhyming words:

tried	sunniest	bumpier	lumpier
cried	funniest	bumpiest	lumpiest
lazier	berries	fries	flying
cherries	crazier	flies	frying

4. Fill in the missing letters in the words to answer the riddles. Then tell you how many syllables the words have.

A lot of joy.	__appiness	(happiness)
Going quickly.	__urrying	(hurrying)
When someone is *more* funny than one other person.	funni__ __	(funnier)
When someone is the *most* silly of several people.	silli__ __ __	(silliest)
Making the same thing.	__opying	(copying)
More than one rabbit.	__unnies	(bunnies)
A word to describe something that sparkles and is bright.	shin__	(shiny)
Someone who tries hard.	tri__ __	(trier)

5. Read these sentences and complete them with one of the words. Then have him tell you how many syllables the choice words have:

The plane was _______ at a fast speed.
trying crying <u>flying</u>

This is the _______ dog. He will not do these tricks.
fastest <u>silliest</u> nicest

Joan is the _______ girl. She's going on a trip to Boston.
mucky lucky <u>luckiest</u>

The slim clown was _______ than the fat clown.
sunny funny <u>funnier</u>

Mom will bake the _______ for the parties.
cooking cooked <u>cookies</u>

This is a much _______ day than yesterday.
window windy <u>windier</u>

______ is better than wealth.

Happiness Emptiness Luckiness

The babies were ______ loudly.

cries crying trying

CHAPTER 9

Stage III: The Harder Ones

The emphasis now should be on reading, reading, READING. Your child needs to get his nose into books and stories to practice all the skills he has learned so far; and it's the best way for him to learn the new, more difficult sounds.

He won't find it as difficult as you think. Remember, he has been pronouncing most of the words he will meet correctly in his speech for some time. He now knows most of the important phonics rules, and, if he doesn't recognize a word, you have taught him to figure out its meaning from the context.

So: First load up on simple stories. You can see if they are at his level by having him read a page, and count off a finger for each word he can't figure out. If he uses up all fingers and thumb (can't read five words), it's too difficult.

Second, read with him. Sometimes take it in turns. Read one paragraph to him, and have him read the next. Sometimes read the whole story to him—but *always* have him follow the words as you do so—and at other times have him read it all to you. Play it by ear according to the difficulty of the book and your moods.

Third, as he reads, have him sound out the words applying the rules he learned. If he has forgotten the rule, remind him of it, and later, when you have finished the story, play some games to review it with him.

Fourth, put the emphasis on COMPREHENSION. Ask him the meaning of words, and ask him questions to make sure he has understood what he has read. Be careful, as always, to make the questions enhance the story for him, not spoil it.

Fifth, if he comes to a sound he hasn't learned yet, give it to him. Then look it up in this section and spend the next lesson teaching it to him. Use the same kinds of games and activities you used to teach the other phonics rules, as well as the activities I give.

Step 1: Silent Letters

You can have fun with this lesson. Explain that some letters really like to fool you. Or perhaps they get shy. Whatever it is, sometimes they keep very quiet and have no sound at all.

Once he has learned a few of the words, he will soon get the idea. Also, his own speech will help him, for he has already learned how to say the words correctly.

RULE:

Sometimes letters have NO SOUND.

EXAMPLES:

K:	know	knew	knob	knock	knife	
	knee	knit	knot	knowledge	knuckle	
W:	write	wrote	wrap	wrong	whole	
	wreath	wrist	wreck	answer	wrong	
T:	often	soften	listen	glisten	fasten	
	whistle	hasten	rustle	bustle	hustle	
L:	half	calf	calm	palm	folk	yolk
B:	thumb	numb	dumb	crumb	lamb	
	comb	doubt	bomb	plumber	debt	
H:	hour	John	ghost	honest	rhythm	rhyme

ACTIVITIES:

1. Take each letter one by one. Read the words to him, and then ask him, "Which is the silent letter?" Have him underline the silent letter, and then read each word to you. Have him reread the words several times. Then give him activities like these to do.

2. Underline the silent letter in these words, and then read the words aloud:

knee	wrist	thumb	limb	knuckle
whole	knife	listen	half	wreath
fasten	wrong	knowledge	crumb	ghost
yolk	whistle	answer	doubt	knot
wrap	knit	often	writer	soften
hour	lamb	wrote	honest	calm

3. Find the rhyming words:

half	hour	knit	hot	listen	knife	wrote	kite
calf	our	knot	hit	life	glisten	write	boat

4. Fill in the missing vowels in the words to answer the riddles. Then read aloud the word and give the silent letter. You can also ask him the sounds of the vowels for review.

When you put all the parts together it's this.	wh__le	(whole)
Saying the truth is this.	hon__st	(honest)
A baby sheep.	l__mb	(lamb)
To give this in reply to a question.	__nswer	(answer)
When you do something frequently.	__ften	(often)
It comes between your arm and hand.	wr__st	(wrist)
It comes in the middle of your leg.	kn__ __	(knee)
They can come from cake or bread.	cr__mbs	(crumbs)
When you're not right you're this.	wr__ng	(wrong)
You cut with it.	kn__fe	(knife)
You can tie it in a rope.	kn__t	(knot)
You use your ears to do this.	l__sten	(listen)

5. Read these sentences and complete them with one of the words. Next, underline all the silent letter words in the sentences. Then give the silent letters in these words, and all the choice words:

Ann cut the cake with a knife and swept up the ______.
bombs thumbs <u>crumbs</u>

Jane wrote a ______ page in answer to her mom's letter.
ghost honest <u>whole</u>

In half an hour I will ______ up the presents.
wreck write <u>wrap</u>

Jack ______ it was John's ghost by the way he whistled.
know <u>knew</u> knot

They had ______ chops and calf's liver for lunch.
dumb <u>lamb</u> calm

The old ______ can't hustle and bustle like kids.
<u>folk</u> yolk whole

John fastened the ______ onto the door knocker.
wreck wring wreath

Dad said, "I ______ if we will get there in half an hour."
dumb debt doubt

6. Increase his word bank. Give him the meaning of the homonyms, and then have him put them in the correct sentences. Make sure he reads the completed sentences aloud.

hole: The dress had a big ______ in it.
whole: Jack ate the ______ cake.

knew: Mom gave Joan six ______ books.
new: Fred ______ he was going to be late.

ring: Patty liked to wear ______s on her fingers.
wring: Kathy will ______ out the washing and hang it out to dry.

knot: Marc's jump rope has a ______ in it.
not: "I will ______ comb my hair," said Tom.

need: I really ______ your help.
knead: Dad will ______ the bread.

write: Sandra held up her ______ arm.
right: Ethel will ______ a letter.

These are the trickiest silent letters. Don't teach them until he has learned the difficult vowel sounds (see later lessons for these):

GH: sleigh weigh eight freight neighbor caught
daughter naughty taught slaughter ought bought
brought sought thought fought though although
high sigh fight might light right sight flight
night blight bright slight fright
bough
straight

Other tricky silent letters:

C: scene muscle scent science scissors scenery
N: autumn column hymn
G: gnat gnaw sign resign reign campaign
S: island aisle
P: cupboard raspberry receipt

Step 2: Some Consonant Variations

The sounds in this lesson will take you two seconds to explain, but a good deal longer for your child to learn. So give him plenty of practice.

Explain that some consonants have sounds you don't expect, while sometimes two consonants work together to make the sound of one consonant. But once you know which these are, they pose no problem.

Lesson 1: The F Sound

RULE:

The F sound can be made by PH, and GH, as well as F.
The lauGHing dolPHin is a Funny Fish.

EXAMPLES:

PH:	phone	photo	dolphin	Philip	elephant
	phonics	graph	alphabet	nephew	Ralph
GH:	rough	tough	enough	cough	laugh

ACTIVITIES:

1. Don't teach this lesson until he has learned the unusual vowel sounds for the GH words. After you have explained the rule, introduced the example words, and played several games, have him do these activities:

2. Read these sentences and complete them with one of these words:

Phyllis can say the ______ fast.
pamphlet <u>alphabet</u> photograph

When will Philip take the ______?
<u>photo</u> phone phonics

Jack laughed so much he began to ______.
<u>cough</u> rough tough

Mom will teach Francis the ______ rules.
graphs <u>phonics</u> phones

Fred took a photo of the ______ at the zoo.
elephant telephone fruit

The boat trip was ______ and Francis had had enough.
tough enough rough

3. Put these words in their correct order so they make sense:

answered Mom phone the	(Mom answered the phone.)
meat Tom tough the chewed	(Tom chewed the tough meat.)
was the rough road	(The road was rough.)
boy coughed the sick	(The sick boy coughed.)
a took photo Philip	(Philip took a photo.)
the the swam dolphin sea in	(The dolphin swam in the sea.)
Dad's Ralph is nephew	(Ralph is Dad's nephew.)
elephant fed Fiona the	(Fiona fed the elephant.)

4. Underline the consonants that make the F sound in these words. Read aloud the words, and then write them in three columns under F, PH, and GH:

feet	photo	finger	phone	tough
graph	laugh	frost	elephant	fist
enough	flower	phonics	nephew	foot
forest	rough	fat	dolphin	fix
phonics	cough	foolish	Phyllis	pamphlet

5. Fill in the missing letters in the words to answer the riddles.

Add a tiny insect and you have a huge animal.	eleph___ ___ ___	(elephant)
Add a word meaning to cut and you have a relation.	nep___ ___ ___	(nephew)
If meat is this you have to chew it a lot.	___ough	(tough)
It can remind you of past events.	pho___ ___	(photo)
Someone who has no parents.	___ ___phan	(orphan)
It's made up of all the letters.	alpha___ ___ ___	(alphabet)
It lets you talk to people a long way away.	ph___ ___ ___	(phone)

When you do not want any more. ___nough (enough)

6. Read these sentences and complete them with one of the words. Circle all the words with the F sound in the sentences, and then underline all consonants that make the F sound in these words, and the choice words.

The ______ were playing in the sea as Ralph fished.
nephews orphans dolphins

Dad had a ______ time fixing the faucet.
rough tough enough

7. Match the meanings with the words and put them into sentences to show he really understands their meanings.

tough	rules to help you read
laugh	the opposite of smooth
rough	a small book, or brochure
phonics	something very strong or difficult
pamphlet	you do this when you are amused or happy

Lesson 2: The K Sound

RULE:

The K sound is made by:

K:	**key**	**CH:**	**choir**	**(this is the other sound of CH)**
CK:	**back**	**QU:**	**queen**	**(QU has the sound of KW)**
C:	**candy**	**QUE:**	**antique**	

EXAMPLES:

K: king kid kite keep milk market bake
CK: sick sock black block cricket jacket duck
C: cat can cot coat collar clap crisp
CH: chorus stomach school mechanic ache Chris
QU: quick queen quack quote quiz quit
QUE: antique unique physique technique

ACTIVITIES:

1. He's already learned that K, CK, and C have the K sound. However, it's just as well to remind him that C has the K sound *only* when it is followed by A, O, or U. Ask him why this is so. Hopefully he will remember it's because:

"When C is followed by E, I, or Y, it has the sound of S."

If he's forgotten this rule, review the lesson on C on page 208.

He should not come across many words with CH, QU, or QUE until he gets into much more difficult books, for there are very few words containing them, and most of them are fairly sophisticated. The best way to deal with them is on an individual basis as he comes across the words in his reading. Tell him the sound, pronounce the word, and then have him say it. Check to see that he knows the meaning of the word, as he may not have heard it before.

After he has met several CH, QU, or QUE words, do these activities with him.

2. Match the meanings with the words:

ache	something very old
quote	something different from anything else
antique	a dull pain
unique	another word for "to say"
quiz	someone who mends things
quit	weariness
fatigue	a test
mechanic	to give up

3. Fill in the missing letters in the words to answer the riddles:

Another word for tummy.	___ ___omach	(stomach)
The wife of a King.	qu___ ___ ___	(queen)
Add a small insect to make this old.	___ ___ ___ique	(antique)
A duck makes this sound.	qu___ ___ ___	(quack)
A group that sings.	ch___ ___ ___	(choir)
Where you go to learn.	sch___ ___ ___	(school)
When the earth moves.	qu___k___	(quake)
When parts are the same, they are this.	___qual	(equal)

4. Read these sentences and complete them with one of the words. Circle all the words with the K sound, and underline the letters that make it.

This chair is so old it is quite an ________.

physique technique antique

Jack gave a ______ when Dick squeezed the liquid.
squeal strike school

Chris ______ school because he wanted to work as a mechanic.
quote quite quit

The choir sang a ______ of the Christmas carol.
chord chorus cloud

Karen had a stomach ______ from eating so much candy.
ache sake take

Kitty squeezed an ______ amount of juice into the glasses.
quiz equal queer

"Don't ______ me on that," he said.
quit quill quote

Ted had ______ toothache.
chronic chrome chord

Lesson 3: The Sounds of S

RULE:

S usually has the sound you hear in Sam. But it can also have the sound of Z and SH.

Sam loves sugar.

EXAMPLES:

S: Sally sack silly cheeks seeds sand
Z: rose close leaves music frogs toes
SH: sugar tissue sure unsure insure issue

ACTIVITIES:

This lesson is mainly review, because I bet he has already been reading the "Z" words, relying on his own speech for pronouncing them correctly.

There are few SH words, so deal with them as you come to them.

Step 3: Some Vowel Variations

A positive approach is needed here! Emphasize the similarities rather than the differences. Explain that although there sometimes seems to be no pattern at all in our language, in actual fact there is, for the variations often come in "families."

These are the word families your child should know.

Lesson 1: Unusual Long Vowels

RULE:

Some vowels have a LONG sound when you expect them to have a short sound.

EXAMPLES:

Long O words:

The OLD family: old, bold, cold, fold, gold, hold, mold, sold, scold, told

The OST family: ghost, host, most, post

The OLL family: poll, roll, toll, stroll

Long I words:

The IND family: bind, blind, grind, find, hind, kind, mind, rind, wind

The ILD family: child, mild, wild

The IGH (silent GH) family: high, sigh, blight, bright, fight, flight, fright, light, might, night, plight, right, sight, slight, tight

ACTIVITIES:

1. After he has learned to pronounce the "families" correctly and played several games to practice identifying them, have him do activities like these:

2. Read the words aloud. Underline the vowel. Then circle all the words with a long vowel sound:

roll	rob	miss	most	cost	kid	child
chill	kind	stroll	doll	fright	fox	block
sick	high	lot	fold	frost	ghost	got
high	hit	sold	rock	quick	ship	gold

song lost right rip shop post pill
wild hot hold lip light top told

3. Find the rhyming words:

fight	mist	cold	colt	right	child	toll	box
fist	mind	Bob	bold	wild	write	fox	told
kind	might	bolt	cob	will	chill	fold	poll
miss	kiss	roll	toast	mild	find	night	kind
kite	high	most	told	rind	child	sigh	bite
my	tight	scold	pole	right	bite	bind	pie

4. Read these sentences and complete them with one of the words. Circle all the words with a long vowel sound:

This toy costs the ______.
boast post most

Jack ______ his Mom he had seen a ghost and was frightened.
toll toad told

Dad ______ the old clock each night.
finds winds blinds

Nan might find time to ______ the letters.
toast lost post

The cold wind blew his hat right out of ______.
fight might sight

That ______ is wild; he needs to be scolded.
chip cheese child

The ______ old man is a most kind host.
blind bind blink

They took a poll to ______ out who was most popular.
fight flight find

Ted sold his ______ coins to John last night.
bold gold goal

Mom folded in the flour and then ______ out the pastry.
sold told rolled

5. Increase his word bank. Have him give a word from one of the families that has the opposite meaning of these words (antonyms):

low (high) dark (light) least (most) hot (cold) let go (hold)
bought (sold) dull (bright) mean (kind) adult (child)
day (night) left (right) loose (tight) young (old) new (old)
praise (scold)

Lesson 2: More Word Families

RULE:

Some word families have very unusual vowel sounds.

EXAMPLES:

The ALL family: ball, call, fall, hall, mall, small, stall, tall, wall, almost, always, also, altogether (When ALL is added to the beginning of a word, one L is dropped.)

The ALK family: chalk, talk, walk

The ALT family: halt, malt, salt, Walt

The ALD family: bald, scald

A strange U family: bull, full, pull, push, pussy, bullet

An O family that has the sound of short U: above, dove, glove, love, shove, shovel

ACTIVITIES:

1. After following your usual procedure for introducing new sounds and words, give him activities like these to do:
2. Find the rhyming words:

halt	hall	scald	bald	dove	malt	wall	walk
ball	malt	ball	fall	mall	shove	talk	Walt
talk	chalk	full	bull	salt	stall	malt	tall

3. Fill in the missing letters in these words to answer the riddles:

You sometimes use this in cooking to make the food tastier.	_alt	(salt)
One way to get from one place to another.	_alk	(walk)
If you upset hot water on yourself you do this.	_ _ald	(scald)
They keep your hands warm.	_ _oves	(gloves)
The entrance to a house.	_all	(hall)
When you can't get anything more in, it's this.	_ull	(full)
The opposite to big.	_ _all	(small)
The opposite to push.	_ull	(pull)

4. Read these sentences and complete them with one of the words. Circle all the words that belong to the unusual word families:

Tom halted in the ______ before hauling his heavy case upstairs.

mall call hall

They ______ and pushed the car, trying to shove it out of the mud.

fooled pulled picked

"Put on your ______, as it's almost freezing," said Mom.

doves loves gloves

Jan ______ talks a lot when she goes for walks with Kathy.

almost also always

Tom played ______ against the old wall.

ball small call

Joan upset a ______ cup of hot milk and scalded her hand.

bull full fall

Wayne loves to ______ the snow and make a tall snowman.

shower shout shovel

The old man was almost ______.

ball bald scald

Walt put a lot of ______ on his lamb chop.

pullet pussy salt

Several doves flew ______ the tall houses.

altogether a lot above

5. Increase his word bank. Have him give a word that belongs to the unusual word families that has the same meaning as these words. (synonyms):

speak (talk) stroll (walk) stop (halt) hairless (bald)
not quite (almost) overhead (above) shove (push) filled (full)

Step 4: Some Tough Sounds

Yes, these are the real toughies. But apart from the sight words, and some rare exceptions, they pretty well wrap up phonics. How about that? Teaching the lessons wasn't so difficult, was it? And these aren't, if you both realize you are nearly at the end of the road!

So take a deep breath and get to it.

Lesson 1: Those IE and EI Words

Do you still have trouble reading and spelling those IE and EI words? Well, this lesson may even help you!

RULE:

The vowel team EI has the long E sound, but the vowel team IE can also have the long E sound.

EXAMPLES:

EI:	either	neither	ceiling	seize	receive	deceive
	deceit	conceit	perceive	leisure	weird	conceive
IE:	field	grief	belief	believe	brief	thief
	shield	yield	niece	piece	fierce	pierce
	achieve	relieve	chief	priest	shriek	tier

ACTIVITIES:

Have him read and learn these words. Go over the meanings, as he may not know some of them.

RULE:

The vowel teams EI and EY usually have the sound of long E. But sometimes they can have the sound of long A.

EXAMPLES:

EI, EY as long A:

eight	weigh	weight	freight	sleigh	neighbor
vein	rein	reindeer	reign	skein	veil
they	whey	obey	prey	survey	convey

ACTIVITIES:

1. After he has read and learned these words, and you have gone over their meanings, play games differentiating among these words and the EI and IE words. Then give him activities like these:

2. Circle all the words with the long E sound. Then underline all the words with the long A sound.

seize	obey	field	sleigh	pierce
neighbor	leisure	chief	reign	tier
priest	shriek	weird	chief	they
thief	reindeer	believe	prey	receive
shield	skein	veil	fierce	ceiling

3. Find the rhyming words:

achieve	wait	veil	pale	they	beef
seize	receive	prey	Wayne	grief	beard
weight	sneeze	skein	say	weird	play
priest	believe	sleigh	shriek	chief	leaf
deceive	feast	ceiling	tray	whey	weave
eight	late	peek	feeling	conceive	pray

4. Fill in the missing letters in these words to answer the riddles. Then underline the vowel teams, and give their sound:

The head of a tribe.	__ __ief	(chief)
Yarn often comes in this.	__ __ein	(skein)
You see them at Christmas if you're lucky!	rein__ __ __ __	(reindeer)
Laws are for you to ________.	__bey	(obey)
A relation.	__iece	(niece)
All rooms have one.	__eiling	(ceiling)
It carries blood around your body.	__ein	(vein)
Another word for "bit" or "part."	__iece	(piece)

5. Read these sentences and complete them with one of the words. Underline all the vowel teams, and give their sounds:

Ann gave a piercing shriek when she cut the ______ in her wrist.

pain <u>vein</u> vale

They were all relieved the _______ has been caught.
priest chief thief

"I _______ you deceived me," he said.
belief believe receive

The eight reindeer pulled the _______.
sleigh weigh weight

They seized the chance for a _______ time of leisure.
leaf beef brief

The priest was kind to the _______ family.
grieving achieving deceiving

Mom's _______ will not obey either her mom or her dad.
piece niece seize

Jan believes the neighbors will sell their _______.
field yield shield

6. Put these words in their correct order so they make sense:

niece is Jacky Dad's	(Jacky is Dad's niece.)
cake Dan piece a of had	(Dan had a piece of cake.)
a gave Pat shriek	(Pat gave a shriek.)
eighty weighed John pounds	(John weighed eighty pounds.)
must laws you obey	(You must obey laws.)
thief seized the the policeman	(The policeman seized the thief.)
ate lion his prey the	(The lion ate his prey.)
in field the grew corn	(Corn grew in the field.)

7. Match the meanings with the correct words:

yield	to take hold of	survey	to fool someone
seize	strange	achieve	a loud shout
gray	to give up	shriek	to accomplish
weird	what a king does	deceive	to look at
reign	a color	conceit	to be full of yourself

Lesson 2: More Words with the OO Sound

RULE:

"Foot" and "boot" are the usual sounds for OO. But:
UE, UI, OU can have the OO sound as in "boot."
OU can have the OO sound as in "foot."

EXAMPLES:

Unusual "boot"-sounding words:

UE: blue, clue, due, flue, glue, true, Sue, subdue

UI: fruit, juice, suit, bruise, pursuit, cruise, nuisance

OU: you, soup, group, troup, youth, route, wound

Unusual "foot"-sounding words:

OU: could, should, would

ACTIVITIES:

Use your usual procedure for teaching him new sounds and words. Go over the meanings, as there are one or two words he probably doesn't know. See after Lesson 4 for activity suggestions.

Lesson 3: Different Sounds for OU

RULE:

There are several pronunciations for OU.

EXAMPLES:

The usual way:	shout, amount, cloud, round, south, mouth
Long O:	dough, though, although, soul, mould
Short U:	The young southern country couple was touched with double trouble, and had a rough and tough enough time.
"Boot" OO sound:	you, soup, group, troup, youth, route, wound
"Foot" OO sound:	could, would, should
OR sound:	ought, bought, brought, fought, sought

ACTIVITIES:

Check that he knows the meanings of the words after you've introduced the sounds and words. See after Lesson 4 for some activity suggestions.

Lesson 4: More Vowels with R

RULE:

OR, OUR, and EAR can sometimes have the ER sound.

EXAMPLES:

OR: word, world, worm, worse, worst, worth, worthy, worship, actor, visitor, inspector, elevator, conductor, instructor, legislator, illustrator

OUR: journey, journal, courage, courteous, nourish, discourage

EAR: earth, earn, learn, early, heard, pearl, search, yearn, earnest

ACTIVITIES:

1. Check that he knows the meanings after he's learned the words. When he's done Lessons 2, 3, and 4, do activities like these with him:

2. Read aloud all these words, remembering how they should be pronounced:

journey	blue	wound	would	soul	fruit
youth	early	though	glue	journal	young
rough	double	heard	couple	mould	you
juice	soup	should	earnest	Sue	bruise
troup	enough	suit	route	worth	true
word	troup	touch	could	nuisance	nourish
country	due	world	tough	group	trouble

3. Find the rhyming words:

soup	wood	you	heard	pearl	loose
could	loop	word	cuff	blue	whirl
dough	sung	should	yew	route	crew
young	so	rough	good	bruise	boot
house	mouse	pearl	sow	soul	found
though	purse	hood	perch	round	droop
worse	trouble	search	curl	troup	hold
bubble	know	flow	would	mould	bowl

4. Fill in the missing letters in these words to answer the riddles. Then underline the vowels, and say what sound they have:

They're made up of letters.	_ords	(words)
It's usually juicy and sweet and grows on a tree or bush.	_ _uit	(fruit)
A jewel.	_earl	(pearl)
A color.	_ _ue	(blue)
It's your name.	_ou	(you)

When you fall you do this sometimes. ____uise (bruise)

Another word for trip. __ourney (journey)

A word for young people. __outh (youth)

When you want something very badly. __earn (yearn)

He moves along in sections. __orm (worm)

5. Read these sentences and complete them with one of the words. Underline the vowels in the words, and give their sounds:

Jack had just fruit ______ for his early breakfast.
soup glue juice

Sue ______ have learned her spelling words for homework.
wood would should

The youth ______ trouped along the road, but they were on the wrong route.
groove group grieve

Although they all searched for Mom's ______, they could not find them.
pearls peaches purses

Dick had courage. He journeyed on in spite of his ______.
would wool wounds

"This is the ______ soup I've ever tasted."
worse worst worth

I ______ that young couple were going on a world cruise.
heard hurt hoop

Mom had ______ getting the Jell-O out of the mould.
touch trouble tool

You should take the southern route, ______ it has the worst traffic.
dough rough although

The ______ was in trouble. He forgot his words.
inspector actor visitor

6. Put these words in their correct order so they make sense:

fruit Joyce the drank juice (Joyce drank the fruit juice.)

nourishing soup is hot (Hot soup is nourishing.)

for the earthworm an searched bird (The bird searched for an earthworm.)

Mom dough the kneaded (Mom kneaded the dough.)

should words her learn Sue (Sue should learn her words.)

blue Clyde a suit has (Clyde has a blue suit.)

got early Dad up (Dad got up early.)

soon cruise ship the due is (The cruise ship is due soon.)

7. Increase his word bank. Have him give one of the words he's learned in Lessons 2, 3, and 4 that has the same meaning as these words (synonyms):

earth (world) seek (search) trip (journey) serious (earnest)
correct (true) batch or bunch (group) pair (couple)
uneven (rough) hurt (wound) follow (pursue)
polite (courteous) twice the amount (double)

8. Give him the meaning of these homonyms, and then have him put them into the correct sentences.

would: Dad made a camp fire from the dry ______.
wood: I ______ go if I had time.

blue: Nan wore her new ______ dress.
blew: The wind ______ strongly.

heard: The ______ of bulls were being rounded up.
herd: I ______ that on the news.

due: The club fees are ______ next week.
dew: The ______ on the grass glistened in the sun.

flue: The bird ______ up into the tree.
flew: The ______ of the chimney would not open.

route: The tree has huge ______s.
root: We'll take this ______ to Uncle Jack's.

Lesson 5: Some More Unusual Vowel Sounds

RULE:

Some words with O have a SHORT U sound.

EXAMPLES:

son, won, ton, come, some, none, done
month, other, mother, brother
above, dove, love, glove, shove, shovel (already learned in Lesson 2)

RULE:

Sometimes A has the sound as in WANT. It often has W before it when it has this sound.

EXAMPLES:

war, warn, ward, toward, outward, forward, awkward, award, reward, wardrobe, dwarf, quart, quarter, swarm

ACTIVITIES:

1. After you've reviewed these sounds and words separately and played several games, see if he can identify them when they are mixed up. Do activities like these with him:

2. Read these words aloud, remembering how they should be pronounced:

wash	want	forward	other	wardrobe
done	quart	water	come	brother
wasp	above	awkward	wander	waffle
none	warn	shovel	month	son
mother	won	wand	swarm	

3. Fill in the missing letters in the words to answer the riddles, and then read the words aloud:

You do this to get clean.	_ash	(wash)
Another word for clumsy.	_ _kward	(awkward)
The opposite of daughter.	_on	(son)

The opposite of sister. ___other (brother)
Wasps do this. ___arm (swarm)
Two pints make this. ___art (quart)
To go ahead. ___ward (forward)
When you eat you do this. ___allow (swallow)
A vegetable that is green or yellow. ___ash (squash)
When you do not have any. ___one (none)

4. Read these sentences and complete them with one of the words. Underline all the words learned in this lesson and then write them in groups with the same sound:

Mother washed and swabbed Ted's _______ sting with warm water.
was wasp want

I want some gloves to keep my hands _______.
won wand warm

Fred swallowed the _______ in one big mouthful.
waffle shovel reward

A quart of milk will be a _______.
awkward quarter wardrobe

Ethel's dad _______ an award in the war.
done none won

Nan and her _______ Frank watched the swallows in the swamp.
mother other brother

I will give a _______ to whoever finds my watch.
award reward forward

Mother warned Joan not to go near the _______ of wasps.
swarm ward wand

Marc's back felt as though he had shoveled ten _______ of snow.
sons doves tons

Next _______ the squash should be ready to eat.
month some come

5. Increase his word bank. Have him give one of the words he's learned in this lesson that has the same meaning as these words (synonyms):

clean (wash) finished (done) four weeks (month) wish (want)
look at (watch) two dimes and a nickel (quarter)
hottish (warm)

6. Give him the meanings of these homonyms, and then have him put them into the correct sentences:

son: Dad took his ______ to the game.
sun: The ______ shone in the blue sky.

one: Ted ______ the race in record time.
won: I'll have ______ piece of cake, please.

some: Kathy found the ______ difficult.
sum: I'll have ______ more cake, please.

Lesson 6: Some Special-ending Sounds

RULE:

When LE comes at the end of a word it sometimes has the sound of UL.

EXAMPLES:

apple	candle	eagle	people	turtle	needle
bubble	table	handle	knuckle	purple	sparkle
marble	thimble	steeple	sample	rifle	circle

ACTIVITIES:

1. After he's learned the words, have him do activities like these:
2. Match the syllables so they make a word:

mar	tle	lit	ple	sprin	dle	han	dle
tur	ble	ea	ble	ri	ple	nee	kle
gig	ple	trem	tle	pur	kle	spar	cle
ap	gle	sam	gle	poo	fle	cir	dle

3. Give a rhyming word for these words:

table	(Mable)	kettle	(settle)
pickle	(tickle)	handle	(candle)
bubble	(trouble)	cuddle	(huddle)

4. Fill in the missing letters in the words to answer the riddles:

A color.	_urple	(purple)
He carries his home with him.	_urtle	(turtle)
It gives light.	_andle	(candle)
It comes between your leg and your foot.	_ _kle	(ankle)
You have several on your hand.	_ _uckles	(knuckles)

You boil water in it. __ettle (kettle)
The referee blows it. __ __istle (whistle)
It's hard to figure out. __uzzle (puzzle)
Water makes this. __uddle (puddle)
You can blow them. __ubbles (bubbles)

5. Read these sentences and complete them with one of the words:

Mother wore her ______ coat with a silver buckle that sparkled.
apple turtle <u>purple</u>

Sam ran across the pebbles to ______ in the sea.
puddle <u>paddle</u> pickle

Jan got out her ______, thimble, and thread to mend her torn skirt.
steeple feeble <u>needle</u>

Dan juggled the apples and ______ a tune.
<u>whistled</u> tickled scribbled

The baby gave a ______ as Dad tickled her.
buckle <u>chuckle</u> candle

The naughty boy jumped in the ______, and got wet up to his ankles.
muddle cuddle <u>puddle</u>

John knocked sharply on the door with his ______.
needles paddles <u>knuckles</u>

Ann ate an apple and drank a ______ of Coke.
kettle <u>bottle</u> thimble

Lesson 7: More SH Sounds

These are all tricky sounds and difficult words, so don't tackle this lesson until you have to!

RULE:

The SH sound is usually made by SH. Occasionally it is made by S (sugar, sure).
The SH sound is also made when words have SI, TI, or CI endings. ALL SI, TI, and CI ENDINGS HAVE UNUSUAL PRONUNCIATIONS.

EXAMPLES:

Sion, tion, cian: SHUN

action nation division addition television occasion
station expression mention magician explosion musician

Tious, cious: SHUS

precious delicious cautious spacious ferocious

Tial, cial: SHUL

facial social partial residential commercial

Tient, cient: SHENT

ancient patient impatient efficient

ACTIVITIES:

1. Most of these words are too difficult for your child to understand until he has a pretty wide vocabulary. However, if you choose the easier words, you can play games to help him learn their sounds and meanings. And you can give him activities like these to do:

2. Underline the SH ending, and then read the word aloud.

precious commercial nation magician occasion
ancient delicious station patient destination
invention admission cautious physician efficient

3. Find the rhyming words:

delicious residential facial racial station cautious
commercial ferocious ancient patient nation spacious

4. Fill in the missing letter in these words to give the names of the people:

Someone who plays a musical instrument.	m__sician	(musician)
Another name for a doctor.	__ __ysician	(physician)
Someone in politics.	__ __ __itician	(politician)
Someone who looks at your eyes.	__ __tician	(optician)
Someone who does people's hair.	__eautician	(beautician)
Someone who works with machinery.	t__chnician	(technician)
Someone who works with electrical things.	__ __ectrician	(electrician)
Someone who does magic	__ __ __ician	(magician)

A Summary of the Main Sounds: Options for Reading

Vowels

A vowel is SHORT when: a syllable has only one vowel and ends in a consonant:

cat pet hill sock cup rab-bit hap-py pup-py

A vowel is LONG when:

a syllable ends in a vowel	go di-et
a syllable ends in the magic (silent E)	time
two vowels come together (the first one is sounded and the second is silent)	coat

Long A:	a	a–e	ai	ay	ei	ey			
	apron	cake	sail	say	eight	they			
Long E:	e	e–e	ee	ea	ei	ie	y		
	equal	these	beets	meat	either	piece	happy		
Long I:	i	i–e	ie	y	igh	-ind	-ild		
	I	dime	pie	cry	right	find	child		
Long O:	o	o–e	oa	oe	ow	ou	-old	-oll	-ost
	go	bone	boat	toe	snow	dough	gold	roll	most
Long U:	u	u–e	ue	ew					
	music	cube	rescue	new					

Special Vowel Team Sounds:

OU, OW: cloud, clown OI, OY: boil, boy EA: bread AU, AW: auto, draw

OO sounds: "foot" sounds: wood, would "boot" sounds: moon, blue, chew, you, fruit

Sounds for OU: cloud, dough, rough, soup, could, bought

Vowels with R:

AR: star OR: fork, warm AIR: chair, stare, bear

ER: her, bird, curl, learn, journey, word

Other Tricky Vowel Sounds:

More sounds for: A: ball, talk, salt, scald, wash U: pull

O: love, some, glove, mother I: native, police

Consonants

C: K sound before a, o, u: cat, cot, cut — S sound before e, i, y: cent, city, icy

G: G sound before a, o, u: gate, got, gun — J sound before e, i, y: gem, ginger, gypsy

S: sand, rose, sugar

TH: that, thin CH: church, ache, chef GH: tough, ghost, eight

F sound: frog, laugh, phone

K sound: key, back, candy, choir, queen, antique

Silent Letters: know, write, often, half, thumb, hour, autumn, scene, sign, island, cupboard

Some Special Endings

ED: planted (ed) jumped (t) climbed (d) LE: apple (ul)

SH endings: SHUN: division, nation, magician SHUL: commercial

SHUS: precious SHENT: patient

Step 5: Increasing His Vocabulary

He now knows all the major phonics rules. But continue to work on his sounds so his reading fluency and speed increase.

The most important aspect now is to increase his vocabulary and comprehension, so he can read more difficult and sophisticated stories and books. The best way to do this is to explain unfamiliar words *as they arise in the context of the story.* However, you can also keep up your games and activities to increase his word knowledge. Here are some word lists that might be helpful.

Sight Words

These are some commonly used sight words your child should know. See if he can read them. If he can't, try going over a few each night with him.

any	beautiful	been	blood	both	break
broad	build	bury	busy	buy	canoe
chef	do	does	door	eye	false
flood	floor	four	friend	give	gone
great	have	heart	has	his	is
key	laugh	live	lose	many	move
of	off	one	once	pretty	prove
said	sew	shoe	sieve	steak	sugar
sure	the	to	too	two	view
who	whose	woman			

Homonyms

Homonyms (those words which sound the same but have different spellings and meanings) often pose a problem. You have already taught him some in the lessons. But here is a list of the most common ones, which you might like to go over with him when you have that odd spare moment together, such as waiting at the doctor's or going on a journey. Introduce them as a game as usual, but make sure you teach him the words as part of a sentence so he can see them working in their context:

break—brake
beat—beet
weak—week
team—teem
see—sea
peak—peek
way—weigh—whey
rain—rein—reign
fare—fair
seam—seem
pain—pane
feet—feat
threw—through
dear—deer
tail—tale
cheap—cheep
stair—stare
pail—pale
steal—steel
claws—clause
berry—bury
principle—principal
bored—board
course—coarse
heard—herd
whose—who's
hole—whole

sail—sale
meet—meat
bare—bear
steak—stake
main—Maine—mane
hair—hare
read—red
read—reed
ate—eight
earn—urn
blue—blew
bread—bred
bough—bow
cellar—seller
piece—peace
hall—haul
soar—sore
wood—would
sleigh—slay
weather—whether
to—too—two
bolder—boulder
cord—chord
your—you're
not—knot
so—sow—sew
male—mail
one—won
straight—strait
sum—some

tide—tied
tow—toe
new—knew
there—their—they're
waist—waste
hoarse—horse
pore—pour
flower—flour
sent—cent—scent
road—rode
ring—wring
die—dye
fourth—forth
here—hear
right—write
gate—gait
heel—heal
capital—capitol
key—quay
fur—fir
be—bee
aloud—allowed
due—dew
loan—lone
wear—ware—where
taught—taut
roll—role
lesson—lessen

Prefixes and Roots

These are for much later, when your child is really reading well. He may meet one or two of them in the third or fourth grade, but he won't meet most of them until much, much later. As you can see the words are difficult and sophisticated. I have included them because they can increase your child's vocabulary by leaps and bounds. If he can "translate" the meaning of prefixes and suffixes (all those Greek and Latin words we have "borrowed" to form many of our words), he can break words down into their parts and often figure out their meanings.

Prefixes come at the beginning of words. "Pre" is a prefix meaning "before."

All these prefixes mean "not," or the opposite. When they are attached to the beginning of a word they reverse its meaning:

un—unhappy	dis—disorder	mis—misspell	im—impatient
in—informal	ir—irregular	il—illegal	a—atypical

in and im can also mean: into, insight, import

Other common prefixes are:

ex	out of	exit
de	from	depart
pre	before	prefix
pro	forward	proceed
ante	before	anteroom
co	with	co-operate
bi	two	bicycle
auto	self	automobile
inter	between	international
hetero	different	heterogeneous
micro	small	microscope
pan	all	panamerican
peri	round	perimeter
tele	far	television
trans	across	transport
re	again, go back	refill
ad	to	advance

sub	under	submarine
per	through	perceive
post	after	postpone
semi	half	semicircle
hemi	half	hemisphere
anti	against	antitoxin
intra	within	intramural
homo	same	homogeneous
ortho	straight	orthopedist
poly	many	polygram
syn	together	synthetic
super	beyond	supernatural
hyper	above	hypertension

These roots form the basis of a wide variety of words in our language:

pos, pons	to place	position
duce, duct	to lead	deduct
scrib, script	to write	script
mis, mit	to send	transmit
dict	to say	dictate
cede, ceed, cess	to yield	recede
fort	strong	fortitude
flect, flex	to bend	flexible
meter	measure	thermometer
fac, fact	do, make	factory
voc	call	vocation
chron	time	chronology
pel, puls	to push	propeller
spec	to see	spectators
ject	to throw	inject
tract	to pull	tractor
tain	to hold	container
vers, vert	to turn	reverse
cred	believe	credible
equ	even	equal
ped	foot	pedal
junct	join	junction
volve	roll, turn	revolve
phon	sound	phonics

PART FOUR:

Now That Your Child Can Read: Some Suggestions for Developing Interest and Comprehension

CHAPTER 10

Getting Your Child to Read and Enjoy Books

Books are like food. Your child "eats" what he's given, and enjoys what he's used to. If you surround him with books as he grows up, he'll automatically reach for one when he's bored, or has some free time, just as he automatically reaches for a chocolate-chip cookie or a crisp juicy apple when he's hungry. So have lots of books in your home. Big books, little books, fat books, thin books, hardbound, paperback, and for the very young, fabric books. But be sure they are *fun* books, full of interesting, exciting, and enthralling stories and information, covering as wide a variety of topics as possible: adventure, mystery, biography, fantasy, comic, folklore, poetry, sports, science, nature, and, of course, reference. And don't forget if you can't afford all the books you'd like to have, there is always the public library not far away, which can supply you with an ever-changing supply.

Take books with you when you go on a trip in a car—not only on long trips, but also when you think you might have some spare time, such as waiting for Mom while she's in a store, or for Dad to arrive on the commuter train. Take them on camping trips to read at night around the campfire. Take them on hikes and picnics to read when you take a rest. Take them to the park to read under a shady tree. And take them to Grandmother's so she can read them with your child—she'll love that!

Finally, don't forget that your child is the great imitator, so let him see *you* enjoying reading.

When Your Child Goes to School

Most parents spend as much time as possible with their child when he is young, doing the things we've been discussing. However, once he goes to school, it's a different story. They may not be like Mrs. Seager, whom I heard say at a cocktail party:

"Well, I've done my bit with Betty. Now, it's the school's turn to take over."

But many do think they can leave reading entirely up to the school. This is not so. Your child needs your help and encouragement as much, or even more, than before. This is because he now reaches a critical time in his reading "career"—he is learning to actually read. He feels very grown up, and is excited about every new sound and word he conquers. But the reading material, naturally limited to the easiest words and the most simplified stories, is not the most inspiring. It's not at all like the enthralling books you have been reading to him for so long.

"It's baby stuff," he complains to you. "The stories are silly and dull. I don't want to read them."

And, if you are not careful, before you know it, he may be completely turned off reading. But if you keep your reading sessions together going, you can counterbalance this. You can sustain his interest during this trying period, and keep alive the magic of words for him by reading him the most gripping, enjoyable, and amusing books you can lay your hands on.

Devote part of your time to having him read from his schoolbooks so he can practice his newly learned skills, but also let him be the guide as to how much time you spend on them. If he is eager to show off, by all means let him, but don't let them consume the entire session.

As Your Child Begins to Read

As your child gets older and his reading skills and fluency increase, shift the reading emphasis from you to him. This gives him much-needed practice and gives you a chance to check whether his reading skills are improving. Search out simple, high-interest reading books, and have him read these, along with the books he brings home from school. However, continue to read aloud to him. "Don't you think he's too old for that now? Surely he should be doing all the reading?" parents often ask me when I tell them this.

Your child still needs to be read to because, first of all, it helps to improve his skills. Hearing the way you read, and listening to your inflection, rhythm, phrasing, and pauses provide a model for him to copy, and, if you have him read along with you, it exposes him to new words and their sounds. It doesn't necessarily teach him to read these words, but it certainly makes them more familiar, and easier, to learn when he meets them in his reader.

More important than this, it gives your child pleasure, and is the best possible way to sustain his interest and enjoyment in reading. You make the characters come alive, and every event in the story just that much more exciting. You make his spine tingle with suspense as you lower your voice at the crucial moment of a mystery, and make him laugh when you mimic the characters. In short, you make books entertaining, real, and irresistible for him.

At the same time, by reading aloud to your child, you can expose him to all sorts of intriguing, challenging, and sophisticated stories that he is still not yet able to read. For example, if he has enjoyed watching "The Little House on the Prairie" or "Sounder" on television, you can read him their "origins." You can introduce him to some of the marvelous books he will want to read over and over again later on, such as E. B. White's *Charlotte's Web, The Trumpet of the Swan,* and *Stuart Little;* Roald Dahl's *Charlie and the Chocolate Factory;* and all the Beatrice Potter books. And you can read books that might not appeal to him if he were left to read them on his own. A large majority of children today find the old classics pretty heavy going. They have a hard time wading through the long sentences, unusual words, old-fashioned expressions, and many Anglofied colloquialisms. Yet when they are read them they really enjoy them. Some you might try are: Lewis Carroll's *Alice's Adventures in Wonderland* and *Through the Looking Glass;* Kenneth Grahame's *The Wind in the Willows;* Rudyard Kipling's *Jungle Book;* and Robert Louis Stevenson's *Treasure Island.*

When you read longer stories like these, "serialize" them so that you read short excerpts each day. Don't read too much at one time, and always try to end at a particularly exciting moment (like the television serials) so he will be eager for the next day's session.

It is a good idea to continue your reading sessions together for most of your child's elementary school years, for this is the time you need to instill the reading habit so strongly he becomes addicted to books for the rest of his life. And this is the time, believe it or not, that he will have the most time for leisure reading.

As he gets older, and his reading really develops, encourage him to read more and more to himself. Still have him read aloud to you, so you can check his improvement, and occasionally read to him, but now try to turn him into an independent reader. Don't abandon him when he is reading on his own. Stay near him, ready to answer a question, explain a word he doesn't understand, give an opinion, or just be a listener to whom he can describe an exciting event in the story or a strange or interesting character. If possible, try to read the book he is reading, so you can discuss it together (see page 292), for this makes it much more fun, interesting, and meaningful.

Your child will never forget his reading sessions with you. They will be among his happiest childhood memories (and probably among your happiest memories, too).

Choose Appropriate Books

Mrs. Turner was concerned because her ten-year-old daughter, Sally, was showing no interest in reading.

"It's not that she can't read," she told me. "In fact, her teacher says she reads very well for her age. It's just that she *won't* read. She shows no interest whatsoever in books. All she can think about these days, it seems, is horses. She's down at the park every day watching the rangers training their horses, and helping to groom them. What should I do? I've collected various lists of recommended books, and get lots of them from the library, but to no avail."

"Let me look at those lists," I said, and scanned through them. I was familiar with most of them, and they were all books I would have recommended. However, I also noticed there was not a single one on horses! I commented on this, and the light dawned on Mrs. Turner's face.

"Why, how stupid of me," she said. "Of course—I should have got her some books on horses! Can you suggest some?"

"Sure," I replied. "There are lots of horse books a ten-year-old will love." And I gave her Marguerite Henry's *Misty of Chincoteague,* and its sequel, *Sea Star;* and Walter Farley's *The Black Stallion, The Black Stallion and Satan,* and *The Island Stallion* for starters. I also suggested that she start reading aloud *The Yearling* to Sally before she went to bed each night.

Your first consideration in choosing a book for your child is *whether it appeals to him.* Don't worry about all the recommended books, or whether the book is "good" for him. If you do the kinds of things we have been discussing, he will get around to those "good" books eventually, and perhaps even enjoy them! But he won't unless you link his reading with *his* world. So if he is enthralled with bugs, cats, or dinosaurs, get him books on these. If you have just been on a trip to Yosemite, and he was fascinated by the rock formation, the incredible redwood trees, or the beautiful wild flowers, search out rock, tree, or flower books. Or if he has decided he is going to be a great dancer, or musician, get him Noel Streatfield's *Ballet Shoes* or a biography on Mozart, the child prodigy.

And be prepared for your child to go through "fads" in his reading. My student, Jimmy, went through a period when he would read nothing that was not on boats. Julie, on the other hand, wanted "any book, as long as it's funny." Whatever your child's fad may be—sports, mysteries, or science fiction—accept it for what it is, and be happy he is reading! However, at the same time, use his interests to introduce him to as many kinds of literature as possible. Get him a biography of a sportsman, a poem on space, or a good science book on space exploration. Use your imagination, and be subtle. But *never* force a book on your child!

Make sure that the books you choose are at your child's reading level. No matter how interested he may be in the subject, if the vocabulary is too difficult, he will soon become frustrated, or bored, or both. The best way to judge if a book is at his level is to ask him to read a page you select at random. Then have him count off on his fingers each word he can't read. If he can't read five words before he has completed the page, its probably too difficult for him.

It's also important not to go to the other extreme, and choose books that are too far below his reading level. It's fine to have easy ones for fun-type reading, just as it's good for him to reread old favorites. But it's also necessary to have ones that challenge him enough so that his reading constantly improves.

Your best guideline in choosing an appropriate book is to consider its purpose. Is he going to read it on his own? If so, it should be fairly easy, particularly if he is going to read it silently to himself. Is it to be informative, to be read to find out more about a particular interest or hobby? If so, it can be more difficult as you can help him with the words he doesn't know. Is it to be what I call a "rainy day" book? A pure "escape" book? If so, it should be well within his reading capacity. On the other hand, if it's specifically to develop his reading skills, it should challenge him as much as possible. However, any book you choose for this should be short, so it's a realistic challenge, or it should be read in "bite sizes." You should also explain to your child, "This one is really difficult but I thought you would like to try it as your reading is coming on so well." This will give his self-image a boost and generate enthusiasm to tackle it. But when he does read it, be sure to be nearby so you can help him with the words or passages he finds difficult. Remember to congratulate and praise him when he manages to figure out unknown words and finally finishes the book.

If you are going to read the book aloud to him, it can be well above his reading level, for you can help him understand the more difficult vocabulary by your intonation and expression. You can also stop and explain words he doesn't understand. However, if you have to do this often, it means the book is not for him yet. Too much stopping breaks the continuity of the story, which in turn spoils its impact and appeal.

Although children enjoy comics and the odd mediocre escape book (don't we all?), you will find that the reading materials that really hold their interest are the ones that are well written and tastefully presented.

They revel in stories that are imaginatively told, gasping with delight at the colorful use of words, similes, and metaphors. They are enthralled by language that is so intense and powerful that it makes an event, or character, seem real. They love being caught up in a clever author's web of words, and being made to smile, shed a tear, shiver in suspense, shudder in horror, or sigh with relief. In short, they enjoy stories that are so well told they become totally involved, heart and soul, as well as mind, in their events.

It's not easy to select books of good caliber, especially when you consider that more than a thousand new children's books appear on the market each year! One method is to consult your local children's librarian; the manager of the children's section of a bookstore; or your child's teacher or school librarian. Another is to refer to the book lists published by organizations such as the American Library Association, the Children's Book Council, or the Association for Childhood Education International (for more, see page 430). You can refer to the book lists that periodically appear, especially around Christmastime, in magazines and newspapers. These are usually well researched and comprehensive, but most refer only to recent publications.

Another guide to excellence in children's books can be found in the Newbery, and Caldecott Award, lists. They provide the titles of books that have been chosen respectively as "the most distinguished contribution to American Literature for children" and "the best-illustrated book for children," each year. The equivalent to these in Great Britain, which is also useful to know, as so many British books appear in our bookstores, are the Carnegie Medal, for the outstanding author, and the Kate Greenaway Medal, for the most distinguished illustrated book. Other important American awards include the Laura Ingalls Wilder Award and the Regina Medal Award.

You will find a list of book suggestions, categorized under age and subject, beginning on page 365. The following are general guidelines to use in making your own selections.

What to Look for When Choosing a Suitable Book for Your Child

•First glance through the book quickly to get an initial impression. Ask yourself: "Would my child enjoy reading this book? Is it appealing? Does it have something to say? Is it entertaining, enriching, and instructive? Do I want him to spend the next week, or so, reading it? Will it be time well spent and enjoyed?" If you have a negative reaction to any of these questions, put the book down right then and there and go no farther.

•Try to find out if the book is on a recommended list. See if the author is well known, if he's written other books, and how popular they are.

•Check the publisher. If it is a well-known house you can usually be pretty sure that the subject of the book has been well researched and the author is an authority in the field.

•If the book is fiction, see that the story is simple and straightforward, with plenty of action. See if it's true to life, or contrived, for even fiction should be believable. Are the characters realistically presented and can your child relate to the events? I always look to see if the book contains humor, not sarcasm or cynicism, which are beyond children's comprehension, but the direct kind of humor that appeals to them. Not all books should be humorous, of course, but a light touch is always a plus in winning a child's interest.

•Study the subject matter. Is it constructively and positively presented, and as far as you can judge, accurate? Compare its presentation with other books dealing with the same topic, and see how it stands up to comparison.

•Observe the author's writing style. Is it distinctive? Does it have a special quality? Is it explicit? Does it flow easily? Is it grammatically correct, uncomplicated, but not oversimplified? Are slang and colloquialisms avoided? Are words used imaginatively and in good taste? Do they make the story or subject matter *come alive?*

•Look at the illustrations, because they play a very important part in children's books. Not only are they the No. 1 attraction for most children, but also they are usually a good indication of the content of the book, because they reflect the author's philosophy and approach. Look to see if they are attractive, colorful, realistic, tastefully and simply executed, and have "character." An example of the best kind of illustrations for children's literature can be found in Beatrice Potter's books. They are simple, alive, and always make you want to smile.

•Consider the book's physical characteristics, because children often decide whether they want to read a book by its appearance. Does it make you want to pick it up, touch it, and finger through its pages? If it has an attractive, pretty cover, uncluttered pages, print that is clear and easy to read, and paper that looks and feels nice, your child will probably want to read it. Size is also important. If a book is excessively large, or extremely small, he will have difficulty in handling it, and consequently be unlikely to enjoy reading it for long.

If you are buying the book, it's also a good idea to check that the book is well bound and durable—for you never know, it may become one of the favorites, and it would be a catastrophe if it were loved to pieces. This is not to say that paperbacks should be excluded. Many of the finest children's books are available now in paperback editions, and they are a remarkably inexpensive way to expand your child's library. The only problem is that they tend to fall apart with too much handling, and especially the vigorous handling of the typical youngster. You can remind your child to "be careful," but you must also be careful not to mar his enjoyment of the book by making stipulations that are hard to keep.

Choosing your child's first books is one of your most important tasks, for the fun, or boredom, he asssociates with them will largely determine his future attitude to reading. It requires thought and time on your part, and it involves much more than going to the library or bookstore and randomly taking a book off the shelf in the children's section.

Be assured, however, that nobody is as well qualified as you, for no one knows your child's interests, hobbies, dreams, likes, and dislikes better than you. You are the best judge whether a book will grip him with delight or receive a completely negative reaction. Except for one person—your child!

Involve Your Child in the Choice

There is no better way to choose appropriate books and stimulate your child's interest in reading than to involve him in their selection. This is obvious and natural, and yet how few parents do it. It is very likely he will select some poor books, but it is just as likely you will too! On the whole, however, you will find he is quite perceptive and critical in his choice, and the sense of participation it gives him is much more likely to make him want to read the books.

The best method is to make the choice together. You guide your child as far as the literary quality is concerned, and let him guide you as far as its general appeal is concerned. Remember, you can always give him a little "nudge" into a new direction if he is choosing the same kinds of books, or ones on the same subject.

Make Trips to the Library and the Bookstore

The sooner you take your child to the library and local bookstore, the better the chance he will develop an interest in what they have to offer. Include him in your visits when he is still a baby. If you don't go regularly, start doing so now. They will then be familiar places, and the visits a natural part of his life.

As soon as he is old enough, explain the appropriate behavior in libraries and bookstores, so he won't be embarrassed by making mistakes or doing something wrong, such as speaking in a loud voice or muddling up the books on the shelves. If he knows what is expected of him, he will also be better able to concentrate on his choice of books. When he is still older (around the second grade) show him where to find the different types of books: fiction, biography, science, and so on. Encourage him to select from these different sections so he varies his reading matter. When he is about nine or ten introduce him to the card catalogue in the library, so he can begin to look for special books, or ones on particular subjects. He will feel very proud when he can do this, and it will give him a sense of "power" that will, in turn, increase his interest.

Introduce your child to the children's librarian so they become acquainted. You will be thrilled with the outcome of this personal contact. Having been specially trained in children's literature, she can offer him a wealth of information far beyond your limited knowledge. But more than this, once she knows your child, she will very likely give him special attention, and perhaps even slip him a "goodie" now and then, such as a new book. If she offers a "story hour," which most librarians do, have your child attend. He will not only love this, but it will show him that other children love it too—which all helps to instill in him that reading is something everybody does and enjoys.

Give Your Child a Library of His Own

One of the most effective ways to interest your child in books and reading is to give him a library of his own. This is not as impossible as it may sound, because it's not something you do all at once! If you did acquire a whole library overnight, it would not only be expensive, it also would not achieve your purpose—for the sudden appearance of such a vast number of books would probably so overwhelm your child that he would not know where to begin, so not begin at all! Also, it's very likely you would tend to buy books just to "make up" the number, rather than for their particular appeal to your child.

No, the fun is in acquiring a library, and the way it will stimulate, and sustain, your child's interest is by *gradually* collecting books as he needs or wants them. Then they will be tailored to his growing and changing interests and needs, and will be loved, treasured, and *used*.

There is no substitute for ownership to make something seem special and important to a child. Make it clear from the start that this is *his* library. If he knows that the books are specifically for his pleasure and use, he will not only develop a great pride in them, but he will also want to continually refer to them. They will become beloved friends and play an important part in his life.

Provide a special area where he can keep his books together. This not only furthers his sense of ownership, but also helps him keep them in an orderly fashion. Also, he is far more likely to read them if he knows where he can always find them. The best place is his bedroom, as this is already his private domain. However, if this isn't possible, a few shelves set aside, perhaps with a sign saying "Billy's Books," will do. If you have more than one child, the best arrangement is to provide one area for the books they commonly own and share, and another for their own special books.

Wherever the library is set up, see that it's accessible and that the shelves can be reached easily. A highly suitable and adaptable bookcase can be made from unfinished hardboard cubes about eighteen inches square with one open side, which can be bought fairly cheaply at the lumber store. They can be lined up, or stacked, if you fasten them to the wall. And if you paint them in bright colors, they look very attractive.

However, these cannot accommodate the larger books. An alternative that does, and that is even more adaptable but less stable, is to use plain boards and bricks. You can adjust the height of the shelves to any size book and easily add more as the library expands. Then, of course, you and your child can build a "proper" bookcase together. If you do this be sure to measure the books you already have so that each one has a "home."

The best way to encourage your child to use his library is to set up an area nearby where he can read and enjoy his books. See that it is quiet, away from distractions, with good lighting and a pleasant setting. Give him a nice big comfortable chair in which he can curl up, or a soft rug he can sprawl on, or preferably both of these. You can also add a desk and chair for homework and more serious study. Make him responsible for keeping this area in an orderly, neat fashion. Let him arrange the area as he wishes, just as you should let him organize his books on the shelves in his own way. This doesn't mean you can't offer helpful suggestions, such as grouping the books under special categories, but the final decision should be his. Children are more orderly than you may imagine, and, although his organization may not be clear to you, you can be sure that it's meaningful to him. And that, of course, is what matters!

Once you have acquired a good basic library, keep your child's interest alive by gradually increasing it through birthday and Christmas presents and other special-occasion gifts. Suggest to grandparents and other relatives and friends who take a special interest in your child that they give books sometimes, instead of games and the inevitable candy. To ensure they choose ones you know he will enjoy, give them a list of titles, subjects he is currently interested in, and most important, are at his reading level. Remember, there is nothing more frustrating to a child, and likely to put him off reading, than a book he can't tackle. When it is a special present, it makes it even worse.

Don't limit the acquisition of books to special days. In fact, probably the best time, in terms of stimulating your child's interest in reading, are those very "ordinary" days when nothing much is going on, and he is eager for something to do. What better opportunity to pop down to the bookstore, have him select a book, and come home and read it! And, if the piggy bank isn't too full, you can drop into the library and get a temporary addition to his library!

Other good times to capitalize on are cold, wintry days, which are a bane to all youngsters. On days such as these, your child will thoroughly enjoying roaming around a bookstore or library choosing a book, and dashing home to read it in a nice warm place. Stifling hot midsummer days are equally good, as bookstores and libraries are usually air conditioned.

Another successful way to stimulate your child's interest in books, and at the same time build up his library, is to have him join a book club. There are some very good ones now for children. Belonging to his own club will make him feel very important, and he will eagerly wait for the mailman to bring the latest offering. Also, as he knows the books are specially for him, he will avidly read each and every one he receives. (See page 429 in the appendix for a list of book clubs.)

Another alternative is for him to have his own private book club. Have him save up money each month or so (you can add a little extra to his pocket money for this so he doesn't have to give up other things he wants), and then go down to the bookstore to make his own selection. By the way, when you make these trips, only go when you have plenty of time, for there is nothing more frustrating than saving your money up for a long time and then be hurried into making your choice. It's like dreaming of a delicious meal and then being told you've only two minutes to eat it in!

Not all the books need necessarily be new to capture your child's interest. He will be delighted with a hand-me-down from an older child he admires, and thoroughly enjoy a book "scavenged" from the inevitable secondhand bookstall at the local church bazaar or school fair. He will be quite happy to trade the books he doesn't want to keep in his permanent library with a school, or neighborhood friend, and, believe it or not, he may even enjoy those books *you* enjoyed as a child and have packed carefully away in the attic.

To make your child's library most beneficial, include as many different kinds of books as possible, and don't forget to add a children's magazine or two. They have special appeal for youngsters because they are more current than books and have a wide variety of articles and stories. These are always fairly short with simple vocabulary, and so are quick and easy to read. They also usually include various kinds of activities that are fun to do, such as puzzles, cutting out, simple experiments, and things to make—and that often require careful reading to do! (See list in the appendix page 427.)

Let Your Child Read Anything and Everything

Not all the literature your child reads will be the kind you will want him to keep in his permanent library. However, this doesn't mean you should prevent him from reading it. Let him read anything, and everything, for the more he reads, the more he will want to read. And the more he reads, the better he will be able to discriminate between good and inferior literature. Let him read the inevitable comics. They are pretty harmless, and I am quite sure you still read the cartoons in the daily newspaper, and probably before anything else, too! If you have started him off early with the reading habit they will become merely casual, fun-type reading, just as they are for you.

If you introduce your child to excellence from the beginning, and give him interesting and enjoyable books that stretch his imagination and grip his emotions, he will grow up convinced that reading is worth all the time and effort. He will come to love his books, just as he loved his stuffed animals and all his other toys when he was a toddler. And he will be well on his way to becoming a lifelong reader.

CHAPTER 11

Ways to Help Your Child Get the Most out of a Book

Reading a book merely at the level of an interested reader naturally has its benefits and brings enjoyment. But, as in music and art, knowledge of its finer elements can greatly increase understanding, appreciation, and satisfaction. This chapter will hopefully help you know more about literature so you can help your child appreciate its finer points.

But a word of caution. Don't overdo the "reading appreciation." Don't delve too deeply into books until your child is reading fluently with good comprehension, and is into the more involved, and sophisticated books (he should *at least* be reading the kinds of books listed for seven- to eight-year-olds at the end of the book). Wait until he has become a regular bookworm, is *eager* to go into a book more thoroughly, and is mature enough to handle and *enjoy* it. Even then, don't do it with every book he reads. Select certain ones that you think will be particularly enhanced by a more thorough scrutiny.

As usual, you will have to rely on your parent intuition in deciding which books to choose, and how thoroughly to go into them, and, of course, on your child's reaction. He will let you know if he is not interested. His eyes will glaze over, he will begin to fidget, and suddenly he won't be so eager for your reading sessions together.

However, if you think of yourself as a friendly guide, whose role is to make reading as pleasurable as possible, you won't go far wrong.

Read the Book Yourself

Start by reading the book yourself! This, I'm afraid, takes time. But you can't possibly help your child understand it better unless you know what it's about. And read it *before* he does, so that you can prepare him for unfamiliar situations or references; give him background information if the story takes place in another country or historical period; and provide him with other relevant and interesting "tidbits," such as telling him about the author and his reason for writing the book. This means homework for you. But it's well worth it, because it enables your child to relate to the book much more easily.

Let Your Child Get a General Impression First

When you introduce a book to your child have him glance through, or "scan," the entire book first. Let him look at the cover, the chapter headings, the length of the chapters, the illustrations, and any introductions or comments by or on the author. This not only gives him a general impression and "feeling" for the book, but also arouses his interest and curiosity.

Ask Questions

The best way to help your child get the most out of a book is to ask him questions about it. But don't ask too many, or you will spoil rather than enhance his enjoyment. Limit them to a few relevant ones, which help him to:

•Understand generally what the book is about, so he sees the relationship and significance of all the facts, details, and events.

•Note its main aspects and events, so he doesn't miss a crucial point; and the order in which they occur, so he follows the writer's train of thought and reasoning.

•See the facts as they are present (and not muddle them with facts he has learned elsewhere) and interpret them in relationship to the book as a whole.

•Understand words in their context.

•Summarize and evaluate what he has read, discriminating fact from opinion, recognizing points of view, drawing conclusions, and making judgments.

In fact, point out the main, essential points necessary for him to fully *comprehend* what he is reading.

To make these questions as meaningful as possible, relate them to specific incidents and unique characteristics in each particular book. For example, instead of saying, "What are the characters like?" ask more perceptive questions, such as, "Why do you think Mr. Mole talked that way? What does it tell you about him?" or, "What is the significance of the clothes Cinderella and the ugly sisters wore? What does it tell you about the way the stepmother treated them?" or, "What did the other children in the neighborhood think about Mary? How do you know this?"

Ask your questions in such a way that he can answer them *successfully*. If he is incorrect, don't tell him he is wrong, or give him the answer. Instead, raise more questions, and subtly draw his attention to the key points so he eventually gets them. And don't ask "trick" questions, because this will only frustrate him and make him lose interest in the book.

The more absorbed your child becomes in a book, the more he will get out of it. Therefore, don't be so eager with your "helpful" questions that you interrupt his train of thought and cause him to lose the thread of the story. Try to gauge the appropriate time to ask them—when there is a natural break in the story, such as at the end of a conversation, or description, or at the end of a chapter. Sometimes wait until he stops and asks you a question. Don't feel you always have to ask him the questions immediately after he has finished reading, although this is usually the most helpful, for there will be occasions, particularly if he has been reading for a fairly long period, when he will want to dash outside and play or do something active. If this is the case, store up your questions and ask them later when he is more receptive.

Personalize It

Things always mean much more if they are personalized, so relate the book to his own life. Help him to compare the experiences, ideas, and values he is reading about with his own. Ask him if he agrees or disagrees with the opinions stated by the characters, or if he would have done the same thing given the same situation. These may seem sophisticated aspects to discuss with a youngster, but they are by no means beyond him, especially if you began raising them early on in your reading sessions together.

Encourage Your Child's Own Interpretations

Be careful not to bias his opinion about the book when you ask your questions. He will get much more out of it if he is left to formulate his own ideas, and conclusions, as this will force him to *think* as he reads. Your role is to ask the kind of questions that draw his attention to the key aspects and important details, so that he has sound criteria to base his judgments on. You can begin doing this with his very first picture books, by asking him such things as: "What has the dog got in his mouth? Where do you think it came from?" instead of saying, "Look, the dog has stolen the bone." "What is the girl doing? Why do you think she is doing that?" instead of, "Oh dear, the girl is crying because she's lost her kitten."

Another way you can help your child read between the lines is to ask him to put what he has read into his own words. This makes him focus on the key points and shows you if he has missed an important detail or misinterpreted it in relationship to the context of the story.

As he grows older and his experience with books increases, you can also have him compare one book with another. Ask him to tell you the similarities as well as the differences. And have him say why he preferred one more than another.

Remember that the purpose of your questions is to further your child's understanding and enjoyment of a book. So make sure he is not reading just to answer your questions! (as children often do at school, I'm afraid). If this happens, he will never learn to enjoy a book for its own sake, nor experience that meaningful personal interchange, or communication, with the author that results in true insight into his thoughts. The best way to focus his attention on the book, rather than on your questions, is to gradually encourage him to formulate and answer his own. You can help him do this by having him first ask *you* questions. He will love doing this, and it will give you a chance to see if he is asking the right kind. See if they help him recall facts and events accurately. Are they ones that probe, that help him understand the book's significant points and deeper meanings? If they are not, you can help him by saying: "That question was too easy. Give me a more difficult one that really makes me think." or, "I can't give you the answer to that because the book doesn't tell me about it." He will soon get the idea, and subconsciously will start formulating and answering questions as he reads.

By putting the initiative onto your child, you encourage him to become an *independent* reader, which, of course, is your ultimate goal. It is only when he need no longer rely on others that he will really get the most out of a book.

Help Your Child to Assume Certain Responsibilities

Before he can become a truly independent reader you must also help him to assume other responsibilities, the most important being the ability to decipher the meaning of a new and unfamiliar word. You can, and should, teach him how to use a dictionary, so he can look it up. But this is not the most satisfactory method, because it causes a break in his reading. A much better way is to show him how to figure out the meaning of the word by seeing it in the context of the sentence, or paragraph, in which it appears. This keeps his attention still focused on the book, and makes it less likely for him to lose the gist of the story. Another disadvantage of using the dictionary is that it offers so many definitions of a word, he is quite likely to choose the wrong one, and so still be no farther in understanding its meaning. Also, if he gets into the habit of using the dictionary frequently, he may begin to use it as a crutch, and thus actually become less independent than before.

One of the best ways you can help your child see the relationship of words is to show him how to read in phrases, those "gulps" I talked about in explaining the reading process. This will also help him to increase his speed and fluency, which in turn improves his comprehension. But here again, your child must assume the responsibility. No matter how many reading skills and techniques you show him, he won't increase his speed or comprehension unless he has the determination, patience, and desire. This means that somewhere along the line you must also help him to develop certain personal characteristics that enable him to meet the challenges of reading. (See Chapter 3, "The Importance of Emotional and Physical Well-being.")

You must particularly help him to concentrate so that he can become totally involved in the book. And, above all, you must help him to react to what he is reading. It's not until he can respond to the thoughts, ideas, and feelings expressed, as well as perceive their implications and relationships, that he will get the most out of a book. One specific way you can help him do this is to suggest that he underline important parts of the book, mark significant passages, or jot down his impressions or ideas in the margin. Many parents discourage or even admonish their children for doing this, saying it shows a lack of respect, or "reverence," for books. However, you will find he has a much better feeling for what the book says, and develops a much closer rapport with the author, if he can add his reactions as he reads. Also, the fact that he has contributed something, however minor or little it may be, tends to create a bond between him and the book, which draws him back to it again. And when this happens, he may find points previously missed and new aspects to appreciate and enjoy.

Your Child Must Have the Intention

Of course, you will never be able to help your child get the most out of a book unless *he* has the intention of getting the most out of it! The best way to encourage him to have a positive approach is to give him a reason for reading the book. This is easy, because no matter what the book is about, there is always a reason for reading it. The joy of books is that each one has something to tell, and a special reason for its existence. So even if he doesn't have a personal reason for reading the book, such as to find out about shells so he can organize his collection, he can always read it to "see what it has to say." If he learns to approach a book in this way, he will probably find that a book, which at first didn't appear particularly interesting, had something to offer after all!

Make Your Child Aware of the Author's Techniques

As your child matures and his tastes, along with the books he reads, become more sophisticated, you can further his appreciation of what an author is saying by making him aware of *how* he is saying it. A writer is like a composer in that he uses different methods and techniques, according to the thoughts, ideas, and feelings he wishes to express. It is the way he uses and combines these that ultimately decides the effectiveness and success of his work. However, in helping your child delve more deeply into the finer aspects of a book you must see that he never loses sight of the book as a whole, for then he will come away with a disjointed, confused impression, rather than a clearer understanding of what the author is saying.

Make Your Child Aware of the Different Literary Forms

The best way to help your child appreciate the various methods and techniques that authors use to convey their "messages" is to introduce him to the different literary forms early on in your reading sessions. It's also a good idea to refer to them by their names fairly soon, as this helps him to differentiate among them and gradually recognize their essential qualities and characteristics. So instead of saying, "Let's read this," get into the habit of saying, "Let's read this story [or rhyme or poem]."

Gradually, as your reading sessions progress, draw your child's attention to the unique characteristics of each literary form, *but* do it in an unobtrusive, casual way so that it highlights, rather than distracts from, the essential substance of the work. For example, when you read a poem to him, comment: "That had a nice jingle, didn't it?"

or, "Weren't the words fun? Did you notice how some of them had the same sound?" or, "Did you notice that some of the words sounded like the rain they were describing?" or, after reading a description of a garden, say, "My, I could almost smell those flowers the way he described them. Weren't his words vivid?"

If you develop your child's reading appreciation subtly and quietly in this way, you will find he will not only enjoy each book much more, but he will also become a truly critical reader capable of evaluating a story, poem, or book objectively on its intrinsic merits. It is, of course, when he reaches this stage that he appreciates them to their fullest.

Fiction

Fiction is popular with all ages, but particularly with children. It's full of excitement, laughter, pathos, mystery, adventure, and romance, for it encompasses just about any and every subject. There are stories about animals, goblins, and gnomes, people from outer space, and even talking flowers and furniture. It can be in the present, the past, and the future. And yet, for all its variety, fiction has one essential characteristic: It is always based on real-life situations. Although fictional works are often referred to as "stories of make-believe," and the author "makes up" a story, they are nevertheless interwoven around some identifiable human experience. Thus, although Beatrix Potter's books are about animals, all the things they do are essentially human. Mrs. Tiggy-Winkle cleans her house. Jemima Fisher goes fishing. And poor Peter Rabbit gets punished. Likewise, although the characters act somewhat strange in Lewis Carroll's *Alice* books, they are easily identifiable as human beings, and they participate in normal, everyday happenings, such as a tea party (remember, Carroll was English!). Even Alice's remarkable change in size occurs through a simple act we do so frequently we never think twice about it—taking a drink.

As you read various stories with your child, help him to see this subtle intermingling of fancy with fact. But, more important than this, help him to blend them together in his imagination so they become a very real and meaningful experience for him. As I said earlier, the more he can personalize the events he reads about, and feel part of them, the more he will enjoy the book.

You can make a story come alive, and more significant, for him by drawing his attention to the part played by the events, the characters, the setting, and the author's style, for these are the four basic means the author uses to tell his story.

The Events

The events are the most vital aspect of fiction, for they provide the excitement and suspense that keep the reader turning the pages to see "what happens next."

You can make the events meaningful and exciting for your child by seeing he doesn't "read over" or miss the important ones, and that he understands their significance in relationship to the story as a whole. With his first books this is simply a matter of asking, "And then what happened?" for the stories are simple and the events usually follow each other in a natural time order. For example, in *Cinderella,* the ugly sisters go to the ball leaving Cinderella behind; then the fairy godmother arrives and transforms her, then she arrives at the ball and falls in love with the prince, and so on.

However, as the books become more complex, the author presents the events in the order in which he feels they will have the greatest impact on the reader. So instead of describing them as they occur in real life, he switches back and forth, from the present to the past, and even, sometimes, to the future. The scenes that go back in time are called "flashbacks," and are usually introduced to provide necessary background information. The scenes that go forward in time are called "foreshadowing." They suggest a future outcome, and are used to arouse the reader's curiosity or heighten the suspense.

The best way to help your child see a logical pattern in these events is to explain, as I do to my students, that a story is like a jigsaw puzzle. Just as you have to put together all the pieces to form a complete picture, so you have to weave together all the events to understand the story. You can also point out, however, that the events do fall into a logical pattern in that they always gradually build up to a climax, and then resolve themselves into some kind of conclusion. You can help him spot the key events that bring about the climax, pinpoint the climax, and ask him to predict the outcome.

The Characters

The more closely your child can identify with the characters and share their emotions and feelings, the better he will understand and appreciate their role in the story. You can have a lot of fun helping him gain an insight into their personalities. The most obvious is to have him note the descriptions of their physical characteristics, such as their facial features and physique, the clothes they wear, and the way they walk, for this is the main way an author depicts his characters. However, you can also draw his attention to the kinds of things they say, such as the opinions or preferences they express. How much, for example, we learn about Mr. Mole through his simple statements. You can have your child "listen" to the words, grammar, or dialect they use, as these indicate the kind of people they are; or observe the kinds of things they do, such as the way they react to certain situations, and the choices and decisions they make; and the kinds of things they say about one another.

Most of the characters your child "meets" in his early storybooks are pretty stereotyped—the wicked fox, the good fairy, the mischievous monkey, the kind, poor couple, and the beautiful princess or heroine. However, soon, even in some of the books listed under my suggestions for third- and fourth-graders, the key characters are more fully developed and become more like real people. They have weaknesses and strengths, loves and hates, and fears and desires. They often undergo some personality change, or acquire a new awareness of themselves, or life, through some experience related to the story. Make your child aware of these factors, and help him see the relationships among the various characters and understand their roles, so that he shares their emotions and feelings and sees the world in terms of their values. It is only when he can do this that he will completely understand why they do the things they do and see them as they really are.

The Setting

The more feeling your child has for the setting, and the more vividly he can picture it, the better he will be able to interpret the story as a whole. It not only provides the background against which the action of the story moves, by telling of its geographical location, the period in history, and the social milieu of the characters, but it also plays a significant part in the characterization and gives meaning to the events.

I have already suggested that you give your child background information if he is not familiar with the environment of the book. However, understanding the setting is more than just knowing about the place, or area, in which a story occurs. It is being able to capture the mood, or atmosphere, created by the author, and this can be achieved only by *guiding him back to the book*. Make sure he doesn't miss important details in the descriptive passages. Draw his attention to the less obvious, subtle means the author uses, such as the way he describes the characters' clothes (are they dark and drab, or bright and colorful?) and the weather (is it stormy and overcast, or sunny and clear?). An author, also, often uses the comments of the characters to create a certain mood, or feeling, so make your child aware of the relevance of these too. By helping him understand and "see" the setting, you help him to feel the "power" of the story —so much so, that he may even be moved to laugh aloud, or have a quiet cry. When this happens you know he has truly appreciated and enjoyed the book, for we love a good cry just as much as a good laugh!

The Author's Style

The author's style, more than any aspect, give a book its unique personality and individuality. It is this that enables him to describe the same scenes, people, and events as other writers, and yet create very different pictures or interpretations for the reader.

His style is affected by his personality, experience, and the era in which he lives. This is partly why the children of today are not "sold" on the old classics and writers like Dickens. Their works contain "old-fashioned" words, and long, elaborate, and complicated descriptions, typical of an earlier period. But they love E. P. White, whose terse, crisp, and functional narrative is "right on."

Don't stress the author's writing style in your discussions with your child, but subtly make him aware of it by drawing his attention to such things as the tone of the book. He needs to know whether it's serious, amusing, whimsical, or sarcastic, so he can interpret the story correctly.

If the author uses sophisticated techniques, such as symbolism (when he uses characters and situations to represent other characters and situations), don't go into it until you are quite sure he is mature enough to understand it. For example, you will only spoil the story of *The Tortoise and the Hare* if you try to make it anything more than a simple race between two animals, when you first read it with him. However, when he goes back to it later, you can explain how the tortoise symbolizes one type of individual, while the hare symbolizes another type, and the race is a depiction of the conflicts and competitions that occur in human society. Likewise, when he first reads *The Lord of the Flies,* help him to enjoy it merely as a rather exotic adventure story. Only later show him how each character symbolizes an aspect of man's personality, and that the story is really an analysis of man's relations with each other.

The more you can help your child appreciate an author's use of symbolism, the more fascinated and involved he will become in the story—at least that is what I find with my students. This is especially the case when the author blends together every aspect of his book—the events, the characters, and the setting—to create a complete, little imaginary world, or "microcosm," to comment on the larger world we live in, as Golding does in *The Lord of the Flies,* Melville does in *Moby Dick,* and Swift does in *Gulliver's Travels.*

It is, of course, the author's words, and how he uses and manipulates them, that explain the events, bring alive the characters, describe the setting, and tie them all together to tell the story. However, here again, don't constantly draw your child's attention to the words. Don't "analyze" passages to "see why they're effective." More teachers have ruined books for children by doing this, for not only is it boring and annoying, but it also destroys the general impression the author is trying to create. As the saying goes, he will not be able to "see forest for the trees." Instead, point out a particularly vivid word, colorful simile, or effective phrase or sentence that *specifically* helps him to understand a situation or character better and see them more clearly in his imagination. When a writer creates special sounds and rhythms to create a certain effect or mood, have him "listen" to the words as he reads them. For example, when he reads *Moby Dick,* point out how Melville's description of the sea makes you almost hear the lapping of the sea, and feel its rolling motion, when you listen to the wonderful, rhythmic pattern and blending of the similar-sounding words:

> It was while gliding through these latter waters that one severe moonlight night, when all the waves rolled by like scrolls of silver, and, by their soft, suffusing seethings, made what seemed a silvery silence, not a solitude: On such a silent night a silvery jet was seen far in advance of the white bubbles at the bow. Lit up by the moon, it looked celestial; seemed some plumed and glittering god uprising from the sea.

This passage is an excellent example of a writer's masterly use of language, even though its style is somewhat "old-fashioned," for every single word contributes to the total effect. Let's hope when the time comes for your child to read *Moby Dick,* he will appreciate its power and beauty, for then he will truly participate in the enthralling and exciting adventures in *Moby Dick*. And you will know you have succeeded in helping him get the most out of fiction.

Poetry

The literary form that relies most heavily on effective use of language is, of course, poetry, for unlike the fiction writer, who has almost limitless possibilities to develop his ideas, the poet is confined to a limited number of words. Each one, therefore, is chosen with infinite care and thus each one needs to be observed carefully, rather as you would look at a jewel—holding it up to the light and turning it to catch and savor its many colors and sparkles. Yet, when you first introduce poetry to your child, don't draw his attention to the words. This is not only because he may not understand all their meanings, but also because you want him to respond to it generally, as he would to a piece of music; for poetry is much like music in that it must be experienced in its totality to be appreciated.

Poetry has something more to say than just the meaning of its words. If this were not the case, the writer could just as well, and much more easily, write a few informative sentences. No, the uniqueness, value, and appeal of poetry, and the way it differs from prose, lies not so much in what it says but in *how* it says it—and even beyond this, in some intangible that can never be fully explained or analyzed. Unlike fiction, which unfolds a story, or an article in a magazine that gives specific information, poetry conjures up a picture, or image, that appeals to all our senses, and involves us so totally that reading it becomes an experience in itself. Notice, for example, how Robert Louis Stevenson's delightful but simple poem creates a reaction in you that goes beyond just feeling and seeing the sun.

Summer Sun

Great is the sun, and wide he goes
Through empty heaven without repose.
And in the blue and glowing days
More thick than rain he showers his rays.

Though closer still the blinds we pull
To keep the shady parlor cool,
Yet he will find a chink or two
To slip his golden fingers through.

The dusty attic spider-clad
He, through the keyhole, maketh glad;
And through the broken edge of tiles
Into the laddered hayloft smiles.

Meantime, his golden face around
He bares to all the garden ground,
And sheds a warm and glittering look
Among the ivy's inmost nook.

Above the hills, along the blue,
Round the bright air with footing true.
To please the child, to paint the rose,
The gardener of the world, he goes.

If you introduced your child to nursery rhymes when he was young he will have already learned to go beyond the words to sense the mood and feeling of a poem. Didn't he react to *The Grand Old Duke of York* by briskly clapping his hands, and gently rock when you read him *Rock-a-bye Baby?* And that of course is what poetry is all about—it must be reacted to before it can be truly understood.

Some good poems to introduce your child to early on are those by Robert Louis Stevenson, Dorothy Aldis, A. A. Milne, and Henry Behn. He will enjoy them because they are about familiar subjects that he can relate to—for example, such things as going to bed, which A. A. Milne describes so delightfully in one of my favorite poems, called *In the Dark:*

> I've had my supper,
> And *had* my supper
> And had my supper and all;
> I've heard the story
> of Cinderella,
> And how she went to the ball;
> I've cleaned my teeth,
> And I've said my prayers,
> And I've cleaned and said them right;
>
> And they've all of them been
> And kissed me lots,
> They've all of them said, "Good night."

Or about the rain, which Longfellow depicts so well in *Rain in Summer,* making us hear it as well as see it, particularly in the second verse, which goes:

> How it gushes and struggles out
> From the throat of the overflowing spout!
> Across the windowpane
> It pours and pours;
> And swift and wide
> With a muddy tide
> Like a river down the gutters runs
> The rain, the welcome rain.

Or about eating, as in this fun one:

> I eat my peas with honey,
> I've done it all my life.
> They do taste kind of funny
> But it keeps them on the knife.

Or about household mishaps, which an anonymous poet puts rather well in this poem, called *Mr. Nobody:*

I know a funny little man,
As quiet as a mouse,
Who does the mischief that is done
In everybody's house!
There's no one ever sees his face
And yet we all agree
That every plate we break was cracked
by Mr. Nobody

'Tis he who always tears our books,
Who leaves the door ajar,
He pulls the buttons from our shirts
And scatters pins afar;
That squeaking door will always squeak,
For pantries, don't you see,
We leave the oiling to be done
by Mr. Nobody.

The fingermarks upon the door
By none of us are made;
We never leave the blinds unclosed,
To let the curtains fade.
The ink we never spill; the boots
That lying round you see
Are not our boots—they all belong
to Mr. Nobody.

Poems like *Mr. Nobody* are also good in accustoming your child to the unusual word order that poets often use to create a special effect, or develop a certain rhythmic pattern. But don't point this out to him unless he specifically asks about it, for the fewer explanations the less likely you will destroy the "magic" of the poem.

Introduce your child to as many different kinds of poetry as possible, so he grows up understanding that it can cover the widest variety of topics, ideas, moods, and feelings, and is not limited to just "serious stuff" or descriptions of "babbling brooks" or the "joys of nature," as one of my students complained.

You can have a lot of fun with humorous poems, such as the "peas" one quoted above. And poems by Edward Lear in his *Complete Book of Nonsense,* and by Lewis Carroll and John Ciardi. Your child will also enjoy the gentle humor of Dorothy Aldis, the more daring humor of Alfred Noyes, and the "tongue in cheek" humor of Ogden Nash.

Then, of course, he will love adventure poems, or poems that "tell a story." They are exciting, and they are also good for helping him follow a poet's thoughts to their logical conclusion. Particular favorites with youngsters are: Edward Lear's *The Owl and the Pussycat* and *The Walrus and the Carpenter,* both of which have the most delightful choice of words, and enchanting rhythms; *The Pied Piper of Hamelin; There Was a Crooked Woman* (which is especially popular for its repetition); *The Duel* by Eugene Field, and, of course, all the adventures of Christopher Robin and his friends.

Don't avoid the sad poems. You will be surprised how your child empathizes with them. They can be about a lost pet, the passing of summer, the "death" of a flower, or a poor pig who could not jump, as in Lewis Carroll's *The Melancholy Pig:*

There was a pig who sat alone,
  Beside a ruined pump.
By day and night he made his moan:
  It would have stirred a heart of stone
To see him wring his hoofs and groan,
  Because he could not jump.

Or a moving story of a blind boy, such as the one by Calley Cibber:

The Blind Boy

O say what is that thing call'd Light
  Which I must ne'er enjoy:
What are the blessings of the Sight:
  O tell your poor blind boy!

You talk of wondrous things you see;
  You say the sun shines bright;
I feel him warm, but how can he
  Or make it day or night?

My day or night myself I make
 Whene'er I sleep or play;
And could I ever keep awake
 With me 'twere always day.

With heavy sighs I often hear
 You moan my hapless woe;
But sure with patience I can bear
 A loss I ne'er can know.

Then let not what I cannot have
 My cheer of mind destroy:
Whilst thus I sing, I am a King,
 Although a poor blind boy.

This poem is more suitable for older children, and yet many ten- and eleven-year-olds can identify with it. When you read poems like this with your child help him to go beyond the pathos, and identify what the poet is really saying. For example, Cibber is saying that the poor blind boy is not really poor, but quite happy in his blindness. If you can do this, you certainly will help him get the most out of a poem.

Other kinds of poems your child will particularly enjoy are ones about animals, particularly if they are about his pet cat, dog, rabbit, or turtle; special days, particularly if you read them on the particular day; things he has just done, such as going on a camping trip or a picnic; or things he has just seen, such as a lion at the zoo or an eagle on a hike. A beautiful, compact description of an eagle, by the way, can be found by Tennyson. In only six lines he captures every aspect of this majestic and cruel bird. Read it to your child sometime and see if you can help him to see the eagle as Tennyson does.

The Eagle

He clasps the crag with crooked hands;
Close to the sun in lonely lands,
Ringed with the azure world, he stands

The wrinkled sea beneath him crawls;
He watches from his mountain walls
And like a thunderbolt he falls.

Use this poem, or one like it that illustrates a remarkable use of words, to show your child how poetry differs from prose. Have him look up the description of an eagle in the encyclopedia, and compare it with Tennyson's. Ask him what differences he notices in the two descriptions. They both tell a lot about an eagle. But which one reaches beyond its feathers, beak, and wings, and bares its soul? And which one helps him understand an eagle better, and perhaps even share his experiences?

Have your child read aloud *The Eagle* so the words have the greatest impact on him. See if he speeds up when he says the last line. If he does, you know he has experienced the poem as Tennyson wanted him to.

Always encourage your child to read the poems aloud, for poetry is written to be heard. It can only be truly appreciated when meaning, and sound, are blended into a harmonious whole. Sometimes suggest he learn a poem, or part of one, by heart. Then he won't be hampered by the format of the poem, and can really put feeling into the words. This is not as difficult for him as you might think, for children find it fairly easy to memorize, particularly if the thing to be memorized is enjoyed and has a catchy rhythm. In fact, I bet he already knows most of those old favorites you have read together over and over again. Try him out and see!

Don't, however, ever force your child to learn a poem. And be sure he *never* recites it parrot fashion as a "party piece"! The only reason for him to memorize a poem is so that he can appreciate and *enjoy* it more. Not so he can become a showman.

As you introduce your child to the greater poets, and the poems become more sophisticated, he will need more help interpreting the language. This is because poets use certain literary techniques that need to be understood to be fully appreciated. This is a difficult time for you because, on the one hand, you must help him understand the special meanings and connotations, and yet, on the other hand, you mustn't let him lose sight of the mood or feeling the poet's trying to convey. It is a time when your child is most likely to lose interest and be "turned off" poetry. So forewarned is forearmed!

You can prevent this, in part, by introducing him to the works of the masters early on so that he's already familiar with them. The best poetry book for this is *A Child's Book of Poems,* with pictures by the superb artist Gyo Fujikawa (see publisher and other books illustrated by her under "Tips and Titles"). It has the most marvelous collection of poems by such poets as Blake, Browning, Coleridge, Dickinson, Emerson, Herrick, Keats, Longfellow, Rossetti, Shakespeare, Shelley, Stevenson, Tennyson, Wordsworth, and many more. I recommend this book to all my students, and, in fact, many of the poems included here can also be found in it.

The literary technique most frequently used by poets is figurative language. This is the use of comparisons, or "figures of speech," to make descriptions more effective. They are popular with poets because they convey a great deal in a very few words, or, as one writer said, they "say more with more intensity." At the same time, they conjure up vivid images by appealing to our senses. They emphasize significant points and details giving them greater impact, and give the emotional intensity that is unique to poetry.

The best way to deal with these figures of speech is to explain them only when they are really necessary to understand the poem as a whole, or a particularly significant detail or description. Even then, do so fairly quickly—avoid any deep analysis!—so you don't disrupt the continuity of the poem or destroy your child's interest. It's better that he miss some of the depth and power of a poem, if discovering it takes away the enjoyment!

The following are some of the most commonly used figures of speech. I include them to help *you* identify and interpret them. Don't use the terms with your child. Just make sure he understands their importance in the context of the poem he is reading.

Similes are probably the most commonly used. They compare two unlike things, and are usually introduced with the words "like" or "as."

Examples: He swam *like a fish.*
They were quiet *as mice.*
I wondered lonely *as a child.* (Wordsworth's *Daffodils*)
The moon *like a flower.* (Blake's *Night*)

Metaphors make a comparison boldly, and directly, stating one thing *is* another.

Examples: He is *a little demon.*
Her dress was a *dream.*

Tennyson uses metaphors in *The Eagle.* Did you notice them? First, he uses one to describe the eagle:

"He clasps the crag *with crooked hands.*"

And then he uses one to describe the sea:

"The wrinkled sea beneath him *crawls.*"

Personification gives the attributes, or characteristics, of a human being to objects, animals, or even abstract things, such as ideas.

Examples: The skies *wept.*
The thunder *roared* in anger.
"----- *a lady, sweet and fair,*
Who comes to gather daisies there."
(Blake describing the moon)

A very good poem for introducing personification to your child is *The Snowman,* for a snowman already seems like a real person:

Once there was a snowman
Stood outside the door
Thought he'd like to come inside
And run around the floor,
Thought he'd like to warm himself
By the firelight red;
Thought he'd like to climb up
On that big white bed.
So he called the North Wind, "Help me now, I pray.
I'm completely frozen, standing here all day."
So the North Wind came along and blew him in the door,
And now there's nothing left of him
But a puddle on the floor!

You can see if your child really understands personification by asking him who the "people" are. And if they are really people.

One of the poets' favorite subjects for personification is nature. Read this gem of a poem with your child, and notice how the poet (unfortunately unknown) extends the figurative language to describe the whole "sewing" process. When the comparisons become so closely interwoven into the poem it's called "analogy."

Sewing

If Mother Nature patches
The leaves of trees and vines,
I'm sure she does her darning
With the needles of the pines;
They are so long and slender,
And somewhere in full view,
She has her threads of cobwebs
And a thimbleful of dew.

Exaggeration. Poets often exaggerate to emphasize a significant point, heighten an effect, or arouse a particular response.
Examples: There were *millions* of people at the game.
You could have knocked me down with a *feather*.
The exaggeration always has a certain element of truth, and is probably most effective in humorous writing, such as in this fun poem by Mary E. Wilkins Freeman, *The Ostrich Is a Silly Bird:*

The ostrich is a silly bird
With scarcely any mind.
He often runs so very fast
He leaves himself behind.
And when he gets there, has to stand
And hang about till night,
Without a blessed thing to do
Until he comes in sight.

In a more serious vein, you can point out the use of exaggerations to your child in some of the poems already mentioned. For example, Tennyson uses it in *The Eagle* when he describes the eagle as being "*Close* to the sun in lonely lands." Wordsworth uses it in *Daffodils* when he describes them as "stretched in *never-ending* line."

Allusion is a reference to something, someone, or some event in history, or literature, such as Pandora's box or Achilles' heel. You may have to do a little homework to explain these to your child, but he will need to understand them to get the full meaning of the poem. For example, Christina Rossetti's enchanting *My Gift* will have little meaning for him unless he is acquainted with the story of the birth of Christ.

> What can I give Him,
> Poor as I am;
> If I were a sheperd,
> I would give Him a lamb.
> If I were a wise man,
> I would do my part.
> But what can I give Him?
> I will give my heart.

Irony is employed when poets (or any writer, for that matter) use words to convey their *opposite* meaning, such as calling an irritating commercial jingle "that melodious song," or a sickly smile "that engaging expression." Irony is most effective, and fascinating, when it's used subtly. But it needs a thoughtful and perceptive reader to fully appreciate it. Nevertheless, time and time again, youngsters amaze me by "getting the point." Read this delightful description of a crocodile by Lewis Carroll to your child and see if he "gets it."

> How cheerfully he seems to grin,
> How neatly spreads his claws,
> And welcomes little fishes in,
> With *gently smiling* jaws!

When he is older try him out on this moving poem by Blake, called *The Chimney Sweeper,* which shows a more sophisticated form of irony, and see if he sympathizes with the young chimney sweepers. Notice how much more effectively the irony conveys their misery than a direct approach would have done.

> When my mother died I was very young
> And my father sold me while yet my tongue
> Could scarcely cry 'weep! 'weep! 'weep! 'weep!
> So your chimneys I sweep, and in soot I sleep.
>
> There's little Tom Dacre, who cried when his head,
> That curled like a lamb's back, was shaved; so I said,

"Hush, Tom! never mind it, for, when your head's bare
You know that the soot cannot spoil your white hair."

And so he was quiet, and that very night
As Tom was asleeping, he had such a sight,
That thousands of sweepers, Dick, Joe, Ned, and Jack,
Were all of them lock'd up in coffins of black.

And by came an Angel, who had a bright key,
And he open'd the coffins and set them all free;
Then down a green plain leaping, laughing, they run,
And wash in a river, and shine in the sun.

Then naked and white, all their bags left behind,
They rise upon clouds and sport in the wind;
And the Angel told Tom, if he's be a good boy,
He'll have God for his father, and never want joy.

And so Tom awoke, and we rose in the dark,
And got with our bags and our brushes to work.
Though the morning was cold, Tom was happy and warm;
So if all do their duty, they need not fear harm.

Did you notice how Blake uses very common, everyday words? Yet he weaves them together so well they not only create a very real and vivid picture of the boys' plight, but, also a tremendous sense of drama that makes you become emotionally involved. This is the sign of a true poet. And it's when your child feels this sense of drama, becomes emotionally involved, and finds some intangible that goes beyond just the meaning of the words that you know he has learned to really appreciate poetry.

You will have taught him not only to "hear" and "see" a poem, but also to "live" a poem—and shown him, as Archibald MacLeish says,

A poem should not mean
But be.

You will have made reading poetry a fun and enjoyable experience for him, so that he naturally and eagerly comes to you and says, as Longfellow says in *The Day Is Done,*

Come, read to me some poem,
Some simple and heartfelt lay,
That shall soothe this restless feeling,
And banish the thoughts of day.

Nonfiction

Your child will read more nonfiction than anything else, as it accounts for as much as 90 per cent of all printed matter. It is the writing method used to give facts and information, so it covers every conceivable subject and is used in all sorts of forms: articles, reports, documents, letters, biographies, autobiographies, textbooks, and books like this, which give information on a specific topic. The ones you will read mostly with your child will probably be special-interest books, and those stories about people that enthrall all youngsters. But don't forget to introduce him to articles. They are particularly good for children because they are short, don't take long to read, and yet give a lot of information.

Whatever your child's reason for reading, the important thing for you to do is to train him to read the facts *as they are given*. This may sound obvious and simple, but it's not as easy as it sounds. In fact, a large majority of reading problems stem from passing over or misinterpreting details, or even reading in details that aren't there! The best way to help him to read accurately is to ask him simple, specific questions that require specific, factual answers. Then later, show him how to make up his own questions so he learns to check up on himself.

You can also help him to read more perceptively and beneficially by showing him how to vary his reading according to his purposes. For example, if he wants to find out specific information, tell him to read slowly, noting every detail and fact, perhaps underlining or circling significant parts, or jotting down notes in the margin. On the other hand, if he needs only general information, tell him to skim through the book more quickly, but suggest that he still may find it useful to mark important passages in case he wants to refer to them again. You can also show him how to save time by using the Contents, and back index, to find out pertinent information.

The nonfiction books that he will probably enjoy most are the biographies (written by someone else) and the autobiographies (written by the actual person). This is because he can vicariously step into the shoes of someone who is famous, has achieved success, or has done something particularly interesting, which is often of a heroic or dangerous nature (the more heroic or dangerous the better!). Stories such as *The Diary of Anne Frank* and *Helen Keller,* both tremendously popular, enable him to escape his mundane life (no reflection on you, but there inevitably has to be an "ordinariness" to his life!). For a short while, he can participate in all kinds of adventures and experiences that he probably will never have the opportunity, nor perhaps the courage, tenacity, or faith, to do himself.

When you read these stories with your child help him to really get to know the personality. Draw his attention to the way he thinks and feels; the kinds of things he does; and the way others react to him. Ask him what he thinks is special about the person, what makes him different from other people and capable of doing what he did. If it's a historical biography, help him to see the personality in relationship to the era in which he lived, but in such a way that he can relate to him as another very real human being and not as a remote "historical figure."

When your child is older you can also teach him to evaluate the author's attitude to his subject, or, if it's an autobiography, how objectively the writer presents his facts, for this will enable him to view the account in its proper perspective. You can do this by asking him questions about the kinds of traits, or qualities, he learns about the personality, and if these are attractive; the kinds of incidents the writer relates, and the impression they give about the individual; and whether he gets to know the whole man, or only a certain aspect of his character. If the account tends to emphasize one aspect, try to find another one that is more impartial or shows the personality in another light. This will not only enable your child to view him in greater depth, but will also give him an opportunity to see how extensively writers' approaches and techniques differ, even when they are writing about the same subject.

PART FIVE:

Working with Others to Help Your Child Read

CHAPTER 12

Working with the School

The school and the family should work together in the development and education of a child. It's a team effort, with the parent responsible for creating the best home environment and the school responsible for teaching the basic learning skills. Unfortunately, however, parents and school personnel sometimes fall short of their obligations. So far in this book I have talked about how you, as a parent, can play your part in helping your child to read. Now we'll see how you can evaluate if your child's school is doing its part in teaching him the necessary skills.

Reading should be at the heart of an elementary school program, not only because a child is ready and eager to learn at this time, but also because he cannot learn the other subjects unless he can read. It should be taught in regularly scheduled, *daily* "reading" classes, which concentrate entirely upon the reading process. Specific skills should be introduced, and all the activities should be geared to improving reading ability. These classes should be taught by a teacher who is knowledgeable in the intricacies of reading and who has completed special teacher training courses in the subject. Preferably this is your child's regular grade teacher, who knows your child well, but if she is not qualified, someone who is qualified should teach the class.

Reading instruction, however, should also permeate the whole curriculum and be taught indirectly through *all* subjects. Every opportunity should be seized by *all* the teachers to implement and reinforce the skills acquired in the actual reading class.

How to Evaluate a School's Reading Program

The only way you can evaluate the reading program of your child's school is to visit the school and ask some very specific questions. I know a personal visit might be difficult, particularly if you both have jobs, but it should only take a few hours *if* you know what to look for and the kinds of questions to ask.

Visiting the School

Call the school before your visit so they will be expecting you, and let them know the following:

1. the purpose of your visit is to find out about your child's reading program
2. you would like to set up appointments to meet the principal or chief administrator; the person in charge of reading throughout the school; and your child's reading teacher.
3. what you would like to do during your visit—sit in on your child's reading class, and, if you have time, some of his other classes; look at his textbooks and other reading materials; and see some of the children's work

Usually the school will be most co-operative and happy to make the arrangements you request. However, visits are always disruptive and involve people's extra time and effort, so you might meet some resistance. Nevertheless, persevere in a pleasant but firm way, because you need to know the kind of education they are providing for your child if you are to help him make the most of it.

Also before the visit, you should make a list of the questions you want to ask each of the people you will be meeting. This will not only save you time, but will also ensure that you cover all the aspects. It will also indicate to the school that you know what you are talking about and are really serious about getting to know the program so you can work with the school to help your child.

Questions to Ask the Principal and/or Reading Co-ordinator

Even though the principal is not usually directly responsible for the reading program, you should still try to meet with him, for a school always reflects the philosophy and feelings of the person in charge. If he is personally committed to reading and feels it is of the utmost importance that the children in his school learn to read, you can be pretty sure the rest of the faculty will feel this too. The principal can also give you the best picture of how reading fits into the school's overall educational program, whereas the reading co-ordinator or your child's grade teacher are more likely to interpret it from their much narrower perspectives. However, if the principal is too preoccupied with administrative duties, try to meet his deputy. If this fails, you will have to be content with the reading co-ordinator, who is a "must."

The questions you ask these administrators should be of a general nature, concerning the school's reading program as a whole, and cover such topics as:

1. *What is the basic philosophy of the school concerning reading? Is the school genuinely committed to teaching children to read? Does the curriculum emphasize reading? How important is reading in relationship to the other subjects taught?*

2. *Does the school have a definite, well-planned, and well-organized reading program? Every school should have a sequentially developed and co-ordinated reading program. It should be written down so everyone is familiar with it, and it should specify exactly which skills are taught at each grade, or reading level. Such a plan enables the children to learn in an orderly, controlled way; it avoids*

unnecessary repetition; it prevents important skills from being omitted; and guards against conflicting methods and techniques being used.

In some schools you will find the teachers teaching what they feel is right, or what they like to teach, with no regard for what a child has learned already, or will learn in the next grade. A definite plan enables the teachers to work closely together and *reinforce* each others' programs. As well as avoiding much wasted time, it gives the teachers and children definite objectives that have to be achieved, sets standards, and provides a clear basis for evaluating student progress.

Ask to see the curriculum, and, if possible, get a copy to take home so you can study it more thoroughly. Use the check list of essential skills on page 344 to see that they are all covered.

3. Which method do you use to teach reading?

There are many methods for teaching reading, and new ones are constantly appearing. However, there are three main ones most frequently used in our schools today: the "sight" method, which teaches through the memorization of whole words; "phonics," which teaches the identification of words by learning the visual patterns and sounds of the letters; and the "language" method, which uses the development of other language skills, such as speaking, listening, and writing, to teach and reinforce reading skills. Hopefully you will be told that your school employs all three methods, for they are all necessary to give your child a good foundation in the basic reading skills and develop not only his mechanical skills, but also his comprehension.

4. How do you evaluate the success of your reading program? Do you have a means for evaluating each student's progress? If so, what means do you use? How do you discover if a child has just fallen behind in his work, or has a real reading problem?

It is great to have a beautifully developed plan, but it is not going to be very useful if there is no means to see if its objectives are being reached. There should be a definite means for checking each student's progress to ensure that he is acquiring the skills and making measurable improvement in his reading ability. This should be done

by the school's own informal tests, but "standardized" tests that have national "norms" for comparison with other children across the country should also be given. There are also standardized "diagnostic" tests that can be administered to your child to see if he has a real reading problem (more about these standardized tests later on).

5. Are special provisions made for a child with reading problems or particular weaknesses? Is there a special remedial reading specialist—someone who is trained to give the standardized diagnostic tests and work with my child if he has a problem? If not, does the school have "outside" experts they can call upon or to whom parents can refer?

Every school should have a reading specialist to work solely with the children having reading problems. The child's reading teacher should teach the basic skills and cope with the normal, everyday reading difficulties, but real problems should be left to the expert who is specially trained and has the *time* to work alone with the children.

6. How do you take care of normal individual differences? How do you cope with the children who learn more slowly or more quickly than the rest of the class? How do you group the children for their reading lessons?

Children develop and learn at different rates. It is important, therefore, that the school provide some means for taking this into consideration. The usual and most satisfactory method is to group the children according to their reading levels. This can be organized in two ways: within each grade, or throughout the entire school. In the latter instance a certain time each day is devoted to reading, and each student meets with other students who are reading at the same level no matter which grade they are in, or what age they are. This can be an effective method as long as not too much time is lost getting the children to their different classrooms. Another method for coping with children's different rates of learning, which has become increasingly popular during the past few years, is "individualized instruction." This is when the children work entirely on their own with a teacher, or teachers, giving each one help when needed. This is the most effective method, theoretically, for children learn much more easily and rapidly when attention is focused on their specific needs. However, a teacher has to be really expert in teaching reading and extremely well organized to work with a group in this way. He also has to have plenty of time so he can reach each child and cope with the extra preparations necessary to meet each child's special needs.

7. What is the size of the reading classes or groups? How many teachers work with each class?

The best way to teach a child to read is on a one-to-one, student-teacher basis. This, of course, is impossible in the normal school situation, but the smaller the class, the better. It is most helpful if the teacher has an assistant who can work separately with the ones in need of extra help or reinforcement. He need not necessarily be specially trained, as he works under the reading teacher's direction and is only coping with minor difficulties. He could be a volunteer parent, a teacher trainee, or even an older student.

8. How much time each day is devoted to reading instruction? Are there daily reading classes that are devoted entirely to teaching specific reading skills and improving a child's reading? Is reading also emphasized in the other classes?

There should be classes devoted entirely to reading instruction each day. The *minimum* length of these classes should be forty-five minutes. On top of this there should be plenty of reading reinforcement in the other classes, as well as extra time for "fun" reading.

9. When do you start teaching the children to read? When do you expect them to be reading fluently with good comprehension?

The reading program should begin the first year of a child's schooling. Kindergarten should prepare your child for reading by developing all those important prereading skills discussed in Part II, "Preparing Your Child for Reading," particularly in the last three chapters. So if your child is in kindergarten, make especially sure his time is being spent profitably. See that he is learning to think for himself and reason, becoming more familiar with language and words, and being exposed to all kinds of new experiences that will help him to relate to what he reads later on. Is he developing concentration, patience, and perseverance? Is he being exposed to books and reading materials, and being read to? Is his interest in reading being stimulated and encouraged? Is he learning that written language is merely spoken language and recognizing some common, familiar words in print (building a useful little "sight" vocabulary)? Is he becoming familiar with the letters and their sounds, and realizing that they fit together to make words? Most important, check that these are being developed easily and naturally in a relaxed, informal setting, through a wide variety of fun games and activities, stimulating toys and materials, "playing" alone and with others, and even going on field trips, for then the learning will be enjoyable and unpressured, and he'll be eager and ready for first grade and the real business of reading.

By the time a child reaches sixth grade he should be reading quite sophisticated books on a variety of subjects with fluency and comprehension. In other words, he should be an accomplished reader by the end of elementary school.

10. What facilities and resources do you have to improve and encourage reading? Do you have a school library? If so, how often do the children visit the library? What role does the library and the librarian (there is a librarian, isn't there?) play in the school's reading program? Can the children visit the library when they want to and choose books as they please, or do they have to go with their class at specified times? Does each class also have its own library?

Every school should—*must*—have a library. It should not be a remote place that is visited only on "special" occasions. It should be easily accessible and play a very meaningful part in the school's entire educational program, but especially in the reading program. The children should be encouraged to visit it frequently, during recess and lunch breaks, and even after school.

The library should be manned by a qualified librarian who is intimately involved in the reading program and familiar with the reading skills being taught at each level. He should work closely with the teachers, supplying appropriate books and materials for their various reading projects, and be prepared and available to help the children choose appropriate books for their reading level when they visit the library.

An imaginative, involved librarian can do wonders to promote interest in reading in a school. If you have time you should visit the library and see what kind of librarian your school has. You can tell very quickly by glancing around the room. Is it inviting? Are there books on display? Are there attractive bulletin boards? Has an attempt been made to make the books appealing, so you feel you cannot resist the temptation to pick one off the shelf? Is the librarian with the children, or is he busy behind a desk "cataloguing"?

You should also check to see if the library is well stocked. Does it have books on a wide variety of topics? Are these topics suitable for elementary-level children? Are there plenty of books for each reading level? For boys and girls? Are there books of high interest but low reading level for the slower readers? Are there challenging books for the advanced readers?

If you have a chance, you should spend some time with the librarian. You could ask him the above questions, and it would also be a wonderful opportunity to ask advice about which books he thinks your child should be reading, or would like to read, for you cannot have too many ideas on this. It might also stimulate him to take a special interest in your child when he visits the library—which certainly could not hurt!

11. What other resources do you have to make your reading program effective? Do the teachers have plenty of books and materials to draw upon to provide a wide variety of reading activities for the children? Is money allocated in the budget each year for reading materials? Is there a special reading resource room equipped with remedial reading materials where the reading specialist can work with the children with reading problems?

All of the items mentioned above are necessary for a good reading program. However, a word of caution: Even though the school may have beautiful facilities with plenty of resource materials, the most important factor is the *way* they are used, and this depends upon the teachers—which leads us to the next question.

12. Are the reading teachers skilled, knowledgeable, and well trained in teaching reading? Are they enthusiastic, and do they have a good rapport with the children? Do they stimulate the children so they want to learn to read and are excited about books and reading? Are they using the facilities and resources available to their best advantage to improve the children's reading?

As mentioned earlier, reading teachers should have special training, but unless they are enthusiastic and can capture the children's enthusiasm, they will not be very successful. They must also be resourceful and imaginative, varying their approach and using a variety of methods and techniques to meet the many interests and needs of their students.

Visiting Your Child's Classroom

You have a chance to find out what kind of teacher your child has when you visit his class. However, a word of caution: You will never see the class as it normally functions, for your very presence (particularly being a parent) creates a certain amount of tension and affects the atmosphere. Nevertheless, your visit will give you a good indication of the kind of education your child is receiving.

It is best to visit your child's classroom before your conference with his teacher, as it will be much easier to formulate your questions after you have seen him "in action." However, make sure you really use the visit to gain the information you want. I have seen so many visiting parents spend the entire time watching their child. You see Johnny every day at home—this visit is to see if he is learning, and particularly if he is learning to read.

It will help you to focus on the task at hand if you again make a check list of the things to look for. Refer to it while you are observing, and methodically check off each item after you have considered it. Do this as inconspicuously as possible, as the teacher may not like the idea that you are, literally, checking up on him!

It is absolutely essential that you develop a good rapport with your child's teacher, because you need to work closely together. Greet him warmly when you arrive; make sure your presence causes as little disruption as possible; and quickly fade into the background (grab a chair at the back of the room) so he can get on with his job. Remember to tell your child beforehand that you are coming so he is not surprised when you arrive. Wave to him, but do *not* go over to him and make a fuss of him or any of the other children whom you may know.

These are some of the things you should look for:

1. General organization and appearance of the classroom.

You can learn a lot about a teacher and what is going on in the classroom by its general organization and appearance. As you want to know particularly about the reading program, you should first look to see if there is *an emphasis on books and reading.*

Look at the bulletin boards—are they just covered with pretty pictures, or are they intended to stimulate reading or teach a specific reading skill, such as word recognition or vocabulary development? Can you see the children's *own* reviews of books, or drawings stimulated by books they have read? Are there lists of "good books to read" suggestions made by the children as well as the teacher?

Are there "reading centers"—self-teaching areas that have all sorts of reading materials, games, and puzzles where the children can work on their own to practice reading skills?

Are there a class library and reading areas with a wide variety of books (reference and leisure type) and a comfortable place where they ran be read and enjoyed to their fullest?

Is there evidence, or are there examples, of special reading projects going on? For example, is there a model of a community they have read about, or a forest scene compiled from information they have gathered from their reading?

2. How are the children grouped for their reading lesson?

You can ask specific questions about how and why they are grouped when you have your conference with the teacher. Your task now is to note how many are in each group; the student/teacher relationship (does the teacher have an assistant?); and how much attention each child receives. Remember, the more individualized help, the better in teaching reading.

However, do not panic if you find the teacher working with the class as a whole. Sometimes this is the best method—for example, if he wants to make sure everyone knows a specific skill. But make a note to check with him when you meet later, that he does work in small groups, or individually with the children during the reading classes.

If your child is in a totally unstructured, "individualized instruction" situation, with each child working entirely on his own, make sure the teacher is supervising them carefully and is aware of what each one is doing.

3. What are the children doing?

Look to see if the children are absorbed in what they are doing. Do they seem to *understand* what they are doing? Do they appear to be actively involved in the "learning process," or are they merely "passive observers"?

Are they learning specific reading skills and being given the opportunity to apply them? (When you meet with the teacher you should check the exact skills he intends to cover during the year.)

Make sure that the children, without the direct supervision of the teacher, whether alone or in a group, are working on specific assignments to improve their reading skills.

Particularly look to see if the children are given practice in reading aloud. If they are not, make a note to ask the teacher about it.

4. How are they being taught?

It is extremely important to find out what methods the teacher uses to teach reading. Are the children learning by rote and memorization, or are they learning by understanding the basic concepts and principles or "rules" of reading.

Research indicates that children do not retain knowledge learning by rote. For example, if they are given words to memorize for "vocabulary development" (heaven forbid, but it happens all the time!), they may get a 100 per cent right the day after they have learned them, but a few weeks later they may well have forgotten most of them! It is essential, therefore, that your child acquire a real understanding of the reading process and has a good foundation in the basic, essential skills.

You will probably find it difficult to assess if your child is being taught to read in the most effective way, especially as your visit is short. However, you may have had some indication already from the kind of homework he has been bringing home. Has *he* been given lists of words to memorize, or has he been asked to learn basic rules, which he then applies to learning words demonstrating the rule? You can also, of course, ask the teacher directly which methods he uses. However, the only way you can really tell whether the children are learning through understanding is through your own observation.

Does the teacher "lecture" the children? Is it a one-way process, with the teacher doing the talking and the children the listening? Or does the teacher ask the children questions and get them involved and reacting to what he is saying? Does he, in fact, make the children *think?* Does he encourage them to ask questions? Does he give *reasons* for things, or merely state them as "facts to be learned"? Does he put the children "on the spot," or is he patient, encouraging and willing to wait for answers?

In regard to specific reading skills, you should look for such things as:

- Are the children learning words by sounding them out, analyzing them by their structure and applying the basic phonics rules, or are they just told, "This word means 'cat'—remember that."?
- Do they learn the meaning of words by observing them in their context? Does the teacher call the children's attention to certain characteristics of a word to help them discover the meaning, such as, "What letter do you notice at the end of the word? How does that change the meaning of 'dog' to 'dogs'?"? Does he say, "See if you can tell the meaning of the word by looking at all the other words around it."? Or does he just tell the children the word so they can "get on"?
- When a new phonics or reading concept or rule is introduced, are the children told to memorize it or to learn it through applying it? Are they given exercises and activities that give practice in its use, or are they "tested" on it or required to repeat it "parrot fashion"?
- If the children are given tests and quizzes, what kind are they? I'm all for quizzes *as long as* they test general comprehension. For example: "Spell 'ice' *and* say why the 'c' has an 's' sound." Or, "Spell these words—'horn,' 'lawn,' 'auto' and 'arm'—and say which is the odd man out and why."
- Are the children given a wide variety of exercises, activities, games, etc., that require them to use words in many different ways?

•*Is plenty of actual reading going on?* Silently and out loud? To the teacher and to one another?

•If a child makes a mistake, or misinterprets or mispronounces a word while reading, is he reprimanded, laughed at, or not given a chance to correct himself? Is another child asked to "give Marion the word"? Or does the teacher carefully guide him to the correct word?

5. *What texts and reading materials are being used?*

Again, it will be difficult for you to evaluate the quality, suitability, and effectiveness of the books and materials. However, you *can* assess if the children are interested and absorbed in them and enjoy using them.

Notice if they are attractive, appealing, and inviting. There is absolutely no excuse if they are not, because there are some simply wonderful, imaginative, and stimulating texts and reading materials and activities on the market today.

When you talk with the teacher you can ask some specific questions that will give you an indication of their acceptability as far as educational standards are concerned.

Do not be concerned if you come away from your visit to the classroom feeling you have not learned very much. Remember, the purpose was to gain a *general* insight into your child's "learning environment" (to put it in educational jargon), and just get an idea how he is being taught to read. Your interview with the teacher will give you a much clearer view of the reading program if you ask perceptive and specific questions.

Questions to Ask Your Child's Teacher About the Reading Program

I am presuming your child's reading teacher is his grade teacher, as this is usually the case. If he is not, you may have to vary your questions slightly, as he will naturally not be teaching all the other subjects, or working with your child throughout the day.

First, a word of caution—again! Remember that the teacher is probably giving up his free time to meet with you (that much-valued coffee break, or time to correct assignments or prepare classwork), and you have already disturbed a precious class period by your visit.

Also, he may not be used to having a parent ask *him* questions, demanding specific answers to specific questions. Most parents sit and listen to a teacher talk. He may feel "put on the spot" and resent the questions. They may well put him on the defensive. Obviously it is very important that you find out the answers to your questions, but there are ways, and ways!

So keep in mind:

1. First of all, you must build a rapport with the teacher. Let him know that you are not trying to be critical but just want to know more about his reading program so you can help your child become a better reader. You are not being a demanding parent, just a co-operative one. Once you have put him at ease, you will find he will answer your questions very willingly, and may even enjoy sharing with you some of his ideas on reading.
2. Keep the interview short.
3. Make your questions specific but not "challenging."
4. Don't pretend you know more than you do.
5. *Don't* say, "I've just read a book about reading and it says . . ."! ! I hope you find this book useful; but don't thrust it down the teacher's throat!
6. Don't flourish your list of questions and ostentatiously check each one off. On the other hand, don't hide them or surreptitiously refer to them like some nervous actor who has forgotten his lines. Be quite open and say nonchalantly: "I hope you don't mind, but I have jotted down a few notes to remind me of some of the things I wanted to ask you."
7. Finally, its not so much the questions you ask but *how* you ask them.

Now for your questions, or what you want to find out:

1. What are your qualifications, background, and experience?

It is best to ask the principal about these, for it certainly would put the teacher on the defensive if he felt you were questioning his ability to teach your child. However, if you have been unable to find out, you must try to get the information subtly during the conversation. For example, you could casually ask: "Did you take your course in reading locally?" or "How long have you been at this school?"

The point of your questions is to see if he is knowledgeable, skilled, and experienced in teaching reading—with the emphasis on experienced. Hope that he has had at least three years teaching reading. I always tell my teachers that the first year *they* are learning from the children; the second year it's fifty-fifty; and it's only during the third year they make a real contribution! This may be a slight exaggeration, but there is some truth in it.

2. How important do you think teaching reading is? How much emphasis should be given to reading at this age level?

Keep your fingers crossed that he will say, "It is No. 1 priority!"

3. Which reading skills do you consider important? How would you define reading? What particular reading skills do you teach at this age level?

Let the teacher explain to you in his own way which skills he feels are important, mentally noting which ones he excludes from your reading skills check list on page 344. Only when he has completed his review should you go through your own check list. On this occasion you could produce the actual list and ask him to comment on it.

Then ask him which specific skills he intends to cover during the year. Find out if he has a definite, sequentially planned curriculum to teach these skills. Is this his own plan, or is it part of the school's planned reading program? Even though the principal may have assured you that the school has a reading curriculum, the teacher may not actually be referring to it or using it! Be that as it may, what you must find out is: Does this teacher have what appears to be a well-thought-out, comprehensive curriculum that will teach your child the essential reading skills and make a significant impact on his reading ability?

4. How much time do you spend teaching reading?

Hopefully he will tell you that he spends a minimum of one class period (approximately forty to fifty minutes) *each* day teaching the basic skills and concentrating entirely on reading improvement, and that he also uses the other classes to reinforce reading skills.

5. What methods do you find most successful in teaching reading?

This is a slightly more tactful way of asking how he teaches the skills. Hopefully he will say, "By having the children understand the key concepts, which they can apply," as we discussed earlier.

6. *How do you group the children?*

You had an opportunity to observe how many were in each group, or if the class was taught as a whole or entirely on an individual basis during your visit. Now you want to find out *how* they are grouped so you can assess if the teacher is paying attention to individual needs.

As I commented earlier, the most usual, and probably the most efficient, way to group children is by their reading *levels*. However, there should be other groupings as well to provide variety and stimulation. For example, groups can be formed around children with a common problem or deficiency. These are short-term, providing intensive practice in specific skills. Groups can also be formed around children with a common interest. These are again short-term, enabling children to read about a particular topic that motivates them, and is disbanded when they have satisfied their curiosity and shared their experiences. This kind of grouping is most effective once in a while because it gives students at different reading levels a chance to work together and help one another.

If the teacher has a completely individualized program with each child working at his own level and speed, ask him how much time he spends with each child and how he manages to keep track of what each one is doing and the help they need. His answers will indicate if he is truly reaching each child and if he is well organized—which is essential in individualized instruction.

If he teaches the class as a whole, ask him how he takes care of the children reading at different levels and with different needs.

7. *How do you cope with children with special reading needs?*

However the teacher may group the students or teach them, there are still going to be some students who need extra attention. What does he do about these children? Is there someone he can call upon to work with them alone, such as a remedial reading teacher? Does he suggest that the child be tutored by someone "outside" the school? Is the responsibility put on the parent to cope with the problem? Or does the school consider it is their problem?

8. Do you have a means to evaluate your reading program and ascertain the achievement and progress of the children?

The teacher should give frequent tests of his own construction to see whether the children are learning the skills he is teaching. They should be varied, and hopefully not of the multiple-choice, fill-in variety—although they can occasionally be useful to test specific skills. They should cover all aspects of reading—the mechanics, reading comprehension, *and* speed and fluency of reading.

The teacher, or the reading co-ordinator or specialist, should also regularly administer the standardized tests, which are discussed in detail on pages 341–42. These enable you to judge how your child is achieving in comparison with other children his age in the rest of the country.

9. Which textbooks do you use for teaching the basic reading skills? What other materials do you use in your reading program?

Ask to see copies of the texts so you have a general idea what they are like. Notice if they are teaching specific reading skills. Look at the copyright date to see if it is up-to-date. If you have time, or better still, if you are allowed to, take a copy home to study at your leisure. Read a story or two and check to see the kinds of assignments and activities given. Are they "thinking" questions? Or do they entail "busy work"?

If you have a chance, also look through the other books and materials so that you know the kinds of activities your child is doing. This will be helpful if you plan to do some work with him. In fact, the teacher might even lend you some of them—but more about that later.

10. What do you think about homework?

Homework should be given frequently to reinforce the skills being taught during the reading class, so let's hope the teacher feels it is important.

Ask him *what your role should be* in regard to homework assignments. Would he like you to actually review your child's work sometimes? Or would he prefer that you "left him to it"? Teachers vary on this. But let him know you are happy to work with your child—

hearing him read, or asking questions to see if he understands a story —if this is what the teacher would like.

11. What do you do to promote special interest in books and reading?

As well as teaching your child to read well, hopefully his teacher will encourage and inspire your child to read. Does he have special reading "projects" to get the students interested in certain topics? Do they visit the school library frequently? Do they have a chance during class time to just read for the fun of it—and *no* questions asked? (How many teachers ruin a book by asking for a book report or giving a test on it!) Has he checked to see that every student in his class has a public library card? Does he encourage the children to bring books to school as well as take schoolbooks home? Does *he* seem to enjoy books and reading and let it "rub off" on the students?

You will have noticed that some of these questions are the same, or similar, to those you asked the principal, but hopefully, the teacher's answers will help you evaluate the school's reading program specifically in terms of how it is helping *your child* improve his reading *now*—at his present grade level.

However, having learned about the program and having had a chance to assess the competence of his teacher, you still have to find out how your child is actually doing. Is he making progress in his reading? If so, is his progress normal for his level? Does he have any special reading difficulties or problems? Are they serious or minor? Is he reading at the appropriate level for his age?

As you can see, there is a great deal to find out. The best way to cover all your questions is to visit twice. Make the first visit very early in the school year, spending this time visiting the principal and your child's classroom and teacher to find out about the program. Then make a second one about six weeks to two months into the semester to see how he is progressing. This is a good time, because it is long enough for the teacher to assess your child's abilities and improvement, while not too late to cope with a problem if he has one.

How to Evaluate Your Child's Progress and Reading Level

Your second meeting with the teacher should be much easier, for you now know one another and have established common ground on which to base your discussion of your child's progress; you know and understand the teacher's reading program, and he knows and understands your interest in helping your child.

You should let the teacher know well before the meeting that you wish to talk specifically about your child's reading ability and progress. This will give him time to make his evaluation and collect together any necessary data to answer your questions. There are five major questions you should raise during the meeting:

1. What progress has he made?
2. How is he doing in relationship to his abilities and potential?
3. How is he doing in relationship to the rest of his class and the standards set by the school?
4. How is he doing in relationship to other children of his age in other parts of the country?
5. What are his main strengths and weaknesses?

Your discussions should cover *all* aspects of the reading process so that you have a truly comprehensive picture of your child's abilities, for he may be extremely proficient in one area but quite weak in another. So once again refer to the check list on page 344.

1. What progress has my child made?

You want detailed information from the teacher indicating exactly how much your child's reading has improved, so do not be content with vague generalities and such comments as, "Oh Johnny is doing fine," or, "He's coming along nicely." Admittedly they seem nice and reassuring, but they do not really tell you anything. *Pin the teacher down to specifics.* Ask for a review of your child's accomplishments in each aspect of reading.

Most teachers keep a record or report book of their daily observations of students and the results of their work. Ask to see his notes on your child, or, if he feels they are too personal, ask him to comment on them. Try to get him to explain his achievement on specific assignments. For example: "Johnny got ninety words correct out of one hundred on this vocabulary test." "He began in Book A, and now is halfway through Book B." "He had trouble with this phonics rule, but after a lot of practice he now seems to understand it."

Also ask for a review of his grades, if grades are given. Are they above or below average? Are they consistent? Grading levels vary from one teacher to another, so ask him to interpret them for you. Are they acceptable in his grading terms? See if your child has been given any tests. How well has he done on them? Do they show he has made any improvement?

Ask to see the work your child did early on, and the work he is doing now, so you have something tangible on which to base your evaluation of his progress. Notice if the assignments are more difficult or merely repetitions of earlier ones. Check to see he is not only perfecting skills but also learning new ones.

Particularly ask to see the main reading text. Ask where your child is in the book now compared to where he was earlier. Notice how many pages he has covered. Does the amount seem reasonable for the amount of time he has spent working in the book? What does the teacher say about this? Also, find out if he is making as much progress in his silent reading as he is in his oral reading.

2. How is my child doing in relationship to his abilities and potential?

This, of course, is the most important question, and the one of greatest concern to parents. Naturally they want their child to do as well as he possibly can. On the other hand, they do not want to put him in a situation beyond his capabilities. But how do you judge the abilities and potential of your child? This is really a tough one to answer, for even experts in the field of learning are not entirely satisfied with their ability to assess these characteristics.

However, there are some indications that might help you evaluate whether your child is working at the appropriate level; for example, his behavior and attitude at home. If he appears frustrated and uptight; says he does not like school, or does not want to go; or complains of a stomach ache or of not feeling well just before the school bus arrives, you can be pretty sure he is under some pressure at school. It may not be due to his work, but it is something that you should discuss with his teacher during the conference. Restlessness and reports of bad behavior at school could also be indications of problems concerning his work. In this case it might mean the work is too easy and he is bored.

The way he deals with his homework could be another indication. Does he spend hours doing it, agonizing over every part? Does he get upset because he cannot do it? Is "homework time" a period of tension in the household, or does he whiz through it and say, "Oh this is easy"? However, do not assume, if this happens, that he really does find the work easy; it may be that the work is actually too difficult and he cannot do it. On the other hand, it may indicate that he is being just downright lazy! The way you can check up on this is to look at the homework assignment and see for yourself how he has done it.

If you are concerned that your child may be reading above or below his level, have him read to you from his main reading text. Ask him to read the story that he is currently working on at school. If he stumbles and stutters over the words and does not understand what the story is about, obviously it is too difficult. When this occurs, go over the stories he has already covered and see if he reads and understands these any better. If he also finds them difficult, the book is too hard for him. Another easy and pretty reliable method is the one I mentioned earlier in the discussion on choosing appropriate books. Have him read a page and count off the words he cannot read on his fingers. If he uses up all his fingers before he completes the page, it is probably too difficult for him. On the other hand, if he reads the story quite effortlessly, with the appropriate pauses and expression, and can answer all your questions about what he has read, then go ahead in the book to stories he has not yet read at school. If he finds all these easy, he probably needs to be in a more advanced book.

Having your child read to you from his text gives you specific information upon which to base your questions to the teacher. But a word of caution once again. If his reading has indicated an inappropriateness, do not immediately assume that he is wasting his time or that the teacher is completely incompetent. He may have a very good reason for having your child work in that book. The teacher may have deliberately chosen an easy book to build his confidence or reinforce certain skills, or a difficult one to stimulate him to learn new skills.

You should, however, express whatever concerns you have during the conference, because it may be that he has misjudged your child's ability. Also, I am sure the teacher would appreciate learning how your child fares away from the supportive environment of the classroom. Remember, the more information you can give him the better he can help him.

Even though you may have no indication of problems at home, you should ask his teacher if he is satisfied that your child is reading at his ability level and working up to his potential. If the teacher is experienced, and has taught your child's age level for several years, he should have a pretty good idea. Find out, though, if he is expressing just his own feeling or if the other members of the faculty, particularly the reading co-ordinator, feel this too.

If your opinion differs from the teacher's, and you are convinced he does not have your child working at the right level, he can be given an intelligence or scholastic ability test. These tests provide I.Q. or mental-age scores, and although there has been much questioning of late whether they do in fact indicate a child's intelligence, they are pretty good indicators of reading potential. One of the most comprehensive of these is the Wisc-R (Wechsler Intelligence Scale for Children-Revised). It is an individual test that requires a specially trained administrator. However, there are other tests frequently given in schools that are much easier to administer and can be given to groups. It may well be that your child has been given one of these, so ask his teacher if he has. Some of these tests are:

Otis-Lennon Mental Ability Test
S.R.A. Primary Mental Abilities Test
California Test of Mental Ability
Kuhlman-Anderson I.Q. Test

Another way of estimating a child's reading potential is by testing his listening ability. Some of the tests that do this are:

Botel Reading Inventory
Brown-Carlsen Listening Comprehension Test
Durrell-Sullivan Reading Capacity Test
Stroud-Hieronymus Primary Reading Profiles

3. How is my child doing in relationship to the rest of the class and the standards set by the school?

This is not nearly as an important question as how he is doing in relationship to his potential, but every piece of information helps you get a better picture of your child's accomplishments. The kinds of questions to raise are:

- •In which reading group is he—top, intermediate, bottom?
- •In which level reading book is he—top, intermediate, bottom?
- •Has he learned as many new skills as the majority of the class?
- •Does he take a longer or a shorter time to grasp a new skill or concept?
- •Does he take a longer or a shorter time to complete assignments?
- •How do his grades and class test results compare with the other children's?
- •Does he read as many books from the library, or in leisure reading time, as the other children?
- •Does he enjoy reading, or is he as interested in reading as the others?

You have already asked the teacher if he is satisfied with his reading standard, but you should also ask how the school sets their standards. As mentioned earlier, most schools give tests based on the specific skills outlined in their reading program. Ask to see the results of the tests given to your child's class and compare his score with those of the other children. Ask what was the average score and the mean score (the middle score in the ranking) and how your child ranked in relationship to them.

4. How is my child doing in relationship to other children of the same age, on a national level?

In order to give a comprehensive evaluation of reading achievement, I said a school should also give standardized achievement tests. These are specially devised tests that are generally accepted to be valid (measure what they are supposed to measure) and reliable (provide consistent results). They also provide norms that enable a child's performance to be measured against all other children at his age level and not just against his classmates.

Standardized reading achievement tests are also useful because they provide information on a child's performance in each of the main aspects of reading. The categories vary slightly with each test, but they essentially test for: word skills; word meanings; comprehension; and speed and accuracy. The following are some of the highly recommended reading achievement tests:

Stanford Achievement Test
Gates-MacGintie Reading Tests
Metropolitan Reading Test
California Reading Test
Durrell-Sullivan Reading Capacity and Achievement Test
Iowa Silent Reading Test

Interpreting Standardized Reading Achievement Tests

You may have seen the results of standardized reading achievement tests on your child's report card, but they probably did not mean much to you, right? This is because you did not know how to interpret the scores to make them meaningful. Here are what some of the terms and scores mean:

Raw score: This is the total number of correct answers in each category; for example, 80 means 80 correct out of a certain number of questions.

Grade score: The raw score means little on its own, but it can be converted into a "grade" score by means of a conversion scale. A grade score gives the level of performance; for example, a grade score of 4.8 is typical for students in the eighth month of the fourth grade. Thus, if your child has a grade score of 3.6, he is reading at the level of the sixth month of the third grade.

Stanines: Raw scores can also be converted into "stanines." A stanine is a value on a simple 9-point scale of standard scores (whence the name: "sta" for standard; "nine" for nine-point scale). The scores are expressed along the scale, with 1 ranking low; 9 ranking high; and 5 always representing the average performance; for example, if your child had a stanine of 8 he would be performing well above the average (see figure below).

Percentile rank: Percentile rank also indicates performance in terms of low, high, and average. As the figure below shows, there is a fixed relationship between percentile ranks and stanines; for example, if your child had a stanine of 8 he would fall in the 89–96 percentile.

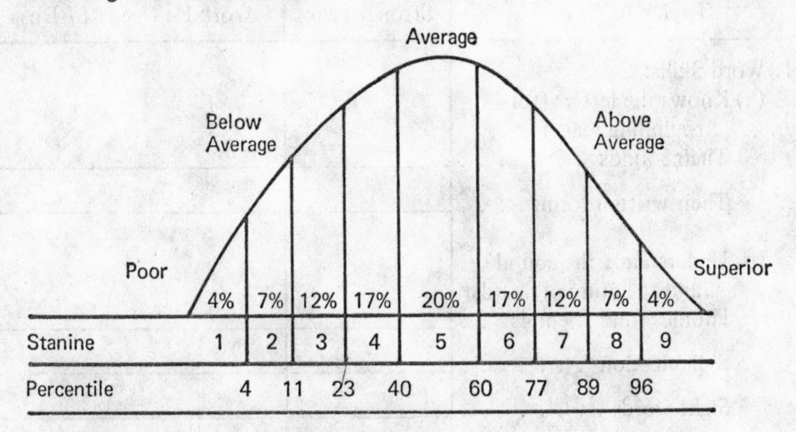

Try your skill in interpreting the scores:

QUESTION: Johnny has a stanine of 3. What is his percentile rank? How is he doing?

ANSWER: His percentile rank is between 11 and 23. He is achieving below average.

QUESTION: What is the average percentile rank? What percentage of students fall in this rank?

ANSWER: The average percentile rank is between 40 and 60; 20 per cent of students fall in this rank.

5. What are my child's main strengths and weaknesses?

This final question is intended to summarize all the various aspects of your child's reading ability that you have discussed during the conferences. The most effective way to do this is to make a check list like the one below. This can then be used as a guide for developing a specific reading program for you to work on with your child if you and the teacher feel it is necessary.

Topics to Cover	Strong/Weak	Work He Needs to Do
1. Word Skills: (a) Knows the letters (for beginning readers): Their sounds		
Their written forms		
(b) Understands the sound and structure of words: Phonics fundamentals . .		
Syllabication		
Sight words		
2. Reading Comprehension: (a) Word meanings and vocabulary development		
(b) General comprehension . .		
(c) Ability to note details and see their relationships and significance		
(d) Ability to draw conclusions and evaluate what has been read		
3. Application of the Skills: (a) Accuracy		
(b) Fluency and speed		
(c) Oral reading		
(d) Silent reading		
4. Attitude: (a) Tries hard		
(b) Interested in and enjoys reading		

How to Work with the School to Improve Your Child's Reading

Hopefully, by the end of your second conference you have built up a rapport with your child's teacher and he realizes that you are not just a "pushy," demanding parent, but genuinely want to help your child improve his reading. If you and the teacher decide that your child will benefit from additional help at home he will probably be delighted to give you assignments and books and materials you can work on with him. However, remember that this means a lot of extra work on the teacher's part, so do not be too demanding. Also, *do* assure him that you want to *reinforce his program* and are not planning to set up shop in competition with him. He is the reading specialist and presumably has a very definite plan of skills he wishes to teach his students.

If your child does need extra help, now may be the time to use the lessons in this book. However, be sure to do this in conjunction with the teacher. Ask him to give you the specific skills your child needs to work on, look them up in the outline of the skills on pages 135–36, and go to work! Or take the book to him and ask him to check off the lessons your child needs to work on.

If you work with your child to generally reinforce the teacher's program, the way you can be most helpful is to:

1. Be generally supportive—praising your child when he does particularly well, being sympathetic when he is having a hard time, and encouraging him when he has a difficult assignment. Let him know that you are interested in how he is doing, boost his morale, and give him confidence. See that he tries hard and puts all his effort into his schoolwork;

2. Reinforce the reading skills he is currently learning in class. Ask the teacher which skills he is working on and what he would like you to do to help your child in terms of: (a) specific assignments and (b) general things;

3. Supervise homework. Be sure, though, to ask the teacher *what role* he wishes you to play in regard to homework. Obviously he does not want you to do it for your child, but you could (a) make sure he *does* it—and does it well, (b) do such things as listen to

him read and ask questions to make sure he understood a story, and (c) go over phonics "rules" with him;

4. Work on your child's particular weaknesses and ask the teacher in this case for *specific assignments* that you and your child can do together (such as working on the lessons in this book).

5. Ask for some fun-type reading projects—games and activities that will reinforce and improve your child's reading skills but not seem like "schoolwork."

6. Ask for a list of books that he recommends for leisure-time reading.

7. Finally, you can be of great help by telling your child's teacher as much as you can about him—his interests, experiences, concerns, and needs; for the more the teacher knows about your child the better he will understand him and be able to help him.

If, by any chance, you find your child's teacher is unwilling to spend time with you to discuss your child's reading, or you are getting no response or help from the school but are concerned about his progress, you can review the lessons in this book with him. By doing this you will, at least, ensure that he covers all the basic skills. Start at the beginning and progress lesson by lesson, skipping the ones he knows.

If, however, you feel your child needs more than a review of the skills and has a problem that is too serious for you to deal with, you should seek special help—which is the topic of the next chapter.

CHAPTER 13

Getting Help When There Is a Problem

If you think your child has a reading problem, don't panic, for it is more than likely something minor that can be easily corrected. On the other hand, don't delay in checking into it, for if it is serious it should be treated as soon as possible.

How do you know if your child has a serious reading problem? You have probably heard and read a good deal about reading disability in recent years, yet, if you are the typical parent, you are probably more confused than ever. This is because it is an extremely controversial subject. Research is comparatively recent, and there are many different opinions concerning its identification, causes, and treatment. Even the terms used to describe it vary enormously, but probably the one you have heard most often is "dyslexia."

Signs of Reading Disability

One of the reasons why research in reading disability has been so difficult is that there is no clear, cut-and-dry pattern of behavior, or similar symptoms, that you can check off, as you can when your child has mumps or measles. No two children have exactly the same characteristics. Consider these children with reading disability, and you will see what I mean.

Andrew was six when he came to be tested. Mr. and Mrs. Weintraub, like many parents of children with reading disability, were disturbed about him. They knew he was not a happy child, and they had a vague feeling he was not "progressing as he should," as they told me. But they could not put a finger on any particular cause.

Andrew was an attractive, well-built, fresh-faced boy with curly hair and deep brown eyes. But he was obviously having emotional problems. During the interview the brown eyes were downcast, there was a constant scowl on the handsome face, he stuttered when answering my questions, and I noticed his nails were bitten down to the quick.

After discussions with the Weintraubs, and talking with and testing Andrew, I also discovered the following: He had a very short attention span, was impulsive, hyperactive, and in constant motion; he found it difficult to understand simple directions, such as, "Take three steps forward" and "Open the box and take out all the blue blocks"; he was unable to construct simple forms out of the blocks, could not follow a simple sequence of pictures and "tell their story"; and he showed no interest at home in looking at books or listening to stories.

Gerry was seven and in the second grade when her parents, Mr. and Mrs. Fleming, brought her to me. She was a thin, slight child, extremely nervous and tense, and obviously resentful of being subjected to an interview and tests.

Her parents told me she had been a happy, healthy, bubbly youngster, but as soon as she started first grade she began to have problems. She lost weight, started to have headaches and stomach aches, and frequently had terrible nightmares. At first they blamed the school, but now, they told me, after discussion with Gerry's teacher and principal, they felt the problems were related in some way to her development.

Gerry's other symptoms were: temper tantrums; bursting into tears when faced with minor problems or disappointments; tiring easily; and unwillingness to put much effort into tasks, whether academic or household chores. She also had a hard time telling right from left and demonstrated poor physical co-ordination, not being able to consistently catch a ball, ride her new bike, or hold a pencil properly and write neatly. And she had not learned to read, being unable to associate the correct sounds with the letters.

John had more obvious symptoms of reading disability. He was repeating third grade, and was still having a terrible time learning to read. He had prevalent perceptual problems, constantly reversing letters, mistaking "b" for "d," or transposing words, reading "was" for "saw"; he muddled up the order of the letters, and even missed out letters, reading "bend" for "blend"; and he made the same mistakes in his writing.

John was a bright boy. He had an I.Q. of 128. He could think and absorb quite difficult concepts, and had an extremely good memory. But he had always had a problem with language. When he was six months old he had been unable to distinguish among dissimilar sounds, and he could not talk, except for a few odd words and his own strange "jargon," by the time he was two. Even when he was four he spoke in disjointed sentences and had very poor pronunciation.

Cindy was also bright and in the third grade. Her problem was that although she could reason well and could solve quite difficult problems, she was inconsistent. She made silly mistakes often in the simplest assignments, or gave what appeared to be the first answer that came into her head. She also had visual perception difficulties like John, which had completely turned her off reading and any subject which involved reading. She had, in fact, "turned off" so completely that she had become a "dreamer," and even showed signs of living in a fantasy world of her own. Her parents told me she constantly talked about her two pals, Jenny and Jane, and the many things they did together and places they visited. She had also developed a very low esteem of herself, showed no enthusiasm for special treats or outings, and was generally despondent, which naturally greatly disturbed her parents.

If your child has some of the characteristics of Andrew, Gerry, John, or Cindy don't immediately jump to the conclusion he has a reading disability. A child can develop emotional problems or nervous habits like stuttering for all sorts of reasons. It is also quite normal for children to confuse "b" with "d" and read words backward occasionally when they are learning to read. It is when these behaviors become excessive and form a pattern that makes it extremely hard for your child to learn and read that you should become concerned.

The following are signs that could indicate your child has reading disability. If you think he may, compare them carefully and objectively with his behavior. Then, if you still feel he has a serious problem, seek help.

•Actual reading problems.

The most obvious signs are actual reading problems, such as the inability to identify the letters and their sounds or see letters and words as they really are, as well as a general inability to come to grips with the reading process. There is also likely to be disinterest, and even active dislike, of books and reading or any subject connected with reading.

•Related problems in writing.

Perceptual problems which show up in reading are frequently also reflected in the child's writing. He makes reversals and leaves out letters, and perhaps syllables, even when he is copying. He has difficulty with the "mechanics" of writing, being unable to form the letters neatly and legibly, and he is usually unable to express his thoughts coherently in writing.

•Language problems in general.

Perhaps the strongest indication of reading disability is the child's inability to deal with language generally. He is frequently unable to express his thoughts verbally, as well as in writing. His vocabulary is limited, his sentences garbled and cluttered, and he may even stutter. Often he was extremely slow in learning to talk, and sometimes he has difficulty in understanding what is being said to him. For example, if you ask him, "How old are you?" He may reply, "I'm very well, thank you," thinking you asked him how he was.

•Right-left confusion.
Difficulty in identifying right from left, and signs of confused right-left dominance, are also common characteristics of children with reading disability.

•Poor co-ordination.
Poor co-ordination and a tendency to jerky movements or clumsiness, and poor eye-hand co-ordination. Sometimes there is a general lag in all physical development, such as slowness in learning to crawl, walk, catch a ball, or ride a trike and bike.

•Hyperactivity and impulsiveness.
Inability to focus on one thing, easily distracted, and short attention span.

•Memory problems.
Difficulty in remembering even for a short time. For example, if you show him how to set the table for dinner, he may forget how to do it by the time you give him the cutlery and plates. On the other hand, many children with reading disability have very good memories, and it is only when memorizing is related to learning a language skill, such as remembering how to read or spell, that they have problems. Actually, the problem does not stem from poor memorization but from the inability to perceive the correct letter formation to be remembered.

•Emotional instability.
The frustrations related to reading disability often result in emotional problems: rapid changes of mood; restlessness; depression and excessive crying; undue anxiety; temper tantrums and unco-operativeness; lack of initiative, daydreaming and passiveness.

•Problems at school.
Learning problems at school, particularly in reading and language-related subjects, are also possible indications of reading disability,

particularly if your child is trying hard. A negative attitude to these subjects, or to school in general, is also another sign: if he develops headaches, stomach aches or complains of feeling sick just as the school bus is about to arrive; or he refuses to do his homework; or he complains about his teacher or the other students in the class. Behavioral problems are yet another sign: being disruptive in class and overaggressive with classmates or, on the other hand, being passive and not participating in class activities and discussions.

What to Do if You Suspect Your Child Has a Reading Disability

If you suspect your child has a reading problem, first of all make sure it *is* a reading disability. If it can be corrected merely with some extra practice and help from you or the teacher, it is not serious. Also check that it is not due to some other cause such as some physical, neurological, mental, or psychological handicap.

Talk to Your Child's Teacher

Begin by talking to your child's teacher and any other people who have contact with him to see if they have noticed any signs that indicate he might have a problem. If they have, ask them if they feel it is due to laziness, inattention or lack of effort, or if it is more serious than this. At the same time, if you have not already done so, ascertain how well your child is being taught (see the previous chapter as to how to go about this), for his problem could be due to poor teaching.

Have a Good Physical Checkup

Take him to the doctor to have his sight and hearing tested, and to have a thorough neurological and medical checkup.

Consult a Specialist

If all indications are that he is basically healthy, consult an expert or a team of professionals who can evaluate not only your child's specific reading difficulties, skills, and abilities, but also his intellectual skills and potential abilities, his language and speech development, and his general behavior.

Check with your child's school, or contact the special education department of your local school district to see what diagnosis service they have. Since the passing of the Education for All Handicapped Children Act (Public Law 94-142) in 1977, all public schools are obligated to provide diagnosis by a qualified person or team.

However, if you are not happy with what they have to offer, there are other places you can go. There are special reading clinics and centers in many cities that specialize in such evaluations. These may be private organizations, or they may be connected to a hospital or university. Your pediatrician or school can probably tell you about these, or give you a list of diagnostic specialists in your area. But, if they're not forthcoming, consult the sources at the end of this chapter.

Become More Knowledgeable

Finally, read and learn as much as you can about the subject, as this will help you to evaluate and deal more effectively with the professionals with whom you will come into contact, and help you understand their professional jargon.

Diagnosis

Check the Qualifications of the Examiner

Before you submit your child to a thorough diagnosis, be sure to check that the examiner, or examiners, are fully qualified. If they have not been recommended by someone whose opinion you respect, or if you have any uncertainty about their qualifications, ask them about their background. Inquire how long they have been testing and working with children with reading disability. If they will give you the names of families who have used their services, call the families, and ask if they were pleased with the way the examiners treated their child, administered the tests, and made their evaluation.

Make Sure the Diagnosis Is Thorough

Make sure the diagnosis will be thorough. The examiners should not only give your child a comprehensive series or "battery" of tests, but they should also spend *time* with him so they really get to know him. An experienced diagnostician can gain a tremendous amount of information by talking to a child, working with him informally, and generally observing the way he moves, looks, and reacts to various situations. It also relaxes your child for the actual tests so that the results are more likely to be an accurate assessment of his abilities.

The examiners should also include an interview with you to hear your concerns and what you feel your child's particular strengths, weaknesses, and problems are. Also, with your permission, they should consult your child's teacher, or at least have him answer a questionnaire, so that they get his views about your child. In other words, they should pursue every possible avenue that will help them to understand your child and his problems.

Ask About the Tests

Find out which tests they intend to give, and why. Check that they are standardized tests, based on adequate research, and have met standards set by the American Educational Research Association, or the National Council of Measurement in Education. Or at least be sure they have national norms so you know that your child's results are valid and can be compared with those of other children.

Make Sure You Are Given a Plan for Remediation

Ask what information the tests will give, and ascertain if it can be used to develop a definite and comprehensive program for helping your child overcome his reading disability. Make it quite clear that you want more than a nice, neat, typewritten account of the test results. You want *specific* suggestions, and a clear plan that can be acted upon. Also, make sure the test results and suggestions are explained fully. Ask questions if there is any aspect you don't understand.

Discuss the Plan with the Appropriate Personnel at Your Child's School

When you receive the diagnosis and proposed plan for your child's treatment, discuss it with the appropriate personnel at his school. If the testing was done within the school district, they will also receive, with your permission, a copy. If it was not, send them a copy before your meeting so they can come up with specific suggestions for implementing the plan. Again, under the Handicapped Child Act, all public schools are obligated to provide an "appropriate program" for your child if it is shown he has a severe reading disability.

Other Options

If you are not satisfied with their program or the teacher they assign to work with your child (more about evaluating the teacher in a moment), you can request changes. Or you can take other routes, as in the testing. The reading clinics and centers usually also provide remedial programs. There are schools that specialize in working with children with reading and learning disability, and there are independent tutors who specialize in working with these children.

Finding a Good Remedial Teacher

The best method for finding a good remedial program or tutor is word of mouth. There is no substitute for a personal recommendation from someone whose child has actually participated in the program or been taught by the teacher. Ask your friends, neighbors, and parents of your child's classmates or friends to see if they can help you. You may dislike discussing your child's problems with them, but it is the most likely way you will find the most effective treatment for his problems. So swallow your pride and start asking!

If this fails, ask the school or your pediatrician, or check the sources suggested at the end of this chapter. You can also look for advertisements in your local newspaper. However, be sure to check out the program and the teacher *thoroughly*. Beware of any program that offers gimmicks, sure-fire methods, a "system" that takes care of every child's problems, instant success, or outstanding progress in a short period of time. There are no shortcuts in learning to read, and there are certainly no "instant" remedies to cure reading disabilities. So be wary of anyone who tells you there are!

The cost for private remedial programs vary enormously. Tutoring may cost from $10 to $50 an hour. Special courses, such as those offered by reading centers, which last for a certain length of time, vary according to the number of hours and your child's reading disability. Schools that your child attends daily charge between $4,000 and $5,000 for a school year, and twice this if it is a boarding school. However, some states will assume these costs, so be sure to contact your state education authorities.

Treatment

There Is No One Method

There is no one method of treatment, program, or magical formula that will remedy all reading disability problems. This is because each child's problems are different. Whereas one child may find it difficult to learn the letters, another may not be able to remember their sounds. And whereas one child may not be able to remember a word, even though he is exposed to it numerous times, another may be a whiz at memorizing but leave out letters or syllables. Each child has different strengths, weaknesses, methods of learning, and interests, which should all be considered in setting up his program.

Another reason for the variety of "remedial" programs, as they are often called, is that teachers prefer different approaches. They find they are more comfortable teaching in a certain way, and, at least if they are good, they develop their own special methods and techniques.

Ingredients of Successful Treatment

It is generally agreed, though, that whatever method or approach is used, the most effective programs are those that give the child a feeling of *success* right from the start; provide a systematic, step-by-step procedure for teaching the skills; include the development of general language skills; involve as many of the senses as possible; and combine comprehension with the teaching of the mechanics of reading.

The Key Is the Teacher

The key to your child's treatment, above all else, is the teacher. She is the one who really counts. She can be the fairy godmother who, at last, makes learning to read an exciting, joyous, successful experience; or she can be the taskmaster who makes it agony all the way. Leave no stone unturned in your search for the right person.

First of all, see that she is a specialist in reading disability, who has not only received special training but has also had *plenty of experience* working with children with reading disability. Spend time interviewing her. Get to know her. Ask yourself: "Would I like this person to work with my child? Do I feel comfortable with her? Is she the sort of person who will spend time talking to me, answering my questions? [for you will have many as your child's treatment progresses]. Is she sympathetic? And yet does she seem to be realistic and down-to-earth? Is she the kind of person who will be firm and yet understanding in her dealings with my child?" Finally, have your child meet her. Find out his reactions. Does he like her and feel confortable with her? Do their "chemistries" match? In other words, is she the kind of person who has not only the qualifications and background to help your child but also the ability to make him *want* to and *enjoy* learning? If you don't have a nice "warm" feeling about her, stop right there and look elsewhere for your "fairy godmother." Don't despair, she's around somewhere!

Your Involvement

Be prepared to work closely with your child's tutor. Consult with her frequently, ask her what you can do at home to make her lessons more effective, and follow your child's progress carefully. In other words, don't simply turn your child over to the tutor and leave it at that, for it has been my experience that the more involvement and effort on the part of the parents, the sooner a child overcomes his problems.

If your child does have a reading disability, don't despair. With your encouragement and support and the help of an understanding teacher, he will overcome his problems. He will learn to read. Before you know it, he will be back to regular classes and doing just fine. And just to give you another note of encouragement—Albert Einstein, Thomas Edison, and Nelson A. Rockefeller all had reading disabilities and look what they accomplished!

Where to Find Help

Association for Children with Learning Disabilities
4156 Library Road
Pittsburgh, Pa. 15234
(412) 341-1515

This is a marvelous organization, which you will find most helpful. It has over two hundred state and local affiliates comprised mainly of parents with problems and concerns similar to yours. Write to them to find out about the group nearest to you, and then contact this group. You will probably find it will not only be able to supply you with information on diagnostic services, remedial programs, special schools, tutors, professional counseling, recreation, and camps, but, in addition, its members will be able to give you invaluable recommendations and advice from their personal experiences.

The Orton Society, Inc.
8415 Bellona Lane
Towson, Md. 21204
(301) 296-0232

A great organization to contact. They contend they "never turn anyone away," and they do their utmost to help you. You will talk to people who understand your problems and what you are looking for.

Dr. Orton was a pioneer in research in reading disability and the organization consists of professionals and parents concerned with reading and language disabilities.

They have twenty-two branches throughout the United States, each one being cognizant of the facilities, resources and help available for children with reading disability in their area.

Closer Look
Box 1492
Washington, D.C. 20013
(202) 833-4163

This is a national information service, funded by the Office of Education's Bureau of Education for the Handicapped, concerned with all the handicapped. However, if you write to them explaining your specific needs, giving the age of your child, they will, as their brochure says, "Put together as much information as we can to help you out."

They will give you information on the special education personnel in your state, so you can contact the appropriate state school administrator to see if there is a suitable program for your child in your local public schools. They will explain your child's rights in regard to the local school providing an adequate program for your child, and the procedures for obtaining this.

They will help you find a parent group, or organization, in your area concerned about your child's special needs, and they will send you helpful booklets, pamphlets, and lists of recommended reading.

American Association of University Affiliated Programs for the Developmentally Disabled
1100 17th Street, N.W., Suite 908
Washington, D.C. 20036

(202) 333-7880

This organization, funded primarily through the U. S. Department of Health, Education, and Welfare, will provide you with a list of universities that offer a wide variety of services for the developmentally disabled. Even if the university in your area does not provide the services your child needs, contact them, as they can often refer you to an organization that does.

Academic Therapy Publications
P.O. Box 899
1539 Fourth Street
San Rafael, Calif. 94901

Their journal is helpful to both parents and teachers, and many of their publications are directed to parents.

Can't Read, Can't Write, Can't Talk Too Good Either
by Louise Clarke
Penguin Books, Inc.
72 Fifth Avenue
New York, N.Y. 10011

1973; reprinted, 1976

Although this book is written by the mother of a child with a severe language disability, it provides some useful information concerning the facilities and services in individual states, including public and private schools, clinicians, and referral centers.

You will also find the book interesting and helpful. As the author says, it is a very personal document, beginning with an account of the struggles of her bright and determined child and his family in understanding and coping with his severe language disability. It also includes a guide to evaluating if your child has dyslexia, and describes some programs in schools working with disabled children.

These books, which you may be able to obtain from your local library, also contain useful information on facilities and resources:

The Academic Underachiever
Porter Sargent, Publisher
11 Beacon Street
Boston, Mass. 02108

1971

The information may be somewhat outdated but the book gives tutorial, remedial, diagnostic, and academic resources in prep-school programs and clinics.

Directory of Facilities for the Learning Disabled and Handicapped
by Careth Ellingson and James Cass
Harper & Row, Publishers
10 East 53rd Street
New York, N.Y. 10022

1972

This book is expensive (twenty dollars), and the information may also be a little out of date, as it was published in 1972. It lists and describes diagnostic facilities for both children and adults in the United States and Canada, and includes information on remedial, developmental, and therapeutic programs.

APPENDIX

Book Suggestions: Some Tips and Titles

On the following pages are some book suggestions to start you off on your reading program. All these books have proved to be popular with children, but don't forget: Interests and tastes differ, and what may give enjoyment to one child may not to another. So don't be disturbed if each and every one does not appeal to your child. However, I hope you will find enough that will stimulate his interest and show him the pleasure books can give. If you need more ideas, a list of sources of recommended children's books, some of which are updated annually, is given at the end of the Appendix.

The age levels given are only approximate, for the appeal of a book varies with the maturity and reading level of your child. Also, you may wish to read aloud one of the more difficult books when your child is quite young, and then give it to him again later on to read for himself.

THE FIRST FIVE YEARS

ABC Books

Apples to Zippers: An Alphabet Book by Patricia Ruben. Garden City, N.Y.: Doubleday, 1970.
Good! Your child will quickly identify with the black-and-white photos of children.

All About Arthur: An Absolutely Absurd Ape by Eric Carle. New York: Franklin Watts, 1974.
You'll like this one. It uses woodcuts and photos to show how letters are actually used.

ABC by John Burningham. Indianapolis, Ind.: Bobbs-Merrill, 1967.
Beautiful. It gives one simple word for each letter and has lovely colored drawings.

Brian Wildsmith's ABC by Brian Wildsmith. New York: Franklin Watts, 1963.
Illustrated by the author, it has splashes of colorful drawings for each word.

ABC Bunny by Wanda Gág. New York: Coward-McCann, 1933.
Also illustrated by the author, this is a tried-and-true favorite. Through the use of rhymes and outstanding lithographs, the adventures of a small rabbit are told.

Gyo Fujikawa's A to Z Picture Book by Gyo Fujikawa. New York: Grosset & Dunlap, 1974.
Yes! Yes! Yes! This one is a must, as are all the books illustrated by this superb artist. Interesting and often unusual words are given for each letter, accompanied by darling illustrations, often in color.

Nutshell Library by Maurice Sendak. New York: Harper & Row, 1962.
Your child will love to hold these tiny books. The set contains an alphabet book, a counting book, a book of rhymes, and a book about the months.

All Butterflies: An ABC by Marcia Brown. New York: Scribner's, 1974.
Check this one out. Both you and your child will love the beautiful woodcuts using bright colors, as well as black and white.

ABC of Cars and Trucks by Anne Alexander. Garden City, N.Y.: Doubleday, 1971.
Definitely for your child if he loves cars and trucks. It has brightly colored and clear drawings for each letter.

In a Pumpkin Shell: A Mother Goose ABC by Joan Walsh Anglund. New York: Harcourt, Brace, 1960.
Sweet. It combines favorite nursery rhymes with each letter of the alphabet. As always, Anglund's illustrations are delicate.

Good Night Little ABC by Robert Krans, illustrated by M. M. Bodecker. New York: Dutton, 1972.
Small-sized, for little hands. A dear book! Perfect for bedtime.

Jambo Means Hello: A Swahili Alphabet Book by Muriel Feelings, illustrated by Tom Feelings. New York: Dial, 1974.
Great if you want something different. It gives one Swahili word for each letter of the alphabet, and a map of Africa showing the countries where Swahili is spoken. It also has lovely illustrations.

Anno's Alphabet: An Adventure in Imagination by Mitsumasa Anno. New York: Crowell, 1975.
Unusual. Try it!

Cloth Books

Baby's Farm Animals. New York: Grosset & Dunlap, 1956.
Yes! It has mother animals with their babies in nice-sized, colored pictures.

My Animal Friends. New York: Platt & Munk Perma-Life Book.
Good. It has colored pictures of animals that your child will recognize. And each picture is explained by one simple sentence.

What's in My Pocket? New York: Fisher-Price Company. (Obtained from your local department or toy store, or write to Fisher-Price Toys, Inc., 200 Fifth Avenue, New York, N.Y. 10010.)
Good.

All by Herself and *All by Himself*. Hoover Products. (Check your local department or toy store for these.)
Nice self-help books with zippers to pull, buttons to unbutton, laces to tie, and so on. Other good cloth books are also produced by Western Publishing.

Touch Books

Pat the Bunny by Dorothy Kunhardt. New York: Golden Press, 1962.
Buy today! This is the best touch book. You and your child will love reading and touching this book together.

The Rabbit Who Slept and Slept. New York: Grosset & Dunlap, 1977.
Your child will like feeling a piece of the rabbit's blanket as you read the story.

Santa's Beard Is Soft and Warm by Bob Otterm and JoAnne Wood. New York: Golden Press, 1974.
Yes! This book has some Christmas-type items to feel on each page, and, of course, Santa's beard is one of them.

Counting Books

There are numerous fun and imaginative counting books on the market. Here are a few your child will enjoy.

Anno's Counting Book by Mitsumasa Anno. New York: Crowell, 1977.

My Golden Counting Book by Lillian Moore, illustrated by Garth Williams. New York: Golden Press, 1957.

Brian Wildsmith's One, Two, Threes by Brian Wildsmith. New York: Franklin Watts, 1965.

Numbers of Things written and illustrated by Helen Oxenbury. New York: Franklin Watts, 1968.

Numbers, illustrated by John J. Reiss. Scarsdale, N.Y.: Bradbury, 1971.

Wordless Books

Changes, Changes by Pat Hutchins. New York: Macmillan, 1971.
Super! Your child will love "reading" this book to you! Brightly colored blocks are used by a wooden couple to make many things they need.

A Boy, a Dog, and a Frog by Mercer Mayer. New York: Dial Press, 1967.
Funny. Children from preschool to junior high enjoy the humor in this book—and so will you. Also look for the other four books about this frog.

A Birthday Wish by Ed Emberley. Boston, Mass.: Little, Brown, 1977.
Clever. It has a comic-strip layout with funny sight gags.

Brian Wildsmith's Circus. New York: Franklin Watts, 1970.
Any book by Wildsmith is a winner, and this is no exception.

Who's Seen the Scissors? by Fernando Krahn. New York: Dutton, 1975.
Fun. Detailed illustrations show a pair of scissors romp through town cutting things as they go.

Jacko by John S. Goodall. New York: Harcourt Brace Jovanovich, 1972.
This book recounts the adventures of a monkey who has escaped from his organ-grinder master.
Also look for Goodall's other books:

Shrewbetinna's Birthday. New York: Harcourt Brace Jovanovich, 1971.

The Midnight Adventures of Kelly, Dat, and Esmeralda. New York: Atheneum, 1973.

The Adventures of Paddy Pork. New York: Harcourt Brace Jovanovich, 1968.

Paddy's Evening Out. New York: Atheneum, 1973.

There's a Nightmare in My Closet illustrated by Mercer Mayer. New York: Dial, 1968.
Nice and scary!

Deep in the Forest by Brinton Turkle. New York: Dutton, 1976.
Another good one.

Bedtime Stories

Goodnight Moon by Margaret Wise Brown. New York: Harper & Brothers, 1947.
A must! This book will definitely become a favorite. A small bunny bids good night to familiar objects in a bedroom.
Also look for her two other charming bedtime books:

A Child's Good Night Book by Margaret Wise Brown. Reading, Mass.: Addison-Wesley, 1950.
This book depicts animals getting ready for bed, and children saying their nighttime prayer.

The Runaway Bunny. New York: Harper & Row, 1972.

Sleepy Book by Charlotte Zolotow. New York: Lothrop, Lee & Shepard, 1958.
Yes! This book has lovely illustrations of children and animals going to sleep.

The Snow Parlor and Other Bedtime Stories by Elizabeth Coatsworth. New York: Grosset & Dunlap, 1972.
Both you and your child will find this book interesting. It contains five stories ideal in length for bedtime reading.

Bedtime for Frances by Russell Haban. New York: Harper & Brothers, 1960.
Yes! Your child will identify with the badger in the story who tries to put off going to bed!

Curl Up Small by Sandal S. Warburg. Boston, Mass.: Houghton Mifflin, 1964.
Isn't the title nice? And the book is equally appealing. It's about a baby and some animals who go exploring but get too sleepy to continue.

Dr. Seuss' Sleep Book by Dr. Seuss. New York: Random House, 1962.
Not as "gentle" as the other bedtime books, but your child will enjoy it. It shows imaginary characters going to sleep throughout the world.

Sleepytime illustrated by Gyo Fujikawa. New York: Grosset & Dunlap, 1975.
This is a hardboard book, so it's nice and sturdy. Once again Gyo Fujikawa provides enchanting pictures. This time they're of children preparing to go to bed and then going to sleep, as well as some darling ones showing how some animals sleep.

Mother Goose Books

Mother Goose illustrated by Gyo Fujikawa. New York: Grosset & Dunlap, 1968.
This is for you! The illustrations are outstanding.

The Real Mother Goose illustrated by Blanche Fisher Wright. Skokie, Ill.: Rand McNally, 1965.
No child or adult can help but love this fiftieth-anniversary edition of an old classic. The illustrations are fantastic.

The Mother Goose Treasury compiled and illustrated by Raymond Briggs. New York: Coward-McCann, 1966.
A beauty! Buy, buy, buy! It has twice as many fresh illustrations as rhymes.

Mother Goose illustrated by Tasha Tudor. New York: Walck, 1944.
This one has delicate, old-fashioned illustrations in soft colors.

Brian Wildsmith's Mother Goose. New York: Franklin Watts, 1965.
A super edition with brilliantly colored illustrations of animals as well as humans.

Tall Book of Mother Goose illustrated by Feodor Rojankovsky. New York: Harper & Brothers, 1942.
The unusual shape of this tall book appeals to children, and the humorous and bold illustrations modernize the favorite Mother Goose rhymes.

Ring O'Roses: A Nursery Rhyme Picture Book illustrated by Leslie Brooke. New York: Warne, 1977.
Amusing. Twenty of the favorite Mother Goose rhymes are illustrated with drawings that make you smile.

Book of Nursery and Mother Goose Rhymes compiled and illustrated by Marguerite de Angeli. Garden City, N.Y.: Doubleday, 1954.
This is a lovely, large book with almost four hundred verses illustrated in soft watercolors.

Picture Books (for four-, five-, and six-year-olds)

The Very Hungry Caterpillar by Eric Carle. New York: William Collins, 1969.
This is a must! It has wonderfully colored pages that a caterpillar "eats" through!

Where the Wild Things Are by Maurice Sendak. New York: Harper & Row, 1963.
This would be a great gift. It has unusual illustrations that children love, and it won the Caldecott award. It's about Max, who tames the wild things in his dreams.

Corduroy by Don Freeman. New York: Viking, 1968.
You'll both love this. A wonderful teddy bear is the star of the

story. Also great is his *A Rainbow of My Own.* New York: Viking, 1966.

Big and Little by Joe Kaufman. New York: Golden Books, 1967.
Wonderful color illustrations show clearly the concept of big and little.

The Biggest House in the World by Leo Lionni. New York: Pantheon, 1968.
Super!

The Little House by Virginia Lee Burton. Boston, Mass.: Houghton Mifflin, 1943.
This book won the Caldecott award. The pictures, full of detail, depict a little house and its surrounding environment. Also, don't miss her *Mike Mulligan and His Steam Shovel.* Boston, Mass.: Houghton Mifflin, 1939, which will soon become an old friend. And *Katy and the Big Snow.* Boston, Mass.: Houghton Mifflin, 1943.

Why Mosquitoes Buzz in People's Ears by Verna Aardema, illustrated by Leo and Diane Dillon. New York: Dial, 1975.
Another winner by the Dillons! It too received the Caldecott award.

A Friend Is Someone Who Likes You by Joan Walsh Anglund. New York: Harcourt, Brace, 1958.
A dear book.

The Grouchy Ladybug by Eric Carle. New York: Crowell, 1977.
Be sure to get this. The pages grow as the ladybug meets larger animals.

Little Auto by Lois Lenski. New York: Walck, 1934.
Yes—even though it dates back to the thirties. It's one in a series about Mr. Small.

Blueberries for Sal written and illustrated by Robert McCloskey. New York: Viking, 1948.
This will be a favorite. Also McCloskey's *One Morning in Maine.*

Umbrella by Taro Yashima. New York: Viking, 1958.
This book is full of color, as well as having a good story.

The Story of Babar by Jean De Brunhoff, translated from French by Merle S. Haas. New York: Random House, 1935.
Another old-timer. This one, with lovely bright pictures, has a terrific story about Babar the elephant. Your child will ask you to read it over and over again!

Tomten by Astrid Lindgren. New York: Coward-McCann, 1961.
Ask the grandparents to buy this one. Super colored winter scenes tell about Tomten, a Swedish folklore character.

A Tree Is Nice by Janice May Udry, illustrated by Marc Simot. New York: Harper & Brothers, 1956.
Glorious pictures. The book shows the importance of trees.

Do You Know What I'll Do? by Charlotte Zolotow, illustrated by Garth Williams. New York: Harper & Brothers, 1958.
A terrific team effort by author and illustrator. It's a tender story about a little girl and her baby brother. Also get their *Over and Over*. New York: Harper & Brothers, 1957.

Ira Sleeps Over by Bernard Waber. Boston, Mass.: Houghton Mifflin, 1972.
Real, touching, and funny. It's a must if your child sleeps with his stuffed animals. It's about a little boy who has to make the decision whether to take his teddy bear when he stays overnight with a friend.

Richard Scarry's Best Word Book Ever written and illustrated by Richard Scarry. Racine, Wisc.: Western Publishing, 1963.
This is a great vocabulary builder. There are fourteen hundred pictures, with a word for each picture.

The Little Engine That Could retold by Watty Piper. New York: Platt & Munk, 1976.
Yes. The positive attitude of the little engine is catching.

The Carrot Seed by Ruth Kraus, illustrated by Crockett Johnson. New York: Harper & Brothers, 1945.
This is bound to be a favorite.

The Muffin Muncher by Stephen Cosgrove. Bothell, Wash.: Serendipity Press, 1975.
Yes—buy!

Morris's Disappearing Bag: A Christmas Story written and illustrated by Rosemary Wells. New York: Dial, 1975.
Be sure to get this one.

Whistle for Willy written and illustrated by Ezra Jack Keats. New York: Viking, 1964.
Get this, and his *Hi, Cat!* New York: Macmillan, 1970.

Animal Stories (for three-, four-, five-, and six-year-olds)

Millions of Cats written and illustrated by Wanda Gág. New York: Coward-McCann, 1928.
An old-time favorite. No child's library should be without it.

Make Way for Ducklings written and illustrated by Robert McCloskey. New York: Viking, 1941.
A wonderful book, one of my absolute favorites. It's about a family of ducks who live in Boston.

Sylvester and the Magic Pebble by William Steig. New York: Windmill/Simon and Schuster, 1969.
This book is great for stimulating your child's imagination. Sylvester, a donkey, finds a magic pebble and is turned into a large rock. It has lovely bright illustrations and won the Caldecott award. Also look for his *Caleb and Kate*. New York: Farrar, Straus & Giroux, 1977.

Norman the Doorman by Don Freeman. New York: Viking, 1959.
A very imaginative book, with beautiful illustrations.

Johnny Crow's Garden by L. Leslie Brooke. New York: Warne, 1903.
Great! It gets better over the years. Johnny Crow's garden is visited by many animals.

Once a Mouse by Marcia Brown. New York: Scribner's, 1961.
Another winner of the Caldecott award.

The Tale of Peter Rabbit and *all* the books by Beatrix Potter. New York: Warne, 1900s.
I've never met a child who didn't fall under the magic of these books. Buy as many as you can for your child's library. He'll grow to love each and every one.

Baby Farm Animals by Garth Williams. New York: Golden Press, 1959.
Great illustrations.

Baby Animals illustrated by Gyo Fujikawa. New York: Grosset & Dunlap, 1963.
Once again, lovely pictures, this time with sweet, descriptive sentences about each animal, including the sound it makes.

The Cat in the Hat written and illustrated by Dr. Seuss. New York: Random House, 1957.
A priceless story about a cat that goes visiting on a rainy day. You'll both have a good laugh over this one. Also, *The Cat in the Hat Comes Back*. New York: Random House, 1958.

Little Bear by Else Holmelund Minarik, illustrated by Maurice Sendak. New York: Harper & Brothers, 1957.
An easy-to-read book of four charming stories about Little Bear. Your child will enjoy Sendak's illustrations, which are very popular with kids today. Also look for: *Father Bear Comes Home,* 1959; *Little Bear's Friend,* 1960; and *Little Bear's Visit,* 1961, all published by Harper & Brothers.

Lyle, Lyle Crocodile written and illustrated by Bernard Waber. Boston, Mass.: Houghton Mifflin, 1965.
Your child will enjoy the adventures of Lyle, who adopts a human family. Also, *Lyle and the Birthday Party,* 1966, and *Lovable Lyle,* 1969, both published by Houghton Mifflin.

Fantasy (for three-, four-, and five-year-olds)

And to Think I Saw It in Mulberry Street by Dr. Seuss. New York: Vanguard, 1937.
Still a winner. Buy it today!

Winnie-the-Pooh by A. A. Milne. New York: Dutton, 1954.
An absolute must. You can't let your child grow up without getting to know Pooh! They'll become lifelong companions.

May I Bring a Friend? by Beatrice Schenkde Regnier. New York: Atheneum, 1974.
Another Caldecott winner. The illustrations are really excellent.

Burt Dow, Deep Water Man by Robert McCloskey. New York: Viking, 1963.
Another marvelous book by McCloskey. Kids love Band-Aids, and this story is about whales and Band-Aids!

The 500 Hats of Bartholomew Cubbins by Dr. Seuss. New York: Vanguard, 1938.
Another funny fantasy by another popular author.

Tico and the Golden Wings by Leo Lionni. New York: Pantheon, 1964.
Gorgeous illustrations!

In the Night Kitchen by Maurice Sendak. New York: Harper & Row, 1970.
A story about a little boy who fantasizes about living in a baker's night kitchen.

Laughter (for three-, four-, and five-year-olds)

Where's Wallace? by Hilary Knight. New York: Harper & Row, 1964.
Fun. An orangutan escapes from the zoo and hides in the illustrations of the places he explores.

Whose Mouse Are You? by Robert Kraus. New York: Macmillan, 1970.
Cute! A question-and-answer approach.

Flap Your Wings by Philip D. Eastman. New York: Random House, 1969.
Amusing, with gorgeous pictures.

Tell Me a Mitzi by Lore Segal. New York: Farrar, Straus & Giroux, 1970.
Three funny stories about a city family.

And It Rained by Ellen Raskin. New York: Atheneum, 1969.
An amusing book on how to have tea in a rain forest.

Albert's Toothache by Barbara Williams. New York: Dutton, 1977.
Funny. Albert has a toothache in his toe!

Giants Come in Different Sizes by Jolly Roger Bradfield. New York: Random House, 1966.
Yes, funny, with good illustrations.

American Experience (for three-, four-, and five-year-olds)

Will I Have a Friend? by Miriam Cohen. New York: Macmillan, 1967.
About a kindergartener who wonders if he'll find a friend on his first day at school.

Sam, Bangs, and Moonshine by Evaline Ness. New York: Holt, 1966.
All about truth.

Wake Up, City by Alvin Tresselt. New York: Lothrop, Lee & Shepard, 1956.
The book describes a city waking up.

Stevie written and illustrated by John Steptoe. New York: Harper & Row, 1969.
About a small boy's resentment in having to share his mother, and his possessions, with a little brother. See also Steptoe's *Uptown,* 1970; and *Train Ride,* 1971, both published by Harper & Row.

The Rice Bowl Pet by Patricia M. Marlin. New York: Crowell, 1962.
About apartment living.

Tom and the Two Handles by Russell Hoban. New York: Harper & Row, 1965.
A humorous story about two friends who always get into a fist fight.

On Mother's Lap by Ann H. Scott. New York: McGraw-Hill, 1972.
Great crayon drawings of an Eskimo family.

Peter and Mr. Brandon by Eleanor Schick. New York: Macmillan, 1973.
About a small boy who discovers new sights in the city.

What's Good for a Three-year-old? by William Cole. New York: Holt, 1974.
Three-year-olds tell about what they think is the most fun.

Girls Can Be Anything by Norma Klein. New York: Dutton, 1973.
Yes. Buy today!

Peter's Chair written and illustrated by Ezra Jack Keats. New York: Harper & Row, 1967.
This book has gorgeous illustrations. It tells about Peter's jealousy of his new sister.

Life in Other Lands

Gilbert and the Wind by Marie Hall Ets. New York: Viking, 1963.
Excellent. It's about a little Mexican boy who plays with the wind.

Crow Boy by Taro Yashima. New York: Viking, 1955.
Sensitive illustrations. About a Japanese boy.

The Story About Ping by Marjorie Flack. New York: Viking, 1933.
A great favorite of children past and present. It's about a Peking duck who is lost on the Yangtze River.

Jeanne-Marie Counts Her Sheep by Françoise. New York: Scribner's, 1960.
A simple, appealing story about a little French girl and her sheep. Also look for *Minous*. New York: Scribner's, 1960.

My Teddy Bear by Chiyoko Nakatani. New York: Crowell, 1976.
Warm illustrations of a small Japanese boy and his best friend, a teddy bear.

Religion

Noah's Ark by Peter Spier. Garden City, N.Y.: Doubleday, 1977.
Gorgeous. An absolute must. It won the Caldecott award.

Nine Ways to Christmas by Marie Hall Ets. New York: Viking, 1959.
A beautiful Christmas book about a little girl in Mexico preparing for a Christmas party. Also a Caldecott winner.

The Story of Christmas, a Picture Book illustrated by Felix Hoffman. New York: Atheneum, 1975.
Yes! Lovely lithographs and story of the Nativity.

Brian Wildsmith's Illustrated Bible Stories edited by Phillip Turner. New York: Franklin Watts, 1969.
Another good one by Wildsmith.

The Jewish Sabbath by Molly Cone, illustrated by Ellen Raskin. New York: Crowell, 1966.
This book contains stunning woodcuts.

The Littler Drummer Boy written and illustrated by Ezra Jack Keats. New York: Macmillan, 1968.
Buy it. Another beauty by this sensitive writer and illustrator.

The First Christmas by Robbie Trent, illustrated by Marc Simont. New York: Harper & Brothers, 1948.
Great for the very young.

A Christmas Story written and illustrated by Mary Chalmers. New York: Harper & Row, 1971.
This tiny book, with simple and dear illustrations, tells the story of a small child's search for a star for the top of a Christmas tree.

Tales of Long Ago (for four- and five-year-olds)

Thy Friend Obadiah by Brinton Turkle. New York: Viking, 1969.
A super book, with beautiful pictures. Set in old Nantucket, it's about a Quaker boy and a seagull.

Hercules by Haidie Gramatky. New York: Putnam, 1940.
The story of an old-fashioned fire engine.

Andy and the Lion by James Daugherty. New York: Viking, 1938.
An old favorite. It's a tale about kindness remembered.

Poetry and Ballads (for three-, four-, and five-year-olds)

A Child's Book of Poems illustrated by Gyo Fujikawa. New York: Grosset & Dunlap, 1977.
This is the poetry book that I said earlier is an absolute must. If you can afford to buy only one book for your child, this is it! Another must is her *Child's Garden of Verses* by Robert Louis Stevenson. New York: Grosset & Dunlap, 1957.

A Frog Went a' Courtin' by John M. Langstaff, illustrated by Feodor Rojankovsky. New York: Harcourt, Brace, 1955.
A ballad telling the story of a frog who marries Miss Mousey, with great illustrations.

The World of Christopher Robin by A. A. Milne. New York: Dutton, 1961.
This book is, of course, a must. It combines Milne's two books *When We Were Very Young* and *Now We Are Six*.

Madeline's Rescue by Ludwig Bemelmans. New York: Viking, 1953.
The adventures of a small Parisian girl told in verse. A real favorite. Also, *Madeline*. New York: Viking, 1939.

Hailstones and Halibut Bones by Mary O'Neil, illustrated by Leonard Weisgard. Garden City, N.Y.: Doubleday, 1961.
"Fresh" poems about colors.

Fireside Book of Children's Songs by Marie Winn, illustrated by John Alcorn. New York: Simon and Schuster, 1966.
Full of songs about everyday events in the life of a child, as well as some singing games.

A Child's Garden of Verses by Robert Louis Stevenson, illustrated by Brian Wildsmith. New York: Franklin Watts, 1967.
Another attractive version of Stevenson's delightful poems.

Poems to Read to the Very Young by Josette Frank, illustrated by Dagmar Wilson. New York: Random House, 1961.
A good introduction to poetry.

The Night Before Christmas by Clement C. Moore, illustrated with paintings by Grandma Moses. New York: Random House, 1962.
You'll both enjoy this one.

There'll Be a Hot Time in the Old Town Tonight by Robert Quackenbush. Philadelphia, Pa.: Lippincott, 1974.
A musical story about the Chicago fire, with excellent illustrations.

Folklore, Fairy Tales, and Legends (for three-, four-, and five-year-olds)

The Fairy Tale Treasury selected by Virginia Haviland, illustrated by Raymond Briggs. New York: Coward, McCann & Geoghegan, 1972.
Save up for this one! It contains thirty-two nursery favorites and has excellent pictures.

Stone Soup: An Old Tale retold and illustrated by Marcia Brown. New York: Scribner's, 1947.
The witty folktale is nicely illustrated. Also look for *The Bun: A Tale from Russia;* New York: Harcourt Brace Jovanovich, 1972.

Journey Cake Ho! by Ruth Sawyer, illustrated by Robert McCloskey. New York: Viking, 1955.
A folktale about a wandering pastry.

The Mitten: An Old Ukrainian Folktale retold by Alvin Tresselt, illustrated by Yaroslavia Mills. New York: Lothrop, Lee & Shepard, 1964.
Yes!

Tall Book of Nursery Tales compiled and illustrated by Feodor Rojankovsky. New York: Harper & Brothers, 1944.
This will quickly become a loved member of the family.

The Five Chinese Brothers by Claire H. Bishop, illustrated by Kurt Wiese. New York: Coward-McCann, 1938.
An old favorite.

More Fables of Aesop retold and illustrated by Ezra Jack Kent. New York: Parents' Magazine Press, 1974.
Another winner by this writer and illustrator.

Mystery, Suspense, and Adventure (for three-, four-, and five-year-olds)

You're the Scaredy Cat by Mercer Mayer. New York: Parents' Magazine Press, 1974.
An adventure into the backyard to camp out.

The Three Robbers by Tomi Ungerer. New York: Atheneum, 1962.
Simple, colorful illustrations tell the story of three robbers who set up a beautiful castle for lost or unhappy children.

Frog and Toad Together by Arnold Lobel. New York: Harper & Row, 1972.
Five adventure stories about these two best friends.

Paddy Pork's Holiday by John S. Goodall. New York: Atheneum, 1976.
Colorful illustrations make Paddy's adventures on a walking holiday seem very real.

Clyde Monster by Robert L. Crowe. New York: Dutton, 1976.
This monster is afraid of the dark because he thinks someone may be under his bed.

Mr. Gumpy's Motor Car by John Burningham. New York: Crowell, 1976.
Great. Also try, *Mr. Gumpy's Outing*. New York: Holt, 1971.

The Secret Birthday Message by Eric Carle. New York: Crowell, 1972.
Your child will love this.

Rooftop Mystery by Joan M. Lexan. New York: Harper & Row, 1968.
Absorbing.

The Snowy Day written and illustrated by Ezra Jack Keats. New York: Viking, 1962.
Beautiful pictures, acknowledged by the Caldecott award. About the adventures of a little boy on a snowy day.

FOR SIX- AND SEVEN-YEAR-OLDS

Animal Stories

Country Bunny, and The Little Golden Shoes by Du Bose Heyward. Boston Mass.: Houghton Mifflin, 1974.
Charming—buy it! It's about a mother bunny and her children.

Leo the Late Bloomer by Robert Kraus. New York: Dutton, 1973.
Yes, the colorful pictures are super. It's about a little tiger who finally "blooms."

The Big Snow by Berta and Elmer Hader. New York: Macmillan, 1948.
Award-winning illustrations showing how animals survive the winter.

Curious George by H. A. Rey. Boston, Mass.: Houghton Mifflin, 1941.
This is a favorite of all children. Curious George is a mischievous monkey who gets into all sorts of trouble.

Amos and Boris by William Steig. New York: Farrar, Straus & Giroux, 1971.
A neat book with great pictures. A mouse and a whale become very good friends.

The Biggest Bear by Lynn Ward. Boston: Houghton Mifflin, 1952.
You'll both enjoy reading about this bear.

Three Billy Goats Gruff by Marcia Brown. New York: Harcourt, Brace, 1957.
Imaginative illustrations help tell this old Norse tale about a horrible troll and three billy goats.

The Church Mice by Graham Oakley. New York: Atheneum, 1977.
Excellent illustration of Sampson the cat who leads a group of mice through many perils.

Harry the Dirty Dog by Gene Zion. New York: Harper & Brothers, 1956.
Your child can't help but love Harry. Get this book and all the others in the series.

Rabbit Hill by Robert Lawson. New York: Viking, 1944.
A warm and humorous story about a human family moving into a rabbit family's domain.

Biography

Abraham Lincoln by Ingri and Edgar d'Aulaire. Garden City, N.Y.: Doubleday, 1957.
A great edition, with outstanding pictures, which won the Caldecott award. Also get *George Washington,* 1936, *Benjamin Franklin,* 1950, and *Buffalo Bill,* 1952, all published by Doubleday.

Picture Life of Martin Luther King, Jr., by Margaret B. Young. New York: Franklin Watts, 1968.
A brief text accompanies pictures in this easy-to-read book.

And Then What Happened, Paul Revere? by Jean Fritz, with pictures by Margot Tomes. New York: Coward, McCann & Geoghegan, 1973.
An exciting and funny story that blends fact and legend about Paul Revere.
Also look for this author's *Will You Sign Here, John Hancock?* 1976 published by Coward, McCann & Geoghegan.
A lighthearted story of one of our Founding Fathers with robust drawings. And her *Where Was Patrick Henry on the 29th of May?* 1975, *Why Don't You Get a Horse, Sam Adams?* 1974, also her

latest 1977 book called *Can't You Make Them Behave King George?* all published by Coward, McCann & Geoghegan.

Fantasy

Velveteen Rabbit by Margery Williams. Garden City, N.Y.: Doubleday, 1958.
A super story of a stuffed rabbit who wants to become real.

Many Moons by James Thurber. New York: Harcourt, Brace, 1943.
The excellent drawings gained the Caldecott award. Your child will love this story about a little princess who wants the moon.

Thumbelina by Hans Christian Andersen. New York: Scribner's, 1961.
Soft water colors enhance this story of a tiny heroine.

Lion by William Pène du Bois. New York: Viking, 1956.
Excellent pictures by the author.

My Father Dragon by Ruth Gannett. New York: Random House, 1948.
Yes, try it.

The Maggie B written and illustrated by Irene Haas. New York: Atheneum, 1975.
A neat story with beautiful illustrations. A little girl sails away for a day on her dream ship with her baby brother.

Aesop's Fables retold by Anne Terry White, illustrated by Helen Siegl. New York: Random House, 1964.
A great edition of these fables, which every child should know.

Cinderella by Charles Perrault, retold and illustrated by Marcia Brown. New York: Scribner's, 1954.
Beautiful—an absolute must for the library. Also save up for

Marcia Brown editions of: *The Steadfast Tin Soldier* by Hans Christian Andersen; *Dick Whittington and His Cat; Puss in Boots; The Flying Carpet;* and *Once a Mouse.*

The Fairy Tale Treasury selected by Virginia Haviland, illustrated by Raymond Briggs. New York: Coward, McCann & Geoghegan, 1972.
Yes, you must have this lovely book too! It has thirty-two fairy tales from all over the world that your child should know. He'll not only enjoy them but also the many super illustrations. Also get Haviland's *Favorite Fairy Tales in England* and *Favorite Fairy Tales Told in France, Scotland, Germany,* and other lands.

The Shoemaker and the Elves by the Brothers Grimm, illustrated by Adrienne Adams. New York: Scribner's, 1960.
Gorgeous colored illustrations help to bring alive this tale, which has enthralled many generations of children. Yes, of course, another must!

Laughter

Lentil by Robert McCloskey. New York: Viking, 1940.
Another children's favorite by Robert McCloskey. This one has particularly interesting illustrations.

The Story of Ferdinand by Munro Leaf. New York: Viking, 1936.
This book has been popular for a long time. You'll both enjoy it too.

My Friend Charlie by James Flora. New York: Harcourt, Brace & World, 1964.
Great. All about the crazy antics of Charlie.

House on East Eighty-eighth Street by Bernard Waber. Boston, Mass.: Houghton Mifflin, 1962.
Yes!

The Dog Who Thought He Was a Boy by Cora Annett. Boston, Mass.: Houghton Mifflin, 1965.
Fun.

The Amazing Bone by William Steig. New York: Farrar, Straus & Giroux, 1976.
Funny. You'll like this too. Pearl Pig finds a talking bone.

The American Experience

Boats on the River by Marjorie Flack. New York: Viking, 1946.
Dramatic illustrations of all kinds of boats.

The Day We Saw the Sun Come Up by Alice Goudey. New York: Scribner's, 1961.
This book gives good information, and has beautiful pictures of the sunrise.

Nobody Listens to Andrew by Elizabeth Caudill. New York: Holt, Rinehart & Winston, 1964.
A story about a boy's first day at school, with outstanding illustrations.

Song of the Swallows by Leo Politi. New York: Scribner's, 1949.
A Caldecott winner.

Book of Moon Rockets for You by Franklyn Branley. New York: Crowell, 1970.
This book is easy to read, with accurate information.

Benjie by Joan Lexan, illustrated by Don Bolognese. New York: Dial, 1964.
About a very shy boy who overcomes his shyness to help his grandmother.

City Rhythms written and illustrated by Ann Grifalconi. Indianapolis, Ind.: Bobbs-Merrill, 1965.
An unusual book. A young boy becomes aware of city sounds.

Life in Other Lands

Pelle's New Suit by Elsa Besko. New York: Harper & Brothers, 1929.
An old favorite with beautifully colored pictures. A Swedish boy gets a new suit and sees how it is made from the beginning to end.

Amigo by Byrd B. Schweitzer. New York: Macmillan, 1963.
A small Mexican boy sets out to tame a prairie dog for a pet.

Wee Gillis by Munro Leaf. New York: Viking, 1938.
Another old favorite about a Scottish boy. You'll love the gorgeous illustrations.

Ola by Ingri and Edgar d'Aulaire. Garden City, N.Y.: Doubleday, 1939.
A Norwegian boy takes the reader on a tour of interesting places in his homeland.

Little Pear: The Story of a Little Chinese Boy by Eleanor F. Rattimore. New York: Harcourt, Brace, 1931.
Yes, you'll both enjoy this one.

Mei Li by Thomas Handforth. Garden City, N.Y.: Doubleday, 1938.
This story is about a Chinese girl who goes to the New Year's Fair in the city. It won the Caldecott award.

The Girl Who Loved the Wind by Jane Yolen. New York: Crowell, 1972.
An oriental girl is aroused by the wind to branch out from her protected environment.

The Day the Hurricane Happened by Lonzo Anderson. New York: Scribner's, 1974.
Lovely water color pictures illustrate the Virgin Islands setting.

Religion

A Certain Small Shepherd by Rebecca Caudill, illustrated by William Pène du Bois. New York: Holt, Rinehart & Winston, 1965.
A sensitive story about a young mute boy from Appalachia. Caudill and du Bois have created a classic.

Prayer for a Child by Rachel Field, illlustrated by Elizabeth Orton Jones. New York: Macmillan, 1973.

A child's thankfulness is expressed in gentle verses and beautiful pictures. A Caldecott award.

Christmas Eve by Edith Hurd, illustrated by Clement Hurd. New York: Harper & Row, 1962.
A nice story about the animals in Bethlehem on the first Christmas Eve.

Runaway Jonah and Other Tales by Jan Wahl, illustrated by Uri Shulevitz. New York: Macmillan, 1968.
Exciting illustrations. Wahl recounts her favorite Old Testament stories.

The Christ Child by Maud and Miska Petersham. New York: Doubleday, 1931.
Beautiful retelling of Christ's birth and his childhood, illustrated with water colors.

The Shepherd written and illustrated by Helga Aichinger. New York: Crowell, 1967.
A picture book story of a shepherd's journey to the manger.

Tales of Long Ago

The Plymouth Thanksgiving by Leonard Weisgard. Garden City, N.Y.: Doubleday, 1967.
Stunning pictures help to tell about the Pilgrims' first year in this country.

Little Runner of the Longhouse by Betty Baker, illustrated by Arnold Lobell. New York: Harper & Row, 1962.
An Indian boy and his mother celebrate the New Year. An "I can read book."

Dan Frontier by William Hurley, illustrated by Jack Boyd. Chicago, Ill.: Benefic Press, 1962.
All about a pioneer boy in Kentucky. Follow this up with *Dan Frontier and Wagon Train.*

The Little Girl with Seven Names by Mabel Hunt. Philadelphia, Pa.: Lippincott, 1936.
A good story that continues to be a favorite of today's children.

Sam the Minuteman by Nathaniel Benchley, illustrated by Arnold Label. New York: Harper & Row, 1969.
An excellent story about Sam and his father, who fought the British at the beginning of the Revolutionary War. Another "I can read book."

Poetry and Ballads

Free to Be—You and Me edited by Francine Klagsbrun, with a Foreword by Marlo Thomas. New York: McGraw-Hill, 1974.
Excellent. Nonsexist poems, songs, stories, and cartoons.

Nibble, Nibble by Margaret Wise Brown, illustrated by Leonard Weisgard. Reading, Mass.: Addison-Wesley, 1959.
A wonderful picture/poem book about insects and animals.

Sung Under the Silver Umbrella, Association for Childhood Education International, illustrated by Dorothy Lathrop. New York: Macmillan, 1972.
A good collection of poems for young children.

Listen Rabbit by Aileen Fisher. New York: Crowell, 1964.
A story, poem, and picture book about a boy who tries to tame a rabbit.

Time for Poetry edited by May Hill Arbuthnot and Shelton L. Root, Jr. Glenview, Ill.: Scott, Foresman, 1968.
Ask the grandparents to buy this. It's great for reading aloud.

Alligator Pie by Dennis Lee. Boston, Mass.: Houghton Mifflin, 1975.
Yes, try it.

Everett Anderson's Year by Lucille Clifton. New York: Holt, Rinehart & Winston, 1974.
About the monthly experiences of a young boy.

On the Day Peter Stuyvesant Sailed into Town by Arnold Lobel. New York: Harper & Row, 1971.
Rollicking verse tells of life in the New Amsterdam colony.

Jack Jonett's Ride by Gail Haley. New York: Viking, 1975.
Ballad like verse tells of a historical event in American history. Illustrated with colored linoleum cuts, it takes place in Virginia.

It's Halloween by Jack Prelutsky, illustrated by Marylin Hafner. New York: Greenwillow Books, 1977.
Easy-to-read poems about Halloween with fun illustrations.

Folklore, Fairy Tales, and Legends

Chanticleer and the Fox by Geoffrey Chaucer. New York: Crowell, 1958.
A good story with a happy ending and colorful pictures that won the Caldecott award. What more could you want?

Once a Mouse: A Fable Cut in Wood by Marcia Brown. New York: Scribner's, 1961.
Another super book by Marcia Brown, which also won the Caldecott award. Woodcuts retell this old fable.

Told Under the Green Umbrella, Association for Childhood Education International, illustrated by Grace Gilkison. New York: Macmillan, 1935.
A great collection of famous folk and fairy tales.

Anansi the Spider by Gerald McDermott. New York: Holt, Rinehart & Winston, 1971.
An African folk tale.

Tikki, Tikki Tembo retold by Arlene Mosel, illustrated by Blair Lent. New York: Holt, Rinehart & Winston, 1968.
Yes, you'll enjoy this.

John Henry an American Legend by Ezra Jack Keats. New York: Pantheon, 1965.

Another good Keats book. This one is the story of our famous American hero.

Andy and the Lion written and illustrated by James Daugherty. New York: Viking, 1938.
Many children over the years have enjoyed this book, and I'm sure your child will too.

The Goblin Under the Stairs by Mary Calhoun. New York: Morrow, 1968.
The story of an English house elf, a boggart. Good illustrations.

Even the Devil Is Afraid of a Shrew retold by Valerie Stalder, illustrated by Richard Brown. Reading, Mass.: Addison-Wesley, 1972.
A Lapland folktale, with lovely colored pictures, about how a peaceful man gets rid of a nagging wife.

Who's in Rabbit's House? (A Masai Tale) retold by Verna Aardema, illustrated by Leo and Diane Dillon. New York: Dial, 1977.
Different. It's an African tale told by making the reader feel part of an audience watching a play.

Mystery, Suspense, and Adventure

The Case of the Cat's Meow by Crosby Bonsall. New York: Harper & Brothers, 1945.
A great mystery! Four young boys search for a missing cat. Also try his suspense-filled city story *And I Mean It, Stanley*. New York: Harper & Row, 1968.
A nice ghost story.

A Ghost Named Fred by Nathaniel Benchley. New York: Harper & Row, 1968.
A nice ghost story.

Big Max by Kin Platt. New York: Harper & Row, 1965.
All about a missing elephant.

The Case of the Stolen Code Book by Barbara Rinkoff. New York: Crown, 1971.
Excitement and mystery abounds in this one!

The Secret Three by Mildred Myrick. New York: Harper & Row, 1963.
A terrific book.

The Mixed-up Mystery Smell by Eleanor Coerr. New York: Putnam, 1976.
Full of suspense from beginning to end. Your child will love it.

Binky Brothers, and the Fearless Four by James Lawrence. New York: Harper & Row, 1970.
Yes. He'll like this one too.

Bored, Nothing to Do by Peter Spier, illustrated by the author. Garden City, N.Y.: Doubleday, 1978.
To overcome boredom, two friends build an airplane that really flies!

Come Away from the Water, Shirley by John Burningham. New York: Crowell, 1978.
Good illustrations tell about Shirley at the seashore with her parents.

FOR EIGHT- AND NINE-YEAR-OLDS

Animal Stories

Trumpet of the Swan by E. B. White. New York: Harper & Row, 1970.
A super story, and an absolute "must" for your child's library. It's about a voiceless swan who learns to play a trumpet and finds his fortune.

Misty of Chincoteague by Marguerite Henry. Skokie, Ill.: Rand McNally, 1974.
You'll enjoy reading aloud this story to your child. It's about a horse called Misty. He is owned by a brother and sister, and becomes famous. Marguerite Henry's other two books on horses are also good: *King of the Wind,* 1976, and *Stormy—Misty's Foal,* 1963, both published by Rand McNally.

Mr. Popper's Penguins by Richard and Florence Atwater. Boston, Mass.: Little, Brown, 1938.
A humorous story, with illustrations to make you laugh. A penguin family moves in with Mr. Popper.

Lassie Come Home by Eric Knight. New York: Harper & Row, 1971.
An old favorite. The famous collie travels four hundred miles to return home after being sold.

The Wind and the Willows by Kenneth Grahame. New York: Grosset & Dunlap, 1967.
One of the classics. Great to read aloud. It's a tale of magic and humor about some adorable small animals who assume human personalities.

The Enormous Egg by Oliver Butterworth. Boston, Mass.: Little, Brown, 1956.
A funny, funny story. You'll both enjoy it! A dinosaur is hatched from an enormous egg and a boy finds he has many problems.

Abel's Island by William Steig. New York: Farrar, Straus & Giroux, 1976.
An adventure story about a mouse who leads an easy life until he's separated from his family on a desert island.

Biography

Langston Hughes, American Poet by Alice Walker. New York: Crowell, 1974.
Good, and easy to read.

Louis Armstrong by Genie Iverson. New York: Crowell, 1976.
Another easy-to-read book. It tells about Armstrong's life, from his childhood to when he became known as the "King of Jazz."

Arthur Mitchell by Tabi Tabias. New York: Crowell, 1975.
About a black man's dream to be a leading ballet dancer coming true.

Sir Henry Morgan, Buccaneer by Ronald Syme. New York: Morrow, 1965.
About a seventeenth-century pirate who was knighted by a king.

Jeanne d'Arc by Aileen Fisher. New York: Crowell, 1970
A good introduction to the story of Joan of Arc.

A Special Bravery by Johanna Johnston. New York: Dodd, Mead, 1967.
This book tells about the accomplishments of fifteen outstanding black people from Revolutionary times to the late 1960s.

The Great Houdini by Anne Edwards, illustrated by Joseph Ciardiello. New York: Putnam, 1977.
The story of one of the greatest magicians and escape artists of all time!

Fantasy

The Borrowers by Mary Norton. New York: Harcourt, Brace, 1953.
Yes, yes! This book, about some unusual miniature people who live under the floorboards of a house, is very popular with this age group.

Charlotte's Web by E. B. White. New York: Harper & Brothers, 1952.
Another winner by White, and another "must" for your shopping list. This story is about a spider, a pig, and a little girl who can "talk" to the animals.

Charlie and the Chocolate Factory by Roald Dahl. New York: Knopf, 1964.
A fantasy for all ages! Put it on the "must" list.

Mary Poppins by Pamela Travers. New York: Harcourt, Brace, 1934.
Year after year children delight in reading the fun and magic that exudes from Mary Poppins. Your child will be no exception. A delightful book. Also read: *Mary Poppins Comes Back; Mary Poppins Opens the Door;* and *Mary Poppins in the Park.*

Adventures of Pinocchio by Carlo Collodi. New York: Macmillan, 1969.
A good edition of the old-time favorite.

The Bee—Man of Orn by Frank P. Stockton, illustrated by Maurice Sendak. New York: Holt, Rinehart & Winston, 1964.
Children particularly enjoy Sendak's illustrations of this nice fantasy.

Peter Pan by James M. Barrie. New York: Scribner's, 1950.
A classic. No child should grow up without reading Peter Pan!

Miss Hickory by Carolyn Bailey. New York: Viking, 1946.
An imaginative text, with fine lithographs, which won the Newbery award. It's about a doll who has to become self-reliant when she is forced to live outside for the winter.

Laughter

Henry Huggins by Beverly Cleary. New York: Morrow, 1950.
Very funny. Buy it! Henry gets into all sorts of amusing situations. Also try *Henry and the Paper Route; Henry and the Clubhouse; Henry and Beezus;* and *Henry and Ribsy.* Your child will also enjoy Beverly Cleary's stories about Ramona, the young sister of Beezus. *Ramona the Pest,* 1968; and *Ramona and Her Father,* 1977. All are published by Morrow.

Capybobby by Bill Peets. Boston, Mass.: Houghton Mifflin, 1966.
Great! A funny, warmhearted, personal story.

The Reluctant Dragon by Kenneth Grahame. New York: Holiday House, 1953.
Another Grahame that has become an old favorite. In this one a boy makes friends with a peaceful dragon.

Monster Too Many by Janet McNeill. Boston, Mass.: Little, Brown, 1972.
Fun!

McBroom Tells the Truth by Sid Fleischman, illustrated by Kurt Werth. New York: Grosset & Dunlap, 1972.
Funny! McBroom tells how his eleven-acre farm produces three or four crops a day.

American Experience

The Little House in the Big Woods by Laura Ingalls Wilder. New York: Harper & Brothers, 1953.
Yes! The author tells of her childhood growing up at the edge of a big wood in Wisconsin around the 1870s. This is one of a series made famous by the television program developed from her *Little House on the Prairie*. However, her books have always been popular with children, and your child will also enjoy them. The others are *On the Banks of Plum Creek; By the Shore of Silver Lake;* and *Farmer Boy*.

A Week in Leonora's World: Puerto Rico by Eliot Elisofon. New York: Crowell, 1971.
A peep into life in Puerto Rico.

Mississippi Possum by Miska Miles. Boston, Mass.: Little, Brown, 1965.
Great illustrations. A baby possum escapes a Mississipppi River flood with a black family.

Did You Carry the Flag Today, Charley? by Rebecca Caudill. New York: Holt, Rinehart & Winston, 1971.
Charley is allowed to carry the flag if he's been good in school all day.

The Courage of Sarah Noble by Alice Dalgliesh, illustrated by Leonard Weisgard. New York: Scribner's, 1954.
An eight-year-old girl and her father go into the Connecticut wilderness to build a home.

Strawberry Girl by Louis Lenski. Philadelphia, Pa.: Lippincott, 1954.
Yes. It won the Newbery award.

The 17 Gerbils of Class 4A by William Hooks. New York: Coward, McCann & Geoghegan, 1976.
A student brings his gerbils to school because he's moving away, and the class has to learn how to care for them.

The Accident by Carol Carrick. New York: Seabury Press, 1976.
This is a sensitive story, with good illustrations. It tells how a young boy deals with the loss of his dog, who is killed.

One Morning in Maine written and illustrated by Robert McCloskey. New York: Viking, 1952.
Wonderful! It's about a young girl who loses her first tooth.

"The Whistling Teakettle" and Other Stories About Hannah by Mindy W. Skolsky, illustrated by Karen Ann Weinhaus. New York: Harper & Row, 1977.
Four wonderful stories about Hannah, a Jewish girl who lives in New York.

Life in Other Lands

The Happy Orpheline by Natalie Savage Carlson. New York: Harper & Brothers, 1957.
A nice story about some French children who live in a poor orphanage. They are so happy they don't want to be adopted.

Janet Reachfar and the Kelpie by Jane Duncan. New York: Seabury Press, 1976.
Good. Color paintings depict the rural Scottish Highlands.

Pippi Longstockings by Astrid Lindgren. New York: Viking, 1950.
Another "must." Your child can't grow up without becoming friends with this Swedish tomboy and learning about all her outlandish experiences.

Heidi by Johanna Spyri. New York: Macmillan, 1962.
Another classic that should be part of your child's library. It's about lovable Heidi who lives in the Swiss mountains.

Religion

Told Under the Christmas Tree by Association for Childhood Education International, illustrated by Maud and Miska Petersham. New York: Macmillan, 1962.
A good collection of Christmas and Hanukkah stories and poems.

Small Rain by Jessie Orton Jones, illustrated by Elizabeth Orton Jones. Baltimore, Md.: Penguin, 1974.
An excellent selection of Bible verses chosen especially for children.

Festivals for You to Celebrate by Susan Purdy. Philadelphia, Pa.: Lippincott, 1969.
A good reference book.

Happy Christmas compiled by William Kean Seymour and John Smith, illustrated by Beryl Sanders. Philadelphia, Pa.: Westminster Press, 1968.
Great for reading aloud around Christmastime. It contains a wide variety of stories, poems, and songs, such as an excerpt from Beatrix Potter's *The Tailor of Gloucester;* Christina Rossetti's poem, *A Christmas Carol,* and an excerpt from E. R. G. R. Evan's *South with Scott.*

Christmas edited by Alice Dalgliesh, illustrated by Hildegard Woodward. New York: Scribner's, 1962.
A Christmas must. Put it on the list for Santa Claus. It's a marvelous collection of stories and poems, old and new. It has the story of the first Christmas as told in the Bible, and Kenneth Grahame's modern version. Also descriptions of an old-time American Christmas by Laura Ingalls Wilder, and tales of Christmas in several countries. And more! Lovely black-and-white illustrations.

Joy to the World by Ruth Sawyer, illustrated by Trina Schart Hyman. Boston, Mass.: Little, Brown, 1966.
Six tales of Christmas richly illustrated.

Tales of Long Ago

The Bears on Hemlock Mountain by Alice Dalgliesh, illustrated by Helen Sewell. New York: Scribner's, 1952.
An eight-year-old has to brave a journey over a mountain and meets the bears she dreaded.

Little Pear by Eleanor Lattimore. New York: Harcourt, Brace, 1931.
An old story, which is still a favorite.

Thee, Hannah! by Marguerite de Angeli. Garden City, N.Y.: Doubleday, 1940.
A story about a lively young Quaker girl growing up in old Philadelphia.

Aaron and the Green Mountain Boys by Patricia Lee Gauch. New York: Coward, McCann & Geoghegan, 1972.
A really interesting story based on true facts. It's about a nine-year-old boy during the Revolution.

The Drinking Gourd by F. N. Monjo, illustrated by Fred Brenner. New York: Harper & Row, 1969.
A simple but engrossing story about a New England boy who helps to save a slave family during the Civil War.

Poetry and Ballads

Bronzeville Boys and Girls by Gwendolyn Brooks. New York: Harper & Brothers, 1956.
Short poems about the city life of black children.

The Hunting of the Snark by Lewis Carroll. New York: British Book Centre, 1976.
Humorous nonsense—glorious!

All the Silver Pennies by Blanche Jennings Thompson. New York: Macmillan, 1967.
A favorite.

Rocket in My Pocket: Rhymes and Chants of Young Americans compiled by Carl Withers. New York: Holt, 1948.
Essential!

You Read to Me, I'll Read to You by John Ciardi. Philadelphia, Pa.: Lippincott, 1962.
All of Ciardi's poems are fun. Also get his *The Reason for the Pelican,* 1959, and *The Man Who Sang the Sillies,* 1961.

The Laura Ingalls Wilder Songbook: Favorite Songs from the Little House Books compiled by Eugene Garson, illustrated by Garth Williams. New York: Harper & Row, 1968.
A chance to appreciate the songs on their own.

Nightmares: Poems to Trouble Your Sleep by Jack Pretulsky, illustrated by Arnold Lobel. New York: Greenwillow Books/Morrow, 1976.
Great for monster lovers!

A Pack of Riddles compiled by William R. Gerler. New York: Dutton, 1975.
Super, terrific, fun! And it has amusing illustrations, too!

Folklore, Fairy Tales, and Legends

This Time, Temper Wick? by Patricia Lee Gauch. New York: Coward, McCann & Geoghegan, 1974.
Yes, buy this one! It's a legend of a strong, brave girl.

The Long-tailed Bear and Other Indian Legends by Natalie Belting. Indianapolis, Ind.: Bobbs-Merrill, 1961.
You'll both enjoy reading these legends.

Ol' Paul, the Mighty Logger by Glen Rounds. New York: Holiday House, 1976.
Ten tales of Paul Bunyan.

Tales for the Third Ear from Equatorial Africa by Verna Aardema. New York: Dutton, 1969.

Interesting, easy-to-read tales about the adventures of crafty animals.

The Legend of Scarface: A Blackfoot Indian Tale adapted by Robert San Souci, illustrated by David San Souci. Garden City, N.Y.: Doubleday, 1978.
An Indian brave journeys to the land of the sun to ask for the hand of his sweetheart.

The Wonder Ring: A Fantasy in Silhouettes by Holden Wetherbee, illustrated by the author. Garden City, N.Y.: Doubleday, 1978.
A wordless story of a young boy's fantasy, involving a wicked stepmother, a giant, and a princess.

D'Aulaire's Trolls by Ingri and Edgar d'Aulaire. Garden City, N.Y.: Doubleday, 1972.
Kids adore the d'Aulaires' books, especially their bizarre illustrations! This one is full of colorful stories about Norwegian trolls.

How Wilka Went to Sea, and Other Tales from West of the Urals by Mirra Ginsburg, illustrated by Charles Mikolaycak. New York: Crown, 1975.
Tales about central Russia with striking colored, full-page illustrations.

Favorite Fairy Tales Told in India selected by Virginia Haviland, illustrated by Blair Lent. Boston, Mass.: Little, Brown, 1973.
Magic stories from India, with attractive illustrations.

When Shlemiel Went to Warsaw, and Other Stories by Isaac B. Singer, illustrated by Margot Zemach. New York: Farrar, Straus & Giroux, 1968.
Traditional and new Jewish tales. These stories are fun.

Wiley and the Hairy Man adapted and illustrated by Molly Garrett Bang. New York: Macmillan, 1976.
Very good. An American folktale about a young black boy and his smart mother who outwit a hairy creature.

Mystery, Suspense, and Adventure

Encyclopedia Brown: Boy Detective by Donald J. Sobol. New York: Nelson, 1963.
Children love this and all the other Encyclopedia Brown books, which tell about mystery cases solved by a ten-year-old boy.

Harriet the Spy by Louise Fitzhugh. New York: Harper & Row, 1964.
Harriet spies on everyone, and kids enjoy doing it with her!

The Tower Treasure: Hardy Boys Mystery Series by Franklin W. Dixon. New York: Grosset & Dunlap, 1927.
The Hardy Boys books are not great literary works, but they have been encouraging children to read ever since they were first published more than fifty years ago. Great "escape" books.

The Ghost of Blackwood Hall: Nancy Drew Mystery Stories by Carolyn Keene. New York: Grosset & Dunlap, 1948.
The same comments as above apply to the Nancy Drew books, which are now written by the daughter of Dixon.

Basil of Baker Street by Eve Titus and Paul Galdone. New York: McGraw-Hill, 1963.
All about a very intelligent mouse detective.

Tim and Lucy Go to Sea by Edward Ardizzone. New York: Walck, 1958.
Tim and Lucy have an adventure at sea.

First Adventure by Elizabeth Coatsworth, illustrated by Ralph Ray. New York: Macmillan, 1950.
A very good story of the adventure of a boy and his dog.

Emil and the Detectives by Erich Kastner, translated from the German by Eileen Hall, illustrated by Walter Trier. New York: Penguin, 1959.
A detective story in which Emil is the victim. This book and the

other ones by Kastner have delighted children all over the world since they were first printed in the 1930s. The other ones are: *Emil and the Three Twins; The Flying Classroom;* and *Lottie and Lisa.*

Five Find a Secret Way by Enid Blyton. New York: Atheneum, 1972.
All children adore this English author's absorbing and exciting stories. Load up!

FOR TEN- AND ELEVEN-YEAR-OLDS

Animal Stories

The Incredible Journey, A Tale of Three Animals by Sheila Bunford, illustrated by Carl Burger. Boston, Mass.: Little, Brown, 1961.
An absolute must. Buy it for the library, as it's bound to become a favorite. It's about a cat and two dogs who depend upon one another for survival on their journey home through the Canadian wilderness.

Gentle Ben by Walt Morey. New York: Dutton, 1965.
An outstanding story of a boy and an Alaskan bear.

Jungle Book by Rudyard Kipling. New York: Grosset & Dunlap, 1950.
A well-known classic, but best read aloud.

The Cricket in Times Square by George Selden. New York: Farrar, Straus & Cudahy, 1960.
Yes—a must. This very funny story about a cricket and his friends, who live in Times Square, is a real favorite with children of all ages.

The Story of Dr. Dolittle by Hugh Lofting. Philadelphia, Pa.: Lippincott, 1920.
Another all-time favorite. A medical doctor, who becomes a veterinarian, understands the sounds of animals. Try the other Dolittle books too.

Owls in the Family by Farley Mowat, illustrated by Robert Frankenberg. Boston, Mass.: Little, Brown, 1961.
Funny. A true story about a boy whose two pet owls cause many disruptions in his home.

Pagoo by Holling C. Holling. Boston: Houghton Mifflin, 1957.
Beautiful illustrations describe the story of a hermit crab.

Benjamin West and His Cat Grimalkin by Marguerite Henry. Indianapolis, Ind.: Bobbs-Merrill, 1947.
Amusing! A story about Benjamin's struggle to study painting.

Biography

They Were Strong and Good by Robert Lawson. New York: Viking, 1940.
Excellent. Personal accounts of a family told by grandparents to a child. It won the Caldecott award. Great for developing an appreciation of family history.

Mary McLeod Bethune by Eloise Greenfield. New York: Coward, McCann & Geoghegan, 1977.
An interesting account of Mary Bethune.

Pete, Soccer Superstar by Louis Sabin. New York: Putnam, 1976.
Yes, if your child is a football fan.

Black Pioneers of Science and Invention by Louis Haber. New York: Harcourt Brace Jovanovich, 1970.
Informative and interesting.

The Runaway Slave: The Story of Harriet Tubman by Ann McGovern. New York: Four Winds Press, 1965.
Easy-to-read, gripping story, full of information about the Civil War.

Indian Capture: The Story of Mary Jemison by Lois Lenski. Philadelphia, Pa.: Lippincott, 1941.
The true story of Mary Jemison, who was captured by the Indians and had to decide whether or not to return to her own people.

Daniel Boone by James Daugherty. New York: Viking, 1939.
A vivid account of this early pioneer who has fascinated and enthralled generations of children. A Newbery winner.

Fantasy

The Lion, the Witch, and the Wardrobe by C. S. Lewis. New York: Macmillan, 1951.
Not so well known as his Alice books, but a real winner! In fact, children of today prefer this story of four children who walk through a wardrobe into another land. Also get his other tales, particularly *The Magician's Nephew* and *The Last Battle.*

The Hobbit by John R. Tolkien. Boston, Mass.: Houghton Mifflin, 1938.
This book appeals to all ages. I suggest you first introduce it to your child by reading it aloud. Then you can also enjoy it!

Summer Birds by Penelope Farmer. New York: Harcourt, Brace, 1962.
Original! Three English children are taught to fly.

The Phantom Tollbooth by Norton Juster, illustrated by Jules Feiffer. New York: Random House, 1961.
Humorous and magical.

Half Magic by Edward Eager. New York: Harcourt, Brace, 1954.
Another magical adventure story.

Gnomes by Wil Huygen. New York: Abrams, 1977.
A terrific book with maps, charts, and even recipes, telling you all you've ever wanted to know about gnomes! It has lavish illustrations on every page. A true family keepsake that you and your kids will want to peruse again and again. Buy it! Buy it!

Chitty-Chitty-Bang-Bang by Ian Fleming. New York: Random House, 1964.
About an old racing car that can communicate, swim, and fly.

The Secret Garden by Frances Hodgson Burnett. Philadelphia, Pa.: Lippincott, 1962.
This has long been a true favorite of children. Buy it for keeps!

Just So Stories by Rudyard Kipling, illustrated by Etienne Delessert. Garden City, N.Y.: Doubleday, 1972.
An absolute must!

Laughter

By the Great Horn Spoon by Sid Fleischman. Boston, Mass.: Little, Brown, 1963.
Hilarious.

Homer Price written and illustrated by Robert McCloskey. New York: Viking, 1943.
Terrific. Six really funny stories about a boy and a nonstop donut machine.

Complete Peterkin Papers by Lucretia Hale. Boston, Mass.: Houghton Mifflin, 1960.
Fun to read aloud.

The Alligator Case by William Pène du Bois. New York: Harper & Row, 1965.
Yes, amusing.

The Great Brain by John D. Fitzgerald. New York: Dial, 1967.
Witty.

Alvin Fernald, Foreign Trader by Clifford Hicks. New York: Holt, Rinehart & Winston, 1966.
Your child will love this one. It's full of funny incidents connected with a trip to Europe, and spies.

American Experience

Little Women by Louisa May Alcott. Boston, Mass.: Little, Brown, 1968.

Is there a girl who has not enjoyed this captivating story about four sisters? A must for the library, as it will be read over and over again. Also get Alcott's other books in the series, *Little Men* and *Jo's Boys*.

Caddie Woodlawn by Carol Ryrie Brink. New York: Macmillan, 1973.
An exciting story about a spirited pioneer girl in the mid-nineteenth century. The author, the granddaughter of the real Caddie Woodlawn, based the book on true stories told her by her grandmother. A Newbery winner. Buy it!

Anne of Green Gables by L. M. Montgomery. New York: Grosset & Dunlap, 1970.
Originally written in 1908, this book has appealed to girls of every generation to the present day. It's about a red-haired girl who finally acquires a home of her own after spending years in an orphanage. No girl should miss experiencing with Anne the trials and tribulations, and sorrows and joys, of growing up.

Adopted Jane by H. R. Daringer. New York: Scholastic Book Services, 1972.
Another story about a girl in an orphanage. In this one Jane is sent to a Mrs. Thurman, sister-in-law of the chairman of the Board, for a month.

The Moffats by Eleanor Estes. New York: Harcourt, Brace & World, 1968.
Great for reading aloud. It's about four Connecticut children who have exciting adventures with their mother, despite having little money.

My Brother Stevie by Eleanor Clymer. New York: Holt, Rinehart & Winston, 1967.
About a black girl and how she guides her younger brother.

Blue Willow by Doris Cates. New York: Viking, 1940.
The story of a ten-year-old girl whose family are migrant workers in California.

From The Mixed-up Files of Mrs. Basil C. Frankweiler by E. L. Konigsberg. New York: Atheneum, 1967.
A fun story about a brother and sister who leave suburbia to live in the New York Metropolitan Museum of Art. A Newbery winner.

Rebecca of Sunnybrook Farm by Kate Wiggin. New York: Macmillan, 1962.
Another favorite about a young girl growing up.

All-of-a-King Family by Sidney Taylor. Chicago: Follett, 1951.
A happy, Jewish family story set in New York.

Gabrielle and Selena by Peter Desbarats. New York: Harcourt, Brace & World, 1968.
There's friendship and humor in this story about two eight-year-olds, one black and one white, who exchange identities for an evening.

Noonday Friends by Mary Stolz. New York: Harper & Row, 1965.
About a Puerto Rican family living in New York. Poverty causes Franny humiliation, but her relationship with her younger brother offsets everything else.

Life in Other Lands

The Good Master by Kate Seredy. New York: Viking, 1935.
A warm and humorous story with beautiful illustrations. It's about a city girl who visits her uncle's farm in prewar Hungary.

The Wheel on the School by Meindert DeJong. New York: Harper & Brothers, 1954.
A great story about some Dutch schoolchildren who try to bring back the storks to their village. A Newbery winner.

The Bushbabies by William Stevenson. Boston, Mass.: Houghton Mifflin, 1965.
An engrossing story, set in South Africa, about a young girl and her pet.

The Big Wave by Pearl Buck. New York: Day, 1948.
A must by this superb author. It's about a Japanese boy who finds courage to make a new life after a tragedy.

A Prairie Boy's Winter by William Kurelik. Boston, Mass.: Houghton Mifflin, 1973.
Good text and illustrations combine to tell about the author's boyhood on the prairies of Manitoba.

The Family Under the Bridge by Natalie Savage Carlson. New York: Harper & Brothers, 1958.
A heartwarming story set in Paris. It's about some children and their mother who live under a bridge and meet a tramp.

Religion

A Wreath of Christmas Legends by Phyllis McGinley, illustrated by Leonard Weisgard. New York: Macmillan, 1967.
Unusual. Medieval poems about Christmas legends.

Amahl and the Night Visitors by Gian Carlo Menotti, adapted by Frances Frost, illustrations by Roger Duvoisin. New York: McGraw-Hill, 1952.
A nice edition of this lovely Christmas tale.

Christmas Gif' by Charlemae Rollins, illustrated by Tom O'Sullivan. Chicago: Follett, 1963.
An outstanding collection of poems, stories, songs, and recipes written by black people.

The First Book of Holidays by Bernice Burnett, revised edition. New York: Franklin Watts, 1974.
This revised edition includes ethnic holidays as well as the traditional ones.

Adventures with Abraham's Children by Catherine F. Sellew, illustrated by Steele Savage. Boston, Mass.: Little, Brown, 1964.
A history of the Hebrews, full of adventure and heroism.

Are You There, God? It's Me, Margaret by Judy Blume. Scarsdale, N.Y.: Bradbury, 1970.
A must! This is about a preteen's concern about growing up and which religion she should follow.

Tales of Long Ago

And Then What Happened, Paul Revere? By Jean Fritz. New York: Coward, McCann & Geoghegan, Inc.
Another exciting story by Jean Fritz.

Matchlock Gun by Walter Edmonds. New York: Dodd, Mead, 1941.
This won the Newbery award. Based on a true story, it's about a courageous boy who saves his family from an Indian attack.

Mr. Mysterious and Company by Sid Fleischman. Boston, Mass.: Little, Brown, 1962.
Another winner by Sid Fleischman. It's the story of a family of traveling magicians in frontier times.

Copper-toed Boots by Marguerite de Angeli. Garden City, N.Y.: Doubleday, 1938.
The story of an American family sixty years ago. Also read *Door in the Wall: Story of Medieval London* by De Angeli, 1949, also published by Doubleday. This won the Newbery medal and is about a courageous crippled boy who lived in England during the thirteenth century. It tells how he overcame his handicap.

Winter Danger by William Steele. New York: Harcourt, Brace, 1954.
Good. Strong characterization.

Poetry and Ballads

Golden Treasury of Poetry edited by Louis Untermeyer, illustrated by Joan Walsh Anglund. New York: Golden Press, 1959.
Yes, buy it! Joan Walsh Anglund's illustrations are always tops!

The Sidewalk Racer and Other Poems of Sports and Motion by Lillian Morrison. New York: Lothrop, Lee & Shepard/Morrow, 1977.
Yes, for *girls* as well as boys!

You Come Too by Robert Frost. New York: Holt, 1950.
Frost poems for the young.

Cricket Songs: Japanese Haiku by Harry Behn. New York: Harcourt, Brace & World, 1964.
Children love haiku and they'll especially love this collection with Japanese paintings.

The Voice of the Children compiled by June Jordan and Terri Bush. New York: Holt, Rinehart & Winston, 1970.
Poems written by black and Puerto Rican children, illustrated with photographs.

Oxford Book of Poetry for Children compiled by Edward Blishen, illustrated by Brian Wildsmith. New York: Franklin Watts, 1964.
A lovely collection for your child to read aloud or to himself. He'll love Brian Wildsmith's bright, bold illustrations.

The Great Song Book edited by Timothy John, arrangements by Tomi Ungers. Garden City, N.Y.: Doubleday, 1978.
A lovely collection of sixty-six songs, with great illustrations, for piano and guitar enthusiasts.

Folklore, Fairy Tales, and Legends

The Brothers Grimm: Popular Folk Tales translated by Brian Alderson, illustrated by Michael Foreman. Garden City, N.Y.: Doubleday, 1978.
A good collection of the popular tales.

Pecos Bill and Lightning by Leigh Peck. Boston, Mass.: Houghton Mifflin, 1940.
A tall tale about Pecos Bill that will amuse and amaze your child.

Norse Gods and Giants by Ingri and Edgar d'Aulaire. Garden City, N.Y.: Doubleday, 1967.
A real favorite. The Norse myths are accompanied by outstanding —and imaginative!—illustrations. Another must is the *D'Aulaires' Book of Greek Myths,* 1962, also published by Doubleday.

The Iliad and the Odyssey of Homer retold by Alfred J. Church. New York: Macmillan, 1967.
A good introduction to these "must" tales.

Aesop's Fables selected by Louis Untermeyer. New York: Golden Press, 1965.
Terrific. Large, humorous drawings bring alive these fables, which all children should know.

Beowulf, the Warrior retold by Ian Serraillier, illustrated by Severin. New York: Walck, 1961.
An interesting account of the famous warrior.

The Blue Fairy Book edited by Andrew Lang. New York: Airmont, 1969.
Excellent!

Fourteen Hundred Cowries and Other African Tales by Abayomi Fuja, illustrated by Ademola Olugebefola. New York: Lothrop, Lee & Shepard, 1971.
Unusual. You'll both enjoy these.

Mystery, Suspense, and Adventure

The Adventures of Tom Sawyer by Mark Twain. New York: Macmillan, 1961.
Yes, of course, your library cannot be without this American classic.

Smith by Leon Garfield. New York: Pantheon, 1967.
Set in eighteenth-century London, this is a story about a twelve-year-old pickpocket.

My Side of the Mountain by Jean George. New York: Dutton, 1967.
A great adventure story.

Ghost in the Noonday Sun by Sid Fleischman. New York: Dell, 1973.
Great! About a shanghaied boy, buried treasure, and a wicked sea captain.

Men of Iron by Howard Pyle. New York: Harper & Brothers, 1930.
An old favorite.

Twenty-one Balloons by William Pène du Bois. New York: Viking, 1947.
An adventure in a balloon.

Julie of the Wolves by Jean Craighead George, illustrated by John Schoenherr. New York: Harper & Row, 1972.
An exciting story about a thirteen-year-old girl who becomes lost in Alaska and is looked after by a pack of Arctic wolves.

FOR TWELVE- AND THIRTEEN-YEAR-OLDS

Animal Stories

The Yearling by Marjorie Rawlings. New York: Scribner's, 1962.
Yes. The whole family will enjoy this story about a pet fawn raised by a boy in the backwoods of Florida.

Watership Down by Richard Adams. New York: Macmillan, 1975.
You'll want to borrow this from your child, but you probably won't get the chance until he's finished it! Set in England, it's about a group of rabbits who set out to establish a new home.

Old Yeller by Fred Gipson. New York: Harper & Row, 1964.
A classic story about a boy and his dog.

The Call of the Wild by Jack London. New York: Macmillan, 1963.
A real favorite. An adventure story about a sled dog in the Klondike.

The Red Pony by John Steinbeck. New York: Viking, 1959.
A good introduction to this well-known author. A sensitive story about a boy who discovers the real meaning of life when his pony dies.

National Velvet by Enid Bagnold. New York: Morrow, 1949.
A super horse story, made even more popular by the movie.

A Horse Called Mystery by Marjorie Reynolds. New York: Harper & Row, 1972.
Even if your child is not particularly a horse lover, I'm sure he'll enjoy this book. It has a lively story about a preteen-ager growing up during one summer. Also by Marjorie Reynolds: *The Cabin on Ghostly Pond.*

Born Free by Joy Adamson. New York: Pantheon, 1960.
A true account about a lion raised among humans and then returned to the wild. Good photographs.

Biography

Johnny Tremain: A Novel for Old and Young by Esther Forbes. Boston, Mass.: Houghton Mifflin, 1943.
A classic. Also a Newbery winner. It's about a silversmith's apprentice during the time of Paul Revere.

Lee of Virginia by Douglas Freeman. New York: Scribner's, 1961.
An interesting and informative account of Lee.

Edgar Allan Poe, Visitor from the Night of Time by Philip Stern. New York: Crowell, 1973.
A sympathetic and vivid introduction to Poe.

Three for Revolution by Burke Dairs. New York: Harcourt Brace Jovanovich, 1975.
Portraits of Patrick Henry, Thomas Jefferson, and George Washington.

Malcolm X by Arnold Adoff, illustrated by John Wilson. New York: Crowell, 1970.
Brief, but well written.

Breakthrough to the Big League; The Story of Jackie Robinson by John R. Robinson and Alfred Duckett. New York: Harper & Row, 1965.
Illustrated with photographs, this is the story of the first black ballplayer in the big leagues.

Women's Rights: The Suffrage Movement in America, 1884–1920 by Olivia E. Coolidge. New York: Dutton, 1966.
An interesting account of the battle for women's suffrage is told through sketches of the women who led the movement.

Abe Lincoln Grows Up by Carl Sandburg, illustrated by James Daugherty. New York: Harcourt, Brace, 1931.
A classic. Carl Sandburg brings alive Abe Lincoln's childhood.

George Washington's World written and illustrated by Genevieve Foster. New York: Scribner's, 1977.
Yes, save up for this one, and her delightful account of Abraham Lincoln, called *Abraham Lincoln's World.*

I'm Deborah Sampson: A Soldier in the War of the Revolution by Patricia Clapp. New York: Lothrop, Lee & Shepard, 1977.
Biographical fiction about a girl who joins the Continental Army and must conceal her sex. Entertaining!

Fantasy

Alice's Adventures in Wonderland, and Through the Looking-Glass by Lewis Carroll, illustrated by John Tenniel. New York: Macmillan, 1963.
This is the age when your child will really appreciate Alice and her extraordinary experiences.

Wrinkle in Time by Madeleine L'Engle. New York: Farrar, Straus & Giroux, 1962.

Great—get it! A science-fiction fantasy that won the Newbery award.

The Prince and the Pauper by Mark Twain. New York: Macmillan, 1962.
Another classic. A super story about a poor boy changing places with a prince.

The Owl Service by Alan Garner. New York: Walck, 1968.
Try it!

Earthfasts by William Mayne. New York: Dutton, 1966.
You'll both enjoy this one.

Worzel Gummidge by Barbara Euphan Todd, illustrated by Diana Stanley. Baltimore, Md.: Penguin, 1969.
A funny, happy book about a scarecrow who has three birthdays. Great for making your child aware of the delights of the country. One of a series.

The Happy Prince, and Other Stories by Oscar Wilde, illustrated by Lars Bo. Baltimore, Md.: Penguin, 1968.
Oscar Wilde made up these special fairy stories for his children. Great. They not only tell about princes, giants, nightingales, and roses, but also teach about life and the way to live.

Laughter

Cheaper by the Dozen by Frank B. Gilbreth, Jr., and Ernestine G. Carey. New York: Crowell, 1963.
Clever as well as humorous.

The Teddy Bear Habit, or How I Became a Winner by James Lincoln Collier. New York: Dell, 1970.
Great fun. It's about a comic adventure of a twelve-year-old boy.

Henry Reed's Babysitting Service by Keith Robertson. New York: Viking, 1966.
Henry is enterprising and funny. You'll enjoy reading this one together.

The Future of Hooper Toote by Felice Holman. New York: Scribner's, 1972.
A humorous story about a boy whose feet never touch the ground.

I'll Love You When You're More Like Me by M. E. Kerr. New York: Harper & Row, 1977.
Young people's problems written in a light and humorous style.

American Experience

Meet the Austins by Madeleine L'Engle. New York: Vanguard, 1960.
This story about a spoiled orphan who comes to live with the Austins makes delightful reading.

The Old Man and the Sea by Ernest Hemingway. New York: Scribner's, 1961.
Read this well-known short story by Hemingway together. It's about an old man and his fight to bring home a giant marlin, but it says much more than this. Challenging, but well worth the effort.

Onion John by Joseph Krumgold. New York: Crowell, 1959.
A Newbery winner, about a boy's relationship with an eccentric handyman in his village. Also get his *And Now Miguel,* Crowell, 1953, which won Krumgold another Newbery award. This is a fantastic warm story about a New Mexican boy who wants to be accepted as an adult. Another winner is his contemporary story about a boy's struggle to establish the values he wants to live by, entitled *Henry 3*. New York: Atheneum, 1967.

Sounder by William D. Armstrong. New York: Harper & Row, 1969.
Set in the Old South during the Depression, this story reveals the dignity and strength of a black family.

Mom, Wolfman, and Me by Norma Klein. New York: Pantheon, 1972.
An interesting account of a contemporary problem.

Up a Road Slowly by Irene Hunt. New York: Grosset & Dunlap, 1969.
Another Newbery winner. This tender, revealing story of a girl's growing-up years has established itself as a real favorite. See also her *Across Five Aprils* under "Tales of Long Ago."

Bridge to Terabithia by Katherine Paterson, illustrated by Donna Diamond. New York: Crowell, 1977.
A story of friendship in rural Virginia that has a tragic ending when one friend is drowned. A Newbery medal winner.

Life in Other Lands

Call It Courage by Armstrong Sperry. New York: Macmillan, 1940.
Yes, yes, yes! A Newbery winner, with dramatic illustrations, it's about a Polynesian boy who overcomes his fear of the sea.

Hans Brinker, or the Silver Skates by Mary Mapes Dodge. New York: Lancer, 1968.
A classic. An adventure story set in Holland that is at the same time deeply moving and exciting.

The Black Pearl by Scott O'Dell. Boston, Mass.: Houghton Mifflin, 1967.
Good. A novel about Ramon, a young pearl diver, who finds a fabulous pearl and has many problems to solve. See also his *Island of the Blue Dolphins* under "Tales of Long Ago."

The Good Earth by Pearl Buck. New York: Day, 1931.
Another classic, but I would read this story about China together.

Secrets of the Andes by Ann Nolan Clark. New York: Viking, 1952.
For the imaginative reader. About a Peruvian boy.

Anne Frank: The Diary of a Young Girl by Anne Frank. New York: Washington Square Press, 1972.
Very popular. It's a moving story by an adolescent Jewish girl who had to hide in a warehouse during the German occupation of Holland during World War II.

North to Freedom by Ann Holm. New York: Harcourt, Brace & World, 1965.
Buy it! A boy escapes from prison and travels across Europe to Denmark, meeting all kinds of people on the way.

I, Juan De Pareja by Elizabeth Barton De Trevino. New York: Farrar, Straus & Giroux, 1965.
A good story. It's about the friendship between the Spanish artist Velasquez and his black slave. A Newbery winner.

Stories from Shakespeare by Marchetta Chute. Cleveland, O.: World, 1956.
You'll enjoy reading these aloud to one another. A good introduction to the plays.

The Hammerhead Light by Colin Thiele. New York: Harper & Row, 1977.
Twelve-year-old Tessa protects her uncle who lives in an old lighthouse on the coast of southern Australia.

Religion

One God: The Ways We Worship Him by Florence Fitch. New York: Lothrop, Lee & Shepard, 1944.
Great for building understanding of the Protestant, Jewish, and Catholic faiths.

Holidays Around the World by Joseph Gaer, illustrated by Ann Marie Jaus. Boston, Mass.: Little, Brown, 1953.
A good reference book.

A Treasury of Christmas Songs and Carols edited by Henry W. Simon, illustrated by R. Busoni. Boston, Mass.: Houghton Mifflin, 1953.
Piano music for more than a hundred songs.

The Bronze Bow by Elizabeth George Speare. Boston, Mass.: Houghton Mifflin, 1961.

The story of young people in the time of early Christianity. A Newbery winner.

Your Prayers and Mine by Elizabeth Yates, illustrated by Nora S. Unwin. Boston, Mass.: Houghton Mifflin, 1954.
A collection of prayers from many cultures and religions.

A Pictorial Treasury of Jewish Holidays and Customs by Morris Epstein. New York: Ktav, 1959.
Photographs help to explain Jewish customs and ceremonies.

A Christmas Carol by Charles Dickens. Garden City, N.Y.: Doubleday, 1976.
A deluxe edition of the original text. Read this classic together.

Tales of Long Ago

Witch of Blackbird Pond by Elizabeth Speare. Boston, Mass.: Houghton Mifflin, 1958.
An exciting tale with strong characterizations. This Newbery winner about witchcraft is set in Puritan Connecticut.

Island of the Blue Dolphins by Scott O'Dell. Boston, Mass.: Houghton Mifflin, 1960.
Another Newbery winner. This is a super story, based on fact, about a young Indian girl's fight for survival for eighteen years on a fierce and desolate island off the coast of California.

Across Five Aprils by Irene Hunt. Chicago: Follett, 1964.
This popular story was a runner-up for the Newbery award in 1965. It's a beautifully written book about a ten-year-old boy who becomes responsible for his family when the older men and boys go off to fight in the Civil War. It takes place during the Aprils of 1861 to 1865.

Innocent Wayfaring by Marchette Chute. New York: Dutton, 1955.
A love story set in Chaucer's England of the fourteenth century.

Boy of Old Prague by Sulamith Ish-Kishor. New York: Pantheon, 1963.
About prejudice and superstition in feudal days.

Tituba of Salem Village by Ann Petry. New York: Crowell, 1964.
The story of a strong woman. A slave and her husband, who are sold in Barbados, are brought to Salem. Full of suspense!

Castle written and illustrated by David Macauley. Boston, Mass.: Houghton Mifflin, 1977.
If your child loved building with blocks, this is the book for him! It gives a clear account, with detailed illustrations, on how to construct a Welsh castle and its adjacent town. Kids love it.

The Master Puppeteer by Katherine Patterson, illustrated by Haru Wells. New York: Crowell, 1976.
The story of friendship and loyalty in eighteenth-century Japan involving Jiro, an apprentice of a bunraku puppet theater group.

Poetry and Ballads

Reflections on a Gift of Watermelon Pickle—and Other Modern Verse compiled by Stephen Dunning, Edward Lueders, and Hugh Smith. New York: Lothrop, Lee & Shepard, 1967.
Buy it! This is a fine collection with exciting photographs.

Room for Me and a Mountain Lion, Poetry of Open Space compiled by Nancy Larrick. New York: Evans, 1974.
An outstanding anthology of poems about nature and outdoor life.

Song of Robin Hood by Anne Malcolmson, illustrated by Virginia Burton. Boston, Mass.: Houghton Mifflin, 1947.
A handsome book!

Who Look at Me by June Jordan. New York: Crowell, 1969.
Poems about the black experience with paintings of black Americans by famous artists.

Imagination's Other Place by Helen Plotz. New York: Crowell, 1955.
Poetry about the sciences combining nonsense with the serious.

This Way Delight: A Book of Poetry for the Young compiled by Herbert Read. New York: Pantheon, 1951.
Many great poets are represented in this fine collection. A good introduction to adult poetry.

The Silver Swan: Poems of Romance and Mystery compiled by Horace Gregory and Marya Zaturenska. New York: Macmillan, 1968.
You'll both enjoy reading these aloud and to yourselves.

Folklore, Fairy Tales, and Legends

Bulfinch's Mythology by Thomas Bulfinch, illustrated by Elinore Blaisdell. New York: Crowell, 1962.
A great collection of classical myths. Get this one for the library.

The Story of King Arthur and His Knights by Howard Pyle. New York: Scribner's, 1903.
An old one, but still a favorite.

A Cavalcade of Sea Legends compiled by Michael Brown, illustrated by Krystyna Turska. New York: Walck, 1972.
A rich collection of legends, stories, and ballads having to do with man and the sea.

Twelve Great Black Cats and Other Eerie Scottish Tales retold by Sorche Nicheodhas, illustrated by Vera Block. New York: Dutton, 1971.
Great—nice and scary!

Rootabaga Stories by Carl Sandburg, illustrated by Maud and Miska Petersham. New York: Harcourt, Brace, 1922.
A good collection.

Anpao: An American Indian Odyssey by Jamake Highwater, illustrated by Fritz Scholder. Philadelphia: Lippincott, 1977.
A unique book relating the adventures of Anpao as he journeys through Indian history.

Mystery, Suspense, and Adventure

Treasure Island by Robert Louis Stevenson. New York: Scribner's, 1973.
Timeless! Every generation enjoys this marvelous adventure story.

Adventures of Sherlock Holmes by Arthur Conan Doyle. New York: Harper & Brothers, 1930.
Again, an old favorite. The language is rather adult and British, but your child won't let this hinder his appreciation of the absorbing stories.

Night Fall by Joan Aiken. New York: Holt, Rinehart & Winston, 1971.
A real thriller!

The Egypt Game by Zilpha Snyder. New York: Atheneum, 1967.
Great!

Robinson Crusoe by Daniel Defoe. New York: Macmillan, 1962.
A classic. A must for the library.

Twenty Thousand Leagues Under the Sea by Jules Verne. New York: Scribner's, 1925.
Fascinating. Another must. Also his *Around the World in Eighty Days*. New York: Dodd, 1872.

Adventures of Huckleberry Finn by Mark Twain. New York: Macmillan, 1962.
Your library can't be without this one! A truly American classic. Great for reading aloud.

Alfred Hitchcock's Daring Detectives compiled by Alfred Hitchcock, illustrated by Arthur Shilstone. New York: Random House, 1969.
A great assortment of thrillers by famous mystery writers.

CHILDREN'S MAGAZINES

National Geographic World
Department 00178
17th and M Streets, N.W.
Washington, D.C. 20036

A super magazine, mainly for nine-to-twelve-year-olds. But it appeals to all ages, including adults! If you can afford only one magazine, this is the one to get. It's informative, full of interesting activities to do, and, of course, full of superb photographs.

Cricket
Box 100
LaSalle, Ill. 61301

This magazine is the best as far as literary quality is concerned. It contains a nice variety of stories, articles, poetry, book reviews, activities, including recipes, as well as contributions by children. For eight-to-twelve-year-olds.

Highlights for Children
2300 West Fifth Avenue
Columbus, O. 43216

Another magazine with a nice variety. It contains well-edited, high-quality stories, articles on topics of interest and people, poetry, puzzles, and activities, including games and things to make. For preschoolers through twelve years.

Children's Digest
Children's Digest Subscription Office
Bergenfield, N.J. 07621

This magazine is published by *Parents' Magazine* Enterprises, Inc. It's informative and interesting, appealing especially to eight-to-twelve-year-olds. It contains stories, articles, poems, songs, and book reviews.

Children's Playcraft
Children's Playcraft Subscription Office
Bergenfield, N.J. 07621

Another popular magazine put out by *Parents' Magazine* Enterprises, Inc. This one is for seven-to-fourteen-year-olds. It specializes in games, hobbies, and activities, but is still a good magazine to boost your child's reading, as all the instructions have to be read carefully and thoroughly!

Humpty Dumpty's Magazine for Little Children
Humpty Dumpty's Subscription Office
Bergenfield, N.J. 07621

Despite its inane and off-putting title this magazine, also published by *Parents' Magazine* Enterprises, Inc., is great for four-to-eight-year-olds. They love the stories, poems, songs, coloring pages, and short informative features.

Ebony, Jr.
Johnson Publishing Company
820 South Michigan Avenue
Chicago, Ill. 60605

Stories, articles, poems, puzzles, and activities combine with news and information about black leaders and experiences. A parent's guide is also included at an extra cost.

The Weewish Tree
The American Indian Historical Society
1451 Masonic Avenue
San Francisco, Calif. 94117

A magazine for youth about the American Indian. All the stories, poetry, games, and historical features are written and illustrated by American Indians.

The Golden Magazine
850 Third Avenue
New York, N.Y. 10022

Stories, articles, general activities, and crafts for eight-to-twelve-year-olds.

Child Life
1100 Waterway Boulevard
Indianapolis, Ind. 46202

Articles on general information with an emphasis on science and nature, short stories, plays, and craft projects. For four-to-twelve-year-olds.

Jack and Jill
Independence Square
Philadelphia, Pa. 19105

Adventure and animal stories, articles about science and nature, songs, and plenty of games and articles.

BOOK CLUBS

To join a book club, write to the addresses given below. Be sure to give the age of your child so he receives the appropriate level books. The books will arrive monthly.

Parents' Magazine's Read Aloud and Easy Reading Program
Box 161
Bergenfield, N.J. 07621

Good stories, with delightful illustrations for four-to-eight-year-olds.

Weekly Reader Children's Book Club
1250 Fairwood Avenue
Columbus, O. 43216

Your child will enjoy these well-illustrated books, which include some nonfiction. Despite the name of the club, the books are sent monthly. For five-to-eleven-year-olds.

I Can Read Book Club
1250 Fairwood Avenue
Columbus, O. 43216

These fiction and nonfiction books are published by Harper & Row. Good. For four-to-eight-year-olds.

Junior Literary Guild
Garden City, N.Y. 11530

A nice variety of fiction and nonfiction books. For preschoolers to preteen-agers.

Grow-With-Me Book Club
Garden City, N.Y. 11530

A wide variety of books which include some to read aloud, and some for the beginner reader. A plus is a free illustrated folder with suggestions for related activities, which comes with each book. For two-to-seven-year-olds.

WHERE TO FIND LISTS OF RECOMMENDED CHILDREN'S BOOKS

If you still need more ideas in choosing suitable books for your child, here are some good sources. Many of the lists put out by the organizations can be obtained free.

Children and Books by May Hill Arbuthnot. Chicago, Ill.: Scott, Foresman, 1964.
A terrific book covering all aspects of children's literature, as well as providing excellent book suggestions.

A Parent's Guide to Children's Reading by Nancy Larrick, revised edition. Garden City, N.Y.: Doubleday, 1974.
Another marvelous book. Not only does it give a very comprehensive list of books and reading materials for children, listed under categories and age levels, but it also is full of helpful information on reading in general.

Adventures with Books prepared by Shelton L. Root, Jr., and a committee of the National Council of Teachers of English. Citation Press, Scholastic Magazines Inc., 50 West 44th Street, New York, N.Y. 10036, or National Council of Teachers of English, 1111 Kenyon Road, Urbana, Ill. 61801.
A great list of books that the compilers claim, whenever possible,

combine "the qualities of entertaining reading with literary merit." There are over 2,400 titles with annotations, grouped under subjects. For preschoolers to eighth-graders.

Bibliography of Books for Children, Association for Childhood Education International, Christina Carr Young, chairperson. ASEI, 3615 Wisconsin Avenue, N.W., Washington, D.C. 20016. Revised edition, 1978.
Great. This new edition includes many good suggestions on topics of current interest. The books are categorized under subjects, which in turn are listed under broad age levels. Annotations are given, and there are also title and author indexes, which are helpful.

The Proof of the Pudding: What Children Read by Phyllis Fenner. New York: Day, 1957.
You'll enjoy reading this practical guide. It not only gives an excellent list of books, but also explains their appeal as well as the approximate age level to introduce them to your child.

Using Literature with Young Children by Betty Coody. Dubuque, Ia.: William C. Brown, 1973.
Excellent. The annotated lists of books are great, and the author gives good ideas for stimulating children to read.

Intent upon Reading: A Critical Appraisal of Modern Fiction for Children. Leicester, England: Brockhampton, 1965.
Excellent book recommendations with worthwhile comments.

Adventuring with Books prepared by Elizabeth Guilfoile, editorial chairman, and the NCTE Committee on the Elementary School Book List. Obtained from Signet Books, 1966, or the National Council of Teachers of English, see above for address.
A comprehensive guide to 1,250 books, with concise descriptions organized into 32 subject categories and 60 reading interest level groupings.

Books for Beginning Readers also compiled by Elizabeth Guilfoile and NCTE.
This lists over 300 books for beginning readers.

Guiding Your Child to a More Creative Life by Fredelle Mayard. Garden City, N.Y.: Doubleday, 1973.
This book contains a good list of books for children from babyhood to the end of elementary school. The annotations are to the point, and helpful. There is also a list of sources of recommended children's books.

Children's Books Too Good to Miss by May Hill Arbuthnot, Margaret Clark, and Harriet Long. Western Reserve University Press, 1100 Cedar Road, Cleveland, O. 44106, 1971.
Very helpful. It lists over 200 titles of outstanding books and reading materials for children, giving annotations. It categories them under age level and type of book. Regularly revised.

Best Books for Children, compiled by Eleanor B. Widdoes. R. R. Bowker, 1180 Avenue of the Americas, New York, N.Y. 10036, 1961.
An excellent guide. It gives an annotated list of over 4,000 books chosen for their "literary excellence, pertinence, and timeliness." They are arranged by subject in five age categories. Revised annually.

Let's Read Together: Books for Family Enjoyment, edited by a committee of the National Congress of Parents and Teachers, and the Children's Service Division of the American Library Association. American Library Association, 50 East Huron Street, Chicago, Ill. 60611, third edition, 1969.
There are 750 titles listed with annotations, grouped under age level and interests. For two-to-fifteen-year-olds.

Books, Children, and Men by Paul Hazard. Boston, Mass.: Horn Book, 1944.
A classic in the field but somewhat conservative and outdated for the reading interests of today's child. However, you can keep abreast of new publications by taking the *Horn Book Magazine,* a periodical devoted entirely to children's literature and published six times a year, by Horn Book, Inc., 585 Bolyston Street, Boston, Mass. 02116. Or write for *Fanfare,* published annually in October,

giving a small sampling of the most outstanding books of the previous year.

Children's Books compiled by Virginia Haviland and others. Library of Congress publication. Superintendent of Documents, U. S. Government Printing Office, Washington, D.C. 20402.
Every year Virginia Haviland, head of the Children's Book Section of the Library of Congress, with a committee of experts, puts together a judiciously selected list of the best books of the year for preschool through junior high children. The comments given for each book are succinct and helpful. The books are listed under subjects, and grade levels are given.

Children's Books of the Years, Book Committee of the Child Study Association, 50 Madison Avenue, New York, N.Y. 10010.
An annotated bibliography arranged by subject and age level. Compiled annually, so great for current books.

Children's Books and Recordings, Office of Branch Libraries, New York Public Library, 8 East 40th Street, New York, N.Y. 10016.
An annotated list of books and recordings arranged by subject areas. Compiled annually.

Caldecott Medal Books and *Newbery Medal Books,* American Library Association, 50 East Huron Street, Chicago, Ill. 60611.
Two pamphlets giving the award-winning picture books and best-written books. Compiled annually.

Notable Children's Books, the Book Evaluation Committee of the Children's Service's Division of the American Library Association, 50 East Huron Street, Chicago, Ill. 60611.
Approximately 50 notable publications of the year listed with brief annotations. Compiled annually.

Reading with Your Child Through Age 5 prepared by the Children's Book Committee of the Child Study Association in co-operation with the staff of the Child Study—Project Head Start, 1972. The Child Study Press, 50 Madison Avenue, New York, N.Y. 10010.
An annotated list of over 200 favorites for preschoolers.

Books Before Five by Dorothy White. New York: Oxford University Press, 1954.
Books that a mother found her little girl enjoyed from two to five years.

Picture Books for Children edited by Patricia Jean Cianciola and the Picture Book Committee of the National Council of Teachers of English, 1973. American Library Association, 50 East Huron Street, Chicago, Ill. 60611.
Great. It not only includes a good, annotated list of appealing books, but also comments on various styles of writing and illustrating. You'll enjoy the sample illustrations from some of the suggested books.

Anthology of Children's Literature by Edna Johnson, Evelyn R. Sickels, and Frances Clarke Sayers, illustrated by Fritz Eichenberg. Boston: Houghton Mifflin, 1970.
A rather overpowering anthology, often used as a text for children's literature courses. But try it. You'll find the selections interesting and comprehensive, and the book suggestions thoughtful and helpful.

Teller of Tales. Children's Books and Their Authors from 1800 to 1964 by Roger Lancelyn Green. London, England: Edmund Ward, 1965.
An interesting book written by a well-known writer. It gives an excellent guide to British children's literature.

The Republic of Childhood by Sheila Egoff. New York: Oxford University Press, 1967.
A guide to Canadian children's literature, with some helpful comments on literature in general.

Paperback Books for Children compiled by the Committee on Paperback Lists for Elementary Schools of the American Association of School Librarians, 1972. Citation Press, Scholastic Book Services, 904 Sylvan Avenue, Englewood Cliffs, N.J. 07632.
An annotated list of approximately 700 books listed under five broad categories: picture books; fiction; nonfiction; myths, folk-

lore, and fairy tales; poetry, rhymes, riddles, and jokes. Although not current, you will find this a useful reference.

RIF's Guide to Book Selection, 1976. Reading Is Fundamental, L'Enfant Plaza 2500, Smithsonian Institution, Washington, D.C. 20560.
A great selection of paperbacks for preschool through elementary grades published by this super nonprofit organization, which promotes reading by giving away paperback books. The books are arranged alphabetically by publisher, and have succinct annotations. Particularly good for black, Indian, and Spanish-speaking children.

We Build Together: A Reader's Guide to Negro Life and Literature for Elementary and High School Use edited by Charlemae Rollins, 1967. National Council of Teachers of English, 1111 Kenyon Road, Urbana, Ill. 61801.
An annotated list of intercultural books, categorized under subjects.

The Black Experience in Children's Books selected by Barbara Rollock, New York: Dial Press, 1974. Or available from the Office of Branch Libraries, New York Public Library, 8 East 40th Street, New York, N.Y. 10016.
For children of all ages, this paperback gives over 900 books, categorized under the United States; South and Central America; the Caribbean; Africa; and England, and subcategorized under subject. Short, useful annotations are given for each book.

The Afro-American in Books, revised edition, 1974. Children's Service, Public Library of the District of Columbia, Washington, D.C. 20001.
Another comprehensive list of books listed under subjects, with short annotations.

About 100 Books: A Gateway to Better Intergroup Understanding by Ann G. Wolfe. The American Jewish Committee, 165 East 56th Street, New York, N.Y. 10022, seventh edition, 1972.
A list of books for children concerning contemporary intergroup relations.

INDEX

A (long vowel), 268
AI and AY teams, 179–81
EI and EY sounds as, 256–58
with the magic E, 172–73
A, tricky vowel sounds for, 269
Aa (short vowel), 142–46, 268
ABC books, for first five years, 366–67
Academic Therapy Publications, 359
Academic Underachiever, The, 360
Achievement tests, interpreting, 342–43
Action game, 122
Actual reading problems, 350
Adventure books:
for eight- and nine-year-olds, 405–6
for six- and seven-year-olds, 394–95
for ten- and eleven-year-olds, 415–16
for three-, four-, and five-year-olds, 384–85
for twelve- and thirteen-year-olds, 426
AI (vowel team), 179–81
AIR word sound (when vowel is followed by R), 201–2
ALD word family vowel sounds, 254–55
ALK word family vowel sounds, 254–55
Allusion, in poetry, 312–13
ALL word family vowel sounds, 254–55
ALT word family vowel sounds, 254–55
American Association of University Affiliated Programs for the Developmentally Disabled, 359
American Education Research Association, 354
American experience, books on:
for eight- and nine-year-olds, 399–400
for six- and seven-year-olds, 389
for ten- and eleven-year-olds, 409–11
for three-, four-, and five-year-olds, 378–79
for twelve- and thirteen-year-olds, 420–21
American Library Association, 283
Animal stories:
for eight- and nine-year-olds, 395–96
for six- and seven-year-olds, 385–86
for ten- and eleven-year-olds, 406–7
for three-, four-, and five-year-olds, 375–77
for twelve- and thirteen-year-olds, 416–17
Appreciation, reading, 291–316
author's techniques, 297
before child reads book, 292
by asking questions, 292–94
encouraging child's interpretations, 294–95
general impression or "scan," 292
intention and, 296–97
of literary forms, 297–316
personalizing the book, 294
responsibilities and, 295–96
ARE word sound (when vowel is followed by R), 201–2
AR word sound (when vowel is followed by R), 196–98
A sound (as in want), 263–65
Association for Childhood Education International, 283
Association for Children with Learning Disabilities, 358
AU (vowel team), 223–25
Author's style, in fiction stories, 301–3
Author's techniques, awareness of, 297

AW (vowel team), 223–25
AY (vowel team), 179–81

B, as a silent letter, 244, 269
Baby language skills, 86–91
  eighth month, 91–93
  encouraging "talking," 87
  first sentences, 94–98
  fourth or fifth year, 103–6
  introducing books, 90
  naming things, 90–91
  singing to baby, 89–90
  talking to baby, 87–88
  telling stories, 88–89
  third year, 98–103
Baby talk:
  avoiding, 93
  encouraging, 87
Bedroom, child's, as first classroom, 71–72
Bedtime stories, for first five years, 370–71
Biographical books:
  for eight- and nine-year-olds, 396–97
  for six- and seven-year-olds, 386–87
  for ten- and eleven-year-olds, 407–8
  for twelve- and thirteen-year-olds, 417–18
Book clubs, 429–30
Books:
  developing interest and comprehension in, 275–316
  for eight- and nine-year-olds, 395–406
  fiction, 298–303
  for first five years, 366–85
  getting the most out of (ways to help the child), 291–316
  guidelines for, 280–86
  home environment and, 41
  introducing baby to, 90
  involving child in choice of, 286
  nonfiction, 315–16
  poetry, 303–15
  reading and enjoying, 277–90
  recommended, where to find, 430–35
  for six- and seven-year-olds, 385–95
  suggestions for, 365–427
  for ten- and eleven-year-olds, 406–16
  for twelve- and thirteen-year-olds, 416–26
  See also types of books
Bookstores, taking child to, 286–87
Botel Reading Inventory, 340
Brown-Carlsen Listening Comprehension Test, 340

C, as a K sound, 249–51, 269
C, as a silent letter, 246
Caldecott Award, 283
California Reading Test, 342
California Test of Mental Ability, 340
C and G word sounds (followed by E, I, or Y), 208–12
Can't Read, Can't Write, Can't Talk Too Good Either (Clarke), 360
Carnegie Medal, 283
CH (consonant team), 191–95
CH, as a K sound, 249–51
Characters, fiction story, 300
Children's Book Council, 283
Children's projects, display of, 42
CH sound, 269
CI word ending, as SH sound, 266–67
CK, as a K sound, 249–51
Classroom visit, to evaluate school reading program, 327–31
Closer Look (organization), 358–59
Cloth books, for first five years, 367–68
Communication, first bonds of, 38–39
Comparisons and tension, 47
Comprehension, 123, 144, 191
  developing interest and, 275–316
  interpreting meaning of the story, 124–25
  and phonics, 204
  words and relationships, 124
Concentration, need for, 80–81
Confidence and sense of security, 12–14, 58–59
Consonants:
  beginning blends, 165
  blends, 165–68
  ending blends, 165
  teams, 191–95
  variations, 247–51
  vowels and, 140–41
  See also Syllables
Counting books, for first five years, 368–69
Curiosity, child's, 52–53

Demands, beyond child's capabilities, 47
Diagnosis, reading disability, 353–56
Dictionary, disadvantage of using, 295–96
Diet and food, 62–63
Directory of Facilities for the Learning Disabled and Handicapped (Ellingson and Cass), 360
Disability, reading, 347–61
  diagnosis, 353–56
  signs of, 348–52
  treatment, 356–57
  what to do, 352–53
  where to find help, 358–61
Disorganization and tension, 49
Distinct speaking habits, stressing, 102–3
Durrell-Sullivan Reading Capacity Test, 340, 342

E, as a long vowel, *see* Magic E
E (short vowel), 268
EA (vowel team), 181–83, 228–32
EAR, as ER sound, 259–62
EAR word sound (when vowel is followed by R), 201–2
ED endings, 269
ED pronunciation, 235–36
Education for All Handicapped Children Act (1977), 353
Ee (short vowel), 159–63
EE (vowel team, 181–83
EI (vowel team), long E or long A sound, 256–58
Eighth month (baby) language skills, 91–93
  avoiding baby talk, 93
  baby as imitator, 98
  first sentences, 94
  praising each word, 92–93
  stretching (or expanding) sentences, 94–98
Emotional and physical well-being, importance of, 56–66
  physical development and health, 61–66
  stability and self-reliance, 56–61
Emotionally immature child (how to tell), 57–58
Encouragement, 14–17
Endings, added to words, 235–41
  ED pronunciation, 235–36
  magic E words, 236–39
  rule for, 235
  in Y, 239–41
ER sound, OR, OUR, and EAR as, 259–62
ER word sound (when vowel is followed by R), 199–201
Evaluation, school reading program, 320–44
  child's progress and reading level, 336–44
  questions to ask the teacher, 331–36
  visiting the classroom, 327–31
  visiting the school, 320–27
Events, fiction story, 299
EW (vowel team), 226–28
Exaggeration, in poetry, 312
Eye blinking, 57

Fairy tales:
  for eight- and nine-year-olds, 403–4
  for six- and seven-year-olds, 393–94
  for ten- and eleven-year-olds, 414–15
  for three-, four-, and five-year-olds, 383
  for twelve- and thirteen-year-olds, 425–26
Family bulletin board, 42
Fantasy books:
  for eight- and nine-year-olds, 397–98
  for six- and seven-year-olds, 387–88
  for ten- and eleven-year-olds, 408–9
  for three-, four-, and five-year-olds, 377
  for twelve- and thirteen-year-olds, 418–19
Fiction, 298–303
  author's style in, 301–3
  characters, 300
  events, 299
  setting, 300–1
Filing game, 122
Find the odd man out game, 122–23
Fingernails, biting, 57
Fish game, 122
Folklore, books on:
  for eight- and nine-year-olds, 403–4
  for six- and seven-year-olds, 393–94
  for ten- and eleven-year-olds, 414–15

for three-, four-, and five-year-olds, 383
for twelve- and thirteen-year-olds, 425–26
Fourth (or fifth) year language skills, 103–6
broadening knowledge of words, 104–6
keeping up reading, 106
F sound, 269
F sound variations, 247–49

G, as a silent letter, 246
G and C word sounds (followed by E, I, or Y), 208–12
Gates-MacGintie Reading Tests, 342
GH, as a F sound, 247–49
GH sound, 269
as a silent letter, 246, 252
G sound, 269
"Gulps," reading in, 5–7, 111, 124

H, as a silent letter, 244, 269
Health. *See* Physical development and health
Hearing problems, 65–66
Hobbies and special interests, 41
Home environment, 39–52
books and reading materials, 41
child- or parent-oriented, 44–45
display of children's projects, 42
family bulletin board, 42
happy and tension-free atmosphere, 46–47
hobbies and special interests, 41
learning "climate," 50–52
for learning stimulation, 40–41
places for relaxing, reading, and talking, 41
separate area for child, 43–44
situations that cause tension, 47–50
television, 42–43
Homonyms, 270–71
Hunt and seek game, 122
Hyperactivity, 351

I (long vowel), 268
unusual sound variations, 252–53
with the magic E, 173–74
I (silent vowel), 268
I, tricky vowel sounds for, 269
IE (vowel team), long E or long A sound, 256–58
IGH (silent GH) word family vowel sounds, 252–53
Ii (short vowel), 146–50
ILD word family vowel sounds, 252–53
Imitator, child as, 98
Impulsiveness, 351
Inappropriate times for teaching, 49–50
Inconsistency and tension, 47–48
IND word family vowel sounds, 252–53
Insecurity, feeling of, 58
Instability, emotional, 351
Intellectual skills, developing, 67–85
concentration, 80–81
logical thinking, 82–85
observation, 74–80
seeing type relationships and associations, 81–82
stages of development, 68–71
when child is a baby, 71–74
Interest and comprehension, suggestions for, 275–316
appropriate books, 280–86
as child gets older, 279–80
child's own library, 287–90
discriminating between good and inferior literature, 290
involving child in choice of books, 286
library and bookstore trips, 286–87
problem readers, 347–61
reading appreciation, 291–316
reading and enjoying books, 277–90
schoolbook reading, 278–79
working with the school, 319–46
Iowa Silent Reading Test, 342
Irony, in poetry, 313–14
IR word sound (when vowel is followed by R), 199–201

Jane Ervin Reading Comprehension Series, The, 133
J sound, 269
"Junk" foods, 62

K, as a silent letter, 244, 269
Kate Greenaway Medal, 283
K sound, 269
K sound variation, 249–51
Kuhlman-Anderson I.Q. Test, 340

L, as a silent letter, 244, 269

Language problems, 350–51
Language skills, developing, 86–106
  baby, 86–91
  eighth-month period, 86–91
  first sentences, 94–98
  fourth or fifth year, 103–6
  third year, 98–103
Laughter books:
  for eight- or nine-year-olds, 398–99
  for six- and seven-year-olds, 388–89
  for ten- and eleven-year-olds, 409
  for three-, four-, and five-year-olds, 378
  for twelve- and thirteen-year-olds, 419–20
Laura Ingalls Wilder Award, 283
Learning by doing, 26–29
  lesson involvement and memorization, 28–29
  reciting facts, 27
Learning "climate," 50–52
  answering child's questions, 51
  being a good listener, 50–51
  letting child find solutions, 51
  open-mindedness, 52
Learning equipment, 53–55
Learning interest (of the child), 107–25
  awareness of written words, 108–12
  comprehension and putting it all together, 123
  letters, 112–23
  meaning of story as a whole, 124–25
  signs of, 107–8
  transition from talking to reading, 108–25
  words and relationships, 124
Learning the letters, 112–23
  activities and games for, 121–23
  shape of the letters, 115–16
  sounds, 113–15
  writing, 116–21
Learning to write, 116–21
  activities and games for, 121–23
  capital and small letters, 118–19
  pencil grip for, 117
LE endings, 269
Legends, books on:
  for eight- and nine-year-olds, 403–4
  for six- and seven-year-olds, 393–94
  for ten- and eleven-year-olds, 414–15
  for three-, four-, and five-year-olds, 383
  for twelve- and thirteen-year-olds, 425–26
LE sound (at the end of a word), 265–66
Lessons, reading, 127–273
  area or location for, 131
  best way to teach, 131
  materials needed, 132–34
  outline of, 132–34, 135, 136
  questions to consider (before teaching), 129–30
  stage I (very basics), 137–89
  stage II (some variations, 190–241
  stage III (harder ones), 242–73
Letters:
  silent (no sound), 244–46
  and sounds, introducing, 138–39
  See also Consonants; Learning the letters; Vowels
Library, taking child to, 286–87
Life in other lands, books on:
  for eight- and nine-year-olds, 400
  for first five years, 380
  for six- and seven-year-olds, 389–90
  for ten- and eleven-year-olds, 411–12
  for twelve- and thirteen-year-olds, 421–22
Listening to the child, 50–51
Listing game,123
Literary forms, 297–316
  fiction, 298–303
  nonfiction, 315–16
  poetry, 303–15
Logical thinking, developing, 82–85
Long vowels, 169–85
  difference between short and, 169–70
  magic E, 170–78
  summary of, 268
  unusual variations, 252–53
  vowel teams, 173–85
Lotto game, 123
Love and affection, importance of, 58

Magazines for children, 427–29
Magic E (long vowel), 170–78, 268
  activities, 171–72
  EE and EA teams, 181–83
  EI and EY sounds, 256–58
  long A with, 172–73
  long I with, 173–74

long O with, 175–76
long U with, 176–78
rule, 170
when endings are added to words, 236–39
Matching game, 122
Memory problems, 351
Metaphors, in poetry, 310–11
Metropolitan Reading Test, 342
Mother Goose books, for first five years, 371–72
Motivation, child's, teaching methods and, 17–26
attitude of teacher, 23–24
clear and direct results, 20–22
faith in child, 22–23
model (practice what you preach), 24
particular interests, 18–19
positive approach, 20
relating reason and purpose, 19–20
rewards in moderation, 24–26
turn-off and turn-on remarks, 22–23
Mystery books:
for eight- and nine-year-olds, 405–6
for six- and seven-year-olds, 394–95
for ten- and eleven-year-olds, 415-16
for three-, four-, and five-year-olds, 384–85
for twelve- and thirteen-year-olds, 426

N, as a silent letter, 246
National Council of Measurement in Education, 354
Newbery Award, 283
New Phonics Workbooks, 133
"Nit-picking," 48
Nonfiction books, 315–16
Notebook, using, 133–34

O (long vowel), 268
with the magic E, 175–76
OA, OE, and OW teams, 183–85
unusual sound variations, 252–53
O (short vowel), 268
O, tricky vowel sounds for, 269
OA (vowel team), 183–85
Observation, importance of, 74–80
OE (vowel team), 183–85
OI (vowel team), 217–19
OLD word family vowel sounds, 252–53
OLL word family vowel sounds, 252–53
Oo (short vowel), 150–54
OO (vowel team), 213–16
OO sound, 258–59
Open-mindedness, 52
OR, as ER sound, 259–62
Orton Society, The, 358
OR word sound (when vowel is followed by R), 196–98
OST word family vowel sounds, 252–53
Otis-Lennon Mental Ability Test, 340
OU (vowel team), 219–22
different sounds for, 259
as OO sound, 258–59
OUR, as ER sound, 259–62
O words with short U sound, 263–65
OW (vowel team), 183–85, 219–22
OY (vowel team), 217–19

P, as a silent letter, 246
Patience, parents' lack of, 50
Pencil grip, 117
Perceptual problems, 350
Personification, in poetry, 311–12
PH, as a F sound, 247–49
Phrases of meaning, 124
Physical development and health (of the child), 61–66
diet and meals, 62–63
exercise, 63–64
hearing problems, 65–66
sleep, 61–62
vision, 64–65
Physical exercise, importance of, 63–64
Piaget, Dr. Jean, 70
Picture books, for four-, five-, and six-year-olds, 372–75
Poetry, 305–15
allusion in, 312–13
exaggeration in, 312
irony in, 313–14
metaphors in, 310–11
personification in, 311–12
similes in, 310
Poetry and ballads, books on:
for eight- and nine-year-olds, 402–3
for six- and seven-year-olds, 392–93
for ten- and eleven-year-olds, 413–14
for three-, four-, and five-year-olds, 381–82
for twelve- and thirteen-year-olds,

424–25
Poor co-ordination (jerky movements or clumsiness), 351
Posting game, 122
Potential, reading, 340
Praise and encouragement, 14–17
Prefixes and roots, 272–73
"Pre-operational" stage of development, 70–71
Preparation, preschool, 13–125
emotional and physical well-being, 56–66
intellectual skills, 67–85
language skills, 86–106
when and how to start, 37–55
when child is ready to read, 107–25
Punishment, 48–49

QU, as a K sound, 249–51
QUE, as a K sound, 249–51
Questions, child's willingness to answer, 51

Reading:
book clubs, 429–30
book suggestions, 365–426
compared to talking to a friend, 7–8
fundamental lessons, 127–273
in "gulps," 5–7, 111, 124
interest and comprehension, 275–316
introduction to, 4–8
keeping up (fourth or fifth year), 106
magazines for children, 427–29
note to parents, 1–3
preschool preparation, 35–125
recommended books (where to find), 430–33
teaching and learning methods, 11–34
working with others, 317–61
See also Appreciation; Disability; Lessons; Potential
"Red-letter days" game, 121–22
Regina Medal Award, 283
Reinforcement, school reading program, 345
Religion, books on:
for eight- and nine-year-olds, 401
for first five years, 380–81
for six- and seven-year-olds, 390–91
for ten- and eleven-year-olds, 412–13
for twelve- and thirteen-year-olds, 422–23
Remedial teachers, where to find, 355–56
Remediation, 354
Responsibility, developing sense of, 59–61
Ridicule, 49
Right-left confusion, 351
Roots. *See* Prefixes and roots
R sound (when vowels are followed by R), 196–202
AIR, ARE, and EAR words, 201–2
ER, IR, and UR words, 199–201
OR, OUR, and EAR as ER sound, 259–62
OR and AR words, 196–98
review of, 269

S, as a SH sound, 251, 266
S, as a silent letter, 246
S, as a Z sound, 251
S.R.A. Primary Mental Abilities Test, 340
School:
learning problems at, 351–52
specific assignments, 346
See also School reading program
Schoolbooks, developing interest in, 278–79
School reading program, 319–46
evaluation (what to consider), 320–44
working with school to improve child's reading, 345–46
Security, sense of, 12–14, 58–59
Seeing type relationships and associations, 81–82
Self-restraint, parents' lack of, 50
"Self-talk," encouraging, 101–2
"Sensational" stage of development, 68–69
Setting, fiction story, 300–1
Shape of the letters, 115–16
SH (consonant team), 191–95
SH endings, 269
SHENT endings, 269
Short vowels, 142–62
Aa, 142–46
difference between long vowels and, 169–70
Ee, 159–62
Ii, 146–50
Oo, 150–54

summary of, 268
Uu, 154–58
SH sounds, 266–67
SHUL, SHUN, and SHUS endings, 269
Shyness, extreme, 58
Sight words, 111, 163–64, 270
Silent letters, 244–46
review of, 269
Similes, in poetry, 310
Singing to baby, 89–90
SI word ending, as SH sound, 266–67
Sleep, importance of, 61–62
Sounds of the letters, 113–15
S sound, 269
S sound variations, 251
Stability and self-reliance (of the child), 56–61
confidence and security, 12–14, 58–59
developing responsibility, 59–61
emotionally immature (how to tell), 57–58
importance of love and affection, 58
Stage I lessons (very basics), 137–89
consonant blends, 165–68
introducing the letters, 138–39
long vowels, 169–85
outline of, 132–34, 135
short vowels, 142–63
sight words, 163–64
syllables, 186–89
vowels and consonants, 140–41
Stage II lessons (some variations), 190–241
C and G words, 208–12
consonant teams, 191–95
endings added to words, 235–41
outline of, 132–34, 135
tricky vowel teams, 213–34
vowels with R, 196–202
Y as a vowel, 203–7
Stage III lessons (harder ones), 242–73
consonant variations, 247–51
outline of, 132–34, 136
silent letters, 244–46
tough sounds, 256–69
vocabulary, increasing, 270–73
vowel variations, 252–55
Stanford Achievement Test, 342
Story telling, to baby, 88–89
Stroud-Hieronymus Primary Reading Profiles, 340
Stuttering, 67
Suspense books:
for eight- and nine-year-olds, 405–6
for six- and seven-year-olds, 394–95
for ten- and eleven-year-olds, 415–16
for three-, four-, and five-year-olds, 384–85
for twelve- and thirteen-year-olds, 426
Syllables, 186–89
and vowel teams, 232–34

T, as a silent letter, 244, 269
Tales of long ago, books on:
for eight- and nine-year-olds, 402
for four- and five-year-olds, 381
for six- and seven-year-olds, 391–92
for ten- and eleven-year-olds, 413
for twelve- and thirteen-year-olds, 423–24
Teacher, questions to ask, 331–36
Teaching:
child's motivation and, 17–26
confidence and sense of security, 12–14
hints for specific skills, 29–34
inappropriate times for, 49–50
learning by doing, 26–29
and learning methods, 11–34
lessons (fundamental), 127–273
praise and encouragement, 14–17
preschool preparation, 13–125
Teeth grinding, 58
Television, home environment and, 42–43
Tension situations at home (that discourage learning), 47–50
comparisons, 47
demanding, 47
disorganization, 49
inappropriate times for teaching, 49–50
inconsistency, 47–48
"nit-picking," 48
parents' lack of patience and self-restraint, 50
punishment, 48–49
ridicule, 49
unnecessary restrictions, 48
TH (consonant team), 191–95
Third-year language skills, 98–103
doing things together, 99–100
encouraging "self-talk," 101–2
stressing distinct speaking habits,

102–3
TH sound, 269
Thumb sucking, 58
TI word ending, as SH sound, 266–67
Touch books, for first five years, 368
Treatment, reading disability, 356–57

U (long vowel), 268
with the magic E, 176–78
U, tricky vowel sounds for, 269
UE, as OO sound, 258–59
UI, as OO sound, 258–59
UL sound (when LE comes at end of word), 265–66
Unnecessary restrictions, 48
UR word sound (when vowel is followed by R), 199–201
U sound (short U, words with O), 263
Uu (short vowel), 154–58, 268

Vision, 64–65
Vocabulary, increasing, 270–73
homonyms, 270–71
prefixes and roots, 272–73
sight words, 270
Vowels:
and consonants, 140–41
long, 169–85
long (unusual variations), 252–53
with R, 196–202, 259–62, 269
review of syllables and vowel teams, 232–34
short, 142–62
sound variations, 252–65
teams, 173–85, 268
teams (that are tricky), 213–34
tough sounds, 256–69
word families with unusual sounds, 254–55
Y as, 203–7
See also Consonants; Syllables

W, as a silent letter, 244, 269
W, as a vowel, 183
Wechsler Intelligence Scale for Children-Revised (Wisc-R), 340
WH (consonant team), 191–95
Wordless books, for first five years, 369–70
Word order, 124
Words and relationships, 124
Writing:
perceptual problems in, 350
See also Learning to write
Written words, awareness of, 108–12

Y, words ending in, 239–41
Y as a vowel, 179, 203–7

Z word sounds, 251